SEX WORK TODAY

Sex Work Today

Erotic Labor in the Twenty-First Century

Edited by

Bernadette Barton, Barbara G. Brents, *and* Angela Jones

NEW YORK UNIVERSITY PRESS

New York

NEW YORK UNIVERSITY PRESS
New York
www.nyupress.org

Library of Congress Cataloging-in-Publication Data
Names: Barton, Bernadette, editor. | Brents, Barbara G., editor. | Jones, Angela, 1978–   editor.
Title: Sex work today : erotic labor in the twenty-first century / edited by Bernadette Barton,
Barbara G. Brents, and Angela Jones.
Description: New York : New York University Press, [2024] |
Includes bibliographical references and index
Identifiers: LCCN 2023057207 (print) | LCCN 2023057208 (ebook) |
ISBN 9781479821310 (hardback) | ISBN 9781479821341 (paperback) |
ISBN 9781479821426 (ebook) | ISBN 9781479821389 (ebook other)
Subjects: LCSH: Sex work. | Sex workers. | Prostitution.
Classification: LCC HQ118 .S489 2024 (print) | LCC HQ118 (ebook) |
306.74—dc23/eng/20231227
LC record available at https://lccn.loc.gov/2023057207
LC ebook record available at https://lccn.loc.gov/2023057208

This book is printed on acid-free paper, and its binding materials are chosen for strength
and durability. We strive to use environmentally responsible suppliers and materials to the
greatest extent possible in publishing our books.

Manufactured in the United States of America

10 9 8 7 6 5 4 3 2 1

Also available as an ebook

For all who have worked in the sex industries or provided sexual services and all their/our allies.

CONTENTS

Introduction

BERNADETTE BARTON, BARBARA G. BRENTS, AND ANGELA JONES

As sex work scholars who have been researching the sex industry a long time, we are excited to share with you *Sex Work Today*, a cutting-edge volume illuminating the newest trends in sex work. Sex worker activist Carol Leigh, also known as Scarlot Harlot, who sadly passed away in 2022, coined the term "sex worker" in 1978. She used this term to highlight that sex workers are service professionals and that, as the sex worker mantra goes—sex work is work. Still, much has changed since Leigh coined this term. Here, we present data-driven stories, many of which are written by present or former sex workers, documenting the current landscape of modern sex industries. In the twenty-first century, sex work encompasses a wide array of temporary, professional, informal, formal, and entrepreneurial forms of work. Despite widespread media reducing sex work to "prostitution," commercial sex markets vary widely. They include camming, full-service sex work in various contexts (e.g., street-based, brothel work, and escorting independently online), hostessing, phone sex, pornography, pro-domme work, stripping, sugar relationships, various adult content production, and a wide array of individual sexual entrepreneurship.

Political Context

There is today a war on sex work. Rapidly changing technologies, changing consumer cultures, growing transnational inequalities, and precarious employment draw people to the opportunities and autonomy that exist in sex industries. Yet, most countries criminalize full-service sex markets, causing violence and economic harm. Anti–sex work global movements have turned many well-intentioned and needed policies designed to reduce labor trafficking to policies targeting all sex workers, reducing their effectiveness in stopping trafficking and motivating financial and communication platforms to shut out sexual content. The results have made sex work more challenging, less safe, and more time-consuming, causing more harm worldwide.[1] These repressive policies disproportionately impact the most marginal groups, including Indigenous, Black, Latinx, and other workers of color, disabled workers, trans workers, those in the Global South, and poor workers. This war on sex work affects both legal and illegal workers. The harm is real and must end. To understand these impacts and design better policies, researchers must use intersectional and transnational lenses such as those applied in this book because sex-industry experiences are far from monolithic.

Still, these geopolitical and *necropolitical* (the politics of deciding whose lives matter and whose do not) conditions are only part of the story we want to tell. Repressive policies have also spurred increased sex worker grassroots organizing, political activism, community-based advocacy, and mutual aid groups. Sex workers forge tight-knit communities and programs that support one another, especially during times of disruption, such as a global pandemic or climate events like hurricanes, floods, and earthquakes, where sex workers, due to rampant occupational discrimination and criminalization, receive no state-based aid. Essays in this volume document how sex workers organize and resist these conditions through community action and mutual aid.

Despite increased attacks, sex workers' activism has led to real change. National polls show that support for decriminalizing prostitution in the United States of America has risen steadily over the past decade.[2] Right now, in the USA, for example, district attorneys have declared that they will stop prosecuting all crimes of prostitution.[3] Hawaii, Rhode Island, New York, and Vermont are also considering bills that would decriminalize prostitution. Outside of the USA, since the 1990s, several Australian states and Aotearoa New Zealand have removed criminal penalties against prostitution. Most recently, in 2022 Belgium became the first European country to fully decriminalize prostitution.[4]

In sum, especially in these geopolitical times, sex workers have much to teach policymakers and politicians, scholars in other fields, clinicians and service providers, and general readers about the world's economic and political institutions. Sex work is a financial lifeline for many, particularly marginalized people.[5] The labor itself is often a reprieve from the drudgery of what sex workers often call "vanilla," "square," or "civi" (shorthand for "civilian") labor. Indeed, empirical studies show that workers often prefer the autonomy and freedoms of individual erotic entrepreneurship to so-called traditional labor.[6] While contemporary sex work is still marred by exploitation, racism, sexism, ableism, and cissexism, like any industry, studies show that sex workers, primarily those working online, experience high rates of job satisfaction and, oftentimes, pleasurable work experiences.[7] Thus, exploring the expanding world of *sex work today* provides a unique vantage point to better understand contemporary labor, law and social policy, politics, gender, race, ability, and sexuality.

Origins of the Content

To document a full range of market shifts and experiences, in 2020, we distributed a call for papers through our academic and sex worker community networks. The response was impressive, and we were sorry not to take all the abstracts submitted for consideration. As editors, we had four interrelated priorities shaping this difficult selection process: (1) inclusivity regarding sex work industry segments, worker subjectivities, and geographical and cultural contexts, (2) inclusion of sex worker experts, (3) grounding analyses in intersectional and transnational frames, and (4) ensuring that all papers engage with stratification systems within the industry itself. We aimed to curate an inclusive volume that recognizes the complex ways nation, race, gender, sexuality, ability, documentation status, market positionality, and class affect industry outcomes and experiences.

Our first goal was to ensure that sex workers and sex-working scholars were well represented. Sex workers are the experts on sexual economies, kicking down doors long held shut by academic and publishing gatekeepers. They are speaking out, conducting rigorous community-based studies, and demanding ethical research, especially from academics with no personal experience in sex industries. In this volume, we adhere to the sex worker activist political expression "nothing about us without us." This mantra suggests that even well-intentioned researchers and allies should always partner with sex workers when sharing knowledge about sex industries.

Concerning our second goal, the chapters that follow use *intersectional frames* to highlight how white supremacy, cisgenderism, ableism, heterosexism, and patriarchy overlap and intersect when shaping people's labor experiences in capitalist markets. As the authors discuss, overlapping stratification systems shape sex workers' interactions with law enforcement, state agencies, and social-service agencies in unequal ways. These agencies, sometimes labeled the "criminal justice–social services alliance" and the "rescue industry,"[8] all seek to "save" (presumably cisgender) women from sex work. Some chapters also situate their analyses in *transnational frames*, that is, the ways interconnected and unequal relations between nations, past and present, impact who is defined as a citizen, who can move between borders, how money is moved across borders, and how policies in one country affect people in other countries.

Third, it was critical that all chapters in this book explore how white supremacy, patriarchy, and capitalism encourage horizontal hostility *among* sex workers by manufacturing hierarchies that pit marginalized members against one another. This is visible in what sex workers call "the whorearchy" and "lateral whorephobia."

"The whorearchy" is a stratification system within the sex industry that ranks sex workers by their labor sector. As sex worker Raani Begum explains, the whorearchy divides "sex workers into categories of marginally respectable to least respectable."[9] Queer sex worker and activist Tilly Lawless put it this way:

> The whorearchy is the hierarchy that shouldn't—but does—exist in the sex industry, which makes some jobs within it more stigmatized than others, and some more acceptable. Basically, it goes like this, starting from the bottom (in society's mind): street-based sex worker, brothel worker, rub and tug worker/erotic masseuse, escort, stripper, porn star, BDSM mistress, cam girl, phone sex worker then finishing with sugar baby on the top.[10]

Sex workers who internalize the whorearchy may practice lateral whorephobia. Caty Simon, coeditor of *Tits and Sass*, a sex-worker-run blog, defines the term this way:

> "Lateral whorephobia" . . . is where one kind of sex worker is maybe more privileged than another kind of sex worker, so they'll look down upon and stigmatize them, which happens so often in the community. Pro dommes will say things like, "Well, at least we don't fuck our clients" or "At least we're not whores." Porn stars will say that escorts are dirty. Escorts will say full-service pro-subs take too many risks.[11]

Lateral whorephobia perpetuates sex worker stigma and makes it harder for sex worker activists to forge coalitions across sectors. Additionally, marginalized sex workers in street sectors have entirely different needs than more privileged sex workers and different abilities to allocate time to fight for change. The growth of the sex worker–rights movement and its successes are all the more remarkable in this light. Thus, we encourage readers to reject simplistic, oppressive ranking of varieties of sex work and keep their critical gaze on intersecting systems of inequality as problems, not the workers, while recognizing how social location shapes worker experiences.

As we selected and edited the essays, we observed several noteworthy trends in sex work that we highlight for you now.

Digital Technologies: How the Internet Changed the Game

We know digital technologies have transformed the sex industry; essays in this book explore how. Scholars have long shown how porn content *drove* the technological development of the web,[12] but porn content has driven all sorts of technological changes for three hundred years, from seventeenth-century printed pamphlets to daguerreotypes to modern photos, movies, and magazines to VHS, DVDs, digital streaming, and free tube sites.[13] Today, smartphone technology enables more people to see more pornography, more often, more privately, and younger than any previous generation, and to make their own amateur porn and share it.[14] People interact in real time, thus engendering new categories of sex work like camming. Social media platforms also enable sex workers and customers to connect, and schedule appointments. The Internet has also helped make sex work safer as it allows full-service providers to screen clients, create online tools for reviewing clients, and share information about "bad dates." There are more spaces for indirect sex work that involves no physical contact of any kind. Finally, diversification and increased demand for amateur non-studio-produced pornography have led to the democratization of pornographic industries—people typically locked out of studio porn because of racism, cissexism, ableism, and fatphobia now find new spaces online. In thirty short years, digital innovations have revolutionized the sex industry.[15]

The rise of online sex work has also given workers new ways to market their brands and services. The growth of social media sites such as Twitter, which as of this writing allows adult content (such material is often referred to as "Not Safe for Work," NSFW), is one example. At the same time, online sites require sex workers to do a lot more administrative labor, like curating multiple social media and fan content. For example, modern sex workers must "hustle," creating pornographic content on clip sites such as Onlyfans, taking phone sex calls on NiteFlirt, camming on sites such as Chaturbate, posting escort ads online, and so on to make ends meet. Further, many find online sex work attractive, which increases competition and lowers wages. Chapters in this book cover all these trends.

Governing Sex Work: Criminalization and Carceral Systems

Here, we also examine how shifting laws, policies, and patterns in criminalization shape sex markets, from police harassment and violence toward sex workers on the street to new legislation regulating online spaces. As some of our authors explore, *carceral* approaches to sex work, that is, a focus on punishment and criminal legal institutions to implement policies, often conflate voluntary sex workers with trafficking survivors, and this elision of the crucial element of *choice* immensely harms sex workers. This is visible in the 2018 Stop Enabling Sex Traffickers Act (SESTA) and the Fight Online Sex Trafficking Act (FOSTA), which were passed to take down websites ostensibly promoting sex trafficking but have instead led to a worsening of conditions for sex workers.[16] Similarly, years earlier, Craigslist removed private sections where many sex workers posted free ads.

Just before FOSTA/SESTA passed, authorities also took down Backpage—the primary way sex workers met clients, especially in the men-seeking-men market—as part of an ongoing federal sex-trafficking investigation.

While reducing labor trafficking is universally supported, in practice, research has found, and chapters in this book illustrate, that limiting online communications makes sex workers more vulnerable to violence because it constrains their ability to schedule and screen customers. FOSTA/SESTA also weakened the benefits of online mediated sex work, thus perpetuating a broader set of settler-colonial policies most harmful to people-of-color, Indigenous, and gender-nonconforming sex workers.[17] This US policy also has global implications for sex workers—a reality highlighted in several essays.

The Work of Sex Work: Changing Geographies of Work

The nature and organization of work are changing in ways that make non-sex work and sex work more similar. Employers favor part-time, subcontracted, or independent contractors. These contract, or gig, positions offer lower wages, fewer benefits, and less tangible connections between workers and employers than traditional full-time employment. Given stagnant wages (until the COVID-19 pandemic), coupled with unfulfilling (and, during the pandemic, dangerous) work, especially for already marginalized people, many are opting out of long-term positions in favor of gig work like being an Uber driver, opening an Etsy store, or selling photos and videos on OnlyFans, among other options.

Sex workers, like many contemporary gig workers, labor outside a single physical space—working remotely and moving between workspaces. Even before the global coronavirus pandemic, many people no longer worked in traditional physical offices. Escorts use the Internet for advertising, marketing, screening clients, and facilitating dates.[18] Whether they do administrative labor from home or from Starbucks, these are still workspaces. Escorts meet for "in-calls" at their home, or a separate apartment, or "out-calls" at a hotel or a client's home. For many sexual *and* nonsexual laborers, a hotel room can be a workspace. Sex workers, like other gig workers, contribute to expanding definitions of what constitutes a "workplace" and scholarly understandings of the geographies of work.

Sex Worker Activism and Mutual Aid

There is a long, well-documented history of sex worker activism world-wide,[19] and there is a growing list of alliances and coalitions. The Global Network of Sex Work Projects (NSWP) represents national, regional, and local sex worker–led organizations and networks across five regions: Africa, Asia and the Pacific, Europe, Latin America, North America, and the Caribbean. The Global Alliance Against Traffic in Women (GAATW) is an alliance of more than eighty nongovernmental organizations from Africa, Asia, Europe, Latin America, and North America. Currently, organizations such as the African Sex Worker Alliance (ASWA) organize and advocate for sex workers across thirty-five countries on the continent of Africa. The Asia Pacific Network of Sex Workers (APNSW) is a sex-worker-led organization representing workers in over twenty-two countries. Veshya Anyay Mukti Parishad (VAMP) organizes sex workers in India and South Asia. The Caribbean Sex Work Coalition represents sex workers in Guyana, Jamaica, Suriname, Trinidad, Antigua, Grenada, and the Dominican Republic. The European Sex Workers' Rights Alliance (ESWA) represents more than one hundred organizations in thirty countries across Europe and Central Asia. Plataforma Latinoamericana de Personas que ejercen el Trabajo Sexual (PLAPERTS) has members in seven countries in Latin America, including Ecuador, Peru, Colombia, El Salvador, Nicaragua, México, and Brazil. Sex Workers' Rights Advocacy Network (SWAN) represents twenty-eight organizations across eighteen countries such as Albania, Bosnia and Herzegovina, Bulgaria, Georgia, Hungary, Kazakhstan, Kyrgyzstan, Lithuania, Macedonia, Montenegro, Poland, Romania, Russia, Serbia, and Slovakia.

Further, sex workers have created organizations that reflect the intersectional nature of the discrimination and oppression sex workers face. For example, sex industries are highly racialized, and white supremacy shapes global capitalist markets, and organizations such as the Black Sex Workers Collective and Butterfly Asian and Migrant Sex Workers Network in the United States of America attend to how racism and xenophobia shape labor experiences. As another example, in Kenya, sex workers developed the Queer Sex Workers Initiative for Refugees, representing and advocating for LGBTQ sex workers. Sistaazhood is a community of trans women sex workers based in Cape Town, South Africa.

TABLE I.1: A Global Sample of Local Sex Worker Organizations by Country, 2022

Countries	Organizations
Argentina	AMMAR, Sindicato de trabajadorxs sexuales de Argentina
Australia	Scarlett Alliance
Bangladesh	Sex Workers Network
Botswana	Sisonke
Brazil	APROSMIG, Associacao das Prostitutas de Minas Gerais
Canada	Maggies, Toronto; POWER: Prostitutes of Ottawa-Gatineau Work, Educate and Resist; STELLA
England	English Collective of Prostitutes
Germany	SWAG: Sex Workers Action Group
Greece	Red Umbrella, Athens
India	All India Network of Sex Workers; Durbar Mahila Samanwaya Committee; National Network of Sex Workers India
Indonesia	OPSI: Organisasi Perubahan Indonesia
Ireland	Sex Workers Alliance
Jamaica	Jamaica SW Coalition
Kenya	Bar Hostess Empowerment & Support Programme; Coast Sex Workers Alliance; KESWA: Kenya Sex Workers Alliance; Queer Sex Workers Initiative for Refugees
Malawi	Female Sex Workers Association
Mexico	APROASE, Movimiento de Trabajo Sexual de Mexico
Namibia	Namibian Sex Workers Alliance
Netherlands	SAVE: Sex Workers Against Violence & Exploitation
New Zealand	Aotearoa New Zealand Sex Workers' Collective
Nicaragua	Asociacion de Mujeres Las Golondrinas
Nigeria	National Association of Nigerian Prostitutes
Philippines	Philippine Sex Workers Collective
Romania	SexWorkCall
Russia	Silver Rose
South Africa	Sistaazhood
Spain	Colectivo Caye
Switzerland	ProCoRe: Prostitution Collective Reflection
Tanzania	Tanzania Sex Workers Alliance
Uganda	UNESO: Uganda Network for Sex Work -Led Organisations
United Kingdom	National Ugly Mugs
United States	Adult Performer Advocacy Committee; BAYSWAN; the BIPOC Adult Industry Collective; Black Sex Workers Collective; Butterfly Asian and Migrant Sex Workers Network Coyote RI; Cupcake Girls; Desiree Alliance, Erotic Service Providers Union; HIPS; Prostitutes of New York; Red Umbrella Project; Sex Worker Outreach Project; Sex Worker Advocacy and Resistance Movement (SWARM); St. James Infirmary; Support Ho(s)e; SWOP Behind Bars
Vietnam	Vietnam Network of Sex Workers
Zimbabwe	Zimbabwe Sex Workers Alliance

Table I.1 provides a sampling of the many local sex worker organizations that existed throughout the world at the time this book went to press.

Sex worker organizations protest, lobby, provide direct services to sex workers, and run extensive mutual aid programs. Increasingly, there are sex worker organizations and collectives that conduct community-based research. Groups such as Hacking/Hustling share critical research findings in academic peer-reviewed journals and in more mainstream venues, affecting both policymaking and public opinion.

New Directions

All the essays in this book identify recent trends in sex industries, pinpoint new areas for research, and raise critical questions about the future of sex markets. Given our interest in and focus on technological changes, many explore online sex work. This means that the book does not well highlight experiences in street-based economies and survival sex work, such as trading sex for housing or food. More research is needed on contemporary sex work experiences in street-based economies globally.

Also, given the transnational character of sex industries and the scope of global sex worker activism, we aimed to cover an even greater number of countries, especially in places less well documented. To this end, chapters in the volume explore sex work in Canada, Kenya, Aotearoa New Zealand, the United States of America, and the United Kingdom. We believe anthologies like this one should work to capture and document sex workers' labor experiences, market conditions, and sociolegal conditions, as well as sex worker activism across the Global South. We wish we had received submissions or succeeded in our efforts to recruit people laboring in or writing about the Global South and street-based economies, and we hope to see more future work capturing these contexts.

While far from an exhaustive list, the essays in this volume also raise interesting new sets of questions:

- The definition of sex work continues to expand. For example, the growth of industry segments such as sugaring expands definitions of sex work while exacerbating lateral whorephobia. Sites like Sniffer allow people to sell used panties online, but is this sex work? What are the political consequences of sex work no longer referring to full-service providers only? What are the benefits and limitations of inclusive and expanding definitions of sex work?

- How do we reconcile the increasing visibility of sex work in mainstream discourse (e.g., the popularity of porn-content-hosting sites such as Only-fans) with the persistent stigmatization and criminalization of sex work? If countries are witnessing a normalization and acceptance of certain forms of sex work, then public opinions are improving in many countries worldwide (albeit in uneven and complexly different ways); how will such positive patterns shape sex worker activism, law, and policy?

- Given that for many sex workers, part (or in some cases all) of their labor occurs online, how will sex workers continue to grapple with new aggressive Internet regulation, constantly changing terms of service, and the shrinking of sites hosting NSFW content?

- As technologies continue to grow, what will become of sex industries, and how will such shifts affect sex workers? AI technologies have begun affecting online porn industries. With the increase in AI technologies, will the sexbots in brothels documented in Hanson and Smith's chapter in this book, "Cybrothel: The World's First A.I. Sex Worker," displace human workers?

- Banks and payment processors such as American Express, CashApp, Chase Bank, Discover, Mastercard, Paypal, Visa, Venmo, and others have enacted policies refusing to process payments for sales involving sex work (including legal forms such as porn). Thus, how will the changes in banking, currency, payment, and financial platforms affect the ability of sex workers to manage money and work? What are the consequences of occupational discrimination in banking? How does being cut off from an entire financial system affect sex workers' ability to build credit, acquire housing and insurance, and so on?

- Rather than seeing sex work as distinctly or qualitatively different from other forms of economic life, we ask what sex work can tell us about key aspects of current forms of labor, exploitation, consumption, identity, and social life.

- So much research on sex work is qualitative, ethnographic, or based on small samples. The sexual economy is rarely included in larger-scale economic or social-life surveys. How can we gather more comprehensive, reliable quantitative data at a global level about trends and dynamics in the sex industry?

- How do different laws affect sex workers in different countries? We talk a lot about criminalization versus legalization versus decriminalization. But in what areas do different laws and levels of enforcement at the local, regional, national, or international level make a difference?
- There is still a paucity of data about clients. What can the perspective of the client or consumer of sex work tell us about the sex industry? Since sex industries are built around the white cis male gaze, there is a false assumption that all clients are cisgender men. What about women who consume sex, trans consumers, and even sex workers who see sex workers?

The essays in this volume provide readers with a glimpse into the sociolegal landscapes that govern sex work, sex worker labor experiences, market conditions, the way technology affects erotic labor, and sex worker activism. *Sex Work Today* is an invitation to think collectively and critically about how contemporary sexual commerce can deepen academic and public understanding regarding contemporary labor, law and social policy, politics, gender, race, ability, and sexuality.

Finally, we want to give a huge shout-out to all the individuals whose essays appear in this volume and those who submitted abstracts but were not chosen. Submissions came in just as COVID-19 made clear how profoundly all our lives would change over the next three years. Many of our authors struggled with the economic and professional uncertainty of the pandemic. This was on top of the existing challenges in writing about a highly stigmatized topic. Sex work researchers also face challenges funding research, getting support from colleagues, and otherwise conducting their studies in the face of the strength and financial power of anti–sex work movements and organizations. These difficulties are only compounded if the researcher discloses any personal sex work experience. We are grateful to all those who contributed to *Sex Work Today* and to all those who will read these pages.

NOTES

1 Jones 2022a.
2 Luo 2020.
3 See, for example, Treisman 2021.
4 See "Global Mapping of Sex Work Laws," Global Network of Sex Work Projects (NSWP), last updated December 2021, www.nswp.org.
5 Jones 2021a.

6 Jones 2020a; Berg 2021.

7 Jones 2020a; Berg 2021.

8 Dewey and St. Germain 2017; Agustín 2007.

9 Grant 2014; Knoxx 2014; Sciortino 2016; Begum 2020; Graceyswer 2020.

10 Sciortino 2016.

11 Quoted in Poitras 2015.

12 Attwood 2010, 2017.

13 Cole 2022.

14 Studies find that 95 percent of children have seen pornography before turning eighteen (Brown and L'Engle 2009) and that 59 percent of men look at pornography every week while 49 percent saw their first porn before age thirteen (Sun et al. 2016).

15 Attwood 2017; Jones 2016, 2020a; Cunningham et al. 2018.

16 McCombs 2018; SUPRIHMBE 2018; Petillo 2019; Chamberlain 2019; Peterson, Robinson, and Shih 2019; Morgan 2020; Blunt and Wolf 2020; Mia 2020; Eichert 2020; Mai et al. 2021; Albert 2021; Jones 2022a.

17 Petillo 2019.

18 Screening refers to processes for vetting clients before a full-service sex worker will agree to meet them. These methods vary from worker to worker. Examples include clients providing a link to a LinkedIn profile, a picture of their driver's license, or other identifying documents or online profiles. Workers may require a coffee date in a public place before the meeting. In another article Angela Jones published from this research, they showed how marginalized identities often affect screening procedures and whether sex workers feel they can screen clients at all. For example, an economically precarious trans sex worker may loosen screening out of economic need, with fear of losing the client outweighing the need to implement these harm-reduction practices. See, Jones 2022b.

19 Chateauvert 2014; Smith and Mac 2018.

PART I

The Internet Changes the Game

1

Punishing Sex

How Financial Discrimination and Content Moderation Harm Online Sex Workers

VAL WEBBER

It was a typical Tuesday afternoon. I planned to write a bit more, then log in to cam. I took a break and opened my email. As I read a message from my cam platform, my stomach dropped. "No, no, no," I muttered, as I read the automated alert all online porn workers dread:

> This message is to inform you that your performer account with [Company] has been closed for the following reason: The performer was agreeing to participate in banned content . . .

I mentally scanned my recent shifts, trying to guess what innocuous online show had been the offender. Like any frustrated millennial, I then took to Twitter.

I was mad, but I wasn't surprised. I had cammed for many years in the past, then took a hiatus when I started my PhD. When the funding ran out, I returned to online sex work in an increasingly inhospitable climate: anti-porn sentiment and campaigning had intensified. Pornhub

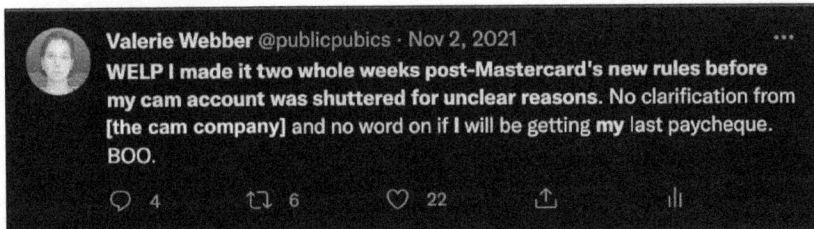

> **Valerie Webber** @publicpubics · Nov 2, 2021   ...
> **WELP I made it two whole weeks post-Mastercard's new rules before my cam account was shuttered for unclear reasons.** No clarification from [the cam company] and no word on if **I will be getting my** last paycheque. BOO.
>
> 💬 4   🔁 6   ♡ 22   ↑   ᵢₗᵢ

Figure 1.1. Tweet from the author's account, November 2, 2021. Courtesy of the author.

had just had its payment processing withdrawn. Then Mastercard announced strict new "specialty adult content merchant guidelines" for all websites accepting Mastercard payments for pornographic content.[1] Impending doom was pervasive across online sex worker communities because this was all-too-familiar territory.

This essay explores the impacts of Mastercard's revised guidelines, which are part of a broader landscape of online adult-content surveillance and moderation that harms sex workers while claiming to protect them from exploitation. It draws on survey data collected from adult-content producers—cam performers, clip artists, and others who create and sell pornographic content online featuring themselves and/or hired performers. Importantly, it also illustrates how these harms affect multiply marginalized workers more severely: Black performers and other performers of color, disabled performers, fat performers, trans performers, and those who produce fetish, kink, or queer content. These guidelines harm individual workers and constrain which sexualities can exist online. In this way, content moderation is implicated in larger ideological projects to police and punish sex and gender diversity.

Payment Processing and Sex Work: The Case of Mastercard

Mastercard has always had special requirements for transactions involving adult content, but the October 15, 2021, policy change added significant criteria, including these:

- Platforms—not producers—acquire and hold copies of all performers' consent forms, personal information, and photo IDs.
- Only verified content providers may upload content, with a process for verifying age and identity.
- Platforms review all content before it is uploaded and monitor livestreams.
- Platforms allow depicted people to appeal for removal of content; create complaint processes for users to flag content that is "potentially illegal or otherwise in violation of the Mastercard standards;" and produce monthly reports on these instances.
- Platforms do not use keywords or search terms that suggest the platform contains child sexual abuse materials (CSAM) or the "depiction of

non-consensual activities" and do not use content that is "potentially illegal or otherwise in violation of the Mastercard standards" to draw traffic.

- Platforms have "effective policies" in place to ensure their sites are not used to "promote or facilitate human trafficking, sex trafficking, or physical abuse."
- Platforms "provide Mastercard with temporary account credentials" upon request so they may view content behind paywalls.

Predicting catastrophic consequences for workers' livelihoods, grass-roots resistance mobilized in the months leading up to the passage of the new policy. Hundreds of sex workers and stakeholders composed a detailed statement, issued on September 1,[2] along with video testimonies, a petition, a social media storm, and in-person protests at banking headquarters in several US cities. Journalists and organizations covered the issue.[3] Some noted that while Mastercard had discussions with evangelical Christian anti-porn groups when drafting the policy,[4] they did not consult with adult-content creators themselves. *After* announcing the incoming guidelines, Mastercard met with two adult-industry organizations but ignored warnings that their policy would deter legal content.[5] Eventually, they also met with a group of sex work advocates. The meeting was disingenuous, however, as Mastercard dismissed the group's concerns, and refused future meetings on the basis that "for a dialogue to be successful, both sides have to have an appreciation for truth and existing laws" and moved ahead with their updated requirements.[6]

Introducing the Survey and Participants

I developed a short survey to collect information from adult content creators about the kinds of content they create and the consequences they experienced due to Mastercard's policy. I built the survey using Qualtrics and launched it via Twitter from November 30, 2021, until January 15, 2022. Percentages have been rounded to whole numbers or one decimal place. Direct quotations are from responses to open-ended text box questions.

A total of 117 surveys were completed. Seventy percent of respondents were from the United States, 10 percent from Canada, 6 percent from

TABLE 1.1: Respondent Demographics

Age	
18–24	13.5%
25–30	35%
31–39	33%
40–49	12%
50–59	3.5%
60+	2%
Prefer not to say	1%

Race	
Black	7%
Hispanic/Latinx	2%
South Asian/Middle Eastern	2%
East Asian/Pacific Islander	1%
Multiracial/Biracial or selected multiple boxes	17%
White	68%
Prefer not to say	3%

Gender	
Trans woman	4%
Nonbinary/Pangender/Genderqueer	20%
Cis woman	60%
Cis man	14%
Prefer not to say	2%

Sexuality	
Queer/Bisexual/Pansexual/Lesbian/Gay	66%
Asexual	4%
Straight	24%
Prefer not to say	6%

Dependents*	
Children	13%
Friend(s)/Partner(s)	21%
Parent(s)/Family	11%
No dependents	54%
Prefer not to say	6%

* Total is more than 100% because five respondents reported having multiple categories of dependents. Most respondents use multiple platforms.

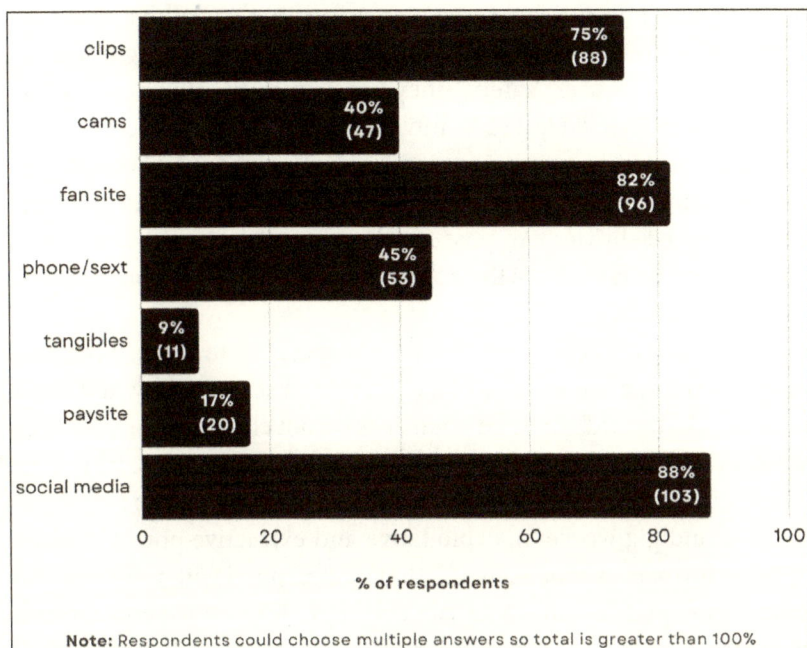

Figure 1.2. Types of platforms used by respondents (% and N). Courtesy of the author.

the UK, 5 percent from western Europe, 4 percent from Australasia, and 1 percent from South Africa (4 percent preferred not to say).

Working at Ruinous Crossroads

The updated Mastercard policy is not an isolated concern. It sits at the intersection of two hostile forces faced by sex workers: discrimination from financial services and biased content-moderation policies.[7] Sex workers, whether operating online, offline, or both, routinely have their bank accounts and other financial products (e.g., American Express, Bank of America, Capital One, CashApp, Chase, PayPal, Venmo, Wells Fargo) closed, their funds seized, and their lives devastated. This happens regardless of whether the sex work they do is legal in their jurisdiction.[8] A wealth of research also shows that sex workers—particularly trans, BIPOC, and politically active sex workers—are disproportionately shadowbanned or removed from online platforms and services ("deplatforming").[9] While platforms describe content moderation as a part of "community guidelines" meant to ensure user "safety," they are primarily influenced by legislation like FOSTA/SESTA and the interests of shareholders.[10] Content-moderation policies target sex workers and pornographic imagery more severely than other kinds of content (e.g., ad revenue–generating celebrities can post nearly nude and suggestive content, whereas sex workers have their accounts flagged, shadowbanned, and shuttered for less).

Porn platforms depend on credit card processors to accept payments, so they must operate within a tangle of strict, discriminatory, and vague policies. Mastercard's updated guidelines do not clearly define what constitutes satisfactory procedures, so risk-averse platforms typically adopt a heavy hand. Like most workers under late-stage capitalism (especially creative and gig workers), exploitative and extractive porn platforms treat performers as expendable.[11] They overrespond with their content-moderation policies since they can afford to kick performers off rather than risk consequences from the financial institutions that affect their bottom line. The result is harsh and unpredictable penalties for hundreds of thousands of workers.

Survey respondents were asked if they had experienced any of the following due to Mastercard's updated policy: (1) having an account closed, (2) receiving an account warning, (3) having to contact old scene partners for updated ID, (4) having to remove content because they could not meet new ID requirements, (5) having to remove content because the theme violated content rules, (6) experiencing delays when having to re-upload content for review, (7) having payments interrupted, or (8) losing access to payment processing entirely. Overall, 90 percent of respondents said they experienced at least one of these negative impacts due to the new Mastercard policy. Over half (61.5 percent) experienced four or more different negative outcomes.

Identification

Traditionally, porn producers are responsible for keeping copies of ID (proving people are over eighteen) and model releases (documenting consent, copyright, and financial agreements), to be made available to platforms or authorities should the legality of the content come into question.[12] Platforms generally require the people uploading or streaming the content to verify their identity, assert that they own the rights to the content, and assert that all performers are consenting adults. Following Mastercard's new policy, platforms demand additional documents: third-party ID verification/facial scans, platform-specific model releases, and/or currently valid ID for all featured performers. If people own older content and cannot contact performers to get images of their renewed ID, that content must be removed even though they have consent forms and ID that was valid at the time of the shoot.[13] As Elaine,[14] a straight, white, cis woman, wrote,

> I am absolutely for following all federal guidelines. . . . But telling me I can't post a scene I own the rights to because I don't have a copy of the person's current ID is ridiculous. She was 18 when I filmed the movie, she didn't suddenly get less [than] 18 over the last ten years.

These additional ID requirements are ostensibly about keeping people safe by ensuring that content was made consensually. In practice, they mean handing over sensitive personal information to platforms that may not protect their databases appropriately. Delilah, a queer, asexual, Indigenous/Latinx, nonbinary trans woman, wrote,

> Requiring sites to keep the private information of ourselves and everyone we work with is a huge security issue, especially since we legally are required to already keep this info ourselves. Any breach in security not just risks our safety but that of everyone we work with.

For performers who already have concerns about doxing and stalking due to sex worker stigma,[15] this added "safety" can have the opposite effect. Among respondents, 42 percent had to remove content because they could not meet these redundant ID requirements.

Flagging, Closure, and Banned Themes

Another detrimental impact people suffered was having an account flagged (58 percent) or closed (32 percent).[16] While platforms have always had a legal duty not to host legally "obscene" content (itself a poorly defined test),[17] Mastercard also disallows a vague category of "brand damaging" content.[18] Platforms interpret and apply these guidelines differently,[19] creating a motley and unpredictable regulatory landscape that tends to ban legal kink categories.[20]

Fifty-eight percent of respondents had to remove content because the theme was banned, mostly content involving "extreme" bodily acts (e.g., squirting, "large" insertions) and consensual power exchange (e.g., BDSM, hypnosis). "They are labeling totally consensual scenes with model releases, IDs, and professional models as 'non-consensual' due to themes in the plot/storyline," said Larry, a straight, white, cis man. Jordan, a straight, Black, biracial, cis man, pointed out the double standard: "My content is fantasy narratives that involve consenting adults. The fact that a vampire can use hypnosis on television to enthrall someone, but I can't do that same scenario in porn, is absurd." This suppression of kink amounts to "the literal censorship of terms and ideas," as Joanie, a queer, cis woman (no racial category selected), put it.

The Costs of Perilous Deplatforming

As the preceding section illustrates, online adult-content production occurs in a landscape of increasing precarity and hypersurveillance. This has impacted performers in three key ways. Workers have experienced (1) decreased income, (2) increased health risks, and (3) increased mental health concerns.

Decreased Income

Online sex work is not a frivolous "side hustle"; 84 percent of respondents said their online work is a primary source of income. Having to remove or re-upload content and having accounts closed or suspended has a drastic effect on people's earnings. Most (75 percent) respondents noticed a drop in their sales due to Mastercard's new policy (19 percent were unsure, and 6 percent had no drop). Among those whose sales dropped, over half lost 50 percent or more of their monthly income (figure 1.3). Respondents also mentioned decreased traffic and engagement as

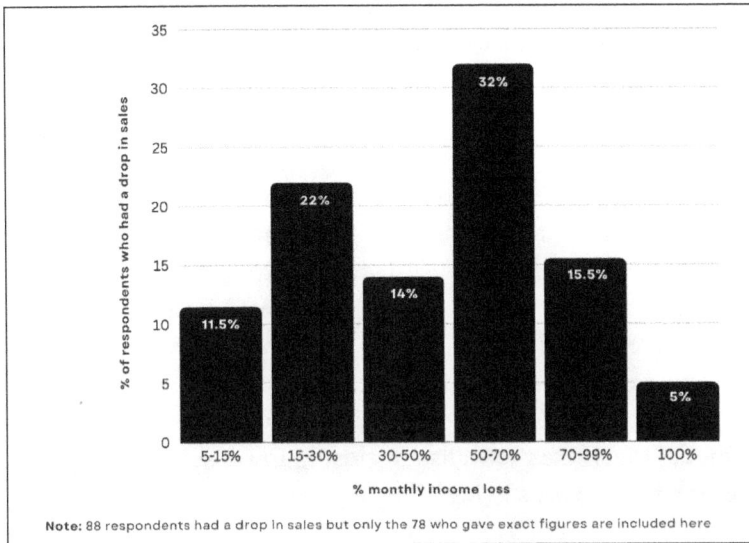

Note: 88 respondents had a drop in sales but only the 78 who gave exact figures are included here

Figure 1.3. Respondents (% and N) whose sales dropped, by percentage of monthly income loss. Courtesy of the author.

customers lost confidence in platforms, particularly on OnlyFans, as they showed indecision around banning adult content altogether.[21] All told, 78 percent said the policy affected their ability to make ends meet.

Respondents shared devastating stories about the consequences of this lost income. "I'm living paycheck to paycheck," wrote queer, white, nonbinary respondent Jae. "I've almost drained my emergency savings," wrote River, a queer, Latinx, nonbinary woman.

Increased Risk

Many respondents noted that to compensate for their loss of online income, they had to return to or take on additional in-person sex work. Others had to return to low-paying, non–sex work jobs. This compounded financial stress with fears of COVID-19 exposure and additional mental and physical strain. "I have had to go back to gig food service work to make ends meet, which has been horrible for both my mental and physical health," said Maude, a queer, white, cis woman. Queer, Indigenous, trans woman Naomi, wrote that she was feeling "extreme levels of stress. Having to go back to in-person sex work during a pandemic is terrifying."

Mental Health

Throughout respondents' stories, there was an overwhelming theme of insecurity and precarity, which took a toll on workers' mental health. Sixty-seven percent said their work-related stress had increased "a lot," and 27 percent said it had increased "somewhat." Respondent Heather, a queer, white, cis woman, wrote, "It's like right now everything is super delicate, and every site has a different approach to the same rules, I feel so insecure about future changes." Carla, also a queer, white, cis woman, lamented, "I feel like the walls are closing in on sex workers who are simply trying to make a living."

Relative Risk: Who Is Hit Hardest

While most respondents reported adverse outcomes, income loss, and increased anxiety, some content creators were more intensely impacted than others. Disabled performers, Black performers, other performers of color, and performers who make fat, trans, queer, or kink content were more harshly targeted and impacted.

Disability

Many sex workers live with some form of disability. Traditional work can be inaccessible, whereas sex work enables people to work less and earn more with a flexible schedule.[22] Therefore, the loss of online income is particularly devastating to disabled workers. Additionally, the prospect of returning to in-person work and the risk of COVID-19 exposure was concerning for many disabled workers. Ari, a queer, Black, chronically ill cis woman, said, "I'm considering brothel work or an extra non–sex work job, but I'm high risk for COVID and very anxious about this." A queer, Latinx, chronically ill, nonbinary respondent, Carmen, wrote that when they started online sex work, they "had hope again for the first time in almost 20 years" but that the economic downturn resulting from Mastercard's policy "has been one of the most gutting experiences of my adult life."

Race, Size, and Content Type

Some performers found themselves more severely targeted by their platforms' implementation of the Mastercard policy. Namely, Black performers were 1.44 times more likely, and other performers of color were 1.32 times more likely, to have suffered multiple detrimental impacts (more than five) compared to white performers. Creators who produce porn with fat performers ("BBW," "BHM," etc.) were 1.73 times more likely to have suffered multiple detrimental impacts compared to those who do not. Those who defined their content as "queer" were 1.71 times more likely to suffer multiple detrimental impacts and 1.4 times more likely to pull content due to theme violations. Finally, those who produce fetish/roleplay and/or kink/BDSM content were 1.56 times more likely to have suffered multiple detrimental impacts and 1.4 times more likely to have to pull content due to theme violations.

The result of these combined policy prejudices is that the performers who fit a cis, white, vanilla, nondisabled, heteronormative ideal have not been as adversely affected as marginalized ones. The sanitization of the Internet does not erase sex per se, but rather narrowly determines what kind of sexuality can exist online. Conservatives, anti-porn Christian fundamentalists, and the governments and corporations they lobby, are not opposed to sex. They are opposed to sex outside the white nuclear family norm.[23]

Broader Connections

Mastercard's updated adult content policy is not a unique situation, nor is its impact on workers. It is just one example of a larger issue whereby sex workers suffer at the intersection of two oppressive forces: discriminatory financial services and unjust content-moderation policies. Appealing to platforms themselves to change has limited effect, so long as they are capitulating to greater economic and political forces. We might consider advocating for the classification of financial services—including online banking tools—as essential utilities to which everyone has an inherent human right. We could insist that governments and corporations involve sex workers in all decision making around online content moderation and identity/age verification to ensure that policies and procedures supposedly intended to prevent harm do not put sex workers' privacy and livelihoods at risk.

As noted above, the Mastercard guidelines were developed under pressure from and in consultation with Christian anti-porn groups, namely, Exodus Cry and the National Center on Sexual Exploitation. Anti–sex work/anti-porn sentiment has been invigorated in recent years, incited by faith-based extremists and carceral feminist groups: from declarations that pornography is a "public health crisis" to violent campaigns for the closure of Pornhub to the passage of disastrous "end-demand" legislation.[24] We are also witnessing an extreme attack on trans folks, queer folks, and abortion seekers,[25] anyone whose existence challenges the moral dominance of the traditional family. Intensive sex and gender policing like this is a key facet of fascist ideology,[26] in particular of white/Christian nationalism, which "not only seeks to maintain ethnic and social hierarchies, but to *politically* enforce a particular type of social and sexual order defined by monogamous, patriarchal, heterosexual marriage relationships and gender roles."[27] History shows that surges in fascism often begin with calls to protect the virility of men and the purity of women and children from the moral decay of "whores," "perverts," and "groomers." Fascism seeks to constrain and control sexual/relational variety so that it can be streamlined to serve specific racial, political, and economic ends.

Scholars, activists, and politicians must make these connections. We must not allow people to dismiss something like tightened content moderation as a frivolous issue disconnected from other struggles. Instead, the suppression, sanitization, and vanillification of sex online must be viewed in context as one piece of a much larger and extremely disturbing movement.

ACKNOWLEDGMENTS

I greatly appreciate everyone who took the time to answer the survey and offer their rich written insights. Thank you also to Ashley Lake, Lucy Hart, Colin and Angie Rowntree, and Steven Rise for consulting with me on various details of this chapter.

NOTES

1 Verdeschi 2021.
2 Acceptance Matters 2021.
3 E.g., Holston-Zannell 2021a, 2021b; Turner 2021a, 2021b, 2021c.
4 Celarier 2021.
5 Turner 2021a, 2021b, 2021c.
6 Cole 2021c.
7 Jones 2021a; Blue 2015; Are and Paasonen 2021.
8 Herrmann and Redman 2021; Tusikov 2021; D'Adamo and Watson 2021.
9 Shadowbanning occurs when platforms make it more difficult to view or discover a user's posts. Blunt and Stardust 2021; Blunt et al. 2020; Lake et al. 2018.
10 FOSTA/SESTA is a 2018 US law ostensibly designed to prevent sex trafficking by creating an exemption to §230 of the Communications Decency Act, making platforms responsible for user-generated content that "promotes or facilitates prostitution." The law is broadly understood to be a failure that has made sex work exceptionally more dangerous. McCombs 2018; SUPRIHMBE 2018; United States Government Accountability Office 2021; Paasonen, Jarrett, and Light 2019; Gillespie 2018.
11 Berg 2021; McKee 2016.
12 These standards are outlined by US Criminal Code §2257. Many producers globally adhere to them because most adult platforms are based in the United States.
13 Some platforms place a greater documentation burden on individual performers and small producers than on larger studio accounts. The irony is that policies intended to reduce exploitation actually push performers to work for studios rather than produce their own content, diminishing their autonomy.
14 All names are pseudonyms. Some quotations have been lightly edited. Regarding demographics: respondents were asked to select one or more options for race, gender, and sexuality. Some of these options were listed as a series of related terms, for example, "Queer/Bisexual/Pansexual" or "Hispanic/Latinx." This umbrella approach was taken in order to offer several affiliated identity markers while maintaining a manageable number of categories that would be adequately populated to be statistically meaningful. In relation to quotations, however, these options have been simplified to single terms in an effort to identify people as accurately as possible while maintaining readability, knowing they may not self-identify with the precise terminology selected.
15 "Doxing" occurs when someone's private information, such as legal name and address, is published on the Internet with malicious intent.
16 Clips, cam, fan site, phone/sext, or tangibles account.
17 Creasy 2012. While countries have different obscenity laws, most adult platforms are based in the United States and/or comply with US law.
18 Mastercard n.d.
19 Ladder n.d.

20 Stegeman 2021; Stardust 2014.
21 Cole 2021b.
22 Jones 2022c; Tastrom 2019a.
23 Rubin 2011.
24 Webber and Sullivan 2018; Decrim Now n.d.; Mac 2016.
25 Strangio 2022.
26 Burnett and Richardson 2021; Roos 2002; Butler 2021.
27 Perry and Whitehead 2022, 5.

2

Sugar Dating

What Counts as Sex Work

KAVITA NAYAR JABLONKA

Since their introductions in the early 1920s, the terms "sugar daddy," a wealthy older man, and "gold-digger," a poorer woman who dates or marries men for money, have challenged traditional values of sexual respectability, in particular the belief that one should not or cannot mix money with intimacy. In the twenty-first century, digital "sugar dating" platforms facilitate arrangements between sugar daddies, mostly economically successful cisgender white men, or, more rarely, mamas,[1] and the "sugar baby," usually upwardly mobile cisgender white women.[2] Launched in 2006, the most popular platform, Seeking Arrangement, boasts forty million active users worldwide, with three sugar babies to every one sugar daddy or mama. Srushti Upadhyay conducted a comprehensive study of user profiles, demonstrating that 80 percent of sugar daddies were white, educated, and affluent (averaging $280,000 a year in income).[3] Among sugar babies, Upadhyay's groundbreaking study showed some racial diversity, with approximately 54 percent identifying as white. Still, while more babies were identified as mixed (19 percent) and Latina (15 percent), there was still a significant lack of Black, Indigenous, and Asian sugar babies. On average, sugar babies are younger and have less education than sugar daddies.

Drawing on interviews, participant observation, and qualitative analysis of US online blogs and forums, this chapter examines the phenomenon of sugar relationships, a form of erotic labor that scholars are just beginning to explore. Because most mainstream sugar dating platforms cater to straight, cisgender men, called "sugar daddies," and cisgender women, called "sugar babies," my data examines sugaring from the perspective of female "sugar babies," and I center their stories. I also recognize that the experiences of cisgender women in straight sugaring relationships do not capture the diversity of participants and breadth of sugar culture. In the following pages, I explain the mechanics of sugar relationships and explore how they differ from, and overlap with, traditional romantic dating *and* sex work. Sugar relationships, like gig work on platforms like OnlyFans, are part of a new wave of commodified relationships complicating how people perceive and define sex work.

What Are Sugar Relationships?

Sugar dating, also called mutually beneficial arrangements, are relationships in which participants exchange youth, beauty, and flattering attention for gifts, money, favors, and social capital. CEO of Seeking Arrangement, Brandon Wade, explains that one person provides "intimacy, companionship or other forms of attention in exchange for personal benefit (e.g., financial support, professional advancement, etc.)."[4] "The relationship resembles a business deal or a financial agreement," one sugar baby (SB) writes. The benefactor provides economic and social benefits, which may include money, gifts, all-expenses-paid trips, professional advice, and networking (colloquially referred to as "help," "spoiling," and "mentoring"), and the recipient bestows relational benefits in equal amounts of companionship, conversation, and sexual intimacy. According to Seeking Arrangement, the average sugar baby earns twenty-eight hundred dollars per month. In practice, benefits range from allowances of a few hundred to a few thousand dollars a month, gifts from an online retail wish list, college tuition, introductions to a network, or even capital investments in a business. Ideally, both parties anticipate some sort of genuine enjoyment in the relationship, and sex may or may not be part of the deal.

Lawyers, psychologists, and journalists alike have begun to question whether sugar relationships are simply a glorified form of prostitution.[5] Sugar babies themselves perceive sugar relationships as different from both "vanilla dating" (when two people date with the hope of falling in love) and escorting. Among sex workers, full-service providers (those who have sex with clients) face far more social stigma than those who perform indirect sex work like stripping, camming, or sugaring. Sugar relationships deliberately obscure the exchange of sex for money to purposely shield sugar babies from the stigma sex workers endure. This form of stigma management benefits sugar workers but simultaneously reifies what sex workers call the "whorearchy" and "lateral whorepho-bia." In sex industries, both clients and workers often see full-service providers, especially those working in street-based markets, as perform-ing the most stigmatized work. Whereas those laboring in the camming industry or as dominatrices, for example, are seen as more privileged. Lateral whorephobia explains why more privileged workers, such as the sugar babies described in this article, might look down upon and per-petuate the stigma full-service providers face.

At the same time, as I will soon explore, fostering the ambiguity that sugar babies may or may not do full-service sex work sometimes results in babies performing more emotional and sexual labor for less money than escorts. When asked what interests young people, mostly young women, to enter into sugar relationships, they offer the same reason as other sex workers: money. In the following pages, I explore how sugar daters challenge and expand contemporary understandings of gender, dating, sex work, and the line between money and intimacy.

Sugar Dating as Traditional Gendered Dating (with Benefits)

At first glance, sugaring is traditional dating, adopting rituals and cus-toms little different from courting practices in the past: two people ex-plore whether they have sufficient "chemistry" to develop a "connection" through shared experiences of commercialized leisure and consump-tion, like dining out, traveling, shopping, and enjoying nightlife. The major difference is that the sugar daddy (or, more rarely, mama) always pays. Such male financial power is one key part of the gendered dynamic in sugaring. Indeed, the terms—"sugar daddy" and "sugar baby"—highlight a nostalgia for heteropatriarchal gender roles, neatly dividing participants by wealth, status, and rational intellect for men, and sexual-ity, subservience, and emotional intuition for women.

The sugar babies I have interviewed say sugar dating is having "a boy-friend with benefits. It has more perks than a traditional relationship." Sugar babies tell me that these relationships provide both "excitement, fun, and adventure" and "financial security/gain" and "mentorship." Sugar babies, like many women, say they prefer to date "established," mature men rather than broke young ones who play video games all day and expect blow jobs on the first date. For example, Elise (all the names used are pseudonyms) explained her attraction to older men: "They generally have more money built up over a lifetime," "their kids are more than likely adults by then, which equals more freed up money for me, lol," and they also have a "massive and varied Rolodex of connections." Dating older men has other benefits. Angie described older men as "less of a physical threat" and less "pressed/thirsty for sex" than younger men. She perceived sugar daddies as more "giving/accommodating because they're used to taking care of family, wives, kids." The women I spoke with, were, as Upadhyay found, primarily young, cisgender, white women who were attracted to the social, cultural, and economic advantages sugar daddies might provide and perceived sexual chemistry as a pleasant but unnecessary element of the relationship.

Some of those interested in sugar dating also appear motivated by the defined nature of the dating script,[6] which romanticizes performances of hegemonic masculinity and emphasized femininity, or in other words, the strong, successful man who supports the sexy, feminine woman. Men with "white knight syndrome," who have the resources and want to be a hero to a vulnerable woman, can follow a simple set of rules: he pays, and she smiles and flatters him. Likewise, women can enjoy being "spoiled" and performing an old-fashioned brand of femininity. Also, for those unsettled by new gender norms in the wake of #metoo and confused by the contemporary dating scene, sugar relationships offer men benefits previously reserved to strip clubs.[7] In strip bars, regular male customers described feeling "young," "virile," and "attractive,"[8] able to openly appreciate women's bodies without repercussions and interact with beautiful women without fear of rejection. Both strip clubs and sugaring not only uphold hegemonic masculinity but also offer a titillating reconstitution of heteropatriarchal gender roles: the sexual assertiveness and public nudity of female dancers, like the directness of some female sugar babies in stating their expectations, terms of engagement, and sexual willingness, transgress norms of respectable femininity in pleasurable ways.

Sugar Dating as Gender Rebellion

Femme sugar babies demonstrate contradictory attitudes: they embrace the expectation that men foot the bill while openly expressing disdain for patriarchal norms of contemporary dating that box women into passive roles. They explain this tension by critiquing "vanilla" relationships as fraught with game playing in which men usually hold the winning hand. In the "Sugar Bowl," women disrupt these dynamics by using their beauty, youth, and charm to make explicit financial expectations. Sugar babies also express frustration with women who give their time, energy, and resources away to men for free. "Do not give up sugaring for a basic ass vanilla boy," one SB warns her peers. They "never know your worth and toss you away after wasting months of your time that you could have been spending making bank." According to some SBs, making money in a dating exchange levels the playing field between women and men.

For this reason, SBs sometimes present sugaring as empowering for women. This is not because SBs are free from oppression but because they believe all dating oppresses women. As feminist Jane Ward explores in her book *The Tragedy of Heterosexuality*, heterosexuality itself is a rigged game sucking up women's love, attention, time, and sometimes money for little in return. Consequently, demanding compensation for typically unpaid acts, like emotional and physical intimacy, is a logical, proactive strategy to ensure a woman's material well-being. Ashley explained:

> Just remember that being paid $2000 per meeting or month is 2000 times better than some dopey 20-something, broke, uneducated loser who wants to feel you up in the back of his Honda civic, cheat on you and try to run game. This is why I don't go for men my age. They just don't deserve me.

I found similar sentiments in the online SB blogosphere. For example, one blogger stated that she is "sick of regular people and their shocked face by saying 'You are too pretty to be single.' Ok, vanilla people, I would rather say I'm too intelligent to stay with stingy and non-rich dudes." Sugar dating resists elements of gender inequality by facilitating greater awareness of double standards, challenging the unpaid emotional labor women perform in romantic relationships, and upending the paradigm of monogamous marriage.

"Sugaring Is Real Work": Sugaring as Sex Work

Constructing sugar relationships as a "job" makes sense to those who identify with the modern archetype of an independent, sexually liberated, and ambitious modern woman. But, using one's sexual capital to advance careers, save money, and build connections is work. "Being in a relationship is a job," Suzannah proclaimed, expressing a widely held contemporary belief that all relationships take work and sugaring is no different, concluding, "I am crazy to not fully take advantage of this situation." Many SBs delay their own romantic interests until they achieve their career goals, financial security, and self-fulfillment.

Female sugar babies engage in "bounded intimacy,"[9] by placing boundaries on their time and energy and ending relationships that demand more emotional involvement than they are willing to provide. As Taylor explained, "Sugaring . . . is not dating. I don't want to see you all the time. I'm busy. I have my own schedule." A blog writer concurred, writing that she does not "vanilla" date because "it's probably going to suck 'breaking up'/hurting him when he becomes too demanding/time consuming." As one SB noted, sugaring is highly skilled affective labor. "Any potential sugar daddy you encounter who is only seeking sex can immediately be redirected towards an escort service. Sugar daddies are paying to be enchanted, and a SB should bring something to his life that he can't buy." She continued: "Any woman can fuck him for the right price. Your job is to make him fall in love every time he sees you."

Many SBs perceive sugaring as an intangible affective experience, harder to quantify and replicate than selling sex. Further, many SBs perceive full-service sex work negatively, as a practice that entails a loss of dignity and bodily autonomy, benefiting men who may, as one noted, "hold money over your head like you have to earn your worth." SBs with these attitudes toward sex work hope that men see them as different from and superior to prostitutes because they offer psychological and emotional, as well as occasional sexual services. Such SBs also distinguish between sexual "taste" and work, seeing what they do as for "perks" or "benefits" and not necessities, thus perpetuating lateral whorephobia.

Positioning themselves above escorts reveals a dangerous and damaging naivety about the value of sugar work relative to escorting. Yes, sugar dating may delay or even exclude sexual gratification, but being an SB may also be much more laborious than full-service sex work. One SB clarified, "They pay escorts to leave, but they pay you to stay." Sugar dating is an elaborate tease that more closely resembles stripping than escorting. Hayley said, "Like strippers, SBs are selling the *idea* of sex" (emphasis added). Alissa concluded, "If he hits it that first night he may as well have hired an escort because he most likely won't be calling you again or your relationship will consist of a pay for play arrangement." All the hours of teasing and getting to know may only be compensated with meals.

Unsurprisingly, groups and individuals differ on how they perceive and discuss "sex work" in sugaring. Some bloggers reject the watered-down Pollyanna version of luxury-brand sugar dating that overempha-sizes the value of fancy meals and flirting. They name this messaging a disingenuous strategy concocted to deceive SBs about the nature of the work while avoiding the stigma of prostitution. "Listen, ladies," one blogger announced,

> This shit is not easy. Stop letting the images of luxury make you think that sex work is all sunshine and rainbows and stacks of money and Chanel bags. If you have a problem being sexual, have internalized whorephobia, or lack street smarts and are just straight up naive, you will not go far, at all.

Some sugar escorts who openly acknowledge the sex work compo-nent of sugaring complain about the infiltration of naïve women seeking "easy money." They argue that this not only results in greater exploita-tion and danger from customers but also lowers consumer expectations about the value of professional services. In other words, sugar babies' intense affective labor may lower wages for escorts while downplaying the risks of what one blogger eloquently describes as "sucking old wrin-kly penis." Sugar escorts assert that sugaring *is* work. They explained:

> This isn't romance . . . it's a job that not everyone can do. So, when you say something like, "I want to get into sugaring because it looks so easy and fun!" you're being insulting and also, you're in for a rude awakening.

> Being a Sugar Baby does not put you above other sex workers. Sugaring is not different. Sugaring is not just about "companionship."

> Stop giving non-sex workers the idea that they can just wake up one morning and get everything in their life paid for.

When one SB asserted, "I don't turn my nose down on anyone and their hustle" but complained about being labeled a "hooker" by patrons at a restaurant where she picked up "whales" (wealthy patrons interested in spending a lot of money), another countered, "We couldn't have you getting mixed up with those dirty hookers now? Can't have people thinking you're a whore!" Another blogger challenged the self-defeating assumption that sugaring is better than escorting: "Hookers go to dinner with their clients too. They just get paid twice what you're getting for it." Ideologies that make false distinctions between sugar babies and escorts harm both groups. Thus, SBs trying to avoid sex worker stigma face a double bind: even if they are not interested in emotional or romantic connections, they might forego a more economically lucrative arrangement to keep up appearances of a "legitimate" relationship rather than suffer whore stigma. Further, considering themselves superior to full-service providers reifies lateral whorephobia, and contributes to the discrimination and stigma full-service workers face.

Some SBs believe they perform *more* unpaid labor than escorts, although they probably do not. One SB turned escort observed, "The biggest draw to escorting is that there's no labor outside working hours, and the pay is better. Unless you're in that ultra-rare category of sugar babies that finds a whale, you'll be spending ten times more time with a guy to get a fraction of what an escort would get." Regardless of whether or not escorts do more unpaid labor, women in "pure" sugar relationship likely earn less than full-service workers. Given the affective labor SBs may potentially engage in, accepting an "allowance" is akin to agreeing to a capped salary or a salary with a commission based on performance. Another blogger explored this: "Sugaring is supposed to be MORE money than escorting because you are 'low volume' and providing a more emotionally available girlfriend type experience. Instead, it's girls who don't want to be labelled 'hooker' taking less money by letting themselves be manipulated by these men."

Situating sugar dating in the spectrum of sex work may offer SBs feminist tools to manage sexism, as Kayla illustrated: "It's crazy to hear a lot of women say they would never do sex work because they don't want to deal with men mistreating them, when in reality men mistreat women everyday . . . whether they're getting paid or not." Some see sugaring as an act of resistance, a form of control over the terms of heterosexual relations, and a creative way to thrive under patriarchal capitalism. Sugar dating is a middle ground between emotion-laden normative intimacies like marriage ("trophy wife" status) and nonnormative intimacies like camming, "online-only" virtual relationships, and full-service relationships between escorts and clients.

Experienced SBs counsel newcomers, "You're going to feel guilty at first. Expect it. Ignore it. You're not a slut, you're not a liar. You are an entertainer." Women warn each other about daddies manipulating new babies by calling those who ask too directly for an allowance "hookers or prostitutes." They explain that these men want to "tap into your insecurity of being seen as a whore so you'll feel ashamed when you bring up HIS side of the MUTUALLY beneficial arrangement." This "whorephobic" ideology works against women who "don't want to be seen as prostitutes" because "men are totally playing along" to get the same services "at a discounted price." They urged SBs to deflect such manipulations and ask for the true value of their services: "Don't let them slut shame you into submission. Be a 'ho and be proud or you'll be dating an old fart for free while your debts keep on stacking."

Framing sugaring as work helps SBs see and demand payment for their labor. "Sugaring is real work," one SB affirms. "Remember this when a man tries to make you do things for free. Do you think he would work overtime for free for his boss? Would he ask his employees to work for free?" The way SBs strain to locate and ascribe value to their labor has implications for all forms of feminized care labor, which feminist economist Nancy Folbre argues comes with a disadvantage she calls the "care penalty," referring to the way emotional ties obscure or discourage workers from ascribing an exchange value to their labor.[10] Women may not even be aware they are doing more for less.

In conclusion, sugar relationships sit on the boundaries between romantic dating/love and sex work. Here I describe these as a specialized sexual sphere that mostly young women negotiate to improve their financial situations. Though sugar dating reinforces intersecting social inequalities—patriarchy, capitalism, and white supremacy—it also offers some individuals a pathway to economic improvement. It challenges ideologies of what constitutes a "good match" in ways that work within, but also subtly resist, patriarchal capitalism. Many questions remain and much intersectional work is still needed to explore how race, nationality, gender, sexuality, and ability shape access to and experiences within the sugaring industry. Still, from the research I and others have conducted, it is clear that sugaring is a form of erotic labor that is part of an ever-diversifying global sex market, expanding public understanding of what constitutes sex work. Further, the tensions between sugar babies and other sex workers, specifically full-service providers, reveal how SBs embrace lateral whorephobia as a form of stigma management but that such behavior and thinking reifies the harmful stigma that criminalized sex workers face every day. Such tensions raise critical issues around how sex workers survive in a world where they face increased crimi-nalization, state-sponsored violence, and enduring stigma created and perpetuated by neo-Victorian laws.

NOTES

1 According to a representative from Seeking Arrangement, in 2021, 14 percent of the users were sugar mamas compared to 86 percent sugar daddies.
2 Upadhyay 2021.
3 Upadhyay 2021.
4 Wade 2009.
5 Attorney at Bruckheim & Patel 2020; Ben-Zeév 2020; Martinez-Ortiz 2017.
6 Illouz 2012.
7 Frank 2002.
8 Frank 2002, 271.
9 Bernstein 2007b.
10 Folbre 2002.

3

"Bitch Wanted a Woke White Medal"

Racialized Emotional Labor and White Guilt in the Digital Sex Industry

SHAWNA FELKINS

Sex workers never sleep, or at least it appears that way while I lie awake in bed for an untold number of nights in a row, my face bathed in the blue light of my phone screen. My thumb moves reflexively in that motion many of us have come to associate with boredom or killing time. I sit in this endless scroll for what feels like minutes, but it's hours. I read the quippy posts, stare at nude photos, and click on short videos where women my age and younger engage in various sex acts in different states of dress.

Most people seeing my Twitter feed would not recognize it as my field site, a digital space comprised of client-facing and non-client-facing accounts of sex workers. Twitter, as I have come to visualize it, can be thought of as a large global network made up of overlapping digital communities. Each user sits at the center of a bubble with their followers and the accounts they follow, and each account has its own bubble. As people gain new followers and find new accounts to interact with, these bubbles inevitably come into contact with each other. As more people (including sex work clients) retreat to the virtual world and sex workers lose advertising platforms in the wake of FOSTA/SESTA,[1] I have watched conflicts increase in frequency and intensity. Such moments of friction provide insights into how group norms are policed and expectations for participation in the community are challenged or reified. Social media spaces also provide more opportunities for interaction between people who might not otherwise meet, resulting in a complicated experience for marginalized sex workers, especially Black and Indigenous sex workers, and other sex workers of color.

In what follows, I summarize critiques of white sex workers as presented to me in interviews with Black and Indigenous sex workers, and other sex workers of color. I highlight the experience of what I call "assuagement work," a specific type of racialized emotional labor. Here, I draw on seven years of research with online sex workers—including informal and formal fieldwork, surveys, and thirty-eight in-depth interviews—to discuss how racism and labor collide in online sex work spaces. Through the stories of Aimee and Nabila, I show that marginalized sex workers do a disproportionate amount of the labor necessary to establish and maintain equitable and safe sex work spaces by noting the dynamics of white privilege and explaining specific ways in which white sex workers and researchers can better support sex workers of color.

Assuagement Work

To "assuage" has two meanings: (1) to "make (an unpleasant feeling) less intense"; and (2) to "satisfy" an appetite or desire.[2] Black and Indigenous sex workers and other sex workers of color often engage in what I call "assuagement work," a type of emotion work that strategically negotiates white fragility and guilt to educate white and otherwise privileged sex workers.[3] When doing "assuagement work," minorities regulate their emotions in work-based interactions while sometimes soothing or assuaging the upset feelings of those in more privileged positions. The following encounters shared in interviews and discussed on social media reveal how white sex workers make demands of and burden marginalized sex workers.

Many of the Asian sex workers that I interviewed described instances of white sex workers appropriating fetishized Asian stereotypes in anime and manga to build their brands. For example, Aimee, a prominent Asian cam model, described many interactions with white sex workers who made comments intimating that her ethnicity was a money maker:

> It's very hard to explain to some people that being fetishized, isn't a benefit. It's actually a form of dehumanization. . . . Sex workers who are white, they're just not really getting it. I'll have girls go, "Oh, but you get, you get such big tips." And then they slide in my DMs, [saying,] "How are you finding these guys? Oh, it must be because you have that Asian look,

and guys love that." They see it as like a benefit sometimes, which is very frustrating because you're trying to explain that no, actually, let me show you my block list of words that people have tried to say in my chat room on a daily basis.

Here, Aimee describes feeling frustrated navigating social interactions with white sex workers who assume (1) that she must make money more easily because she is Asian, thus ascribing a financial benefit to the experience of fetishization, and (2) that sex workers of all backgrounds experience the same types and levels of harassment and violence.

Although all sex workers face stigmatization, BIPOC workers in the digital sex industry, and in the sex industry more broadly, face increased stigmatization and racism from customers, law enforcement, aid organizations, and other sex workers.[4] Because of their proximity to "white-centered, idealized, cis femininity," privileged sex workers benefit from sexualized racism. They then uphold colonialist logic through cultural appropriation and fetishized sexual stereotypes, while benefiting from digital segregation on content platforms and claiming "victim" status because they do not fit into a specific fetish category.

Exacerbating this inequality, platforms reward and reinforce white-supremacist individualism through contests and rankings. To increase their rankings, some white sex workers use racial stereotypes or cultural appropriation like "white anime girls," as Aimee described them. According to Aimee, this is a direct example of cultural appropriation and Asianfishing, which she described as

styling yourself and using graphics and branding elements to look racially ambiguous that's like, "Ooh, I'm half-Asian." You have girls who—they always, get the same black wig with the bangs or a pink wig with the bangs—they're either trying to be an anime Asian person, or they're just straight up trying to play up a lot of stereotypes of Asian women. I've actually seen some girls either Photoshop or do makeup to make their eyes to look more Asian, which is a bit much. There's definitely a lot of performers right now who are trying to look racially ambiguous. And also, I guess a lot of this is "marketing" too. You get people who, like their bio will say, "I'm your uwu waifu," which is, I guess, cute to them. But then as somebody who's been told either, "do you understand English?"

or "your English is really good," it's actually frustrating to see somebody intentionally try to seem like they don't fully speak English.

One extremely controversial aspect of the "white anime girl" aesthetic is the use of "*ahegao*." In Japanese pornography, "*ahegao*," which translates to "a flushed face," refers to a specific affective performance of female pleasure. It is "a portmanteau that combines the word *aheahe*, the onomatopoeia for panting, and *gao*, for face. Ahegao highlights a hyperintense orgasm with visual elements such as frenzied eyes that hardly show the person's pupils, a mouth so wide that a person's tongue is sticking out, and body fluids (tears, sweat, and snot) emerging from a person's body."[5] *Ahegao* is one symbol of historical racist and anti-Asian tropes used to justify physical and sexual violence against Asian women and the colonization of Asian countries and peoples. *Ahegao* is a form of white sex workers in yellowface reproducing colonialist domination and legitimizing them for a new generation.

A "White Woke Medal"

Even as more Asian sex workers speak out against *ahegao*, some white sex workers center themselves in the debate and demand assuagement labor from marginalized sex workers. In one exchange, a white sex worker messaged Aimee asking her to explain what made *ahegao* racist and why it was wrong. While requests like this may seem harmless or well intentioned, answering them involves a great deal of time and emotional labor. Aimee described the discussion about *ahegao* devolving quickly when the white sex worker apologized but claimed that she "had only done it one or two times in the past because guys asked [her] to" and said that "there was no need to be rude. I only asked you a question." When Aimee tweeted about the exchange, calling out the entitlement the white sex worker displayed in her request to educate her for free and then tone policing her, the white sex worker quickly turned to guilt and name calling and demanded that Aimee take down her tweet.

Instead of researching the issue or offering to compensate Aimee for her time, this white sex worker requested unpaid labor from a marginalized person and then displaced her own feelings of guilt onto Aimee. As she described it, "She messaged me out of nowhere to dump her guilt on me and seek reassurance about how it's ok that she did ah*gao in the past. Bitch wanted a Woke White medal from any Asian person she could show off later." These interactions perpetuate the trend of positioning "multiply marginalized people, that are also expected to perform more emotional labor than more privileged groups" as a resource to be used and discarded when there is no more value left.[6] Thus, marginalized people, especially women of color, are forced into the stereotypical role of caretaker and emotional guide on white women's journeys to self-discovery and "wokeness."

When marginalized sex workers speak out against the problematic behaviors of white sex workers, they are often met with intense harassment from white sex workers and their fans. Aimee sent me screenshots she had saved of threads and DMs in which white sex workers tried to defend their use of *ahegao* in their content.[7] After facing several days of such harassment, she deleted the thread. To reiterate, in these kind of interactions, white sex workers demand that BIPOC sex workers do the labor of educating them on racist topics, the work of managing their emotions while discussing the phenomena, *and*, in some cases, handle defensive white sex workers commenting on threads that "not all white women" are guilty.

Rethinking the Whorearchy

Among white sex workers, proximity to clients and police sets up the whorearchy, in other words, a hierarchy ranking sex workers from most to least stigmatized.[8] Lateral whorephobia—when a sex worker perpetuates and weaponizes whorephobia against another sex worker—is an important issue within sex worker communities.[9] Most often, these discussions reveal ways in which more privileged sex workers wield their power and are still willfully ignorant about issues of race, class, gender, ability, and other identities.

As sex-working activist Tilly Lawless explains, the whorearchy is also organized through experiences of marginalization: "For instance, a non-English speaking, immigrant WOC will be seen as 'less valuable' than me (a white middle-class woman) and further down in the chain of things. Often, more marginalized people will be forced to work in lower rungs, for example, trans WOC often won't be hired in brothels and resort to street-based sex work."[10] While the importance of intersectionality in the whorearchy is understood among sex-working activists and sex workers who self-identify as having more leftist or radical politics, sex workers are not a monolith. As with any industry, sex workers come from various backgrounds and have many different political ideologies that impact what views they espouse and how they engage with other sex workers and civilians on social media. As with any industry, the experiences of white women have been historically prioritized in ways that erase the experiences of Black and Indigenous women and other women of color. Nabila, a dominatrix who moved to online sex work during the pandemic, illustrated this:

> A lot of white sex workers I know are like "No, it's all the same. It's an equalizer. We're all in here together. We're all struggling the same way." And I'm like, "But we're not though." There's a level of visibility that I think a lot of [white] sex workers have that paint sex work in a different light than the way Black and Brown sex workers are portrayed. I think there's a lot of, "Oh, Black and Brown sex workers are streetwalkers, they're all poor and uneducated and they're making bad decisions. If they just got their lives together . . . they're all drug addicts. They're all this, they're all that." And there's this petty disgust that's leveled at Black and Brown sex workers, and especially trans women, that is just so gross to me. And I don't see a lot of white sex workers choosing to make that the thing they talk about and raise awareness for and problematize.

Some white sex workers, like otherwise marginalized white people throughout history, use their marginalized status as sex workers to try to "cancel" their whiteness, the same rhetorical strategy used by some white feminists and queer folks. My interviewees noted that when this strategy fails, many sex workers distance themselves from other sex workers through rhetoric steeped in respectability politics,[11] as some sex workers engage in "whorenationalism" by insisting that they are doing "honest work."[12]

One such example is reflected in the proliferation of online sex worker Twitter accounts that include the phrase "No Meetups" in their Twitter bios. This loaded phrase signals to prospective clients that an online sex worker is not interested in full-service work. Direct sex work is criminalized in most countries. As more in-person workers were driven indoors during the COVID-19 outbreak, some were critical of the use of this phrase as stigmatizing and othering for full-service workers.[13]

Digital sex work is classified as mostly indirect (sex work performed without physical contact with the client) with some aspects of direct sex work, since many sex workers do a variety of types of sex work in order to diversify their income streams and survive.[14] As mentioned, some digital sex workers uphold the whorearchy through specific language (i.e., "no meetups") that delineates online work as "legal" and thus morally superior to full-service sex work. Although all sex workers face stigmatization, BIPOC workers in the digital sex industry, and in the sex industry more broadly, face increased stigmatization and racism from customers, law enforcement, aid organizations, and other sex workers.[15] The phrase "no meetups" thus reinforces sex worker hierarchies.

The sex industry exists within larger interlocking systems of power. Accordingly, sex workers bring their own experiences, identities, power, and privilege into online spaces and interactions. As sex workers have pointed out time and time again, some feminists have been interested in sex work as a talking point and an opportunity to live out a moral superiority rooted in white saviorism and paternalism. Several academics have also acknowledged these issues in ethnographic work with sex workers.[16]

For future sex work research, there must be a shift away from the question of "why" people do sex work, since such a question further suggests that sex work is a deviant choice of occupation. White cis women have strategically and historically existed in liminality, in the space between labels of savior and victim, empowered and coerced, and it is their dominance and complicity in white supremacy that has allowed them to control the narrative around sex worker rights and issues. Because of the legacy of the "cult of true womanhood," focusing on white cisgender women in discussions of sex work leads to a flattened discourse that is anything but intersectional.[17]

In trying to think through and name these issues, I hope that I have highlighted a small piece of the thankless and tireless work that Black and Indigenous sex workers and sex workers of color undertake to educate white sex workers, customers, and mainstream culture. My hope is that those of us benefiting from the antiracist labor, knowledge, and theorizations of the experiences provided by sex workers of color will listen, educate ourselves, see being called out on social media as an opportunity to learn rather than argue, and pay people for that labor.

In the preceding pages, I have explored how centering white experiences and feelings in discussions of sex work and in sex work spaces requires that BIPOC sex workers perform "assuagement work." I want to make clear, however, that I think the concept of "assuagement work" is most useful if we realize that it happens *everywhere*. More specifically, it happens in every place where BIPOC are forced to cater to the feelings of white people to survive and thrive.[18] I want to emphasize how much sex work is just like every other job in regard to the racialized, classed, and gendered discourses and interactions that occur. This universality presents researchers with many possible avenues for study. As some of the most marginalized people in our society, sex workers theorize complex issues related to identity, labor, economy, technology and more. New sex work research must be collaborative, accessible, and written for broader public consumption. Feminist research has always been a political project, and sex work research should be no different. Sex workers are experts in navigating institutions and systems, and as such, offer new strategies for understanding power and privilege.

NOTES

1 Stop Enabling Sex Traffickers Act (SESTA) and Allow States and Victims to Fight Online Sex Trafficking Act (FOSTA) were combined into a joint law and passed in 2018 under the premise of preventing human trafficking. The law specifically targeted online platforms by reforming section 230, removing immunity and making platforms culpable for suspected trafficking through their websites. The legacy of FOSTA-SESTA continues to harm sex workers, from the closing of Backpage to the increased surveillance of sex workers in both digital and physical spaces. Blunt and Wolf 2020.

2 *Oxford English Dictionary* n.d.

3 Mirchandi 2003, 721–42.

4 Brooks 2021, 513–21.

5 Santos 2020, 279–90.

6 Carter 2015.

7 On Twitter, users have access to communication through several avenues, but the most private is the Direct Message or DM. Unlike tweets, which are publicly available (outside of the restrictions of privacy settings), DMs are only visible to the people engaging in the conversation, much like a chatroom.

8 Witt 2020.

9 moon 2021.

10 Sciortino 2016.

11 Blewett and Law 2018.

12 In using the term "whorenationalism," I draw on Puar's concept of "homona-tionalism" and its usefulness for understanding how centering respectability and legitimacy by the state only works to protect the most privileged of those in a marginalized group. "Whorenationalism" draws on neoliberal and carceral frameworks that ultimately criminalize BIPOC sex workers and uphold white supremacy. Puar 2007.

13 Friedman 2021.

14 Sanders, O'Neill, and Pitcher 2009.

15 Jones 2016, 227–56.

16 Miller-Young 2014; Jones 2020a.

17 Welter (1966) used the term the "cult of true womanhood" to describe feminine qualities valued in the upper and middle classes during the nineteenth century. "True women" should exhibit four virtues: piety, purity, domesticity, and submis-siveness.

18 Mirchandi 2003, 721–42.

4

"I Didn't Know I Was into Trans Men until I Saw You"

Trans Men Reimagined through Pornography

TRIP RICHARDS

The comment was predictable. Among the heart emojis and other, cruder responses under my nude photo was the reply, "You're so hairy and masculine, Trip. You're the only trans man I could ever be with." I knew this was intended as a compliment, but it felt more like a slap in the face. Am I only accepted because I look stereotypically male? What does this mean for trans men who don't have a full beard or defined muscles? Every time I hear comments like this, it reminds me how trans bodies are amazingly powerful yet still profoundly marginalized.

I am a transgender man and sex worker. I have been involved in the adult industry for more than seven years, including throughout the entirety of my transition. I currently work full-time producing video content. Over these years, I have seen an increasing number of trans men and nonbinary people enter the industry.[1] They perform on webcam, escort, make videos, and offer various other forms of erotic labor. Those who appear on video primarily produce independent content, as I do, but also, to a lesser extent, there are trans men working with studios. The influx of trans men and nonbinary people in these industries reflects several changes in online sexual commerce. Compared to several years ago, trans male pornographic content garners significantly more attention and consumer demand, primarily from gay men. This rise in consumer demand is correlated with the overall growth of amateur pornography online and what feminist scholars and sex workers have called the demystification of pornography, or what I refer to as the "democratization of porn."[2] Pornography itself is rapidly evolving in the twenty-first century, specifically through the growth of social platforms called fan sites, which are designed for monetizing independently created pornography. There are more people than ever showing their bodies and making a living by doing so.

Many of my clients and viewers are cisgender, gay-identified men who had no preexisting experience with trans men. My webcam work included conversations with thousands of viewers over several years. My in-person work involved hundreds of deep, intimate conversations, and my social media presence continues to invite comments and messages today. The most common response from cis gay male viewers seeing my body has been, "I didn't know I was into trans men until I saw you," followed in frequency by the comment, "I fantasized about [men with a vagina] before I knew they existed." The second comment is particularly disruptive because it makes the still-almost-taboo suggestion that vaginas can be separated from femaleness, and thus can be attractive to a gay male audience. Trans and nonbinary people exist at this intersection, representing the forefront of reimagining gender and sexuality.

I firmly believe that the naked trans man is revolutionary and invites viewers to reconsider what it means to "be a man." The presence of trans men in pornography disrupts traditional narratives of masculinity by appearing as a bold alternative to phallocentrism.[3] Nonbinary performers make this point even more explicit by decoupling themselves entirely from a gender. In this chapter, I will present perspectives from performers who were assigned female at birth and who now identify as something other than female, including both trans men like me and nonbinary people. While the sex work experiences of these groups are not equivalent, because gender presentation, race, sexuality, and ability all shape these experiences, I believe the overlap among transmasculine and nonbinary people is significant enough to be considered together in a meaningful way.

In this essay, I argue that trans men's inclusion in pornography remains imperfect and reductive, especially when intersectional issues are considered. First, I explore what forms of trans masculinity are accepted, then how race and racism intersect with transness, and finally, how both online platforms and fellow models can impact the struggle for equity. I discuss these factors through my own experiences and those of several other models. Finally, we share thoughts on how the industry could become more equitable and diverse via the efforts of both online platforms and individuals.

Acceptable Forms of Trans Masculinity

If there is a positive lesson to be learned from trans pornography, it is that viewers are capable of decoupling gender from body parts. They can realize that Man = Penis is not the necessary and natural binary opposite of Woman = Vulva, but rather that each element can exist independently and upon a spectrum. At the same time, it is important to recognize limitations and obstacles to trans inclusion and normalization in pornography.

My own experience is that many viewers make their attraction to trans men contingent on both our masculine appearance (especially beard and body hair) and our willingness to be a sexual bottom (penetrated partner). Consequently, only a minority of videos and other performances have placed trans men in a top (penetrative partner), or dom (dominant or aggressive) role, and even fewer have departed from "traditionally porn-handsome" casting choices (by which I mean white, muscular or slim, and cisgender-passing). Trans men are portrayed primarily as eager bottoms and eager-to-please submissives, because that fits most comfortably within heteronormative and cis-gay-normative storylines. The amount of surprise (and relative disinterest) I encounter when I share my desire to dominate or top a cis male partner exemplifies this. Viewers seem willing to accept only so much departure from gender and sexual scripts.

I feel a measure of guilt at writing a critique of trans inclusion, as a white and cis-passing trans man who has managed to find success and acceptance in the industry. I attribute this largely to my physical appearance and willingness (especially early in my career) to perform in the expected sexual roles. Within about a year of starting my medical transition, I had grown enough facial hair and had masculinized my body shape sufficiently that I was generally assumed to be cisgender as long as I kept my clothes on. Even when my clothes are off, I frequently participate in a strange conversation, explaining to viewers that I was assigned female at birth (and spent twenty-five years appearing as such) and am not a cisgender male who underwent genital modification. I continue to receive these types of questions about my body at least weekly via direct message or comments on posts. It is striking in both frequency and inaccuracy. It also speaks to the fact that viewers (at least the cis male ones) are generally more eager to identify me as a "modified man" than as a "trans man." In other words, "maleness with an original but now-absent phallus" is an easier heuristic for them than "maleness cultivated intentionally in adulthood." I view this as further evidence that maleness (and the expectation of cisgender phallocentrism) is the default social status, with everything else falling one (or several) rungs below maleness in the social hierarchy. Trans people disrupt this assumption, but only when we can be visibly and loudly ourselves.

Because my personal experience is only partially representative of the broader experiences of other trans and nonbinary people, I want to center the voices of other performers. Israel (Izzy) Akino, a heteroflexible Caribbean and Polynesian man, said,

> I feel that there is a whole group of trans men who're tops like myself who don't see themselves represented in porn because people still have this notion that trans men are bottoms, and then it's perpetuated based on the films that are out there. I'd like to break that cycle by being and performing predominantly as a top. [I want there to be] more roles and opportunities for us that are more than just "A Man with a Pussy." Not all trans men are bottoms, and that needs to be shown; otherwise, we perpetuate that belief, and that can be detrimental sometimes.

His words exemplify how, even when trans representation ostensibly exists in porn, it may not demonstrate sufficient diversity in storylines. Thus, it does not disrupt problematic cissexist assumptions but perpetuates them.

Racist Overtones in Pornography

The trans men we currently see in porn are primarily white or white passing, and trans men of color are largely absent. I believe there are several reasons for this, including the reality that trans people of color experience barriers like economic marginalization, homelessness, and violence at even higher rates than their white counterparts.

Even when people of color do make their way into pornography, their bodies are often sexualized in ways that are one-dimensional, fetishizing, and centered on their race rather than their humanity.[4] These storylines often make the racist assumptions about skin color central to the story narrative. When scene descriptions, titles, and tags focus on the color of the performers, the entire scene is framed through race.[5] And when the scene includes racist themes like "thuggery," it makes explicit that Black bodies only exist reductively. All of this is true for cisgender performers of color, and even more striking for trans performers.

I spoke on this point with Max, a performer who identifies as a "Black kinky queer, trans man." I asked him if he felt represented.

> Absolutely not. There is not a single mainstream actor that is even close to how I look. In order to find people who come close to me, I have to peel away my intersections. But even if I was cis, I would be hard-pressed to find a Black person that wasn't typecast to be a "thug" or to be involved in some kind of race play. If I were to look at mainstream trans actors, it's hard to find someone who isn't white and/or with abs. If I were to look at other kinky performers, we see a similar lack of diversity. This was part of why I started my journey into sex work. I was tired of waiting to see someone that looked like me, and I imagined I was not the only one.

Max's words echo those of many other models I have spoken with over the years. Frustrated by the lack of diversity, and the absence of people who look or act like them, they started making their own porn that accurately embodies them.

Mainstream pornography may not fully or independently liberate itself from problematic white-supremacist cis-centric storylines. However, I believe that sex workers can start a conversation that may spill over into nonexplicit contexts, provided that independent performers like Max, Izzy, and myself have accessible spaces in which to tell our stories and monetize them to support our livelihood.

The Future of Democratized Porn

For porn to be a meaningful beacon of social change, it must be seen. If the greatest, most equitable video never gets seen (or purchased), it is ultimately a failure from the standpoint of social transformation and career success. Viewers can drive equality forward—or drag it down—with their purchasing choices. Today, viewers have more options than ever for how to spend their porn dollars.

The most dramatic recent change to the porn landscape has been the development of fan site platforms.[6] Since the launch of OnlyFans in 2016 and the subsequent rise of other, similar platforms such as JustForFans, a sex worker–created alternative, much of the adult industry has been transformed by accessible direct-to-consumer content with a social-media-like interface. On these sites, fans subscribe to their favorite models at a monthly rate that offers them access to the model's entire library of existing content and whatever else the model uploads to their feed while the subscription remains active. Fans can also message, comment, request custom content, and more. Crucially, unlike webcamming or other direct-service delivery, the income from fan-site subscriptions is passive and not explicitly linked to hours of performance.

I spoke with Alice Skary, the model liaison at JustForFans (similar to the better-known Onlyfans platform, though more favored by gay and fetish performers). Alice is also a performer who identifies as a white, pansexual, agender, nonbinary human and uses they/them pronouns. I asked Alice what is fundamentally different about the fan sites versus other forms of direct-to-consumer porn like clip studios and live webcam (both of which have been around for years).

> I've been contemplating that a lot lately, and I think the reason why fan sites really took off like they have is because of the aspect of community. Fan sites create communities, little social hubs. They are, in essence, a way of combining social media, which has so taken over our lives, and our need for entertainment and sexual pleasure all at once.

I also consider the fan sites to be a direct rebuke of pornography's traditional format, controlled by agents and casting directors making their own decisions about marketability.[7] For this reason, I view fan sites as being "democratized porn." Models on the fan sites retain ownership of their material, control its contents and distribution, and profit directly from it. Models also control their own casting choices, working with friends, partners, and other performers with whom they are comfortable collaborating. Each performer can drive traffic directly to their own site via their social media. By offering models autonomy and self-determination, the structure of the fan sites addresses many concerns about coercion that have historically plagued the adult industry.

Fan Sites as Agents of Equity

Even considering this challenge of getting enough exposure, the fan sites offer a more credible opportunity for minority models to monetize themselves than any other portion of the modern adult industry. For example, on JustForFans, a notable number of the top-performing models are people of color. JustForFans also explicitly offers appropriate categories for trans and nonbinary performers.

Alice describes the personal importance of accurate self-identified categories.

> Being able to categorize correctly my gender (nonbinary) and being able to specify my pronouns automatically in my profile details (they/theirs) removed a burden I had been shouldering for so long that it had become second nature to me. I came out as nonbinary over a year ago, but I am still forced to identify as female on many of the platforms I am on since the nonbinary gender options don't exist. Being able to supply my pronouns gives my subscribers information they need to treat me with respect and kindness. It is valuable to be seen as the person I am and not have to pretend I am something I am not.

To the extent that language creates consciousness, websites without inclusive gender options telegraph the fact that only some models (usually cisgender and binary) are welcome. I have personally interacted with multiple sites where the platform's designers literally have never considered the existence of trans men. Even on the sites with a "transgender" option, it is often clear from how it is marketed and branded that they only expect trans women to appear there.[8] For example, I was shocked to find that my default profile image on a popular mainstream site was the silhouette of a busty woman with a large penis. In these instances, the existence of trans men is made completely invisible by the site's categories, search terms, and profile options.

I asked Alice to speak from their position as a model liaison on JustForFans about how a website can help advance equity in porn specifically.

> The first part is to listen to performers about how they like to self-identify and how they like to market themselves and simply create that space. Language for identity and marketing trends both are always changing, so to keep up with it having a staff member who is tied closely to the queer community or paying consultants who are members of this community to look over how we are phrased, organized, categorized, and make sure they are appropriate but flexible.
>
> The second part is to simply shine a light on us, instead of hiding us away or ignoring us. Be proud of our work and showcase it as you would any other talent on your site!

My conversation with Alice highlights the critical role a website can play in advancing diverse porn. They said, "Our content sells well, we just need a place to showcase it properly." The experiences of trans and nonbinary performers, including myself, do indeed demonstrate that consumers' tastes are significantly broader than mainstream/studio porn production would suggest. Or, as Max puts it, "Over time, more trans folks have certainly entered the industry. As well as more Black folks, more Latinx folks, and Asian folks. Regardless, the industry still is not as diverse as the people that consume our work."

Costars as Drivers of Equity

Other performers can directly elevate niche models. For example, performers who create partnered content for their fan page have complete creative control over whom they collaborate with. And since costars are tagged in all partnered content, they benefit from the cross-promotion. Even better than a tag on social media like Twitter, a tag on Onlyfans or JustForfans places that model in front of a paying audience, fans who have already agreed that monetized indie content is something worth supporting.

Speaking personally, I was fortunate to film several scenes with well-known cis-gay performers early in my career. I am exceptionally grateful for those opportunities because they helped establish my place in the industry and introduced me to a large fan base. Since then, I have been gratified at the increasing number of established cis-gay performers who work with, and therefore promote, other transmasculine actors. These established models harness the power of their large following and name recognition to elevate other models. By doing so, they send a clear message to their fans that trans models can and should exist alongside their favorite cis models.

However, I remain critical of the fact that these films have rarely placed the trans man in a top or dom role, and even fewer have departed from "traditionally porn-handsome" casting choices, by which I mean white, muscular or slim, and cisgender-passing.

Max expresses his frustration with the casting choices he has observed.

> Fellow performers or those who cast others in their work need to be honest with themselves. Have they filmed a scene that wasn't two (or more) white people? You want to film a twenty-actor orgy, but is there a single PoC there or a trans person? If there is a single PoC or trans person, are they a token within your friend group? I'm not the dictator of who you can and cannot film with. I don't make or enforce rules. And I realize that most performers are most likely just filming with others they know or others with high follower counts. But I urge performers (and civilians alike) to make friends that don't look like them.

Despite all the progress I have seen in the past few years, I experience a similar sense of frustration and wonder if we are now at a standstill. As my discussion with Max and Izzy exemplifies, even though they produce the diverse and equitable porn they believe in, it still feels marginalized. While trans inclusion and visibility are objectively better than ever, they are often still one-dimensional, as trans people are not allowed to be fully themselves but are only regarded as a "man with a pussy."

The Future of Trans Men in Porn

Trans and nonbinary models, like models of color, have often been told that there is no audience for them. But perhaps this gatekeeping was instead obstructing the desires of the marketplace. Max's words suggest that porn consumers desire more diverse content. This theory suggests that humanity—including its tastes in porn—will inevitably fall into an equilibrium where the available pornographic content is representative of the general population, their bodies, and their sexual preferences.

However, I believe models experiencing instability and violence in their personal life will struggle to succeed, even when they have access to perfectly inclusive platforms and eager fans. Because sex work is a matter of literal survival for many models, the importance of stability cannot be overstated. Living in a transphobic, eurocentric, fat-phobic, racist, ableist society places limits on success that individual models cannot solve on their fan pages. And I am reluctant to put the onus of social change on people who are already marginalized. I believe that minority performers need specific social elevation, including help from costars, to counteract the other barriers they are experiencing.

I asked Alice about the industry's future, and they highlighted the concept of a multifaceted approach toward equity.

> Performers need to collaborate more with diverse co-models. Studios need to give more opportunities to diverse performers. But above all, customers, buyers, fans need to be putting their support and money towards supporting diversity of all types in entertainment. Voting with your dollars and putting your support and love and energy towards normalizing marginalized identities and diverse bodies.

I am inclined to believe that progress for certain minorities will fall far short of true equity without this degree of effort. There are simply too many barriers for trans performers or those producing nonconforming narratives. Trans people face significantly higher rates of poverty, homelessness/unstable housing, and physical violence than their cis counterparts.[9] Trans people of color are even more vulnerable, facing the dual oppressions of transphobia and racism. None of these factors are conducive to producing pornography that will find its way into mainstream markets and do the work of telling diverse stories in a way that meaningfully changes public perception. Without a broad disruption of Eurocentrism and heteronormativity, truly equitable queer porn may never flourish.

Ultimately, we need a coordinated, systematic effort among websites, popular models, and viewers to intentionally and systematically advance diverse performers and storylines. The new digital era of sex work has opened many doors during my years in the industry, but I am only moderately hopeful for further improvements.

NOTES

1 Ballard 2014; Lee 2012, 2015; Noble 2012; Darling 2015.
2 Attwood 2010; Jones 2020a; Bembe 2021.
3 Jones 2020b.
4 Miller-Young 2014; Nash 2014; Zhou and Paul 2016.
5 Perdue 2021.
6 Ryan 2019.
7 Jones 2020a; Berg 2021.
8 Jones 2020b
9 Robinson 2020.

5

Pornography with Heart

The Holistic Potential of Feminist Porn

INKA WINTER AND KELSY BURKE

The commercial pornography industry, like broader society, has long been afflicted by what Patricia Hill Collins calls the "matrix of domination," the ways in which systems of inequality intersect to perpetuate negative and damaging stereotypes about marginalized groups, including women, people of color, and queer, trans, and nonbinary people.[1] *Mainstream porn*, the typical product of the commercial industry, is usually produced and directed by cisgender, heterosexual white men made for an audience of the same. This means that the pleasure of the male consumer is front and center of what is presented on screen. The result is stereotypical-looking women performers (who epitomize the "look" of the porn star—white and thin) who engage in stereotypical porn acts that center on men's pleasure.

But mainstream porn has never exclusively defined the industry, which is especially diverse and multifaceted in the twenty-first century.[2] Other genres persist and are on the rise. *Femme-friendly porn* targets mainly straight women, is usually more story driven than mainstream porn, and often depicts romantic scenes. Such films are generally more sensual and aim for better cinematography, even while the casting can reflect the same stereotypes presented in mainstream productions. *Ethical porn*, often including BDSM and kink porn, prioritizes consent on and off screen. It also includes fair pay for performers, content that aligns with a performer's interests, and respect and consideration for actors throughout the entire production process. Consent involves everyone in the production of the film, including the crew. Therefore, even mainstream porn can be produced ethically. *Feminist porn*, the focus of this essay, goes beyond ethical porn in that the production is done in an ethical way *and* the content not only is femme friendly but challenges stereotypes by depicting diversity across bodies by size, race, gender identity, and sexual expression. Feminist porn often includes the realistic depiction of pleasure, and a collaboration between director and actors to incorporate the latter's own sexual desires. Since people who identify as women have diverse desires and sources of pleasure, feminist porn can be soft or edgy, romantic or hard-core, vanilla or kinky, with or without storylines, straight, queer, cis, trans, bi, or any combination thereof.[3]

Inka Winter, who works as a feminist porn director, has experienced firsthand these different facets of the pornography industry. This chapter, coauthored with Kelsy Burke—a feminist sociologist—weaves together first-person narrative alongside qualitative research of Internet sex workers. We draw from the personal experiences of Winter, who has been independently directing and producing pornography from a feminist gaze since 2017. We supplement this personal account with data collected by Burke between 2016 and 2020 from in-depth interviews with twenty-four individuals who work independently in the Internet sex industry (camming, pornography, sex coaching, or some combination).[4] Not all interview participants worked in feminist porn, but all did describe feminist values informing their work.

This chapter argues that Internet sex work has the feminist potential to transform and expand the genre of pornography in what we dub "holistic pornography." Like holistic medicine, which is characterized as "a form of healing that considers the whole person—body, mind, spirit, and emotions," holistic pornography considers emotional and social factors influencing the pornography industry, and sexual experiences more broadly.[5] If the goal of the sex and porn industry is to generate profits through the display of sexual pleasure, holistic pornography considers the broader context, including social norms, and the emotional and mental health of viewer and performer, as Winter's personal journey (in a different font throughout this chapter) illustrates. If mainstream pornography enforces the social "diseases" of misogyny, racism, and class inequality, holistic pornography "treats" these social problems through direct critique and productive alternatives.

Why Feminists Make Porn

The way I came to direct porn is a very personal one and nothing I ever imagined myself doing. Before I became a porn director, my relationship to sexuality was mixed. Ideologically, I was always what we would now call a "sex-positive" person. Growing up in Europe, I encountered less stigma around sex. Yet, I grew up in the notorious Austrian commune, Friedrichshof, founded by artist Otto Mühl. This cultivated community was an attempt to create a utopian society by abandoning the nuclear family and private property. Sexuality was supposed to be "free," which meant people weren't allowed to have relationships because relationships were seen as a form of ownership over another person. I was exposed to sexuality in a very intrusive way in which sex was an obligatory way to show your commitment to the so-called utopian ideals. The result was an environment where you had to be sexual to belong.

In 1991, when I was twelve, the commune ended because Mühl was arrested for having sex with minors. I then moved to Berlin to live with my mother for a time before I attended boarding school. Growing up separated from my parents, I experienced feelings of abandonment, helplessness, and a lack of control. When I eventually became sexually active, I had sex not for pleasure but for emotional affirmation due to the lack of emotional connection and attachment I grew up with.

I started my own journey of healing myself emotionally when I was sixteen. I found a therapist and began exploring mindfulness, which has become a central part of my life over the years. Relationships are an especially challenging "classroom" in which I am learning to use mindfulness to stay present to my feelings and anxious attachment. In 2008, after having an abortion, I lost my sex drive for about a year. As I started to feel a little better, my partner at the time and I began looking for ways to reignite my sexual interest. We turned to porn in the hopes that it would help me feel turned on. But everything we found had the opposite effect. While on a physical level my body indeed felt some arousal, on an emotional level I felt disgust. I would later learn that studies show that women's bodies can have an arousal response while not experiencing the feeling of being turned on.[6] What I saw in mainstream porn was anything but a turn on. The locations, the lighting, the surgically lit closeup of genitalia, the fakeness and overacting of the woman's enjoyment, the focus on the man's pleasure in often demeaning and aggressive acts towards women in the film—all of this made my stomach feel in knots rather than making me want sex.

As I was continually disappointed and disgusted by mainstream pornography, I decided that if I could not find what I was looking for, I would have to create it myself. So, I did. The intention was not just to create erotic films for women but also to create films that couples could watch together, to bring them closer and connect them sexually and emotionally. Since sexuality is a big part of most people's lives, I believe that healing that part of yourself and your relationship will affect other areas of life as well.

Thus began Winter's journey creating "holistic pornography." Never was her goal to become rich or famous in the porn industry, and indeed, among Burke's interview sample, the motivations were uniformly not to become famous porn stars. Instead, as with other studies of sex workers, respondents described their motivations in terms of flexibility in scheduling, autonomy, and a relatively high hourly rate compared to other job options.[7] They took on multiple "hustles," a phrase used in the majority of interviews, to make a living in a way that aligned with their values, sexual and otherwise. All respondents worked several jobs, in and out of sex work. For example, one performer left her adult agency and the commercial industry to serve as her own agent and marketer to get booked on porn shoots, and also maintains an OnlyFans page and social media presence to advertise her content. Another worked as a phone sex operator, cam model, and porn performer, and also as a freelance writer, podcast host, and adjunct instructor for college classes in women's and gender studies. One cam model and amateur pornographer made a little money on the side reviewing sex toys while working full-time in retail. They, along with one other interview respondent, described plans to leave the industry to pursue alternative careers. The remainder of the people Burke interviewed had no plans to leave sex work, only to continue to grow their content and audience.

Beyond practical motivations like income from a flexible schedule, feminist pornographers reference political motivations for their work, and many identified explicitly as activists. Food analogies were a common way respondents explained feminist motivations. One used the analogy of eating meat. "When we're not critical about the ways in which our meat is processed, and we just go, 'Oh, our meat is fine. Oh, our porn is fine,' and we're blindly consuming them, then we are not talking about all of the unethical practices in these industries." Like promoting conscientious consumption that considers where our food comes from and who and what may have been harmed in the process, feminist pornographers insist on practices that eliminate or minimize harm. Unlike anti-porn activists who want to eliminate the industry altogether, feminist pornographers see the solution as advocating for better alternatives.

One interviewee, Gordon B., who described himself as a "cis mostly het" white man and considers himself an artist and activist, wrote a film for feminist pornographer Erika Lust's XConfessions site to flip the script of the typical porn narrative. "I was really curious as to what it would look like if the male orgasm happened at the beginning of the sex instead of the finish line. Almost like it was the best supporting actor at the Oscars. It's just one moment and then everything really centers on the female character's pleasure." He also wanted themes of consent and communication to be showcased throughout. Rather than having "sexual health information sprinkled in," Gordon B. saw it as "the idea at the core of the film." "I wanted to experiment with work that is sex affirming, and humanity affirming, that is intelligent, that is saying something."

The online sex workers in Burke's study also frequently mentioned spiritual motivations for their work, challenging the narrative that sex work and religion are diametrically opposed to one another.[8] Though the interview sample is not representative of the sex worker community as a whole, it is interesting to note that spiritual references came most often from women and queer people of color. One respondent, Andie, a Black Buddhist, saw spiritual potential in porn that depicts gender-queer and nonnormative bodies. Their work is motivated by the belief that "all bodies are worthy of love. I am worthy of love. I am worthy of care. I am worthy of healing." Similarly, Tia, a Black woman and longtime feminist and queer activist, said she created content online to help clients with "healing erotic wounds." She implied not physical wounds primarily, but rather emotional and spiritual ones. Lisa, another Black queer woman respondent, said that what unites all three of her businesses as a BDSM coach, kinky fitness instructor, and straight (nonsexual) fitness instructor was that she wanted to help Black LGBTQ people "to celebrate their autonomy for their bodies." Both practical and ideological motivations influence feminists who work in the porn industry. And yet, they must confront many challenges in making their work.

Challenges to Making Feminist Porn

The practical challenges of independent feminist porn are plentiful. Some are the general struggles of starting a business and some are more unique to porn. While financing is hard for any business, avenues like venture capital are not readily available to most people in this industry. It can be hard to secure a set since many locations explicitly prohibit nudity and adult films.

Another hurdle is getting a bank account and payment processing. Once, I went to open a bank account and when I said that my business was film production, the banker followed up with a prompt that asked whether my business was associated with the adult industry. When I said yes, she looked at me with confusion like she didn't believe me. She asked me in what way I was associated with the adult industry. When I explained to her what I do, she understood. After she marked my answer on her computer screen, she informed me that I wasn't eligible to open a bank account. I called numerous banks with the same result.

The same is true for payment processing companies like PayPal, Stripe, Venmo, etc. There are only a few companies that specialize in so-called high-risk businesses—which includes adult entertainment—and those charge around 15 percent of your revenue compared to the usual 3 percent that PayPal charges. In addition, there is so much paperwork to fill out that my liaison at the payment company I use has jokingly wondered if next they will ask for a blood sample. I am not allowed to have a post office box as my business address or my stage name on any public records, which means I cannot layer protection between my personal and professional identities. This makes me feel very uncomfortable.

And then there is social media. Not only do sites often have compli-cated and contradictory policies that censor images and content; they also "shadow ban" users (hide a user's content without informing them) with sexual content. Instagram flagged as solicitation a comment I made on a performer's photo saying, "It was nice filming with you." Facebook also flagged as solicitation a post I made asking for women to submit their erotic fantasies to me as part of my work. And most importantly from a business perspective, Instagram and Facebook don't allow any advertising for companies whose products are of a sexual nature. This makes it extremely hard to be found by potential users interested in your content.

Similarly, when Burke asked respondents about challenges within the adult industry, the most common response was not sexism but rather corporate policies and social stigma that created obstacles for working in porn. The business of sex work has hurdles that other career paths do not.[9] For example, most states have "off-duty conduct" policies that permit employers to fire an employee who works part-time in the sex industry. Banks can also refuse to open accounts for sex workers, cit-ing their work as "high risk." These hurdles are not unique to feminists in the sex industry, but they may be more acutely experienced when performers or directors avoid mainstream companies. Feminist sex workers who intentionally limit the types of content they create, and the distribution companies they work with or for, may find financial challenges exacerbated. Many secure online payment companies re-fuse to work with even mainstream pornographic websites, and very few will support sex workers creating content on independent web-sites. Challenges of payment, banking, and advertising inhibit innova-tion, leading many performers to remain within the confines of the commercial industry, taking an attitude of "if you can't beat 'em, join 'em." For example, many performers and creators critique companies like Pornhub and OnlyFans for prioritizing profit over sex workers while continuing to work with those sites because of the lack of lucra-tive alternatives.[10]

The structure of the porn industry forces performers to get creative in order to make a living, find community, and, we argue, make a life that is meaningful and in line with feminist values.[11] When they succeed, the resulting concoction is holistic: expanding the genre of what pornography is, sometimes beyond sexual pleasure to a broader sense of well-being and healing.

Healing through Feminist Porn

Since writing and directing pornographic films, I began to see healing as something that can happen on a porn set. It can happen with talent and crew as well as when the viewer watches the finished film.

On set, one way I hope to empower the talent (whom we call "the performers" in an adult film) and bring healing is through collaboration. I intentionally collaborate with the talent on filming their own sexual fantasies so that we capture what feels representative to who they are, their style, their likes, and how they want to be portrayed. Being able to express your authentic self is healing and strengthens one's sense of self. On my sets, the talent has autonomy over their bodies, and their boundaries are respected. This way, what is captured on film is authentic pleasure. We also consider the talents' pleasure by letting them choose whom they want to perform with and simultaneously we capture real intimacy and connection.

One of my films, *Tell Me What You Like*, shows a woman writing in her diary about the kind of sex she enjoys. While we then show the sex she is imagining, we also have a voiceover narrate what is happening so that the people watching it better understand what about the action is pleasurable. I am currently working on a film that addresses body insecurities and how mindfulness can help with that. It starts with a woman doing a mindfulness meditation naked, in front of a mirror, to be present and to hold space for the insecurities she feels towards her body.

Working with women's fantasies doesn't mean it's all romance. Many couples approach me to film with them and many of the women want to portray their BDSM fantasies. The important thing to keep in mind for these scenarios is to find ways to make the consent apparent in the film. That can be either through words or through a gesture that shows the woman is initiating the scene. In our film *The Alley*, a man follows a woman into an alley where they have sex. The only reason that works is that we clearly see the woman inviting the man to follow her. There are many ways films can be educational in a subtle way, for example by showing behavior in our films that we want to encourage.

Avery Jane is another example, a film about a sex worker and her client. Her wish was to show how she wants to be treated as a sex worker. The concept is almost painfully simple because all she really wanted was to be treated with respect and kindness. She described what she wanted as follows: the client sends a nice message to book her, when she arrives, he is courteous, the money is presented before the onset of the encounter, and he offers her a glass of wine and makes conversation before anything else happens. I asked her if she wanted a message at the end of the film and she said, "Sex work is work." So that's what I put.

The films described here by Winter may seem far removed from the typical streaming clips available on sites like Pornhub. And yet, directors like Winter are making and selling porn. They *are* the porn industry, or at least one arm of it. While some industry insiders have been critical that the label of "feminist porn" has become a marketing tool to generate profits (Pornhub, for example, has its own #feminist tag),[12] feminists who create porn continue to push the industry to produce films that are more than the same reel of predictable gender stereotypes and misogynist acts.

But the genre we are describing as "holistic pornography" does not end there. Feminist pornographers consider porn to be one facet of a holistic effort to reclaim women's, and other marginalized groups', sexualities. Winter, for one, has used her own personal journey and experience directing porn to develop tools she is eager to share with others, like mindfulness-based desire and arousal coaching for individuals and couples. Winter plans to continue making conscious, feminist erotica by incorporating mindfulness into her films, such as by offering boudoir shoots that involve meditations on body positivity and acceptance.

By naming and promoting "holistic pornography," we highlight the fact that pornography, sexuality, and feminism are polysemic categories, containing within them multiple meanings and dimensions. We give space to pornography's potential, while acknowledging challenges and limitations, for individuals who make and view this kind of porn, and to perhaps change the social world in which we live.

NOTES

1 See Collins 1990; Barton 2021; Miller-Young 2014; Williams 1999.

2 Horn 2018.

3 Taormino et al. 2013.

4 This research draws from Burke, *The Pornography Wars: The Past, Present, and Future of America's Obscene Obsession* (2023). Interview participants ranged in age from twenty-three to seventy-six and lived in the Northeast, South, or West. All had at least some college education, with the majority (fourteen of twenty-four) having completed a bachelor's degree. Half of respondents (twelve of twenty-four) identified as white, thirteen identified as Black or African American, and one identified as Creole Cajun. The majority identified as women (nineteen of twenty-four), two identified as men, and three identified as nonbinary or genderqueer.

5 Marks 2022.

6 Chivers et al. 2004.

7 Berg 2021; Thukral and Ditmore 2003.

8 See also Ipsen 2009; Qualls-Corbett 1988.

9 Schulte and Hammes 2021.

10 Peepshow Media 2020.

11 Hamilton and Webber 2020.

12 Johnson 2013.

PART II

Intersections

6

"It's Normal for Me"

Structuring Sex Work around Disability

LINDSAY BLEWETT

In 2007, I was struggling with my mental health—major depressive disorder, generalized anxiety disorder with a side of trichotillomania, and undiagnosed ADHD. In short, I was a mess. My mental health was such that I could not work a straight job. I had gone through at least three to four minimum-wage positions in a period of months, never lasting more than a week at a time. The inability to keep a job and the bills piling up only compounded the issues. Then, a man I had recently ended things with offered to pay to continue seeing me, and before long, I was posting ads offering sexual services for a fee on local ad boards whenever I needed money and felt well enough to work.

These experiences in sex work led me to research sex work and disability at the graduate level. In 2018, as part of my doctoral dissertation, I interviewed twenty-five disabled sex workers from Toronto and Ottawa about their disabilities, labor, and struggles and successes in sex work.[1] I wanted to know how they worked in their bodies—how did they make sex work work for them? Using a feminist, poststructural, critical-disability-studies lens, I discursively analyzed interviewees' thoughts about their bodies, focusing on embodiment, feeling, and perception. Following Margrit Shildrick's point that through "the visual, tactile, and aural contact between flesh-and-blood bodies . . . we both perceive and are perceived by others,"[2] I also examined their interactions with clients and police.[3]

Disabled sex workers generate embodied knowledge—they use their bodies to work and therefore structure their work uniquely around their disabilities.[4] Disabilities, especially visible ones, also structure how they are viewed in and outside of sex work. Disabled sex workers can thus offer strategies that challenge our understanding of both work and bodies, even as they struggle against stigma and capitalism. As Shildrick notes, "We constantly remake ourselves, fashioning new forms of self-perception and performance."[5] I argue that the embodied knowledge participants share challenges normative understandings of time, scheduling, pace, and ideas of disability as fixed. At the same time, this embodied knowledge generates creative and skillful hacks that allow them to, most often, flourish in sex work. Such insights are critical to understanding how disabled workers engage in sex work and provide "alternative maps to living" under neoliberalism.[6] Importantly, the disabled workers described in this chapter highlight the need for research that considers disability and sexual labor together and illustrates the critical need for disabled-sex-worker knowledge in academic research.[7]

Embodied Knowledges

Embodied knowledge refers to the critical insights generated from and on bodies. Embodied knowledge helps us see how ableism (and racism, transphobia, and sexism) are written on bodies. In sex work, a worker's body (e.g., height, weight, race, and hair length) is essential to clients when choosing whom to see. Still, these choices, constructed by clients as individual desires, do not exist in a vacuum and, writ large, result in discrimination. Systems of stratification shape sexual capital in sex industries. As Amia Srinivasan, a feminist philosopher, argues, "Racism, ableism, transphobia, and every other oppressive system make [their] way into bedrooms through the innocuous mechanism of personal preference."[8] Therefore, it is imperative to consider the mutually constitutive effects of various oppressive systems on these workers' experiences of disability and sex work.

The embodied knowledge these workers generate is full of clever exploits, such as skillfully manipulating clients' bodies (and emotions), carefully planning around bodily needs, and using disability advantageously whenever possible. Or, as Linton writes, "The cultural stuff of the disabled community is the creative response to atypical experience, the adaptive maneuvers through a world configured for non-disabled people."[9] In what follows, I show how embodied knowledge generates new insights into sexual labor and disability through disabled sex workers' lived experiences of disability as a relation between bodies, their challenges to capitalist time and productivity, their skillful organization and manipulation of sex work for their own ends, and the limits that coconstitutive elements of systemic oppression place on workers.

The disabled sex workers in my study described their disabilities as extremely context specific and often dependent on their interactions with others, notably clients. For example, both Ramona's and Megan's experiences of disability described below illustrate what Alison Kafer, building on the work of Jasbir Puar, calls an assemblage, wherein "categories of race, gender, sexuality, and disability are considered as events, actions, and *encounters between bodies*, rather than simply entities and attributes of subjects" (emphasis mine).[10]

Megan, a twenty-four-year-old mixed Vietnamese and Chinese cis woman with depression and anxiety who is on the autism spectrum and who escorts, told me, "I don't really identify myself as having a disability. It's normal for me. And I feel like whatever I have is normal." Megan describes how many disabled people feel, having never experienced any other way of being. Instead, Megan only began to observe that she was different in her interactions with others. Negative interactions and uncomfortable expectations in straight workplaces pushed her into sex work. She explains,

> I was frustrated that my manager would make me talk to people and be social with people, and I just couldn't, like I'm just not good at it. I'm not good at just asking about the weather or the type of movies they like, and I was just constantly anxious and frustrated that I wasn't doing a good job at my job because I just wasn't, I didn't feel like I was fit for it. I would look around me, and everyone is just enjoying it, and I'm not enjoying it, I don't like it, I feel so degraded.

Similarly, Ramona, a white, twenty-four-year-old cis woman who escorts, with depression and an eating disorder, illustrated how a client's initial contact could trigger her disabilities. So, she is extremely picky about her interactions with them.

> So, I have to really temper who is talking to me and how because I can't handle that much. So, if you're contacting me and you're like, hey, how

are you, what's going on, then I can't talk to you. I don't have the spoons to deal with that, it's just too much. I wouldn't even talk to my friends like that. Tell me what you want when you want it, we'll deal with it. So, I'm really picky on how people approach me, and I won't respond unless I think that it's going to be an easy interaction for me. Because otherwise, it's just draining, and I get angry and frustrated. And it doesn't go well.

In both instances, Megan and Ramona only felt disabled in their encounters with others, which entailed transforming, in Megan's case, where they worked, and in Ramona's, how they worked. For Megan, this meant leaving her job at Starbucks for sex work to control the number of interactions she had with others. This meant actively avoiding any difficult interactions to conserve her energy, in Ramona's case.

Manipulating Sex Work: Disabled Strategies

Like Megan and Ramona, many of the workers I interviewed tried to work around or adapt to situations where their disabilities might come into play. As Mitchell and Snyder write, "The preservation of disabled bodies . . . depends on managing to invent forms of culture that operate as alternatives to the principles of neoliberalism."[11] Disabled sex workers have their own techniques and strategies for preserving their bodies in sex work. Challenging neoliberal capitalist notions of time was one way disabled sex workers made their own culture in defiance of mainstream labor demands. Several spoke of mainstream labor moving too quickly or taking up too much of their time. Olivia, a Black cis woman who escorts with bipolar 2 and an undiagnosed eating disorder, discussed her civilian work:

So much of my life felt like I needed to be moving really quickly, and it's faster than I personally feel able to move. But I had to move at that pace because I'm part of institutions and stuff and things that don't work on schedules like mine.

Alice, a twenty-five-year-old white agender escort with Crohn's, chronic pain, PTSD, and bipolar disorder, noted that "a big issue when I was working as a hairstylist was that literally I just didn't have time to be healthy. I didn't have time to calm down and be present with myself." Winnie, an Indigenous cis woman and escort with PTSD, told me that sex work "allowed [her] to take care of [her]self in whatever way works best for [her] in the moment, in ways that wouldn't have been possible if [she] had a conventional job."

Sex work allows disabled workers to work on what is known in disability studies as "crip time": as Kafer, a feminist disability studies scholar, writes, "Rather than bend disabled bodies and minds to meet the clock, crip time bends the clock to meet disabled bodies and minds."[12] For example, Olivia also has different styles of scheduling based on her moods. She explains:

> So, if I'm having a really depressive episode where I'm having a lot of trouble with cognition, then I will structure my day down to the minute. Just to be like ok, you need to brush your teeth for this long, then this, and then that, and then that. And then mania, I really have to rein myself in because I'll make too many commitments. So that one's more like there are three main things I need to get done for the day, and everything else can kind of just flow through because my brain will come up with new things to do.

Like Olivia, I have ADHD, depression, and anxiety, so my ability to focus (and my energy) comes in waves. Sex work allowed me to do graduate school on my own timeline rather than conform to the program's time limits, because I could afford to pay the tuition necessary if I ran out of funding.[13]

However, Winnie's and Olivia's positive experiences managing sex work were tempered by the way racism structured how they could work and how they were perceived. Olivia found it difficult to get hired by most agencies, who would tell her, "They already have a Black girl." She also said, "Luxury and Blackness don't go together. They're antithetical in most people's minds," and thus described how she was given a "ceiling" for the rates she could charge because she refused to straighten her hair or wear wigs or weaves—in other words, she refused to conform to Western (white) beauty standards. The very fact of Winnie's homelessness is a symptom of the ongoing colonization of Indigenous people in Canada; forced out of her northern community by poverty and lack of jobs, she moved to the city at eighteen. But with her family unable to support her and with only a high school education, she quickly ended up bouncing from couch to couch with no income to support her.

Black and other people of color in sex work must work harder and more often while having fewer opportunities to make what white, non-disabled sex workers earn, while also needing that extra cushion of time to access care. As Olivia noted, accessing care is like "having a second job," and time in this instance is not liberatory but debilitating: the time needed to find and access care (or stable housing) prolongs harm via the slow wearing down of the body.[14] For example, Olivia noted that if she had not gotten a diagnosis when she did, she would be much sicker or "institutionalized by now." While sex work often provides flexibility, racism requires disabled workers of color to work harder and more often, which can limit the amount of time they can spend finding or receiving care. Thus, racism mitigates any liberatory aspects of crip time that Olivia or Winnie might experience.[15]

While sex work allowed Alice, Natalie, and me to set our own schedules, for Winnie and Olivia, the time issue was more complicated. Winnie's homelessness prolonged harm before her sex work income could provide stable housing. For Olivia, sex work provided more time to seek care, but finding care took longer as a poor, Black woman experiencing psychiatric difficulties. For both women, racism curtailed their earning potential.

The ability to decide what services to offer also allowed the people I interviewed to work around their disability. For example, Jeannette, a white cis woman and escort in her midthirties with a hip injury, cannot do some sexual positions. If possible, she draws out conversation with her clients and humorously describes herself as "more of a lounging whore." I asked her what she thought her strongest skill as a disabled sex worker was. She responded, "convincing rich men to pay for my medical treatments," further illustrating the creative conversational skills required of disabled sex workers who cannot do (or can do but not for as long) the same physical, sexual activity as their nondisabled peers.

In contrast, Holly (white, cis woman, thirty-seven), an escort who described herself as not being good at small talk, said she memorized a list of small-talk-type questions to aid her in her conversations with clients, telling me, "I have scripts," thus cleverly turning a perceived limitation into a finely honed skill. Similarly, Da-in, a Korean escort with lupus and depression, uses her civilian work as a sex educator to hustle clients into duos, where two sex workers serve clients together. She said,

> I can see opportunities. I've had [sex workers] reach out to me and ask to teach them something, and I'm like, for sure, but the best way is in session, and I don't want your money. I think you should get on the job training, paid training. So, I often tell people, hook up the duo. Let's do that. If you ever get a client like, I want you to do these things and you have no idea how to do that? Great, give them a sales pitch, oh my goodness, have you heard of [Da-in]? I've always wanted to learn this, could we do a duo?

Attracting clients through other workers means she does not have to use precious funds to pay for advertising. It is often difficult to pay for ads if you have not been working due to illness or a flareup, and in this way, Da-in can save the money she might have used on advertising to get by when she needs to take time off. This adroit strategy not only helps Da-in get clients (and therefore income) but also helps another worker who gets to learn a skill while also still getting paid.

The Politics of Disclosure: Visible versus Invisible Disabilities

Some disabled workers, like Megan, Natalie, and Alice, strategically disclosed their disabilities to clients as a form of bonding and authenticity, using disability to their advantage. Alice, who has Crohn's Disease, bipolar disorder, and PTSD, sometimes shares about her Crohn's, noting of her last client that "we bonded over the fact that we had both spent the morning in pain." She said it was "nice having clients who were also chronically ill because we can chat about that a bit." Clients increasingly want authentic experiences that closely mirror a real girlfriend's behavior.[16] Clients, as Natalie explains, "appreciate that openness."

However, these strategic disclosures were highly dependent on the type of disability and the sex workers' comfort level; several of the disabled workers I interviewed had either experienced stigma about their disabilities or were extremely wary of the potential stigma that might occur if they did share, particularly if their disability was a psychiatric one. Alice was cognizant that while sharing about Crohn's might be a bonding technique, sharing her struggles with PTSD was not a good idea: "When they hear I have PTSD, they feel almost like a guilt. Bringing that into a session, like the idea of sexual trauma or having been assaulted, it's very scary for some clients. And they feel like maybe that's the only reason I'm in the industry."

For others, avoiding the stigma associated with different bodyminds is inescapable,[17] because ableism (like racism, discussed above) is an embodied knowledge sometimes intimately visible on a worker's body. Maggie, an agender white escort with Ehlers-Danlos, a connective tissue disorder that causes easy bruising, had a client walk out, stating that he didn't want "to be with someone who looks like they've been beaten." For this client, bruising carried an assumption of victimhood rather than illness. The irony is that the loss of income from this client directly affects Maggie's precarity as a disabled sex worker, increasing any violence they might experience due to poverty. Here the client's desire is seen as individual preference, rather than part of a larger system of ableist discrimination.

As Shildrick and Price contend, the "embodied subject is actively and continuously produced through social interactions with other body-subjects."[18] Disability, again, is not a fixed identity but a fluid relation, enacted in our encounters with others. It can be used advantageously in some cases, while in others, workers have no control over how others will understand their embodiments.

Conclusions

Disabled sex workers crip or challenge normative time, using creative organization and manipulation, such as "anticipatory scheduling" or memorizing conversation scripts.[19] As Alison Kafer argues, these actions are read not simply as self-care or self-preservation in order to work but "as [a] refusal of such regimes in order to make room for pleasure."[20] In refusing neoliberal capitalist modes of productivity, the disabled sex workers I interviewed make room for living in ways that can attend to care and pleasure. Da-in's strategy for getting duos allowed her to do more of the work she loved: "I think it's a really neat way to use hustle and this industry for me to do the sex education piece that supports someone's work also. That also I don't have to tap you for your money or your market. I love it." Many spoke of what they can do because of the money or extra time that sex work affords them. Rhonda, a white cis woman and escort with multiple sclerosis, said, "I'm happy, I'm healthy-ish, and it's only because of this job. And I get to pursue all these academic things that I really want to do but couldn't afford before." My experiences in sex work gave me the time and money to pursue graduate school and the time needed to continue doing sex work advocacy alongside school.

The disabled sex workers who shared their experiences and lives with me articulated a vision of work that challenged norms of productivity, time and scheduling, and what counts as work. They found creative ways to work with their disabilities rather than against them and developed skillful ways of managing clients and using their disabilities advantageously to maximize their earnings while also being aware of and sensitive to the stigma surrounding many disabilities, especially those associated with "madness" and nonnormative appearances. This embodied knowledge also challenges normative modes of living and relating to others, illustrating the interconnectedness of bodies in the world.

NOTES

1   For this study, I conducted twenty-five semistructured interviews with indoor sex workers with disabilities, across multiple sectors of the industry. Ages ranged from nineteen to forty-nine, with fourteen cis women, one cis man, one trans woman, three identifying as agender, and two as nonbinary or gender fluid. Most participants identified as white or Caucasian (n=15), while the remaining identified as Black (three), Indigenous (two), Metis (one), mixed Arab (one), East Asian (two), and South Asian (one). Their disabilities ranged from physical conditions such as cerebral palsy, multiple sclerosis, lupus, Ehlers-Danlos Syndrome, and pituitary dwarfism to psychiatric disabilities such as DID (dissociative identity disorder), major depressive disorder, anxiety disorders, bipolar disorder, and PTSD. The interviews averaged an hour and were transcribed by me, then coded by hand, and analyzed using a feminist, critical-disability-studies lens.

2   Shildrick 2012, 26.

3   This chapter focuses primarily on workers' embodiment and their interactions with clients. For a discussion of disabled sex workers and police, Blewett 2022.

4   For a full discussion of embodied knowledge as it relates to disabled people more generally, see Mitchell and Snyder 2015.

5   Shildrick 2012, 27.

6   Mitchell and Snyder 2015, 3.

7 In this chapter, I view "disability" as a useful term for the delineation of research and for attracting participants. However, for the purposes of clarity, I see disability as a historically contingent set of power relations and, following Tremain 2017, 23, recognize that people are differentially subjected to the disability apparatus on the basis of "constructed perceptions and interpretations" of a variety of phenomena, including bodily structure and appearance, cognitive ability, style, mobility, and so on that are contextually specific. Accordingly, I have been specific about the embodied differences of participants where necessary and have used the more general term "disability" as an umbrella term for a wide range of differential embodiments.

8 Srinivasan 2021, 84.

9 Linton 1998, 5, quoted in Shuttleworth 2002, 112.

10 Kafer 2013, 10.

11 Mitchell and Snyder 2015, 3.

12 Kafer 2013, 27.

13 My funding has time limits—PhD students are expected to finish their degrees within six years. One does not receive any funding after that, though one can apply for a program extension based on disability. This program extension guarantees a continued TA placement but does not cover tuition.

14 Puar 2017.

15 For a fuller discussion of racism in sex work, see Brooks 2010a, 2010b; Jones 2015, 2020a; Sayers 2017.

16 Bernstein 2007b.

17 Clare 2017.

18 Price and Shildrick 2002, 63.

19 Kafer 2013, 39.

20 Kafer 2013, 39.

7

"I Was Too Fat"

Anti-Fatness as a Workplace Access Issue

PEYTON BOND

In a piece for *HuffPost*, Emily McCombs writes, "Fat people face discrimination in every aspect of society. Weight discrimination plays a role in hiring, determining wages, and firing. Moving through our society in a fat body means constantly being confronted with others' opinions of it when you're just trying to exist."[1] Drawing from interviews with indoor sex workers about their workplace experience in Aotearoa New Zealand, this chapter discusses the impact of classed branding of brothels on fat workers. I use the word "fat," respecting the language of most participants and scholars in fat studies.[2] I use "anti-fatness" based on the work of Aubrey Gordon, a fat activist and writer.[3]

Sex work often functions as a more profitable alternative to low-paid work (especially for women).[4] Excluding fat workers based on classed branding reinforces existing hierarchies of class, gender, and race and further disadvantages people in an already stigmatized and marginalized industry, within an already unequal capitalist labor market. Anti-fatness has damaging outcomes for fat sex workers, especially around wages and job mobility. Fat sex workers are desirable, yet the production of thinness as the peak of feminine performance in brothel branding perpetuates structural issues of anti-fatness in Western society.

In what follows, I first introduce the study methodology. Then I provide a brief background on sex work policy in Aotearoa New Zealand. With my study design and research context briefly outlined, I discuss brothels and their discursive production of classed branding. Finally, I discuss the adverse effect this branding has on wages and job mobility.

The absence of criminalization in Aotearoa New Zealand means that workers have access to rights and may work without fear of arrest or prosecution. Once criminalization is removed, however, there is space to observe how workplaces in the sex industry replicate the prejudices and hierarchies of the capitalist world.

The Study

In early 2020, I spoke to indoor sex workers about their workplace experience in Aotearoa New Zealand.[5] I interviewed twenty-seven full-service sex workers, including brothel, agency, and independent workers.[6] Experiences of anti-fatness were primarily contextualized in the brothel setting, and this essay focuses on those experiences—though several workers described moving to independent work *because* of the anti-fatness found in brothels.[7] Most Aotearoa New Zealand sex workers operate from brothels and agencies, though there are almost six hundred sex workers advertising on the dominant website for independent workers.[8] Participants widely described independent work as necessitating marketing and technology skills alongside an appropriate space to see clients: independent work is running a business. A brothel or agency is the better option for workers without sufficient time or money to run that business.

This essay explores discussions with the ten participants who spoke specifically about anti-fatness in workplace experiences.[9] Out of those ten participants, eight identified themselves as fat or outlined their own experiences of anti-fatness. Seven of the workers are Pākeha, one worker is Asian, one worker is Asian American, and one worker is Pacific Islander.[10] The ten workers ranged in age from twenty to late thirties, and their time in the industry ranged from six months to thirteen years.

Aotearoa New Zealand: A Brief Background

It is widely accepted that sex work arrived in Aotearoa New Zealand in the nineteenth century alongside colonization. In its early history the country saw a "widespread acceptance" of sex work, unlike other Western countries with similar backgrounds of colonization.[11] Sex work was decriminalized in 2003 with the Prostitution Reform Act (PRA), largely due to the tireless work of the Aotearoa New Zealand Sex Workers' Collective (NZPC).[12] Decriminalization removes much of the power from the state (specifically police) and redistributes the power to labor-law and market control. In a world where workers' rights continue to erode, capitalist power increases, and marginalization and inequalities are rampant: decriminalization, while an essential first step, is not the finish line.

Anti-fatness, for example, is not unique to the sex industry in Aotearoa New Zealand. Individuals perceived as fat or "overweight" are disadvantaged during the recruitment or interviewing stage—and all the way through to promotion. This size-based discrimination has been shown to affect women especially.[13] While employers may not discriminate on the grounds of a range of factors, including age, race, ethnicity, sex, sexual orientation, and disability, discrimination based on weight, physical size, or appearance is not prohibited in Aotearoa New Zealand (and in many places worldwide).[14] The exclusion of weight or fatness means that workers may not file complaints against employers for anti-fatness, even though sex workers in decriminalized Aotearoa New Zealand can now file cases against management: in 2020, a sex worker settled with a business owner in a six-figure sexual harassment case.[15]

Anti-Fatness as a Workplace Experience

Anti-fatness was a common theme in my research interviews. Kitty,[16] at the end of our interview about her work experience, had one thing she wanted emphasized:

I would just be going over and over how fatphobic [the industry is], and that needs to change. People that get fired because they are plus size need to be able to say, "Hey, no." Because you can't protest how you're fired, why you're fired. If they have an unfair reason for firing you, then they come up with something else.

Rose agreed:

The skinny girls are like the "high end," and there are very few places that take girls that are over a size twelve. It's fucking fatphobic out there.

While fatness alone marginalizes workers, further intersections intensify that experience. Research participants frequently noted intersections exacerbating discrimination based on body size, race, class, education, gender, queerness, and dis/ability. When discussing being "curvier," for instance, Ruth also pointed to her privilege:

> I try very hard to remember my privilege. I think also, as a white cisgender woman, I'm very privileged in that sense as well. I'm a little curvier, but work is not difficult to come by.

Ruth acknowledges that she is both white and cisgender: two factors that mean that work—both inside and outside of the sex industry—is easier for her to come by. While her body may not fit into the mainstream, her body being both white and cis privileges her.

Brothels and Branding

While ideas of desirability may vary across cultures, Western society holds thin and white (and well-educated, able-bodied, cisgender, upper/middle-class) women as the ideal standard.[17] Successfully branding a "high-end" brothel requires hiring women who conform to this limited standard and rejecting those who do not. High-end brothels promise discreet and elite services, with professional photos and websites and high rates to match: a high-end agency lists rates as $340 for thirty minutes, while a brothel in the same city lists rates as $150 for the same time. Women on the more expensive website are slim and white and devoid of cellulite; the less expensive website has a greater variety of bodies, and the pictures are less professional, unretouched. The high-end agency emphasizes sophistication, and the pictures are of nude women, but resemble stylish boudoir shots—brothels or agencies that are not "high-end" more often have selfies or stock photos.

Classed Branding and Fewer Bookings for Fat Workers

Brothel branding reproduces anti-fatness and measures of erotic capital: some "high-end" brothels are spaces where classed branding means fat workers get fewer bookings, and still other brothels discriminate against fat workers despite fat workers having success in the space. In the context of a "high-end" brothel, thinness is useful in achieving the desired upper- or middle-class feminine performance. To work in high-end spaces, workers must not only perform emotional, physical, and sexual labor but also work at an aesthetic level to reflect the classed "brand" that the organization is trying to present. Jess worked at places where

> they have pretty much exclusively hired size eight white cis women. . . . Clients come to them for a specific kind of woman. If they are hiring people who fall outside of that category, clients go [elsewhere].

Brothels that hire "size eight white cis women" do so to produce an idealized performance. That ideal is sized, raced, and gendered to allow the business to show its "high-class" status using Western standards as a marketing tool. The marketing tool uses the aesthetic labor of those *within* the ideal while *rejecting* people who exist outside of it. The use of Western standards as a marketing tool means that societal hierarchies, including patriarchy, white supremacy, and cissexism, are both mirrored and reproduced in the workplace—it is those factors that form erotic capital in an aesthetic market. It is in the space of brothel brand development and hiring practices, then, that (as Amy put it), "isms and phobias are really, really engrained" and "actively perpetuated" in the industry. Lila, who works in a high-end agency, once spoke to her manager about it:

> [The workers] are skinny, and conventionally attractive, and mainly white. That doesn't sit 100 percent well with me. But that's hard, where do you draw the line? As [the manager] said to me, "I've hired people with bigger bodies in the past, and they just don't get bookings." And she recommends other agencies where they might do better. It doesn't sit well with me personally.[18]

The other agencies where "they might do better" are unlikely to pay the same as the high-end agency where Lila works. Amy had an experience in which, although she was "allowed" to work in a high-end brothel, the style of the workplace was such that she left quickly:

> While they did let me work there, they weren't the sort of workplace that plus-size girls get bookings. So, I ended that quickly.

Bigger bodies not getting bookings in high-end brothels reinforces the dominant ideology of thin bodies as the most marketable. Fat workers are perfectly capable of making money and getting work (and do): the contradiction here is found in the aim to brand as "high-end." If the branded experience offered to clients is the thin and aesthetically high-classed woman, then bigger bodies will succeed less *in that space*. Fat bodies will instead exist in conflict with the neatly packaged standards of money, class, and desire that make up the constructed ideal. The problem is not with fat bodies: the problem is with workplaces (and Western society) whose imaginaries of erotic capital are predicated on ideas of the acceptable body.

Advertisements for brothel workers are even cultivated to appeal to the assumed desire for thinner women. Anna shares,

> If you're over a size twelve, they will mark you down either two or three sizes smaller than what you actually are. When I was a size fourteen, I was advertised as a size ten. When I went back when I was a size eighteen, I was advertised as a size fourteen. They change your height as well!

This is the case even though Kim (and other participants) found that being curvy *helped* her get bookings:

> There's me and another girl who are quite curvy, and people want us for the curves, and she's got like huge boobs, so they want her for big boobs, and they want me for the hips.

The management changing Anna's size from eighteen to fourteen does not change their body or appearance. Rather, it changes the perception of what the client is purchasing. Anti-fatness operates against workers' bodies and in the brothel/agency's fatphobic branding strategies. Many societies have determined that the most desirable and marketable feminine body is the thin and upper/middle-class white body. This brand and its reliance on structural anti-fatness maintain hegemony.

Class and More Diverse Brothels

While some brothels discriminate against fat workers, it is not the case that all brothels reject fat workers. Brothels that are not branded as "high-class" tend to have more diversity. Kitty describes a brothel that

> had a girl that was a size twenty-two.[19] They have girls of all different shapes and sizes. They are less fancy than some of the other places I've worked at. So, working-class guys come in, that sort of clientele is okay with more plus-size girls.

Kitty suggests that there is not a single version of what men prefer, but rather that class background shapes sexual preferences. She states that the brothel where she worked is not "high-end" or "high-class," and the clients who go there are "okay" with a diversity of bodies, in contrast to "high-class" brothels where expectations of the body and its labor are more rigid. Sex workers must thus work on several levels—they must "do gender" (specifically, white femininity), but they must also "do class."[20]

This is not to say that fat workers are only attractive to or desired by working-class people. Rather, thinness is packaged and consumed as the pinnacle of upper- and middle-class feminine performance, and this is used to brand certain brothels as marketing certain class aesthetics. Brothels that actively hire workers who are not thin (and white, and able to pass as both heterosexual and educated) are more likely to be branded as "working-class" or "low-end," while brothels that are "high-end" do not hire those workers. The branding does not align with an individual preference, but instead aligns with structural issues of anti-fatness within Western society.[21]

The Effect on Wages and Job Mobility

The material impacts of anti-fatness in the sex industry primarily revolve around lower wages and less job mobility. The lower wages are caused by "high-end" places shutting fat people out of "high-end" wages and the systemic anti-fatness that still exists in independent work, while the reduced job mobility comes from the rejection of fat workers by brothels. Dana tried to apply for one agency that was the second-highest-paid place in her city with no success, meaning she had to apply to places where the rates were lower:

> They were completely snooty, high class. And I was too fat. . . . She took my photos and said, "Oh, I just don't think you're going to fit in here, have a look at your photos compared to the other girls." And all the other girls were skinny!

Amy had trouble finding a workplace because of anti-fatness and, once she moved to independent work, still had trouble with rates because of the pairing of high-end and thinness:

> I am plus size, and so working at an agency or a brothel isn't really an option since they are incredibly fatphobic. . . . There's a maximum amount of money you can charge as a fat person. . . . It's like 250, and clients will not pay more than that. Whereas my friends can charge 300, 400 bucks and be fine.[22]

Kitty contextualized the anti-fatness in how it removed her ability to choose a workplace, as some had limits on sizing:

> I would just go to places, and most places would turn me down. They would be like, "Sorry, but we don't take girls over a size twelve. Sorry, we don't take girls over a size eight." . . . Lots of places just don't hire plus size women at all. . . . I would work at whatever place would take me.

While Kitty, a white cis woman, had difficulties based on fatness alone, Maya spoke of a distinct lack of places that would take people outside of cisgender, heteronormative, and thin standards:

> [Brothel] has been the one place where you can find a whole bunch of trans people who are on testosterone, or trans women, one of the few indoor venues that will take trans women at all, because they don't give a shit. If you can't make money, what, you're sitting there using .1 percent

of the Internet? . . . And those are the places that tend to take BBWs, tend to be less worried about you looking visibly queer.[23]

Sex workers who do not fit inside the "ideal" brand have fewer options for workplaces. This lack of job mobility means that workers must either (as Kitty outlined) work where they are hired or turn to independent work. An inability to choose a suitable brothel reduces workers' rights. Avoiding a bad work environment often means leaving it rather than contesting poor treatment—an inability to leave the workplace because of limited options reduces experiences of safety (especially for those who choose to move to street-based work).[24] Although several workers moved to independent work to avoid the anti-fatness they experienced in brothels and had more success there, the move also has its down sides: working alone may mean less security and more labor involved in advertising and communicating with clients. For independent workers who are fat, the labor increases. When Maya went independent, they found that

> there is a disproportionate amount of labour involved in it if you're from a minority group. If you're a trans woman, if you're brown, if you're fat . . . you have to play nice.

Maya traces the implications of being a part of one—or more—minority groups. Workers who are fat but are still white, or are fat but are still cis, will face both less labor and less violence (in the way of poverty, job loss, or physical violence) than those workers whose lives exist at more intersections.

In conclusion, people whose bodies exist outside the Western feminine ideal face substantial prejudice within the sex industry. These limitations are based on exclusionary practices in the name of adherence to a brand. If the brand is "high end" and less accepting of fat bodies, workers have less opportunity for movement between or choices of workplaces and may find that their rates are limited in accordance with perceived distance from the "ideal." Hierarchies within sex work mean that while fat workers are booked, make money, and succeed as sex workers, they are not given the same access to workspaces as other workers. Reduced access, particularly to places branded as "high end," shuts workers out of higher-paid workplaces and decreases job mobility. The marketing and selling of a certain brand are not limited to the sex industry. The late-stage capitalist labor market not only exploits workers' physical and emotional labor but also packages prejudice to take advantage of any aspect that may create their aesthetically "ideal" worker—while actively excluding and harming workers unable to embody that chosen aesthetic. Most participants quoted here are cis Pākehā women; sex workers who are trans, who are Māori or Pasifika, face further discriminations and marginalization as the distance between their bodies and the white, slim, and cisgender "ideal" body grows.

While sex work has been decriminalized in Aotearoa New Zealand since 2003, that does not mean that rights for sex workers have been fully realized—rather, sex workers' rights have been brought to the position of workers' rights more broadly. Alongside decriminalization, other countries should aim to move power to workers, raise welfare payments and consider guaranteed basic incomes, and ensure that people have the financial stability needed to demand their rights. Workers' rights and capitalism cannot coexist, and the rights of the marginalized worker are at the greatest risk of erosion. As Berg writes, "Sex work occupies a margin in discourses of work . . . [and] margins can illuminate the perversity of the center."[25] Fat sex workers, marginalized within sex work and marginalized as sex workers, can thus speak to the conditions of work in the capitalist labor market in a way that casts floodlights on the perversity of work's center.[26]

NOTES

1 McCombs 2022.
2 Pickett and Cunnigham 2017; Pausé and Palmer 2021.
3 Gordon 2021.
4 Bernstein 2007b; Gilmour 2016; Maher, Pickering, and Gerard 2012.
5 I received ethics approval for this project from the University of Otago.
6 Participants primarily differentiated between brothels and agencies by naming brothels (or "parlors") as shift work, while agencies were mostly appointment based. For the purposes of this essay, I use "brothel" to capture both types, as it is an umbrella term for a managed sex work workplace (see: Prostitution Reform Act 2003, NZPC Aotearoa New Zealand Sex Workers' Collective, accessed July 2021, www.nzpc.org.nz/).
7 Though there were still issues of anti-fatness in independent work.
8 Jordan 2018.

9 The research project that this essay draws from does not focus specifically on anti-fatness. Anti-fatness arose when I asked questions about diversity in the workplace or when participants were asked what they especially wanted known about their work experience.

10 "*Pākeha*" is the Māori word for a white New Zealander. Some participants asked for their ethnicity to be described broadly for confidentiality purposes (identified as "Asian," for example, rather than by the specific country they are from).

11 Jordan 2010.

12 Radačić 2017; Easterbrook-Smith 2021.

13 Crandall, Merman, and Hebl 2009; Mason 2012.

14 Pausé and Palmer 2021.

15 Taunton 2020.

16 All names have been changed to protect anonymity.

17 Swami 2015.

18 I use Brooks's definition of "erotic capital," found in Brooks 2010b.

19 All sizing is New Zealand sizing.

20 Trautner 2005.

21 Trautner 2005.

22 Louise 2021; Sage 2021.

23 "BBWs" means "big beautiful women."

24 Armstrong 2014; Gilmour 2016.

25 Berg 2014.

26 de Vries 2015; Crenshaw 1989, 1991, 2017; Yuval-Davis 2006.

8

The "Big Beautiful Women" Awards

Fat Latinas in the Porn Industry

YESSICA GARCIA HERNANADEZ

In 2017, the Adult Video News (AVN) Award Show announced the elimination of its "BBW Performer of the Year" category. The AVN show is widely known as the "Oscars of pornography," its first show having taken place in 1984. The "BBW Performer of the Year" category was introduced to AVN in 2014 to recognize fat adult stars in the genre. "BBW" is the porn industry tag for "Big Beautiful Women." The first BBW award went to fat Latina star April Flores, who started her career in the industry in 2005.[1] As expected, the news of the removal of this award disappointed many BBW stars, fans, and producers. AVN responded to the complaints, explaining that the category was removed because of ongoing declines in BBW performers in DVDs and offered a Fan BBW category instead. The elimination of the award undermined the BBW genre's contribution to the porn industry. According to Pornhub, from 2013 to 2015, searches for "BBW" increased by 47 percent. Fat sex workers were making creative content that challenged the genre's past, and Latinas were critical in transforming the genre. Sofia Rose, a Latina multi-BBW-award-winning actor, was among the top three models searched for on the site.

In this paper, I offer some observations of the BBW Awards Show, an adult award show that took place at Larry Flint's Hustler Club in Las Vegas the Tuesday before the AVN Awards. The BBW show is not directly affiliated with the AVN, but takes place the same week, and I show how fat sex workers are transgressing the history and rules of the genre, and glamorizing fat aesthetics. By juxtaposing the BBW Awards Show with the AVN expo, I argue that the BBW Awards Show widens sex work spaces because it embraces a utopic aesthetic of fat positivity. In the fight to develop and recognize inclusionary porn, the BBW Awards Show disrupts power relations by centering the voice of fans and fat performers in the decision and organizing process of production. They institutionalize porn fandom to strategically build spaces that challenge fatphobia in the mainstream industry and beyond, allowing adult stars to navigate the BBW market in a new way and collectively envision its transformation.

At the time of the announced elimination, I was starting my research on BBW pornography and was particularly interested in the history of Latinas in the genre. As with most women of color feminists, *the personal was political* for me. My investment in historicizing the genre came from the powerful transformative impact the films and writing of fat Latina porn star April Flores had on me in my late twenties. Flores's work opened my eyes to fat pleasure in ways I had never seen on mainstream tube sites. Since my first encounter with her writing and films, I have become a spectator, fan, and critic of fat pornography because it transgresses the thin-normative world of mainstream pornography. I also study the genre, and the history of fat Latinas in the industry, because BBW pornography is an important reference in most "plus-size" erotic markets due to the lack of fat sex-positive figures in mainstream culture. Even when I am not studying fat porn, I am always pulled back to it because of my own fat racialized embodiment. As a researcher and a fat Latina myself, I have negotiated the caricature fantasies that the genre produces about fat bodies in my own dating life—during those hours when I am technically off the clock from the "ethnographic field."

In the rest of the essay, through short ethnographic vignettes and photos, I take a *porn-in-action approach* to center the voices of adult stars, producers, photographers, and fans who frequent BBW adult sites.[2] I explore insights into the politics of porn reception and how the representation of Latinas, in the act of fandom or spectatorship, intersects with the labor and business side of pornography. Further, I consider the contradictions of spectatorship, ask questions about the imagined and intended audience for the genre, and lay out the hierarchies of desire and power that both Latina fans and adult stars negotiate. In a capitalistic industry like pornography that uses labor to construct pleasures, fantasies, and representation, we know that the negotiation of these dynamics is constantly being played out. As Heather Berg shows us, a framework of "porno dialectics" is useful as it helps us find the loop-holes, the contradictions, in a structure that was built to be exploitative in the first place.[3] BBW adult stars negotiate this capitalist market with creative strategies, and the BBW Awards Show gives us a glimpse into those creative strategies.

The BBW Awards Show

The BBW Awards Show was founded by award–winning porn star Eliza Allure, whose vision was to recognize and validate the work of fat porn stars. Allure is one of the top twenty BBW models and has produced BBW content for *Hustler*. In an interview she explained why she created the award show: "I want this event to be dedicated to the talented and hardworking men and women who contribute to the BBW community in positive ways."[4] BBW Award categories have indeed been incorpo-rated into other adult industry award shows such as AVN (from 2014 to 2019), CamCon,[5] and the Urban X Awards, XBiz. Still, Eliza Allure filled a gap in the industry by creating a dedicated space for fat performers, producers, and admirers. Black queer feminist Angela Jones has argued that adult award shows provide social capital to cam performers,[6] and indeed, the BBW Awards legitimate performers of the BBW genre. They help welcome new porn stars into the game and facilitate unofficial men-torship between veteran porn stars and amateur or beginning actors.

I have attended the BBW Awards Show for the past three years (2019–2021). Whenever I get there, I self-park near the parking lot entrance and walk over to a hidden elevator that takes me to the club's private event lounge. As soon as I exit the elevator, I encounter a registration table. In 2020, as I approached the table, a cashier asked, "Are you in the industry?" I responded, "No, but can I purchase my ticket?" With a con-fused face, she replied, "Oh, okay, it will be fifty dollars." She had asked because people in the industry could enter the event for free. However, as I walked away, I wondered if she looked confused about me purchas-ing my ticket because at this event, unlike any other adult event I had attended, I could easily have passed for a Latina adult actor in the BBW genre.

That night my racialized embodiment found belonging among the fat adult stars whose bodies looked like mine. It was a night when fat bodies were celebrated, admired, and desired. Every time I have attended the BBW Awards Show, my "cinesthetic subjectivity," that is, my body that constantly negotiates the onscreen and offscreen experience, to use Vivian Sobchak's phrase, has been moved from seeing identification with fat bodies like that of April Flores on screen to feeling this identification in reality.[7] The racial diversity of the event also shaped why the cashier interpreted my racialized fat body as that of one of the performers. Oddly, because my entry to adult entertainment awards was through the BBW Awards Show, I had an unrealistic expectation that the AVN show would be similar to that night. It was not until after the AVN award show that I realized what a utopic moment the BBW Awards Show is. At AVN, fans ignore fat performers and women of color in favor of white and thin porn stars. The BBW Awards Shows reversed these power dynamics.

The Sponsors

As soon as I passed the cashiers, I encountered the red-carpet photo wall, where the stars converse with each other and interact with the professional photographers who are documenting the event. The photo wall lists the names of the event's sponsors, which are mostly porn companies that produce fat pornography. One recurring sponsor is PlumperPass, a porn production company based in Miami, Florida, that manages more than 458 BBW porn stars and offers more than 2,475 BBW movies. According to XVideos, PlumperPass runs the largest BBW site on the Internet.

For the past four years, the chief marketing officer of PlumperPass .com, Clint Woods, has been the repeat recipient of the Best Multigirl Site award. BBW actresses hold PlumperPass in high regard because of its shooting philosophy. According to Woods, PlumperPass does not "play into BBWs being a fetish." Woods and his colleagues instead focus on providing high-quality shoots for the fans.

Under his definition of fetishization, low-quality shoots appear as less respectable compared to high-quality films because they fixate on the fatness on screen rather than the quality and aesthetics of the porn. When he started in the early 2000s, he recalled companies not investing in hair, makeup, or sets for fat models. Wood views his investment in

Figure 8.1. Models at the BBW Awards Show. The photo showcases two adult stars at the red-carpet area of the show. Public domain, Instagram, @Cdavisions.

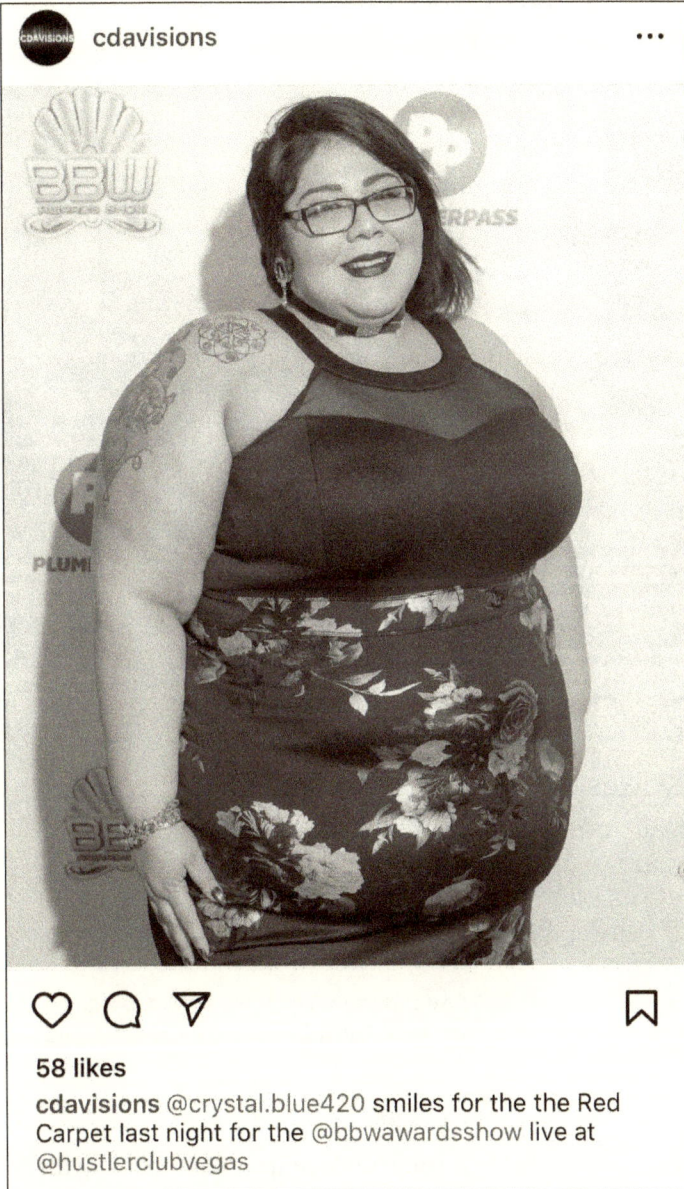

cdavisions •••

♡ ○ ⊳ 🔖

58 likes
cdavisions @crystal.blue420 smiles for the the Red Carpet last night for the @bbwawardsshow live at @hustlerclubvegas

Figure 8.2. A model at the BBW Awards Show. The photo showcases an adult star at the red-carpet area of the show. Public domain, Instagram, @Cdavisions.

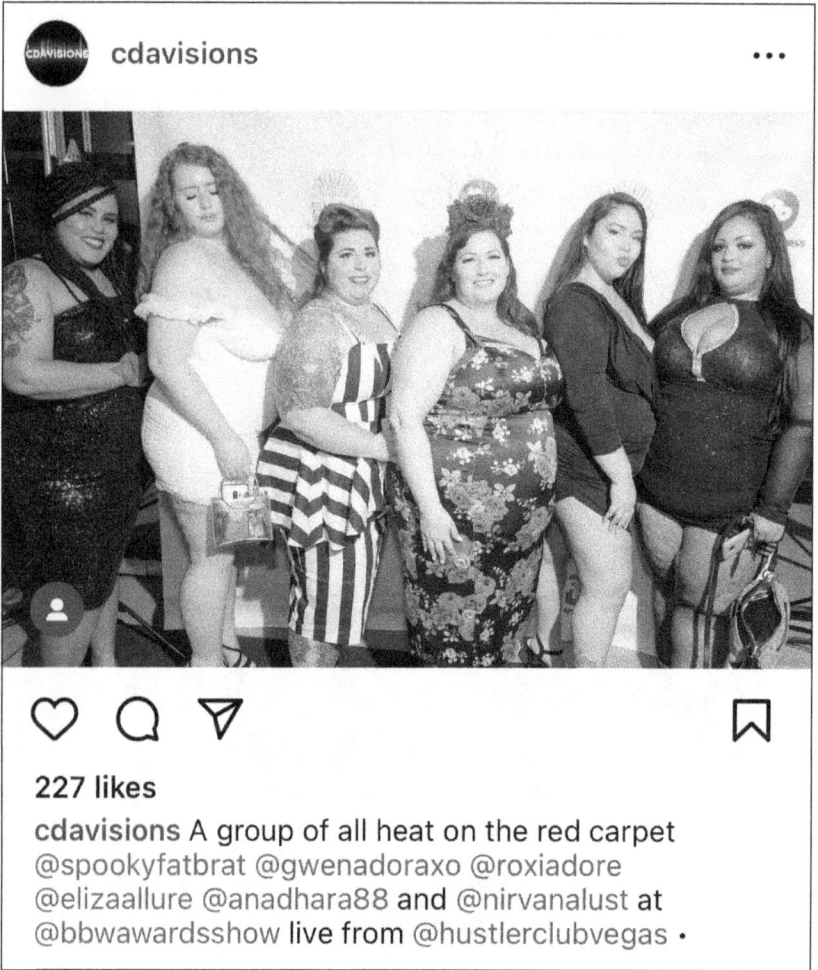

Figure 8.3. Models at the BBW Awards Show. The photo showcases a group of six adult stars at the red-carpet area of the show. Public domain, Instagram, @Cdavisions.

shooting BBW as he would any other genre, demonstrating his commitment to the longevity of the genre.

In recent years, BBW Latina models have been open about degrading treatment from porn companies lacking a commitment to the BBW genre. Cuban actress Angelica Castro and Mexican actor Breana Kahlo contrast the pleasures of shooting with PlumperPass compared to other companies. In a letter she wrote to her podcast audience, Angelica Castro states,

> When I entered the sex industry, I was discriminated against because of my weight with the local [porn] companies and even television stations. Many people did not understand why I was not blond, skinny, or tall with huge boobs. One of the first companies who helped me change the perception I had of me was PlumperPass. They showed me a new world of followers that I did not think existed. They helped me feel comfortable with my body; with my rolls, my excess of cellulite, and above all they made feel sensual and confident with myself. This is kind of touchy because *it is hard to be a porn star and not feel sexy*. . . . They have wanted to pay me less and treat me like a second-class citizen because I did not fit society's norms and the norms of many companies. (translation by author)

Later, Castro explores other difficulties she encountered in the industry, particularly struggling to get paid the money that thin white stars received. In her research on the experiences of Black fat porn actors, Black feminist scholar Mireille Miller-Young has shown that Black porn stars negotiate double oppression in the industry because of their race and size.[8] The experience of Castro and Betty Black (interviewed by Miller-Young) shows that a niche of pornography that claims not to be structured around race is without a doubt structured by sexual racism and fatphobia, and this is most evident in the pay-labor of porn stars.

According to Black erotic laborer Lilith London, clients even low-ball performer prices because they cannot fathom how a fat adult star can charge that much.[9] Castro also notes the affective aspect of her work, which includes "feelings of sexiness" about her own body. People might view Castro feeling sexier as a personal journey, divorced from her porn work. However, Castro does not, and she hints at the power dynamics at play here. Fat bodies are placed at the bottom of the hierarchy within hegemonic hierarchies of desire. The fatphobic structures of mainstream pornography and racist ideologies in porn make companies like PlumperPass more ideal places to work. It is important to note that even though Castro praises PlumperPass, other sex workers have critiqued it for replicating some of the hierarchies of beauty within the BBW genre. Black BBW star Lasha Lane has critiqued the PlumperPass casting process because it creates hierarchies within the fat market. Lasha states, "When it comes to BBW culture, there are usually specific body types that are considered ideal: white women with ginormous boobs, extreme proportions but flat bellies. That is the norm."[10]

Another Multigirl Site nominee in 2020 was Shape of Beauty, a fat production series hosted by the Adult Time platform. Shape of Beauty wants to revolutionize fat pornography by "showcasing hot curvy girls and plump models as muses of adoration and lust." Shape of Beauty is directed by Bree Mills, a multi-award-winning queer director who is revolutionizing lesbian and fat pornography with her porn theater approach, which focuses on improvised character development and chemistry between performers. In 2020, Shape of Beauty had already shot with the top three BBW Latina stars in the industry: April Flores, Karla Lane, and Sofia Rose. The 2020 award show even had a Shape of Beauty's Next Model award. One of the nominees for that category, Breana Kahlo, explains that Shape of Beauty is the future of fat pornography: "I believe that Shape of Beauty is how porn is actually leaning towards; it is more like storytelling and a lot more sophisticated scenes. People are getting more demanding on the quality, and I feel like that's what they are doing."[11] Mills's cinematographic vision queers BBW porn by refusing to incorporate the sexist "gonzo" technique that is often associated with BBW porn.[12] Karla Lane has stated that one of the reasons Shape of Beauty was such a pleasure to shoot with was that Mills listened to her feedback, and she felt she had a say in the final product. The commitment to listening to sex workers is a practice common with queer and feminist pornographic directors.[13] With Shape of Beauty, Mills is joining this legacy, and with its sponsorship at the BBW Awards, they are marking a new era of BBW pornography.

Fat Variety Show

To celebrate fat sensuality, the organizers of the BBW Awards Show incorporated a variety show of rappers, burlesque performers, and a fat stripping contest. The idea was to showcase fat bodies in different erotic

Figure 8.4: Black rapper Mz.OO7 on stage at the BBW Awards. Courtesy of the author.

markets, not just pornography. The invited guest for the 2020 show was Mz.OO7, a Black fat femme rapper performing for a porn-industry audience for the first time. With her fat-positive rap bars, Mz.007 hyped up the room. Because thin white bodies often dominate the stage, the organizers of the BBW Awards intentionally centered fat Black women performers committed to self-determination. For the 2021 online award show, Black rapper Yahlunda even created an original music video. With these cultural productions, fat Black femmes crafted a BBW worldview and philosophy challenging anti-Black racist ideologies that frame Black fat bodies as undesirable. This is important as Black sociologist Sabrina Strings observes that fatphobia is deeply imbedded in a racist project that makes "fatness, an intrinsically black, and implicitly off-putting, form of feminine embodiment."[14] Again, having Black artists perform and facilitate the BBW Awards Show every year imagines what the porn industry can look like when it values Black cultural production and centers Black women in its shows.

The Winners

Several fat Latina sex workers have won numerous awards throughout the years. The BBW Awards are significant because these actresses are not limited to the best ethnic film category; they can also be nominated for other kinks. For the first three years of the awards, the most awarded star at the BBW Awards Show was Sofia Rose, known as a BBW Latina MILF;[15] she is one of the most popular Latina porn stars on Plumper-Pass and the web. Sofia Rose joined the business in 2006 and started her adult career in her thirties. As a Latina in the industry, she has to constantly negotiate a middle ground between the white and Black racial dynamics in pornography.[16]

At the 2020 show, Sofia Rose introduced the New Starlet award, which she had sponsored along with PlumperPass. The winner of this award would have the opportunity to shoot a scene with her for PlumperPass. This award acknowledges that being new to the industry can be very intimidating; by being paired with Sofia Rose, the winner can learn from the living legend of the genre. The winner in 2020 was Mexican porn actor Breana Khalo, who joined the industry in 2019. This award meant a lot to Breana Khalo because she admired Sofia Rose and looked up to her as a mentor.[17] The BBW Awards Show recognizes stars and provides them with a network that supports them during the moments of isolation that sex work entails.

Looking at the PlumperPass accounts for Breana Kahlo and Sofia Rose tells us much about how their bodies are marketed and why PlumperPass appears to be a more friendly place of work. In a trailer video titled *Enter Breana*, we see several intercutting wide shots of Breana's body with closeups of her caressing her stomach rolls. She makes body movements that jiggle her fat in intense, hyperbolic movements. Right after these shots, we see her facial expression as she enjoys the fat in her body. Every scar, stretchmark, pimple, and inch of cellulite is captured in the footage. Sofia's trailers are similar; they zoom into her fat and accentuate these areas. As Laura Kipnis stated, "Fat pornography commemorates bodies that defy social norms, it solicits an erotic identification with bodies that are unresponsive to social control—with voracious, demanding, improper, non–upwardly mobile, socially transgressive bodies."[18]

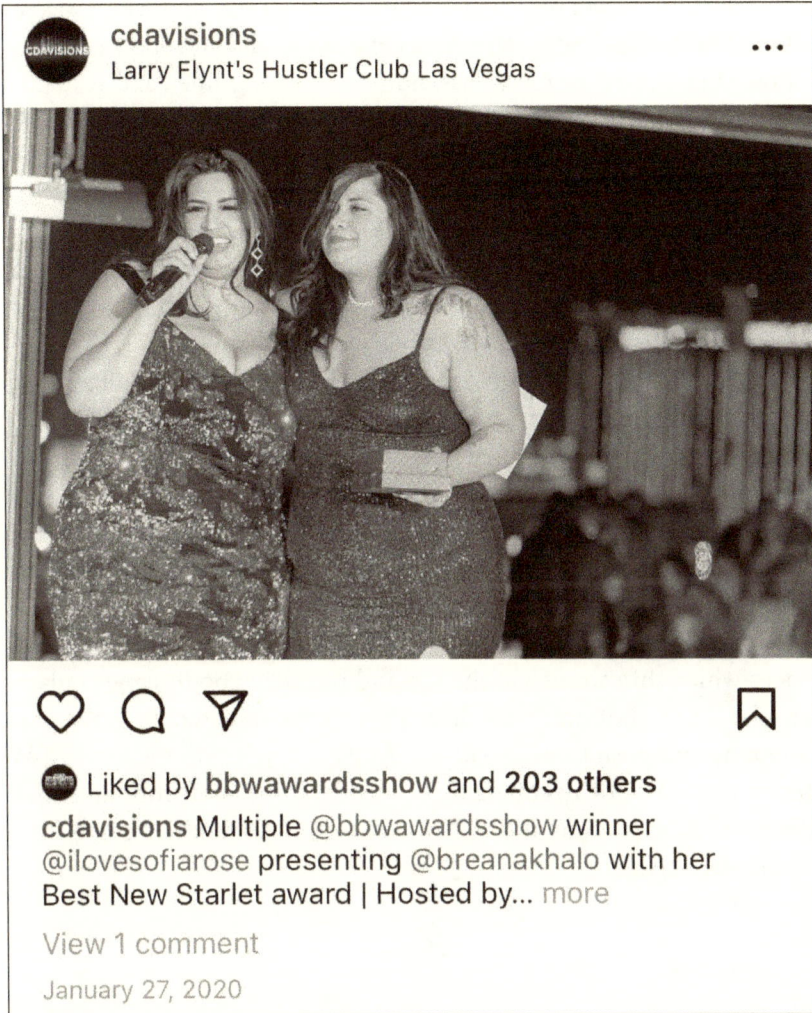

Figure 8.5. Adult star Breana Kahlo (*right*) accepting an award from the BBW legend Sofia Rose (*left*). Public domain, Instagram, @Cdavisions.

The Wrong Exit: Thin-Normative Stages

I left the 2020 BBW Awards Show during the final stage of the stripping contest. I accidentally exited the club through a different elevator that took me through the main stripping stage. Everything went back to normative structures of desire in less than a minute. I entered the main floor at the Hustler Club to see thin white strippers. At this moment, I was reminded of the hegemonic structures of desire that control the sex work industry, organized by race, class, skin color, size, gender, and sexuality. For me, as a spectator, critic, and scholar, this award show opened a new direction in research, one that considers the social capital and validation that fat award shows create for sex workers, and how companies can better create affirming fat erotica. I advocate for porn stars and fans to support BBW pornography as an entire genre recognized for its excellent actors. The BBW Awards has made a good start by crafting a night where all BBWs come together to celebrate body diversity in sex work industries. The one-night arrangement ends too soon, but adult models, fans, producers, and even academics like myself may exit this show feeling reenergized and reminded that fat bodies deserve recognition and that they, too, are sexual beings who are desired and desire. The award show does not eliminate the size or racial hierarchies of desire that have been set by the capitalistic market of the porn industry and AVN; the industry still profits from size-based hierarchies that pay bigger bodies lower rates. Nonetheless, the award show still flips a desire logic that places white, thin women at the top and racialized bodies, particularly fat ones, at the bottom. New directions in the research on BBW pornography and porn more broadly must pay attention to the ways BBW performers of color negotiate these creative modes of work and what affective collaborations and self-production opportunities come from these award spaces.

NOTES
1 Flores 2013.
2 Comella 2014.
3 Berg 2021.
4 James 2018.
5 Jones 2019.
6 Jones 2020a.
7 Sobchack 2004.
8 Miller-Young 2015.
9 Sage 2021.
10 Sage 2020.
11 S&M Show Podcast Network 2020.
12 Kingtown 2019.

13 Taormino et al. 2013.

14 Strings 2019.

15 "MILF" stands in for "Mother I'd Like to Fuck."

16 EricTheYoungGawd 2020.

17 S&M Show Podcast Network 2020.

18 Kipnis 1998.

9

"Looking White"

Sex Workers of Color Hacking White Supremacy

MENAKA RAGUPARAN

In current Western sex markets, systems of white supremacy and anti-Blackness make whiteness the standard for sexual capital and beauty, and "when whiteness is considered superior, white people are considered more attractive by definition."[1] Black feminist scholar Margaret Hunter argues that the politics of skin tone, or colorism, operates as a pervasive and harmful racial stratification in the Western world today. A "beauty queue" exists wherein "the lightest get the most perks and rewards, . . . and the darkest women get the least."[2] This queue works as both social capital, meaning skin color can be used to gain relative advantages, and as a stratifying agent reproducing larger systems of structural racism.[3] Colorism in twenty-first-century sex markets, such as stripping, pornography, and camming, is well documented.[4]

This chapter explores how Black, Indigenous, and other sex workers of color working in the high-end sectors of the Canadian sex markets negotiate their position in the beauty queue. In what follows, I explain how participants in this study invested in their bodily capital and transformed their "looks" to create a particular white feminine impression in the marketplace.[5] This entailed hairstyling practices, clothing choices, exercise, dieting, and sometimes even cosmetic surgery to look "white." Transforming their bodily capital allowed participants to exploit the system of colorism—on the "beauty queue" and within the "raced hierarchy of demand."[6] In most cases, these practices increased their social mobility and avoided race- and sex work–related stigma, and violence,[7] showing us that the relationship between social categories and systemic stratification is not fixed; rather, the intersections between them can both reinforce and contradict the dynamics of power.

In this study I use the term "sex worker" as a general reference to the broad group of people who perform sexual labor. Research participants in this study have been involved in a wide range of sectors within the Canadian sex industry, such as independent in-call/out-call sectors, escort agencies, massage parlors, strip clubs, and online sectors such as pornography and camming. Given the economic precarity of sex work, to enhance their brand and supplement their income, some women simultaneously engage in and/or alternate between street-based sex work and the indoor sectors and in full-service, stripping, and online services. In this chapter, I identify my participants by the type of sex work they performed at the time of the interview.

This study's contribution for understanding new directions in contemporary sex industries and research on Indigenous and other women of color sex workers is twofold. First, this is the first study in Canada to center the insights of Indigenous and other sex workers of color who work in the high-end, independent, and online sectors of the Canadian sex industry. Thus, this study provides significant evidence to challenge popular Canadian assumptions that Indigenous women and women of color occupy only the bottom ranks of the sex industry and therefore are inherent victims of violence, capitalism, and patriarchy.[8] Furthermore, this study also fills a gap in literature that focuses on Canadian Indigenous women passing as white in order to compete in the contemporary Canadian sex industry.

Second, the analysis presented in this study highlights my participants' resilience and resistance to the hold whiteness, anti-Blackness, and white supremacy has on the sex industry. My participants exemplify that white supremacy, capitalism, and patriarchy can be hacked through strategic performance of normative beauty standards. In this regard, this study is setting a benchmark for new research in the field of critical sex work by emphasizing the importance of conceptualizing resistance and resilience even in the most marginalized and vulnerable situations and circumstances.

Interviewing Canadian Sex Workers of Color

The qualitative interviews ask the broad question: How do women of color and Indigenous women experience the indoor sectors of the Canadian sex industry? To answer this, I interviewed forty sex workers from nine cities in Canada between August 2014 and April 2015. Interviews ranged from forty minutes to two and a half hours. Participants were recruited through a targeted snowball sampling technique. I advertised the need for research participants on social media and on my social and academic networks. I also directly reached out to sex workers of color who advertised their services online. Interested women contacted me directly through email, text, or phone call, and I interviewed those who met the study parameters. Participants received seventy-five Canadian dollars as an honorarium for sharing their expertise and time. All participants were assigned pseudonyms to protect their confidentiality.

Thirty-eight participants identified as cisgender women, and two participants identified as gender nonbinary. Thirty-nine participants identified as Canadian citizens or permanent residents, and one participant identified as temporary resident on the visa. Participants were over eighteen years old and belonged to the following groups: Arab (n=2), Black (n=14), East Asian (n=4), Indigenous (n=3), mixed-race (n=11), and South Asian (n=6). The inclusion of Indigenous and a broad range of other women of color marks this as the first empirical study of its kind in Canada.

Performing Whiteness: Branding Strategies among Light-Skinned Workers

Research participants' efforts to perform whiteness varied significantly. Light-skinned sex workers in this study passed as white with little effort. Dark-skinned sex workers, on the other hand, relied on dressing professionally, maintaining a thin body through diet and exercise, and styling their hair by coloring and straightening it to look long and shiny—all of these branding strategies shaped proximity to whiteness.

Mixed-Race Women and Personal Branding Strategies

According to my participants, most clients who frequent indoor sites are white, heterosexual, middle- to upper-class men who desire women who are like them. Therefore, mixed-race participants with light skin tones often benefit from colorism. Among these participants, one of the popular personal branding/marketing strategies involved concealing their "authentic" racial identity and passing as "white" or a white-ish race. Saskia, a mixed-race (Black and white) independent worker, explained how she consciously capitalizes on her white looks and upbringing to satisfy clients' desires, which are often motivated by sexual racism.

> I identify myself as white. Yeah, I was raised by the white side of my family versus the colored [participant's word choice] side, and I am definitely whitewashed. [chuckles] I totally am. . . . I pride myself on that. . . . I always tell all my clients, "You don't have to remind me about how to dress appropriately." . . . I am not walking in looking like a "hooker" [emphasis added by participant]. . . . I'm very conservative. . . . I don't talk, excuse me, with a ghetto accent. I don't use swear words or curse words or slang.

Saskia's efforts to pass as white include masking stereotypical understandings of a sex worker and a Black woman. Thus, when interacting with clients, she dresses conservatively, speaks English fluently without an accent, and avoids expletive language and street talk. In other words, Saskia aesthetically and materially converts her body capital and uses her elegant communication skills to produce a marketable service strategically. Saskia's entrepreneurial tasks also influence impressions of respectability and gender normativity.

Moreover, according to normative narratives, performing the "slick," "classy" woman defies preconceived notions of what and how racialized and Indigenous women are or should be.[9] Therefore, capitalizing on their "slick" and "classy" looks was another popular strategy mixed-race participants used in their personal branding/marketing. Participant Laine, a mixed-race (East Asian and white) independent worker, notes how she capitalizes on her ambiguous skin tones, body size, and "exotic" corporeal features to compete in the mainstream sex markets and increase her opportunity for social mobility.

> I'm mixed, I'm mixed with white. . . . I am also thin. . . . I am your exotic. I am a fucking hot commodity. I am gonna put a damn price tag on this. . . . I am just charging a lot, it's because of the category that I have chosen to go into. I mean something like this [the high-end sectors], you get a lot of white clients, who has money, who has privilege.

Saskia's and Laine's performance of whiteness does not require physical transformation of their appearances. Instead, these mixed-raced participants perform whiteness by appropriating the dominant culture's grooming practices and attire to strategically (re)construct their identities as "white" rather than as racialized.

Kalinda, a mixed-race (Indigenous and white) massage parlor worker, further articulates how she uses her body capital in strategic branding practices.

> I guess because I'm so light, and I dye my hair red. . . . more like a redhead. . . . And it's hard not to take advantage of it sometimes . . . I feel like I get away with charging higher rates, whereas some other girls that I see, who don't pass, there's not as much demand.

Mixed-raced participants' strategies for creating and promoting a competitive (and perhaps even profitable) brand highlight their role as business-savvy individuals. Such an image can cast a shadow on the social and political rhetoric of sex workers as naïve victims. Participants' efforts to perform whiteness and/or pass as white through materially and physically altering their corporeality highlights the complex fluidity of their identities at the intersection of raced, classed, and gendered markers. The stories presented above also illuminate the struggles of sex workers as they experience personal anxiety and community alienation as they perform whiteness. Arguably, the critical benefit of passing as white is that it mitigates the impact of sex work stigma, and the stereotypical assumptions clients may hold about race and sex work.

Indigenous Workers and Personal Branding Strategies

Like other mixed-race sex workers, Indigenous sex workers also capitalized on light skin tones and ambiguous features to conceal their Indigeneity. Some Indigenous participants in this study were purposely vague or lied about their ethnicity to customers.

> When I had my blond hair, it was like, people didn't know who, what kinda background I had. . . . I get all sorts of things like, "So what's your background, Russian? Hawaiian?" I am like, "Hahaha, whatever" . . . and I can play this up, and whatever makes money [laughing]. [Merinda, Indigenous escort]

> I have been advertising myself as French. . . . I have never said I'm Métis. It doesn't look good on my ad. . . . I'm proud to be Aboriginal, but it doesn't really help when advertising. [Coreen, Indigenous worker]

Concealing their Indigeneity allowed some to manage race- and sex work–related stigma and avoid insults, humiliation, verbal abuse, unlawful detention, unwarranted arrests, physical and sexual abuse, and arbitrary arrests that many in this study experienced from police.[10] In this sense, Coreen points out the disadvantage of advertising as Métis or Aboriginal. Similarly, Kim, another Indigenous independent sex worker, explained, "When [clients] see me, they think I'm Italian."

> I would not advertise as an Indigenous sex worker. I just advertise as a BBW [Big, Beautiful Woman] companion or escort or whatever. And I think it would put me more at risk of being a target by predators posing as clients. And I would be more at risk to be visited by undercover police. And I didn't want to be under more surveillance because I identify as Indigenous.

Given the deep-seated assumptions about Indigenous women's sexuality,[11] participants feel that their self-advertising strategies need to focus on demystifying such stereotypes. In this regard, having control over their advertising messages is an invaluable asset.

Intersections of Race and Class: Branding Strategies among Dark-Skinned Workers

Those with dark Black or Brown skin tones could not pass as "white" or vaguely exotic "Russian" or "Hawaiian." Instead, they performed whiteness by adopting middle-class markers such as being well-dressed, thin, toned, groomed, and professional. These participants understand their position in the racial hierarchy of demand. As Tallah, a Black independent sex worker, illustrates,

> I think that, first of all, African Americans are not going to be valued as the prettiest women, that's what is out there, especially in the sex industry.

I think guys want to see, what they see in magazines and on television. . . . So right away I realized that . . . being African [I] wasn't marketable enough. I started to mimic more like the models, so I started changing, you know, arranging my hair differently, make-up, trying to get closer to the Caucasian beauty, than the African American. I exercise five, six days a week, I watch what I eat. . . . Especially because I'm dark-skinned I have to be very, very careful, you know. . . . Yes, I mean guys want a pretty lady, they want a girl in shape.

For mixed-race participants, appropriating cultural images and materials from the dominant culture allows them to strategically (re) construct their identity as "white" instead of racialized. Visibly Black and Brown women, while not in a position to appear white, are well suited to performing whiteness. Doing so positions them higher on the beauty queue and within the raced hierarchy of demand in the industry. This allows them to compete on relatively equal ground with their white counterparts and provides them with access to economic rewards.

Body Size

Hesse-Biber notes that thinness is equated with beauty and vitality in Eurocentric framings,[12] and Pausé explains that fatness is not desirable or valued within capitalist and neoliberal society, such that fatness is received as a disorder and as contrary to the beauty ideal.[13] Given such a normative narrative, maintaining a thin physique is a popular strategy for developing a brand among Black and Brown participants. Teagan, a Black independent worker, explains:

I think also being very petite Black woman changes the way I'm perceived and treated because it's not necessarily very typical. . . . I am a slight little person, you know, so people also project whiteness onto that as well. Between the blond hair and the little itty-bitty body, they're like, "It's almost like you're a white girl."

Research participants who use their body size as a tool for branding and marketing argue that maintaining a lean figure requires discipline.[14]

Transgressing disciplinary practices often results in economic consequences. Reflecting upon a client postservice review, which had a short-term impact on her business, Tallah points out the price she had to pay for indulging.

> I went [out] on a Friday. . . . I don't know what happened, I just ate the whole night. The next day I had a client, and I had one of my worst reviews. . . . He said that I was beefy. Because I have lots of muscles, and what I ate, I had put on the pounds. My body looked bigger because you put fat on top of muscle, I look even bigger. . . . So, he wrote, "I encountered a Black buff girl." Black buff. You know, and I'm like, ugh, . . . that doesn't give a good image. So, I learned my lesson. . . . I mean guys want a pretty lady; they want a girl in shape.

According to Bartley and Bordo, self-regulation and policing in the context of body shaping reify/normalize Eurocentric ideals of feminine beauty.[15] In this sense, Tallah's preoccupation with thinness can be understood as conforming to white cultural demands as part of developing their brand. However, many participants in this study noted that caring for their body increases their self-esteem and enhances their capacity to compete in the marketplace.

Hairstyles as Bodily Capital

Long, flowy hair that is blond and straight or wavy ranks higher on the white-supremacist beauty queue and represents femininity and professionalism within the mainstream culture.[16] Therefore, conforming to hegemonic beauty standards generates a different economic outcome in the marketplace, or, in other words, makes sex workers of color more financially competitive with white women. However, as Banks notes, "Hair shapes Black women's ideas about race, gender, class, and sexuality, images of beauty and power."[17] From this perspective, "Natural hairstyles with African, African-American or Jamaican origins—such as [cornrows], dreadlocks, afros, or braids—have become popular as a way of showing rejection of White-oriented images of beauty and being proud of natural Black Beauty."[18] But since white supremacy constructs natural Black hair as unattractive and undesirable, wearing natural hair reduces opportunities for Black women in the marketplace. Shamika, an independent Black sex worker, reflects upon her position as a Black sex worker and her challenges with natural hair.

> [My hair is] more straight, which is more of work-related. Compared to my hair, which was more natural and kinky and coarse, like afro thing, which is the big trend in the Black community to go natural hair. But natural hair for me won't make me any money. So, I am in between where I would love to have dreads one day, but dreads aren't exactly considered sexually attractive.

Sarena, who alternates between working independently and for a high-end agency, points out one implication Black women face for choosing natural hair styles.

> I shaved my head, and I also went natural [one] time. . . . People stopped seeing me as much when I shaved my head, and I was getting reviews that were like, "She has short, afro hair."

Lola, who works for a high-end escort agency, highlights another dimension of the tension between wearing natural hair and adopting Eurocentric hairstyles:

> There's *no way* [participant emphasis] I will wear my natural hair, not because I'm ashamed of it, but . . . acknowledging that people are really racist and women who don't have . . . straight hair or weave-looking hair or whatever, get discriminated against, by means of not getting bookings or just treated a little bit differently and stuff like that.

Many Black and Brown participants changed their hair to better approximate Eurocentric long, wavy, flowing, shiny hair. This was laborious, sometimes uncomfortable, and caused internal tension. Transforming one's hair texture to resemble white hair is not an easy endeavor. Shemika explains,

> The thing with the hair, where my hair is more processed, it's chemically processed. . . . It's the silky, long flowing hair that's attractive, which costs

me a lot of money to make my hair that way. Where it feels like when I am working, all I'm doing is paying for ads and getting my hair done. Where it all feels like the money that people tell me that we are making, and I am in the same industry as them, and I am not making that money, I was like there's something that I am doing wrong, even though I am not making that, then all my money goes to my hair and ads and everything else to keep my image attractive to make money.

Black and Brown sex workers' negotiation of hair styling practices reinforces the extent to which the Canadian sex industry is shaped by the normative intersecting ideas of femininity, whiteness, anti-Blackness, and beauty. It is noteworthy that a few Black participants wore natural hair, including Afros and varying lengths of braids. Given the various challenges of wearing natural hairstyles, drawing from Zook, I claim that the few participants who have chosen to embrace their culturally appropriate hairstyles are defying the hegemonic beauty tropes with confidence, courage, and "an extra dose of self-esteem just to get through the day."[19] Ultimately, different hair styling practices, whether conforming to and/or resisting hegemonic beauty standards, generate different economic outcomes in the marketplace, increasing or decreasing sex workers' opportunities to compete.

In conclusion, while the primary objective of sex workers' entrepreneurial tasks is to facilitate successful competition within the marketplace and to earn the best wage possible, the execution of these entrepreneurial tasks is entangled in a complex web of historical, social, and political ideologies about race, beauty, and sexuality. Thus, the strategies they enact to develop and promote their brand—most often through appropriations of whiteness—comprise simultaneous actions that are influenced and constrained by the intersections of historical events, social relations, and interpersonal tensions. In this sense, the self-branding strategies highlighted draw attention to the intersection of raced, classed, and gendered markers and the strategic utility of conforming to normative rhetoric, because white tropes of Eurocentric feminine beauty in the marketplace function as cultural and economic currency. In this regard, participants' efforts to compete in the marketplace illuminate the complex fluidity of their identities as they perform approximations of whiteness through materially and physically altering their corporeality. Participants' strategies for creating and promoting a competitive (and perhaps even profitable) brand highlight their role as business-savvy individuals, challenging popular public images that often depict sex workers as naïve victims who lack the responsibility, agency, and capability to assess and avoid risks.

From an intersectional perspective, it is true that some of the market practices within the indoor sectors of the sex industry have the effect of territorializing white sex workers and white clients' experiences and stratifying racialized and Indigenous women's position within the industry. However, intentional appropriation of white culture in the indoor sectors also has the effect of destabilizing aspects of normative raced, gendered, and classed practices, preferences, and assumptions in ways that provide racialized and Indigenous women with opportunities for enhancing their social and economic capital.

NOTES

1 Wade 2014, 1.
2 Hunter 2002, 69.
3 Hill 2000.
4 Brooks 2010a, 2010b; Cruz 2016; Jones 2020a; Mahdavi 2013; Miller-Young 2014; Nash 2014.
5 Bourdieu 1978; Mears 2011.
6 Hunter 2002; Mahdavi 2013.
7 Raguparan 2019.
8 Razack 1998.
9 Zook 1990.
10 Raguparan 2020.
11 Barman 2004; Perry 2005.
12 Hesse-Biber 1996.
13 Pausé 2015.
14 Pausé 2015.
15 Bartky 2003; Bordo 2003.
16 Banks 2000; Craig 2002.
17 Banks 2000, 3.
18 Tate 2009, 9.
19 Zook 1990, 89.

10

"Whorearchy"

Racial Earnings Disparities in Webcam Modeling

ALEX J. NELSON, BRONWYN MCBRIDE, AND YEON JUNG YU

On the webcam site MyFreeCams.com, a webcam model may charge a client between twenty and twelve hundred dollars to witness her bringing herself to orgasm. Why such a difference? While each model chooses her own rates and services, these choices reflect more than individual business strategies. Such disparities in models' earnings and labor conditions reflect deep inequalities in how people value human sexuality.

In this chapter, we explore earnings disparities among webcam models (primarily from the United States, Europe, and Latin America) on a US-based webcam site. After considering existing hypotheses for these disparities, we argue that systemic oppression and intersections of race, ethnicity, class, gender, and nationality produce unequal access to socioeconomic resources and ethno-erotic capital. Race and ethnicity are culturally constructed assets or liabilities in sexual exchanges, and these valuations (and the associated material conditions that reproduce them) reinforce the "whorearchy" and shape individuals' opportunities within the sex industry.[1] We conclude that the economic precarity produced by racially stratified compensation undermines the sexual and labor autonomy of webcam models of color, especially Black women.

Webcam modeling, or "camming," is a form of erotic labor in which a model performs via webcam for a live audience for pay and/or tips. Models' performances can involve conversation, flirting, games, dancing, singing, striptease, simulating sexual acts, and/or engaging in live sex. Performances may synchronize with other erotic content creation and interactive sexual services (e.g., selling used panties, subscriptions to personalized pornographic content). Webcam platforms facilitate these performances by providing a user interface, advertising, and facilitating payments while retaining approximately half of models' earnings. As independent contractors, models purchase their own equipment, props, and outfits for performances, or pay a portion of their earnings to an agency to assist them.

Camming platforms appear to represent the ideal neoliberal sexual marketplace, enabling international sexual-service exchanges between models and clients while creating an opportunity for all market niches to be filled and entrepreneurially savvy models to succeed, regardless of location. The abilities to make a client feel desired, perform pleasure and attraction, market a persona, and avoid bad-faith actors are professional skills that any model can learn. However, business acumen and the quality and creativity of performances alone do not define success: models' earnings are deeply stratified by race and ethnicity. The Internet *has* increased opportunities for sexual commerce but has not created a level playing field for commercial competition.

What We Know about Racial Disparities in Sex-Industry Labor

In the United States, the sex work sectors that enjoy the greatest legal protection—and are considered constitutionally protected speech of artistic value—are stripping/exotic dancing, pornographic film production, and webcam modeling. Notably, white women are overrepresented within these relatively protected sectors.[2] In contrast, women of color, especially Black cis and trans women, are overrepresented in street-based sex work: the most poorly renumerated and stigmatized sector due to its criminalization and stereotyped intersections with poverty and drug use.[3] Working conditions and earnings vary immensely both within and between US sex work sectors. Among independent escorts who have their own website, average hourly rates range from $100 to $1,389 (average $420),[4] while reviews on theeroticreview.com of a larger, more inclusive sample of escorts and street-based sex workers found rates from $10 to $1,100, averaging $150.[5] Consistent evidence suggests that Black women earn significantly less than their non-Black peers in the same sector, across stripping, pornography, escorting, and camming.[6]

Existing literature highlights several factors impacting racial earning disparities in sex work. White supremacy shapes structural racism in employment policies faced by sex workers, wherein some employers in strip clubs or pornography sets explicitly limit the number of Black performers they hire. This systemic racism and discrimination are based on perceptions that link Black women with working-class status, thus being less "exclusive" and desirable.[7] Scholars have also argued that Black women are "hypersexualized" due to past sexual commodification as slaves and historical associations with prostitution, leading to their oversexualization in media (i.e., music videos, movies).[8]

The concept of hypersexualization draws on ideologies of male domination (patriarchy) and relies on an objectifying logic, proposing a sexualizing agent and a sexualized object, for example, men sexualizing women, and white men hypersexualizing women of color. However, this notion is flawed because sexual desirability is a well-documented form of (erotic) capital and an asset that people cultivate. We groom, dress, and move our bodies to evoke desire because being desired can help us achieve our goals and access love, esteem, money, security, and more. Sex work is the labor of making one's persona desirable and producing pleasure for a paying client, converting erotic capital into economic capital. Understanding erotic capital this way frames sexual desirability as an asset, not a stigma, and highlights sex workers' agency.

The concept of hypersexualization alone cannot explain variations in earnings by race and ethnicity among sex workers. We do not see the same racial earnings gap among men in sex work,[9] and while Asian/American women have also been described as hypersexualized,[10] Asian/American and multiracial escorts often command the highest rates in major US markets.[11] Given this gap in both theoretical and empirical evidence, we aimed to examine racial earnings disparities among webcam models. Below, we first present our research methods and empirical findings and then discuss their implications for models of color and the broader erotic services industry.

Our Study on Racial Earnings Disparities among Webcam Models

In August 2019, we designed a novel methodological approach to compare webcam models' relative earnings by their (self-identified) race/ethnicity. We collected our sample, the largest of any current study of the camming industry, from one of the most prominent platforms, My-FreeCams.com (MFC). On an hourly basis for one week, we deployed a commercial web scraper program (Parsehub), which recorded models' usernames and self-identified ethnicities in the order they appeared on the site.[12] This approach allowed us to document each model's hours streamed (HS) by adding the number of hourly runs in which the same models appeared. The key variable, models' earnings, was measured through MFC's "camscore" metric. The platform's default setting on its landing page lists all models currently online by camscore, from highest to lowest earning—a camscore ranking.[13] A model's average camscore ranking (ACSR) indicates how many models, who were online at the same time, appeared in higher positions on the landing page. For example, when online, the top-earning model would always appear first on the landing page, with the highest camscore and an ACSR of 1. The less a model earns, the higher her camscore ranking and the further down the page she appears—a system that exacerbates inequalities.

During our week-long observation in 2019, 15,376 models streamed on MFC. Among them, 4 percent identified as "Asian," 4 percent as "various" (henceforth "multiracial"), 31 percent as "Caucasian" (henceforth "white"), 14 percent as "other," 4 percent as "Middle Eastern," 1 percent as "American Indian" (henceforth "Native American"), 4 percent as "Black," 20 percent as "Hispanic," and less than 1 percent as "East Indian" (henceforth "Indian"). To determine whether a model's (self-identified) race impacted her earnings, we conducted several nonparametric statistical tests.[14]

Our statistical analyses identified significant differences between each racial group's average camscore ranking (ACSR).[15] All but four paired groups differed significantly. The extent of these differences is best understood through the effect sizes of these statistical tests (i.e., Mann-Whitney U test), specifically the "Probability of Superiority" (PS).[16] For example, if we randomly selected one white model and one Black model from our sample and compared their rankings, the probability is that the white model would rank higher 70 percent of the time. These results indicate that, on average, cam models' earnings differ significantly by race.

Notably, Asian models had the lowest ACSR, meaning they earned more than models with other racial identities and received greater visibility on the MFC landing page (table 10.1).[17] The median ACSR was

TABLE 10.1: Relative Earning and Visibility by Race and Ethnicity

Race/Ethnicity	Ranking (ACSR) Average	Hours Streamed (HS) Average	Percentage (Number)
Asian	356	15.1	4 (546)
No Answer	423	12.5	19 (2933)
Multiracial	440	11.5	4 (658)
White	450	11.9	31 (4734)
"Other"	537	14.4	14 (2079)
Middle Eastern	566	15.3	4 (559)
Native American	622	11.8	1 (162)
Black	690	15.3	4 (573)
Hispanic	724	15.8	20 (3075)
Indian	755	20.8	<1 (57)

Notes: N = 15,376; ACSR = Average Camscore Ranking

TABLE 10.2: Comparison of the Earnings and Visibility of Racialized Models and White Models on MFC

Race/Ethnicity	Ranking (ACSR) Median	Median Ranking Difference from White Models	Likelihood of Higher Earnings & Visibility (PS)
Asian	300	+73	57%
Multiracial	366	+66	50%
White	373	NA	NA
Middle Eastern	540	−167	39%*
Native American	608	−235	35%
Black	676	−303	30%*
Hispanic	726	−353	28%**
Indian	771	−398	26%

Note: PS = Probability of Superiority; Mann Whitney U test effect sizes: No asterisk = r < .1; * = r < .3; ** = r < .5.

300 for Asian models and 676 for Black models. Our analysis suggests that any randomly chosen Asian model will have higher earnings than any randomly chosen Black model 79 percent of the time, and prospective clients would have to scroll through 376 models to come across the median-ranked Black model after viewing the median-ranked Asian model. The differences in camscore rankings reveal a pattern of

stratification wherein Asian, multiracial, white, and Middle Eastern models had higher earnings than Black, Hispanic, and Indian models.

Models' streaming hours did not account for but rather exacerbated differences in earnings. Asian, Black, and Hispanic models streamed a similar number of hours on average (15.1, 15.3, and 15.8 hours, respectively) whereas white models streamed significantly less (11.9 hours).[18] Indian models streamed the longest hours (20.8 hours) and had the highest ACSR (ACSR=755) and thus the lowest earnings on MFC. In other words, aside from Asian and multiracial models, models of color—particularly Black and brown sex workers—streamed longer hours than white models but earned significantly less. This critical finding suggests that camming is another market where one cannot merely increase one's working hours to boost one's income, as there are entrenched race-based inequities that "hard work" cannot overcome.[19]

Conclusions

Our data show that webcam models' earnings differ significantly by race, with Black and Hispanic models facing the most severe income disparities.[20] This pattern mirrors those documented in other US sex work sectors (e.g., escorting, porn), highlighting how systems of white supremacy, patriarchy, anti-Blackness, and colorism impact the earnings of women of color. These inequities in earnings have serious implications for racialized sex workers, particularly for Black models' labor conditions and autonomy at work.

Our findings do not support the theory that all ethnic minorities' erotic capital is similarly devalued by hypersexualization. In our sample, Asian models did not earn significantly less than white models. However, our findings mirror broader racial socioeconomic disparities in the US population shaped by patriarchy, white supremacy, and anti-Blackness. White and Asian Americans have higher incomes, educational achievement, health outcomes, and home-ownership rates than Black and Hispanic Americans. The ideology that Asian Americans are a "model minority," as we explain below, perpetuates this inequality and its anti-Blackness.[21]

We theorize that these overarching systems, combined with the socioeconomic inequalities and oppressions based on gender, race, and class that they produce, shape differences in ethno-erotic capital reflected in racial earning disparities among webcam models. Differences in the class and economic status of racial groups shaped by white supremacy closely align with the pattern of earning disparities we observed among webcam models: incomes of Asian Americans exceed those of non-Hispanic white Americans, which exceed those of Hispanic Americans, which exceed those of Black Americans.[22] Based on the relative income and related privilege and status of racial groups, clients are likely to project perceptions of higher class status upon Asian models and lower status upon Hispanic and Black models. This cultural valuation may then enhance the ethno-erotic capital of Asian sex workers through symbolic association of their race with middle- and upper-middle-class status, shaped by the cultural capital that comes with the belief that they are model minorities. However, it is critical to note that despite relatively high earnings, Asian models still experience severe racism, fetishization, and harassment in camming work, while streaming more hours on average than white women to achieve their higher earnings. Asian models' higher incomes may be interpreted as Orientalism—a type of racism. Further, differences in access to economic and health resources in the United States due to systemic racism are likely to shape access to camming resources (e.g., webcams, workspaces, props, costumes) and physical health (e.g., healthy food, freedom from illness), which in turn shape racial disparities in earnings. Our findings suggest that the oppressive structures of patriarchy, white supremacy, anti-Blackness, and the model-minority myth intersect to produce racist sexual stereotypes and physical and material inequalities, producing the ethno-erotic whorearchy exemplified by racial earning disparities in webcam modeling.

Our empirical data demonstrate serious racial inequities in earnings among models on MyFreeCams.com by using the largest sample to date for this sex-industry sector. Our analysis found that certain sex workers of color, namely, Black and brown models, work more hours and earn less money—a disparity that threatens their economic security and labor autonomy.

Racial disparities in earnings and legal vulnerability (in the case of criminalized forms of sex work) reflect more than unacceptable structural inequities: these disparities are also likely to compromise occupational autonomy and choice among sex workers of color, particularly

Black women.[23] Most sex workers remain forced to contend with some level of criminalization, which has been robustly documented to undermine sex workers' labor conditions and ability to screen clients, all of which heighten their vulnerability to violence.[24] Facing financial and legal vulnerability, sex workers may have to compromise their personal boundaries and autonomy to make ends meet. For example, webcam models experiencing financial shortfalls may feel pushed to compromise their physical or emotional boundaries in performances to ensure that they can earn a living. This could involve engaging in role play they find personally demeaning or performing sexual acts they do not want to perform or that are potentially hazardous, particularly for models with disabilities.[25]

Our findings and current evidence indicate that racialized women, especially Black women, are reaping fewer of the benefits of working in erotic economies due to structural racism, which results in these racialized models being undervalued and underpaid. Not earning a living wage in camming may push racialized models offline into forms of sex work that are criminalized, more stigmatized, and potentially more dangerous. In such sectors, sex workers of color then bear a disproportionate burden of the enforcement of antiprostitution laws (i.e., police harassment, arrests, charges) and the legally sanctioned social stigma ascribed to sex work. Further, facing an arrest, eviction, or loan denial limits the options of those already in the most precarious economic situations. Our findings show that racial earning disparities are not primarily the result of the hypersexualization of women of color. This frame could be wielded by abolitionists to call for further criminalization of sex work. Instead, our findings highlight the oppressive structures of white supremacy, anti-Blackness, and patriarchy, which lead to financial discrimination against racialized sex workers. Thus, we suggest that decriminalization and protections against discrimination would disproportionately benefit sex workers of color.

Policy Recommendations

Several public and corporate policies could help address earnings disparities within the sex industry, promote models' sexual self-determination, and minimize harms that disproportionately impact sex workers of color. Governments should affirm the right to sexual autonomy and criminalize discrimination against residents for their sexual practices. Sex workers (whether working in legal or criminalized sectors of the industry) currently have no protection from termination by employers who may object to their erotic labor. For sex workers who do "civilian" work (labor outside the sex industry), the perpetual threat of losing one's job can represent an ongoing source of stress and potential financial hardship that can undermine sexual autonomy.[26] A bill to ban discrimination against sex workers could protect them from discrimination by employers, landlords, the state, and financial institutions. Banks and other financial service providers (i.e., PayPal, Cash App, Venmo) regularly discriminate against and refuse to provide services to sex workers, increasing the challenges of maintaining a profitable erotic enterprise and thus undermining workers' financial stability and autonomy.[27] Furthermore, decriminalizing sex work (as recommended by international policy institutions, including Amnesty International, the WHO, and UNAIDS) will make it safer for both workers and clients, provide greater financial security (which would address many associated impacts of criminalization, including stress, employer discrimination, and police abuses), and reduce the racial income gap by eliminating one source of stigma and punitive sanctions for sex workers.

Beyond legislative shifts, MyFreeCams.com and other webcam platforms could adjust their algorithms to take affirmative action against racial earnings disparities by changing models' order of appearance on their landing page as a default setting (though there is no obvious financial incentive for them to do so). For example, MyFreeCams.com could adopt the "Spotlight" program used by other streaming platforms, e.g., Twitch.tv, where streamers with smaller viewership are featured on the landing page. Currently, approximately 50 percent of what clients pay on cam sites is paid out to the model, while the remainder covers overhead costs or becomes profit for the platform. Platforms could adjust the revenue share to allow marginalized models to retain a larger proportion of their earnings as a step towards leveling the playing field and promoting equitable opportunity among these erotic entrepreneurs. These public and corporate policy changes could help minimize racial earnings disparities in camming as well as broader forms of erotic labor. However, these inequities will never fully dissipate unless broader systems of patriarchy, white supremacy, and their resulting social stratification by gender, race, and class are thoroughly eliminated.

NOTES

1 The "whorearchy" speaks to the hierarchical stratification of identities and interests among sex workers, shaped by sex work stigma. It is derided but nonetheless perpetuated by sex workers as a barrier to community, cooperation, and political activism. See Witt 2020.

2 Dewey and St. Germain 2014; Jones 2020a; Nelson et al. 2020.

3 Dewey and St. Germain 2014; Jones 2020a; Nelson et al. 2020.

4 Nelson et al. 2020, 6.

5 DeAngelo et al. 2019.

6 Brooks 2010a; Miller-Young 2014; Nelson et al. 2020; Jones 2020a.

7 Brooks 2010a; Miller-Young 2014.

8 Brooks 2010b; Miller-Young 2010; Glover and Glover 2019.

9 Logan 2010.

10 Shimizu 2007; Chou 2012.

11 Nelson et al. 2020.

12 Therefore, our data did not rely on self-reports and thus did not suffer from recall biases.

13 Camscore rankings can change in real time as models come online, go offline, and earn money.

14 We first ran a Kruskal Wallace H statistical test to examine differences between racial/ethnic groups. We then ran Mann Whitney U tests to examine whether the differences between each racial/ethnic group were statistically significant and estimate the extent of the differences by calculating each comparison's effect size (r). These nonparametric tests were necessary because the data were ranked and not normally distributed.

15 The Kruskal Wallace H test was statistically significant ($p < .01$). The complete results of each test can be accessed through our project website (www.Virtual -Sexual-Economies.com).

16 "Probability of superiority" is a statistical term that describes an effect size in lay terms for the difference in two sets of ranked data.

17 For example, the largest effect of race on average camscore ranking was between Asian and Black models, with a large effect size ($r = -.5$) and a 21 percent probability of superiority.

18 When we statistically compared differences in hours streamed by race and ethnicity, there were significant differences, but the effect sizes were negligible between Caucasian and Asian models ($r = -.08$) and small for Black ($r = -.12$) and Hispanic ($r = -.18$) models.

19 The dataset presented in this paper only allowed us to analyze self-reported race/ ethnicity and did not enable us to examine the possible effects of colorism, which would additionally require assessment of each model's skin tone.

20 More work is needed to discern the relationship between racial discrimination and colorism. One could compare earnings based on skin tone rather than
self-identified race. However, we lacked the resources to conduct such a tricky
comparison for our sample of 15,376 models for this chapter.

21 Chow 2017; Yi and Todd 2021.

22 Semega et al. 2020; United States Census 2021.

23 Such compromises may include agreeing to see clients that one might normally
decline because they can't/won't verify their identity as a safe and legitimate client
(i.e., not a law enforcement officer or a violent perpetrator). Jones 2020a.

24 Decker et al. 2015; McBride et al. 2020.

25 These personal boundary transgressions might occur at the request of clients
whose demands are made irrefusable by financial precarity. Alternatively, a
model might push her boundaries in a preemptive attempt to attract more and
new clientele, uncertain of the returns doing so will bring. In this way, racialized
economic precarity can actively undermine sex workers' occupational conditions
and autonomy within their labor.

26 Bowen 2021.

27 Holston-Zannell 2021b.

11

Sex Worker Scholars

Navigating Outness in Academic Spaces

LIZZIE BLAKE AND LIA GRAY

Within academia, sex work is a tantalizing, provocative, and politicized research subject, but open sex work involvement can have varied outcomes, including the risk of stigma and harm.[1] Since 2020, as sex workers and academics, we witnessed a student named Celine being doxxed when her sex work was disclosed to a professor without her consent: she subsequently lost her academic positions in a severe, destabilizing blow to her professional development. We also observed Anu, another sex worker whose mental health suffered when they were tokenized and devalued within an academic space purportedly safe for sex workers. Finally, we saw Naomi supported and celebrated for using her lived experience to lead sex worker–centered research.

Whether stigmatized, invalidated, celebrated, or some combination thereof, sex worker scholars are becoming more visible in academic institutions, where there is increasing demand for "out" sex workers to speak publicly on related issues. As a result, it is critical to consider our safety, our needs, and how our involvement shapes broader advocacy towards sex worker rights. Here we explore the following questions: What are the intersectional implications of concurrent stigma and affirmation of sex work in academic spaces? How does having "out" sex worker voices in these settings benefit and/or hurt sex workers marginalized due to their race, class, gender, sexuality, or other facets of oppression who cannot as easily come out? How can we as academics solve issues related to privilege, outness, and safety?

"Coming Out"

"Coming out" is a continual process of sharing lived experiences or components of one's identity with others. For LGBTQ+ folks, coming out can include realizing one's identity, sharing that realization and/or new words or labels to describe that identity with others, and the "continual management" of the new identity.[2] For those living with HIV, or having experience in sex work, coming out may be less of a process of self-discovery, but still includes potential risks associated with being out. One can also "come out" about having sex work experience without personally identifying as a sex worker. "Coming out" entails negotiating othering and stigmatization as the need to come out implies that one's experience or identity is contrary to established societal norms: that just existing in your identity is deviant. For example, for queer folks, the expectation to come out reflects our society's assumption of heterosexuality.

While the requirement to "come out" about aspects of oneself is inherently problematic, under our current systems of oppression—capitalism, white supremacy, heteronormativism, cisgenderism, ableism, and whorephobia, among others—choosing to come out or not remains a critical experience for members of marginalized and partly visible communities. Being out impacts folks' safety, quality of life, the ways we are able to move through the world, and who represents our broader communities within public space. In this chapter, as two white settler sex working academics, we aim to explore the benefits and consequences of "outness" for individual sex workers, communities, and voices, and imagine alternative approaches that promote sex worker rights, value lived experience, and keep sex workers safe.

Coming Out and Sex Work

Historically, sex workers have always navigated issues of privacy, identity, and outness in sex work, their personal lives, and "square"/"civilian" (non–sex work) employment. Like other marginalized, criminalized, and stigmatized communities, sex workers usually maintain certain levels of privacy to protect our physical, psychological, and emotional safety; avoid interactions with law enforcement; and/or reduce experiences of stigma.[3] Since sex work remains criminalized in almost all global settings, being out as a sex worker risks the documented harms associated with criminalization, such as police surveillance, criminal charges, deportation or loss of immigration status, child apprehension, eviction from housing, termination or exclusion from jobs, rejection from loans or other financial services, and more.[4] These potential harms also operate along intersectional lines of gender, race, class, economic status, and disability, with low income, racialized, and trans and gender-nonconforming sex workers facing greater visibility, surveillance, and policing. For example, for working-class and low-income parents, outing can have implications for their families. They may risk losing children to repressive state policies and family-services interventions.

Because being out is only safe in certain spaces with certain audiences, coming out is extremely personal, and sex workers continually work to negotiate our identities to promote our individual safety and well-being. Even though coming out is fraught, broader society and even some folks within queer or sex work communities sometimes judge those who are out or not about their sex work involvement or identity. If someone is out, that person is assumed to be either extremely privileged or extremely marginalized. Those in broader society may also judge people who are not out or who come out later in life, assuming that their decision to not come out was due to internalized stigma or shame, and not because of personal preference, or a decision based on safety or necessity.[5]

Outness is a spectrum. Sex workers may be out to close friends or intimate partners, but not to other family members. Some sex workers are also members of the LGBTQ+ or other communities and may be negotiating multiple closeted identities. Sex workers may be out online, using social media to advocate or discuss issues relating to sex work. Some sex workers use pseudonyms on social media, some use legal names. In square/civilian professional or school settings, sex workers may decide not to come out to teachers or employers, due to fear of their reactions and the potential psychosocial and career consequences of those reactions. However, in some workplaces or academic environments (i.e., a sex worker drop-in center, a university research project focused on sex worker rights), the decision to come out as a sex worker may have different implications.

Setting the Context: Why Does Outness Matter in Academia?

While sex work is still highly criminalized and stigmatized, thanks to decades of advocacy by sex work activists, sex worker rights are more visible.[6] Nonprofit, activist, and academic settings increasingly employ out sex workers. For example, certain funding bodies and academic initiatives (i.e., conferences, journals) have begun to explicitly call for and prioritize funding to community-led projects involving people with lived sex work experience in an effort to narrow the gap between academic research and researched communities.[7] As a result, those with lived sex work experience might be needed for grant applications, conference presentation proposals, and abstract submissions—with research and nonprofit settings seeking sex workers to represent a public face of the issue, and to act as interviewees, writers, project staff, and in other roles while explicitly asserting lived experience.

Fed up with our expertise being minimized and undervalued, sex workers are entering academia to gain greater credibility and direct academic resources towards community organizations of our choosing. Further, due to rising wealth inequality, high cost of living, and stagnant wages under capitalism, and the academic industrial complex, those in academia are increasingly likely to engage in sex work.[8] Thus, as sex work attracts researchers across diverse disciplines, people with sex work experience take up more space in universities, calling for greater attention to how outness is treated and how people with intersecting identities negotiate academic spaces.

Sex worker involvement in academic projects can take several forms. Larger research initiatives spanning one or more faculties may actively hire sex workers as expert consultants. Other community-based projects may take a top-down approach and hire sex worker scholars to execute their projects. Independent researchers may also lead projects on sex work, as "out" sex workers or not. Students in any academic discipline may also bring their experiential knowledge into their studies, presentations, and assignments even without disclosing their background. With sex worker scholars increasingly and more visibly occupying diverse strata of academic institutions, it is critical to consider our individual and community safety, and how our academic engagement impacts the broader sex worker rights movement. While certain spaces within academia reward "out" sex workers, others range from unwelcoming to dangerous. Despite advances in mainstream awareness of sex worker rights, people often experience harassment, judgment, stigma, and discrimination if their sex work involvement becomes known to students, staff, faculty, or administration.[9] As Celine's story illustrated, sex worker scholars have been doxxed (i.e., had their sex work disclosed to professors/employers by other people, without consent) and faced severe academic consequences, including termination of employment and expulsion from research labs and academic programs. These unsafe environments can result in sex workers preferring to keep our identity hidden, which can adversely impact sex workers who must balance traversing diverse academic spaces.[10] Being out only with select colleagues is challenging when some people do not understand the gravity of keeping someone's sex work involvement private. And for academic spaces that do value outness and lived experience, how can we as academics make them safe(r)?

Benefits and Consequences of Outness

In sex work research communities, being out about aspects of one's background, experience, or history can convey credibility and authority.[11] Yet, often only the most privileged of sex workers can be out, and this affects sex worker representation in these elite spaces. There are both benefits and consequences of outness at the individual and organizational level, which we explore below.

To be a sex worker who also holds a square/civilian professional job in academia or elsewhere—which can provide legitimacy when opening a bank account and completing a housing application, and a "cover" when interacting with family and community—is a highly privileged position. Thus, the individuals who can *choose* to disclose their sex work within academia are often middle-class, cisgender white women whose "respectability" and privilege shield them from sex work stigma. In other words, coming out on one's own terms requires sufficient physical and psychological safety to weather material risks, like a loss of income or employment termination.

In sharp contrast, the most marginalized sex workers often have no choice except to be out, due to social and structural exclusion that makes their sex work highly visible, like street prostitution. Low-income, racialized, gender-nonconforming, and/or disabled sex workers may also face barriers to affordable housing, as well as in their experiences of substance use, intergenerational trauma, racism, transphobia, and other forms of discrimination. In this way, individual life circumstances intersect with societally ingrained stereotypes about sex work, respectability, gender, race, and class such that a nonbinary Black or Indigenous person may be seen in the street and assumed to be involved in sex work, whereas a middle-class white woman who is deeply involved in academic sex work research may perpetually "pass" and never be assumed to be a sex worker.

Sex worker researchers and activists embody "duality":[12] we use our lived experience to inform meaningful sex work advocacy while also enjoying the benefits of square employment. At the individual level, being out while working on a sex work research project can allow the scholar to share relevant expertise historically undervalued in academic settings. Consequently, being out allows one to speak with greater authority, gives one's voice greater weight in the organizational setting, and may also facilitate identity cohesion, consistency, continuity, and integrity. Expressing more of one's authentic self and story, and having aspects of one's identity (i.e., researcher, social justice advocate, sex worker, community organizer) coexist in a work environment, without hiding, can engender significant mental health benefits. Being out also minimizes the risk of being doxxed (being exposed as a sex worker without consent) to one's employers.

At the institutional or organizational level, a research project benefits from involving one or more "out" individuals for the following reasons. Research teams can publicly assert that their project includes members with sex work experience who provide credibility and authority to the research process, such as networking within key communities. Additionally, sex worker scholars may also speak to media or provide sound bites (if the person is comfortable being out at that level). Again, this can be a significant asset to funding opportunities/applications that prioritize experiential voices, community-based research, and knowledge translation. Finally, given that research on sex work has historically pathologized sex workers as vectors for disease transmission and denied our personhood,[13] having sex worker scholars on a research team enhances the likelihood that sex worker communities will accept and validate the research and its findings.

Alongside these benefits, there are also individual, community, and project-level risks and potential consequences without sex worker collaborators. For the sex worker, being the single experiential person, or one of few, can result in tokenization. This places a heavy burden of emotional labor to provide insider knowledge, and significant pressure to adequately represent the diverse concerns of a highly heterogeneous community. For example, when our friend Noor disclosed her sex work during an interview for a research position as the face of a high-profile intervention to promote sex worker safety, the interviewers told Noor that she would be more likely to receive the position if she was prepared to come out publicly. This put her in the uncomfortable position of making a major decision about her current and future safety. Noor was also concerned that her relatively privileged status in sex work (as a middle-class cisgender woman) would not accurately represent issues faced by more marginalized workers.[14]

Out individuals in sex work research may also be overworked due to being called on to participate in every interview, media appearance, and more. Some are also undervalued and underpaid in these roles—despite bringing critical expertise and the experiential voice that enables the project to access greater funding—because of internalized stigma, the devaluing of sex worker voices, and funding constraints. Thus, institutions may benefit immensely from having sex worker scholars on their projects without committing to equitable distribution of funding or credit, which can also result in a gross exploitation of student sex workers' labor. Finally, coming out and facing judgment and stigma from one's peers or colleagues can have devastating, long-term impacts on one's psychosocial well-being and career, as well as physical safety.[15] For example, historically, researchers who disclosed that they had sold sex faced internal backlash and stigmatization, with some eventually choosing to leave the academy.[16]

When considering the benefits of being an out sex worker scholar, we recognize that outness is often a choice only accessible to the most privileged sex worker. Further, white, middle-class, cisgender sex workers may even be able to leverage their outness to advance in their academic career, while racialized or lower-income sex workers may never have the physical and psychological security necessary to come out and access these benefits, thereby perpetuating social inequities and oppressive systems of power. The potential consequences of tokenizing privileged sex worker voices and excluding a range of sex workers by class, race, ability, and gender identity are also severe, as this approach neglects the needs of the most marginalized workers, thus producing research that fails to represent and serve them. Interconnected privilege, oppression, and sex work stigma may result in some sex work research spaces being mostly populated by, and safe only for, white, middle-class sex workers. For these reasons, it is important to problematize the desire for out voices in both academic institutions and community organizations and consider alternative avenues to safely foreground experiential voices and diverse perspectives.

New Directions

We are inspired by grassroots collectives, such as Hacking/Hustling, which create an inclusive space by respecting members' and participants' autonomy in sharing and "defining their own experiences."[17] Below, we have outlined transformative alternatives to the in/out dichotomy, as well as low-barrier interventions to support sex workers in academia for institutions and educators, and tips for workers. We hope that these recommendations and this chapter inspire fellow sex workers, academics, and community members to consider new models of amplifying sex worker voices and prioritizing the expertise of individuals with lived experience that do not feature the pitfalls of demanding a singular "out" representative.

Recommendations for Institutions

- Prioritize lived experience in leadership, instructor, and primary investigator positions but do not expect public-facing outness as a requirement for leadership roles.
- Value community work and other forms of lived experience in application materials for leadership positions, teaching positions, or research grants, rather than focusing solely on academic experience. This will allow for more accurate sex work "representation" within your institution.

- Develop grant opportunities that allow for ethical sex work research, like community-led projects with adequate funding to pay experiential researchers, team members, and participants for their labor, time, and expertise.
- Develop services or policies that allow sex workers to safely report institutional violations without fear of consequences.

Recommendations for Educators

- Create a safe environment for sex worker scholars (out or not) by speaking about sex work with respect and dignity. When you speak about sex work as exploitation or something shameful or wrong, you send a signal to all sex workers listening that you are not a safe person to come out to.
- If a sex worker comes out to you, maintain confidentiality. Do not gossip about the sex worker's experience, and do not disclose that person's work to others without direct consent.
- A sex worker's decision to come out to you is not an open invitation to pry. You can acknowledge and appreciate the sex worker's lived experience in the context of the person's research goals without asking personal or overly invasive questions.
- Don't assume identities: you never know if someone has sex work experience or not.
- Don't discriminate against or make assumptions about someone's academic abilities based on the person's sex work involvement.
- Learn about sex workers' rights from community organizations and resources.
- When teaching about sex work, prioritize the use of resources and materials from people with lived experience in sex work over those theorizing about the issue without lived experience.
- Recognize that the sex workers you work with cannot speak for all sex workers and will not know about all sex worker experiences. Do not overburden sex workers with additional unpaid or emotional labor because they have lived experience.

Recommendations for Sex Worker Scholars

- Be cautious in whom you choose to come out to, remembering that once the information is out, it is irrevocable.

- Coming out to your supervisor or classmate does not mean you need to be out to everyone else in your class or on your project. Set clear boundaries with those you do come out to and emphasize the importance of having your direct consent before sharing your sex work experience with others.
- Surround yourself with other sex worker students and trusted allies. Support other sex workers in your institution; make space for them and share resources.
- When/if safe to do so, utilize existing structures within your institution to report violations and microaggressions and demand accountability/get support where needed. This could include an equity, diversity, and inclusion office, a student ombudsperson, or sexual-violence support office. If such supports do not exist, lean on the sex work networks or community supports that you feel safe utilizing and have access to.
- There is no shame in sex work—criminalization and social norms create the stigma. As a sex worker, you are part of a long history of resilience and resistance that is to be celebrated. You will always have support among other sex workers.

Conclusion: Imagining Alternative Avenues to Outness

In this chapter, we have discussed the benefits and consequences of outness for individual sex workers in communities and academic settings. We highlighted and interrogated the increasing demand for out sex worker voices by examining the implications of having a single person (or a few people) represent the face of a deeply diverse community. While well-intended, prioritizing out sex workers can place undue and unfair pressure on spokespeople and create divisions in academic spaces and sex work communities. We urge organizations not to make assumptions about folks' lived experience or lack thereof, and not expect outness from people. This means assuming instead that people are keeping themselves safe, engaging with a good heart, and having something meaningful to contribute to the work.

The demand for outness and the stigmatization that comes with being out hinder sex workers' ability to live safely and freely, and to assert our expertise in ways that feel best for each of us. We hope that problematizing the demand for out voices, and the related inclination to make assumptions about people's lived experience, is valuable to those not only in academic settings but in any work or community setting in which sex workers engage—which is everywhere.

In solidarity, Lizzie and Lia

NOTES

1 Mistress Snow 2019.
2 Orne 2011.
3 Bowen 2013.
4 NSWP 2017; Platt et al. 2018.
5 Glover 2017; Khuzwayo 2021.
6 Mgbako 2020; Gira Grant 2015.
7 Hickey 2020; Lobo et al. 2021.
8 Brooks 2021.
9 Ahearne 2015.
10 Mistress Snow 2019; Sagar et al. 2015.
11 Bruckert 2014.
12 Bowen 2013.
13 Bungay et al. 2021.
14 Sciortino 2016.
15 Heineman 2019; Sagar et al. 2015.
16 Bernstein 2007a.
17 Hacking/Hustling is a collective of sex workers, survivors, and accomplices working at the intersection of tech and social justice to interrupt state surveillance and violence facilitated by technology. You can learn more about them at hackinghustling.org.

12

Ethical Sexual Services

Sexual Assistance for People with Disabilities

GIULIA GAROFALO GEYMONAT AND JULIA GIACOMETTI

In Europe, the term "sexual assistance" is increasingly used to refer to specialized sexual services for people with disabilities, for which providers receive special training. Despite limited availability, these services have gathered public attention internationally. They are controversial even among activists for sex workers' and disability rights. Some fear they can reproduce the stigmas associated with both sex workers and disabled people. Critics question why people with disabilities need special sexual services and why providers need special training. Antiprostitution activists accuse proponents of pushing prostitution under a new name while some sex worker–rights activists ask why sexual assistance is framed as different from what sex workers generally do.

In this chapter, we address sexual assistance, and some of the issues above, through two insider voices: those of a sexual assistant (Julia) affiliated with a grassroots sexual assistants' organization based in Switzerland, and an activist researcher (Giulia) who has done embedded participant observation in this field. Through our dialogue, we discuss the nuances of sexual assistance in Europe, including its contexts, experiences, and relation to different sex work policies. In our views, sexual assistance creates a collaborative space for sex providers, disabled (potential) clients, and professional allies to foster communities centered around providing "ethical" sexual services for all involved parties. Issues surrounding nationality and race remain central challenges in this process, as sexual assistants in Europe continue to be overwhelmingly white and nonmigrant.

The First Time (Giulia)

It was a sunny day in winter 2013, in Paris. I entered a large room and found myself in a crowded public event, with crews from television and radio stations in attendance.[1] Around that time, the Comité Consultatif National d'Ethique (a French government agency advising on bioethics) deliberated on the ethics of sexual assistance, and a disabled-rights organization had called a panel to discuss its pros and cons. I was not surprised that the sexual assistant invited to speak came from Switzerland from a grassroots organization that I will call BodyUnity. BodyUnity facilitates sexual-assistance services and provides training and supervision to sexual assistants. Although sexual assistance is largely ignored by public authorities and regulators, it remains threatened by prostitution laws. Therefore, in France, as well as in other countries with groups pushing for laws to abolish or prohibit sex work, organizations such as BodyUnity are at risk of being prosecuted as "pimping," though they are activist projects careful to remain not-for-profit. Most sexual assistants are also careful not to be publicly out because of the risk of being fired from mainstream jobs or losing child custody rights. Also, at that time efforts were brewing to pass laws criminalizing clients in France. Indeed, since 2016, clients of sexual assistants, like clients of any sex worker, are deemed to have committed a crime.[2] In neighboring Switzerland, where sex work is recognized as a form of work, BodyUnity operates legally. In fact, at that time it operated four different training programs for sexual assistants, a remarkable number for a country of just eight million people.

That day was my first public event on sexual assistance as a sex worker–rights activist and researcher. Recently I had started my two-year research project on a relatively new phenomenon—the conscious engagement by parts of the disability-rights movement with the issue of sex services. Over the last two decades, this activism has taken different forms, including solidarity across movements,[3] collaborations between sex worker activists and disabled activists—such as Touching Base in Australia or TLC in the UK—or the creation of specialized sex services developed across European countries increasingly referred to as "sexual assistance."[4] Some of these practices may remind us of surrogate partner therapy (SPT), sometimes presented as the older cousin of sexual assistance. SPT is in fact distinct and rooted in medical and therapeutic approaches to address sexual dysfunctions,[5] rather than in disabled people's interventions. Sexual assistance is instead based in the disabled-rights approach that frames the sexual problems experienced by disabled people as rooted in social and political processes that see them as asexual, in need of protection, hypersexual, or monstrous and repulsive.[6]

The atmosphere was tense—not unusual with public discussions about sex work. A masked sexual assistant kept the media at a safe distance, revealing how stigma is an important issue, even in legalized contexts such as Switzerland. As I scanned the audience, I noted a group of women's rights activists loudly claiming that sexual assistance is the latest form of exploitation and commodification of women's bodies, and a Trojan horse that the "prostitution lobby" found to give itself legitimacy.[7] However, as the event progressed, I noticed differences compared to sex work conferences I had attended across Europe. The speakers as well as the audience were almost completely white and nonmigrant, something that, I later discovered, characterizes sexual assistance and its activism. Also, the audience was filled with people with disabilities, their carers, and family members, bringing a whole different flavor to the discussion. I felt myself shivering when one panelist, a disabled man, gained the audience's total attention, despite his major challenges with verbal communication. He spoke about his exclusion from experiences of sex and bodily intimacy, which, he said, was a political issue. He talked about disabled people's isolation, segregation and stigmatization, and internalized oppression, and about their dependence on carers and medical technologies, all structural conditions that make access to sexual encounters and knowledge extremely hard. He openly talked about his experiences as a client of sexual services. He was convinced that sexual assistance could be one of the tools to improve disabled people's sexual lives. I was touched. I had never heard such direct disability-rights talk on sexuality, nor a client publicly making a personal and political argument about sex work.

Then came the sexual assistant. Her organization, she told us, was led by sexual assistants and worked with disabled activists and their professional allies in order to promote "ethical" practices of sexual assistance. She talked about the importance of peer training and peer community, about solidarity and intimacy with her clients, and the clarity of the setting and the exchange of money. At that moment, I heard both potential conflicts between the goals of sex workers' rights and disability rights, and yet at the same time the possible remarkable power of their alliance. Was sexual assistance like other forms of "intimate labor," such as care work, where the quality of intimate services and the rights of workers often go hand in hand?[8] Or was it different? In a context where sex work is increasingly criminalized in Europe,[9] I was aware that some criticize sexual assistance for promoting a "good and clean" version of the sex industry, worthy of recognition and protection, while leaving others to their fate or actively persecuting them. Some disabled activists denounce sexual assistance as a dangerous project that reproduces the idea that people with disabilities are undesirable, and their sexuality can be treated—and gotten rid of—yet another need of the disabled that non-disabled people can manage and profit from.[10] I knew indeed that some sexual-assistance activists downplay the sexual content of the encounters ("they do not go 'all the way'") or highlight the sexual assistants' normality ("they are married with kids") or insist on the fact that the clients are "very disabled." Some of that emerged during the panel. But I also knew how "whore hierarchies," or "whorearchies," work. Where prostitution is criminalized, people make efforts to distance themselves from it, especially when speaking in public. What sexual assistants think privately, though, could be quite different. They may prefer to share their thoughts in a safe space, away from the discursive frame of "is this prostitution or not?" and the sharp division between able and disabled people. As I was to find out, for BodyUnity members, producing a clear boundary between prostitution and sexual assistance is not a priority. A multiplicity of identifications is in fact present in the group, with some people who cannot imagine working with nondisabled clients, and others who define themselves as sex workers.[11]

After the talk, I went to speak to the sexual assistant. She told me that BodyUnity was about to begin a new training, and suggested I apply. This is how I started my eighteen-month embedded participant observation. And this is how I met Julia. She was recruited at the same moment, and we both started the training a few months later, I as a researcher and she as a sexual assistant. We were both from Italy, both nondisabled, white, queer women in our thirties. Our time together resulted in a closer bond. My research would not be the same without her. This is the first piece we have written as coauthors.

Why I Prefer Disabled Clients (Julia)

I agreed to write this piece using my sexual-assistant pseudonym, Julia. I consider myself an activist member of BodyUnity. Yet, I am in the closet. This is ironic, as I am out as a queer woman, which was not a painless process in Catholic Italy, but I am back in another closet as a sexual assistant. This is the case for most of my colleagues at BodyUnity and why our privacy is a priority of the organization. It is a delicate balance. We encourage each other, and the new trainees, to be out to our intimate partners. But we recognize the challenge to be out to the world. This means I cannot speak directly about my experience in public, which, though often frustrating, can also teach you how to go beyond individual experience and force you to put yourself in someone else's shoes.

I personally felt I could be good at sexual assistance. When I had mainstream sex work experiences, I was the very intimate type, and I feel very connected to the rights of disabled people. I grew up close to my aunt, who was physically and mentally disabled. For her entire life she dreamed of having her own marriage, but she never had a partner. I wish there were more disabled women clients, but women represent only a tiny minority.

In my case, to be out would put my mainstream job and my parental rights at risk and present the possibility of being rejected by my family of origin even if, in principle, I do not do anything illegal. I hope I will be able to share my whole story one day, perhaps when I am an older woman, as an "ex." That is one reason why I like clients of sexual assistance. They tend to be prouder of their experience of being clients than nondisabled clients are, and many talk about sexual assistance to people around them. It makes me feel less invisible.

The training with BodyUnity has meant a lot to help me acquire self-awareness and self-esteem. I am happy to have trained when I did—a time when I had more money and no kids. These days I just would not be able to afford it. Money is a challenge for most of the other trainees as well. Obviously, we all know participating will be an investment, but we lack a stable income, even though we are mainly in our forties. We mostly work in care, education, body work: all poorly paid jobs! Some of us also have past or current experience in the mainstream sex industry. I think sex workers get interested in training in their forties when it is more difficult to make money, and you may look for different meaning in what you do. I must say I appreciated the detailed screening during my application and the length of our training. You really get a chance to build a community and get involved with the organization. However, people with fewer resources, particularly marginalized sex workers or migrants who do not speak good French, would not be able to take part. Some other sexual-assistance training projects are more open to migrant and poorer sex workers, but this is one of the limits of sexual assistance.

To those who ask if there is a difference between prostitution and sexual assistance—because they always ask, regardless of whether they are "for" or "against"—I answer yes, it is a form of sex work. But I also remind people that many forms of sex work are not accessible to clients with disabilities. I don't consider myself an expert, but I have much experience around sexuality. I recognize some of the trappings of sex when I see them and am committed to challenging the oppressive norms and power dynamics surrounding sexual relations.

I definitely prefer disabled clients over the nondisabled clients I had in the past. My impression is that when people decide to pay for sexual services because they are excluded from other options, they are more likely to show respect for sex workers. Also, when you talk about being stigmatized as a "whore," they often understand because they experience it every day as "crips." I also find that they are more open to the intensity of encounters and look for shared intimacy and pleasure—which is something I like in sex. To me having sex with disabled clients also means not being afraid of getting close to pain and loneliness—theirs but also my own. It also means being open to something akin to spiritual sharing. I think about my regular client, a woman, who sometimes says "sexual assistance saved me." I think about a friend's client who after many years of unbearable chronic pain, decided to end her life, and she asked her sexual assistant to accompany her through assisted suicide— the program offered by the organization Exit in Switzerland.

We discuss these and other issues in our peer supervisions: the relationship with our clients can be a form of love, even though it is bounded in time and space. Also, the boundaries are less rigid than in other kinds of sex work, because with disabled clients you usually end up meeting their caregivers. At times it ends up being messy emotionally—and that is okay too. It is difficult to remain responsible and in control, but also treat your clients as equals without infantilizing them. As the disability activists themselves say, we have the right to fall in love and be in pain too! It is a difficult balance not to feel guilty, frustrated, or angry yourself, or become some kind of "saint" or "savior"! That is why we emphasize throughout—in the nonsexual "preliminary meeting" we have with our potential clients and every time it is needed: that sexual assistance is different from being lovers or friends. It is not just the clients who get confused. Once when meeting a client in an activist space, I told him I was not sure how to behave. I still remember his answer, which was more or less as follows: "Well, I have a doctor I am very close to. If I meet her in the street, we have a nice chat, but we are not friends, and she would not invite me to her daughter's party! That may be a good example for you, even if you are not a doctor!"

We also talk about what it means to experience sexual pleasure with our clients, which some of us do with some clients. I think about Aïha Zemp, a disabled feminist activist and a psychotherapist who apparently was a pioneer in the first trainings for sexual assistants in Switzerland in the early 2000s. She had a clear vision of sexual assistance as a feminist practice to reduce the sexual violence experienced by girls and women with disabilities. Her hope was that women with disabilities could be empowered through safe sexual encounters with sexual assistants, that they could find out what they like and don't like and learn how to say yes and no in practice. She was also convinced that for this to work it was essential for the (able) sexual assistants to share sexual pleasure with the disabled clients. Though I would not fully agree, I certainly hate when people talk about sexuality and disability and forget to talk about pleasure. Sex is not just a problem that needs to be fixed, a tension that needs to be released. I know many people, able or disabled, may think the same of their own sexuality, but isn't that sad?

Money and the Law (Giulia)

Through my years in this field of research, I have realized how hard it can be for sexual-assistance activists to bring up the issue of pleasure.

If they mention it, they risk being labeled "pervs" or fetishists taking advantage of disabled people. Or they risk being told some version of "if you like it so much, or if you believe so much in solidarity, why don't you do it for free?" The Comité Consultatif National d'Ethique that fall of 2012 said much the same thing.[12] They decided that the only ethical practices of "sexual assistance" involved no exchange of money.[13] This was a particularly difficult thing to hear for those who live with disabilities or are close to people with disabilities. Such an approach can be called "a charity model" of sexual assistance.[14] This approach runs the risk of legitimizing the practices—which are not so rare—of carers, nurses, and even friends and family members offering "free sexual help" to disabled people out of goodwill—which can foster codependence, shame, abuse, and incest. The decision of the Comité is also problematic from a sex workers' rights perspective. It erases the recognition of the labor involved in sexual assistance. Since that decision, things have gotten worse in France, as in the rest of Europe.[15] Conversations and policies on sexual services have become more rigid. Client criminalization has become the "ethical" norm around which everyone, especially progressives and feminists, must position themselves.[16] Simultaneously, increasingly restrictive migration laws have worsened the conditions of the sex industry as a whole. This, in turn, has reduced the ability to imagine what "ethical" practices may look like in the sex industry, and which arrangements could facilitate them, in policy and at the organizational level.

However, at the same time, in the last ten years, grassroots groups promoting sexual assistance have become more visible and have established links across countries, including Italy, France, Belgium, Hungary, Spain, and Germany.[17] Rooted in a disability-rights perspective, just like BodyUnity, these organizations are not-for-profit. Offering various kinds of training, they tend to become intermediaries between sexual assistants and disabled people, their carers, and related institutions. These advocacy organizations navigate the difficult issues of consent, autonomy, vulnerability, and power in (paid) sexual encounters between able and disabled people.

How successful these organizations are at least partly depends on the history of the local sex workers' rights and disability-rights movements, as well as, centrally, on the sex work legislation existing in each country. BodyUnity stands out as an organization that is led by sexual assistants as opposed to many others that are led by disabled activists or allied professionals. It is also noted for its collaboration with (other) sex workers' rights organizations. BodyUnity's location in Switzerland also contributes to its success. Switzerland has a strong tradition of sex workers' organizing,[18] and sexuality has been part of the disability-rights agenda since the 1990s. Also, Switzerland represents—along with, within Europe, Germany, Belgium, and the Netherlands—at least partially "integrative" prostitution policies as opposed to Italian and French "restrictive" and "repressive" approaches. According to Petra Östergen,[19] integrative policy—also called "decriminalization"—is an approach that aims to integrate the sex sector into social, legal, and institutional frameworks that protect sex workers from harm. It does so not with criminal law, but through labor laws and other policy tools. The models that are more integrative (or decriminalizing) allow for a more collaborative approach with sex worker communities. As the BodyUnity case shows, these broader collective efforts can include forms of "professional" training within sex work communities.[20] More generally, as various forms of sex workers' organizing indicate,[21] recognizing sex work as legitimate work and including sex workers in the public debate throughout Europe and the globe will result in initiatives that improve their living and working conditions as well as—we can add—the "ethics" of their intimate services around sexual assistance.

NOTES

1 The event, titled "Assistance sexuelle: Présence à l'autre ou marchandisation du corps?," occurred on February 8, 2013, in Paris. It was promoted by the grassroots organization CH(S)OSE, Collectif handicaps et sexualités Ose.

2 Calderaro and Giametta 2019.

3 See for example Fritsch et al. 2016.

4 See Touching Base Inc. (www.touchingbase.org). See also Wotton 2016.

5 See for example Aloni, Keren, and Katz 2007; and International Professional Surrogates Association (www.surrogatetherapy.org).

6 Shakespeare, Gillespie-Sells, and Davies 1996; McReur and Mollow 2012; Kafer 2013; Shuttleworth and Sanders 2010.

7 Jeffreys 2008.

8 Boris and Salazar Parreñas 2010.

9 Jahnsen and Wagenaar 2017.

10 Dufour and Thierry 2014.

11 Garofalo Geymonat 2019.

12 CCNE, "Avis 118 Vie affective et sexuelle des personnes handicapées. Question de l'assistance sexuelle," 2012. Accessed December 9, 2023. www.ccne-ethique.fr.

13 In 2021, the CCNE published another advice involving the topic of sexual assistance for people with disabilities, which was not very different from the one published in 2012. See CCNE, "Réponse à la saisine de Sophie Cluzel, Ministre chargée des personnes handicapées sur l'accès à la vie affective et sexuelle et l'assistance sexuelle des personnes handicapées," 2021. Accessed December 9, 2023. www.ccne-ethique.fr.

14 Garofalo Geymonat 2019.

15 An exception is represented by the decriminalization of sex work in Belgium in 2022.

16 Garofalo Geymonat and Selmi 2019; Ward and Wylie 2017.

17 See for instance European Platform Sexual Assistance, www.epseas.eu.

18 See the network ProCoRe: https://procore-info.ch.

19 Östergen 2017.

20 Garofalo Geymonat and Macioti 2016.

21 See European Sex Workers' Rights Alliance, www.eswalliance.org, and Global Network of Sex Work Projects, www.nswp.org.

PART III

The Work of Sex Work

13

"My Brand Is Girl Next Door"

Authenticity and Privilege among Transfeminine Porn Performers

SOPHIE PEZZUTTO

I am at a Christmas party in Henderson, just outside of Las Vegas, Nevada. A well-known name in the porn industry has invited a handful of close friends and coworkers to her unremarkable house, located in a quiet, suburban cul-de-sac. There is food, wine, champagne, and a tall Christmas tree that is elaborately adorned. As the gathering gets underway, our host props her phone up against the TV and blows smoke into the virtual faces of her fans, who are tuning in to her Instagram live stream, watching some of us play Jenga. I see her feed fill up with comments and emojis from across the world. Another performer lies down on the sofa and records a short clip for her Instagram followers, wishing them a happy Christmas season. A few champagne glasses later our host brings out a big, circular LED light as most of us begin to undress. Like clockwork and with little instructions needed, people start jumping up and down, smiling and laughing while slapping each other's behinds. To the sound of our clinking champagne glasses, we start photographing and live streaming ourselves to the world. This party—like many other social events during my ethnographic fieldwork in the transgender pornography industry—is as much a get-together among friends as it is an opportunity for us to build our brands as porn stars.

The Internet and smartphones have transformed many aspects of sex work, creating what I have termed "porntropreneurs," a portmanteau of "pornographers" and "entrepreneurs," highlighting how, to succeed in today's erotic economy, porn performers are required to embody virtues and skills associated with the creation, ongoing maintenance, and growth of a small online business.[1] Pre-Internet forms of sex work are increasingly digitally mediated while entirely new avenues of income have emerged. Online platforms such as OnlyFans and ModelCentro fuse social-media technology with sex work. Webcamming platforms, like Chaturbate and Camsoda, provide a regular income for a growing number of sex workers. Other apps and platforms, like Snapchat, Skype, and Zoom, were not originally developed with sex work in mind, but sex workers have found creative ways to make money on them.[2]

In this increasingly diverse and digitized sex work landscape, the practice of self-branding has become crucial to success. Self-branding involves the creation of a brand identity through various online and offline practices. As with a corporate brand that becomes synonymous with a particular lifestyle and values, individuals utilize branding strategies to advertise to a target audience not just their skills and services but their way of life and personal values. With the growth of the gig economy, branding has become a career strategy for an increasing number of people across social strata. For many, self-branding is a method of survival enabling them to differentiate themselves in a competitive and precarious labor market. A strong brand helps sex workers tie together their diverse service offerings, distinguish themselves in a globalized marketplace for sex, and forge ongoing, lucrative relationships with their fans. In doing so, self-branding enables sex workers to earn more money across all forms of sex work.

While social and economic conditions of twenty-first-century late capitalism have boosted the need for self-branding, its emergence is also linked to social media.[3] Social media play a key role in sex worker self-branding, enabling the distribution of content globally, instantly, and at no or a very low cost (depending on one's advertising choices). Sex workers use social media to build a unique online presence and get followers to become emotionally attached to them through the production of authenticity. The goal is to ultimately direct traffic from these "free" social media platforms to paying sites and services, such as wish lists, clip stores, cam shows, or in-person appointments.[4]

Unfortunately, many sex workers face significant discrimination on social media alongside other digital platforms.[5] Social media platforms frequently make invisible or shut down sex worker accounts, often without notice, causing significant personal and financial distress. This disproportionately happens to sex workers even as their content is often no less sexual than, for instance, that of models and celebrities. There are many reasons for this online discrimination, but the criminalization of sex work and laws in the United States such as FOSTA/SESTA are key reasons.[6] FOSTA/SESTA has been widely criticized by sex workers and academics as discriminatory, dangerous, and financially harmful to sex workers.[7]

Drawing on ethnographic data and interviews with transfeminine porn performers collected in Las Vegas, Los Angeles, and Australia between December 2017 and February 2022, as well as my own experiences as a trans sex worker, I argue that self-branding has become an indispensable marketing strategy. I demonstrate that it can be a rewarding avenue of self-expression while also demanding of workers new forms of labor, specifically authenticity labor. The way transfeminine performers negotiate this process varies depending on their social position. I conclude that transfeminine porn performers are branding experts, and that their knowledge and skills have mostly been overlooked.

Self-Branding among Transfeminine Porn Workers

Lianna Lawson: So, my brand is the very basic "girl next door," real couple having fun. That's it. Easy.

Korra del Rio: Everyone wants to do the glam thing, but I don't think that's what I am. My brand is the long-distance trans girlfriend who asks her fans, "Oh hey, how is your day going?"

Daisy Taylor: I think I'm kind of like a dorky girl next door almost. There are some girls who are like super glam and are only super glam and that's never been me. I'm just kind of like dorky and I laugh at myself a lot. . . . I think I do have kind of a humorous thing that appeals to people.

My brand as Bunny Marthy can be described as "professional wannabe." I have a young, hot gamer girl look which I sell through my social media, streams, ASMR videos,[8] and amateur porn site Yeabunny.com. I have a youthful aesthetic overall and I'm always super happy, smiling, and crazy on my streams. I love talking, laughing, and playing games with my fans, and creating a bond with them.[9]

Transfeminine porn performers use self-branding to tie together their content under a public identity for consumers to engage with. As trans performer Ryder Monroe put it,

I guess it's just . . . a company almost. It's like your brand is sex. You've branded yourself under that category and you just chose a name and that's like everything under your umbrella of offerings.

Additionally, brand identities help performers differentiate themselves among an increasingly crowded field of sex workers from all over the world. Australian trans porn performer and escort Danika Deep put it as follows:

There's not many no-name mum and dad shops these days and if there are, they are getting branded to be a no-name mum and dad shop, so they're not like a big Maccas [McDonalds] or whatever. Everything needs some kind of point of difference. Some kind of identity, otherwise you get lost in the sea, the ocean.

For many performers the process of articulating their brand is a personally fulfilling journey of self-discovery and self-expression. Performer Natalie Mars, for instance, emphasized how a desire to experience sex and have trans women represented in a certain way were primary considerations in how she built her brand:

Personally, I mean it's not necessarily always financial. It's what I enjoy doing. Sometimes I make porn that I would want to see. It's something that turns me on. And I think there's a severe lack of, especially in trans porn, trans women doing really fetish-y things. It's very formulaic. A lot of my interests are . . . anime influences, like Japanese porn influenced. I love that stuff. It's stuff you see in *hentai*. Its stuff that you . . . don't really see in Western porn very much and I love that shit and I just wanna make that stuff 'cause I want to see that stuff. . . . Personally I got into porn

because I loved porn, I was always a pervert and liked perverted shit . . .
and so doing porn is kind of a dream.

Early in my own sex work career I branded myself as a trans dominatrix instead of the more classic trans girl next door. While there were
many practical, financial, and other reasons that led me to do this, I
found it ultimately personally fulfilling because it helped me explore a
different side of me. This, in turn, led me to reflect on how transfeminine
people are often constricted by highly racialized, intersecting cis- and
heteronormative expectations in how to express gender and experience
intimacy. Prior to sex work I did not properly consider being sexually
dominant, as I had internalized white ideas of femininity, which frame
women as sexually submissive and passive, especially in encounters with
men. In a bid for social acceptance as a transfeminine person, I initially
had shied away from exploring and expressing gender and sexuality beyond this framing. Articulating my own sex worker brand ultimately
allowed me to venture beyond these restrictive norms.

Consumers, in turn, are drawn to brand identities because they play
into their fantasies. Like successful corporate brands, good performer
brands allow consumers to "act, feel and be in a particular way."[10] Fans
take a liking to (or even fall in love with) the fantasy persona they are
presented with and financially support the performer. Experienced performers were aware of this:

Korra del Rio: People follow the Instagram and the Twitter to get the
pictures they wanna jerk off to . . . but even more are there because they
wanna learn more about you, you know? They didn't just see you on a
video and then looked up your name for another video [for no reason].
They sought you out on social media to learn more about you.

Daisy Taylor: The idea of a brand is something that is relatable. Something that people can love. Something that people can . . . put money into.

Performers achieve emotional attachment from consumers through
the production of "authenticity" in their branding. In the words of Daisy
Taylor,

> Truly, I think the core of what a good brand is, is authenticity . . . What interests people most is the human being. People like to watch my porn and stuff, for sure, but Daisy is a character, and there are so many people who went to my YouTube, or there was a long time where I was just going on Instagram and I was going on live every week and there was so many people tuning into that and yeah, cool, the porn star, but seeing me talk about important or nonimportant things . . . seeing me act as me, not as the character, I think is what actually makes people like, "Ah."

Authenticity is achieved through intimate sharing. This can take on many different forms, though most commonly it occurs via social media. Examples are personal tweets on Twitter, behind-the-scenes photos on Instagram, short video clips that take on the form of confessionals on Instagram or YouTube, or Q&As on Instagram. Put in the words of Korra del Rio,

> They're always telling us to just record little bits of everything, all the time throughout the day. That's what the managers and the people running the companies and stuff, they're always like, "You should really Snapchat five or six times a day, just like a five-minute video, a few minutes here, a couple of seconds there, show 'em what you're up to, make them see the human being or whatever."

Despite what it suggests, "being authentic" does not come to performers without effort. As porn-work scholar Heather Berg points out, "Authenticity is both a form of labor and a discourse that conceals labor."[11] Performers must actively produce and manage "authenticity" in their branding efforts. They do so by pushing themselves to engage in intimate sharing and by actively curating what they share. Not only can authenticity labor be exhausting, but I argue that, depending on the social position of the performer, it is more work for some than for others.

Branding Privilege

Transfeminine performers who have class privilege as white, straight, able-bodied, and willing to top are more likely to have an easier time engaging in authenticity labor and therefore find the practice of self-branding empowering. Not only can these performers more easily express their brands on their own terms, but they are often also better positioned to engage in intimate sharing.

Those who are relatively financially stable, for instance, can afford to lose business by not catering to consumer demands that they find objectionable or disempowering. When questioned about her preference for mainstream studios over independent ones, which tend to emphasize self-expression, performer Korra del Rio highlighted how prioritizing self-expression often means forgoing income:

> I respect the indie side of the industry where people strive for a sense of freedom to do whatever they want and to express themselves in whatever ways will grant them happiness and empowerment. But when you don't market yourself to the biggest market, you are either going to have to sell your product for a higher price or consciously make less money. . . . They can't pay me my going rate, so I take a severe cut in order to work with them. The last place I was at was paying four hundred dollars for a hardcore scene, whereas my rate is fifteen hundred dollars with the bigger companies. So, this indie company is going to get to say, "What about our rights? What about our freedoms?" and I look back and think to myself, "Well, what about my car bill? What about my rent?"

Race also shapes experiences of branding. Because whiteness often goes unmarked, white performers can focus their brand identities on things other than their skin color, whereas performers of color must often choose between playing into racially objectifying (yet lucrative) fantasies or making less money. To avoid racial objectification, some white-passing transfeminine performers choose white stage names. As a trans performer of color, branding oneself as racially ambiguous also helps avoid being relegated to niche sites such as Grooby's *Black Tgirls*, which typically have fewer site visitors compared to mainstream websites. Performers of color also have a harder time branding themselves on their own terms because of racist social media algorithms that are built on ideals of white femininity. At the 2019 XBIZ panel on social media success, one participant pointed out that "if the booty is so thick that you cannot tell that person is wearing a G-string it counts as nudity," highlighting how social media nudity algorithms discriminate against certain body types.

Sexuality also impacts transfeminine performers' ability to brand themselves on their own terms. Straight transfeminine performers do not have to feign attraction to men or hide their queer sexuality. Performer Ella Venus, for instance, hid the fact that she had a partner:

> T [my partner] is not part of my brand at all. . . . When fans wanted to take photos . . . then I would be like, "No, T is not going to be in this photo." . . . We've gone out to places and taken photos and just been like, "Don't tweet the photos that have T in them." . . . Like, if fans ask me, "Are you dating anyone?," I just kind of dodge the question because I feel like that maybe ruins their fantasy in a way and that's more of a marketing, a business decision.

Social media is not just a key tool in brand building but also a domain that replicates class and ability privileges. Experienced performers often have extensive knowledge about the user base, algorithms, and terms of use of various platforms, all of which requires a significant level of technical skill, as I have demonstrated elsewhere.[12] Performers who grew up with and can afford expensive technology are more likely to be proficient with it whereas those without these privileges are more likely to perceive this aspect of branding as a challenge and a burden. Those who suffer from bad mental health are also more likely to find the constant need to engage in intimate sharing exhausting.

As Jones points out, people with nonnormative embodiment often make money precisely because customers fetishize their bodies.[13] This means that minorities, such as transfeminine performers, must often choose between playing into objectifying tropes or making less money. For transfeminine performers this specifically means having to enjoy being a top (i.e., being the penetrative partner). Drawing on my own experiences, almost all clients want me to be hard and top them as they see the trans woman's penis as the main point of attraction. Being consistently hard and able to top, however, is something that many transfeminine people are dysphoric about, let alone the fact that it is physically challenging given that hormone replacement therapy (HRT) has the exact opposite effect. As trans performer Natalie Mars poignantly put it in a conversation about this subject, "We're expected to do things we are physically incapable of doing." Consequently, many trans performers elect to skip HRT to better fulfill these physical requirements. Transfeminine performers who are not dysphoric about their penises, and who enjoy being tops and are happy to brand themselves as such, are significantly more likely to find the process empowering.

Branding Experts

The proliferation of the Internet and emergence of social media have created a working environment for sex workers where self-branding has become a crucial marketing strategy. While self-branding can be an empowering practice of self-expression, it takes place within a context where most transfeminine porn performers must strike a balance between self-expression and the demands of the market. Importantly, which performers found this process empowering was dependent on their social position. Performers with class, race, sexuality, and ability privileges, as well as those willing to top, can more easily express their brands on their own terms and are often also better positioned to engage in intimate sharing.

Although transfeminine sex workers are only one example of creative professionals who use self-branding to market themselves and sell their services, they are in many ways particularly reliant on, and thus experts at, employing these techniques and technologies in their daily lives. Not only are sex workers public relations and marketing experts, but they are also uniquely positioned to bring together extensive knowledge about self-presentation and technologies such as social media that increasingly mediate how we see each other. These findings point to the potential for more research that looks at the intersection between sex work, technology, and selfhood.

NOTES

1 Pezzutto 2019.

2 Berg 2016.

3 Marwick 2013, 166.

4 While people can use these platforms free of charge, there is a documented range of increasing costs associated with being on these platforms, ranging from mental health impacts to data harvesting and state surveillance (see: Zuboff 2019).

5 Blunt and Stardust 2021; Stardust 2018.

6 FOSTA-SESTA is an acronym for the Fight Online Sex Trafficking and Stop Enabling Sex Traffickers Act, which was enacted in 2018 by the Trump administration. In short, it criminalizes online platforms and makes them legally liable for the advertisement of sexual services. FOSTA-SESTA has resulted in many platforms preemptively shutting down various forms of erotic and sexual content over concerns of legal consequences and an inability to adequately screen all content. It has also led to the targeted removal of sex workers' accounts even when there is no advertisement of sexual services involved. It has also made the lives of sex workers significantly more financially precarious and dangerous (see: Blunt and Wolf 2020).

7 Blunt and Wolf 2020; Bronstein 2021; Mia 2020.

8 ASMR videos are Autonomous Sensory Meridian Response–inducing videos involving sounds, for example, soft talking, tapping, or humming, that produce pleasant tingling sensations in the body.

9 Bunny Marthy, "Keep Your Brand Consistent across a Variety of Platforms," *XBIZ*, May 31, 2021, accessed December 20, 2023, www.xbiz.com.

10 Arvidsson 2006, 8.

11 Berg 2017, 689.

12 Pezzutto 2019.

13 Jones 2020a, 168.

14

Dominating Pleasure

High Job Satisfaction among Professional Dominatrixes

TANIA G. LEVEY

The professional dominatrix (or pro-domme) is a woman who performs the role of dominant in commercial bondage, discipline, dominance, and sado-masochistic (BDSM) sessions with clients.[1] BDSM is not part of learned heteronormative sexual scripts, and some tasks can be dangerous if not done correctly. Thus, pro-dommes use highly technical skills in these sessions and often undergo extensive training to perform these services. The most visible skills displayed by the dominatrix are physical and technical, such as how to use whips, suspend someone by ropes, and insert catheters for medical sessions. The variability and complexity of scenes also call for creativity and improvisational skills. Further, dealing with clients with stigmatized desires while maintaining an authentic dominant persona calls for interpersonal skills. Professional domination is an excellent case study for examining skill and job satisfaction in sex work because the work involves learning and using a specific set of skills rarely taught in mainstream culture.

Pro-domme work also shows that contrary to public perception, sex workers often experience high job satisfaction and pleasure. In my research on pro-dommes, all sources of data are brimming with stories of satisfaction, happiness, pleasure, and pride in their work. Like those in most occupations, pro-dommes derive job satisfaction from high pay and autonomy, particularly control over working hours and the choice of clients. Though money is not always steady, pro-dommes who secure regular clients and set their own hours report very few complaints. Here, I share stories of job satisfaction that involve exercising these technical, creative, and interpersonal skills using a social-constructionist perspective, meaning that pro-dommes' subjective accounts of skill are taken seriously regardless of how these abilities might be categorized externally.[2]

Job satisfaction is not solely a feature of subjective interpretations of working conditions; we must also consider the gender, race, and class position of the worker and the objective conditions of work.[3] Most pro-dommes are white, cisgender, and college educated,[4] and they benefit from the privilege that comes with these majority locations. While roughly half of my interview sample identifies as lesbian, bisexual, or queer, their feminine display (high heels, corsets, makeup) affords them erotic capital.[5] Dominatrix work is a form of sex work, though pro-dommes benefit from less contact with law enforcement, putting them higher up on the "whorearchy." Research on skills in sex work often focuses on safety, such as identifying violent johns, avoiding sexually transmitted infections, evading arrest, and maintaining bodily control.[6] The professional dominatrix rarely worries about these threats.

Defining various acts as skilled, complex, and creative is important for correcting some misconceptions about sex work. Sex workers have long valued opportunities to be creative and form interpersonal connections with clients. Conceptualizing these as bona fide skills challenges the fear and shaming of sex workers in both public and scholarly arenas. By insisting that social-science concepts such as "skill" be applied to dominatrix work, particularly at a time when the dominatrix is becoming more visible, I further the project of destigmatizing sex work and attend to the parts of the work that promote rather than hinder satisfaction, growth, and self-direction.

The Study

The idea to explore job satisfaction among pro-dommes emerged from a casual lunch with professors while in graduate school. During a discussion on work, I recalled a story told to me by a dominatrix friend. My professors were surprised I was friends with a dominatrix. They were even more surprised when I told them I was friends with roughly a dozen pro-dommes. Participating in the punk and goth music scenes exposed me to BDSM through fashion and fetish clubs, and I lived in

New York City in the 1990s and early 2000s, during a boom in houses (or "dungeons") where dominatrices work.

Because I had valuable access to an occupation most people know little about, an ethnographer at the table urged me to study dominatrix work. Another professor asked jokingly, "I wonder what their occupational prestige score would be?!" This elicited laughter around the table. Occupational prestige measures people's views of the relative worthiness or value of jobs. Typically, doctors, lawyers, scientists, and professors score the highest in occupational prestige. I was struck by their view that dominatrix work having any amount of worthiness was laughable. Professional dominatrices are stigmatized like other sex workers because they receive money or gifts for providing erotic services.[7] Dominatrix work is further stigmatized due to pro-dommes' participation in BDSM, which can elicit confusion, disgust, and even anger from outsiders.[8] Friends working as dominatrices, however, described their work as personally satisfying and even highly meaningful.

Realizing I might be able to address misconceptions about the work, I began conducting in-depth interviews with pro-dommes in my personal network in 2004. I expanded my sample using the snowball method and by posting ads to Twitter and the dominatrix website Max Fisch. I conducted three more rounds of interviews in 2008, 2012, and 2021 for a total of thirty interviews with nineteen current and former pro-dommes and three clients. The last round included interviews with women from previous rounds, allowing me to examine changes over time. My colleague, Dr. Dina Pinsky, and I supplemented interview data with ten published memoirs and ten online blogs and published articles on the themes of stigma and emotional labor.[9] All sources of data were mined for references to skill, satisfaction, fun, and pleasure. This sample cannot produce generalizable claims about all dominatrices; rather, I am interested in the ways pro-dommes construct meaning about their work.

"Learning the Ropes": Technical, Creative, and Interpersonal Skills

The opportunity to practice skills that involve technical expertise emerged most often during pro-dommes' discussions of job satisfaction. Clients visit dominatrices for so many different scenarios that the technical skill requirements seem endless, including intricate rope bondage and suspension ("*shibari*"), whipping and flogging, sensory deprivation, genital torture, anal play, and medical procedures such as enemas. Customers seek dominatrices who are skilled at these tasks to provide pleasurable experiences but also to avoid injury and even death. Tying or suspending clients with rope requires learning how to avoid cutting off circulation. In interviews, several pro-dommes recalled a client who almost died in 2008 during an erotic pseudo-asphyxiation session.[10] Technical skills are not unique to the dominatrix; exotic dancers report greater satisfaction if they are skilled dancers.[11] However, sex workers are less likely to have backgrounds in BDSM, so many of these technical skills are learned from coworkers and formal training provided by houses and professional associations.

Becoming known for a skill contributes to satisfaction as well as the ability to make good money. Former dominatrices Sasha and Renee, both white and in their midtwenties when they started working in the late 1990s, became known as the only pro-dommes at a house who enjoyed and were adept at performing "extreme" scenes such as medical and scat scenes and the infliction of pain using whips, electricity, and "sounding."[12] Lady Karina, white and in her midtwenties and working in Germany, described excelling at a particular skill:

> I'm only [at the house] for one day, so the clients really want to see me. I know I'm extremely good with the single tail, which is something you don't find all that often.... I'm really good in inflicting pain in a very safe way, which is what a lot of the guys crave.

In summary, dominatrix work requires skill at technical acts such as rope bondage and medical procedures, and mastery of these skills enhances job satisfaction through higher earnings and a sense of pride in the work. Because it can take time to acquire technical skills, age works more in dominatrices' favor than it does for other sex workers. Older pro-dommes are rewarded for having more experience. Racism and classism do not seem to affect pro-dommes' ability to acquire technical skills.

The complexity of dominatrix work and the wide range of possible scenarios require pro-dommes to be creative and innovative.

For example, Mistress Vena's client profile contains fifty possible scenarios. Eva, white and in her early twenties, emphasizes the need for a variety of skills in dominatrix work:

> I realized once I stepped in the doors of [a house], that I was so naïve and had no idea of the wealth of possibilities that were available to be explored. I mean, I had some rope that I pinioned between the mattress and the box spring of my bed so I could do bondage and spanking and stuff. But it was all very like "silk scarf on the headboard" kind of thing, you know? Not really anything that involved any level of skill or any real level of risk.

Customers seek dominatrices who are experts in many areas to keep sessions authentic and interesting. One client reports that it is difficult to find "authentic, skilled dommes" who can keep his interest by "constantly thinking up new forms of humiliation and torture." Former dominatrix Marie, white and in her late forties, recalls that she relied on only a few default verbal humiliation scripts in her early years, but over time built up a repertoire that required "imagination and improvisation," particularly for those clients who want something she has never done before. Ms. E., white and in her early thirties, also refers to improvisational skills: "I like everything improv. . . . I do things that they want because they're paying me. . . . But I still do it my way."

Mistress Vena recalls an event that illustrates creativity, improvisational skills, and the benefits of experience: a panicked dominatrix called her into a session to help retrieve a butt plug from her client's anus. The dominatrix and her client had been trying everything to remove the plug. Mistress Vena laughed as she told them the plug would have to come out naturally and advised the client to relax over a bidet. They realized that "losing" a butt plug inside a client's anus could be turned into a torture session, which they named "going fishing."

In summary, expectations to engage clients' interests require a tremendous amount of creativity and improvisational skills, which in turn keeps pro-dommes excited about their work. However, those I interviewed had mixed feeling about directing scenes that perpetuate racist ideology, called "race play." Racism can influence improvisational skills by both limiting and providing racialized narratives. Mistress Vena recalls a Latina pro-domme humiliating white clients by saying "white men cannot sexually please their wives." Several white pro-dommes report feeling conflicted about participating in scenes in which clients want to be humiliated using antisemitic or racist slurs.

All sex workers need strong interpersonal skills, such as knowing how to talk to customers. High-priced escorts must have the ability to blend within a variety of social gatherings.[13] Similarly, because the dominatrix deals with clients with highly stigmatized and sometimes uncommon desires, most pro-dommes identify helping people safely and comfortably explore these sexual fantasies as an important interpersonal skill. Though these abilities have been previously conceptualized as emotional labor and therapeutic,[14] here I discuss them as interpersonal skills.

Marie notes that being a dominatrix requires "a certain level of acceptance of people who have ideas or desires that are outside the norm." Clients may not have told anyone about their desires, including their partners, and while they ask for humiliation scenes, they are also visiting pro-dommes for acceptance. Miss Troy Orleans, Black and in her midtwenties, offers her customers warmth and compassion: "I always say I come from a place of love. I love my clients. I love them for embracing their kink, and honoring themselves for going to see a mistress, and for exploring their desire." Blogger Renaissance Diva writes, "All I have to do is beat him at a steadily increasing level of intensity with a variety of different implements in an empathetic, caring way."[15] Further, sessions like cross-dressing, for example, are about giving clients a safe environment to pursue potentially secret wishes.

Most pro-dommes make clients feel comfortable exploring their desires by conducting lengthy interviews with them before sessions. Mistress Vena and Marie use a checklist of possible scenarios, which is helpful for those who are unable to verbalize their interests. Lady Karina finds that some clients are not yet fully aware of their desires, so she suggests role play to safely explore their fantasies.

Remaining connected during sessions is important to ensure the enjoyment and safety of clients, particularly during scenes of heavy physical torture or sensory deprivation. Being tuned in to even subtle changes in breathing is essential when the client cannot respond due to a gag or hood, or when a client enters a trancelike state known as subspace.[16] In her memoir, Princess Spider refers to staying connected to clients as a skill:

> He just needed a breather, and it was important of me to learn about this, otherwise I could have started punishing him while he was in this tender, vulnerable state, and that could have been extremely damaging. . . . Being able to read people is a great skill in this business.[17]

Like other pro-dommes, Mlle. Antoinette, white and in her late twenties, finds that dominatrix work is much more demanding than other jobs because of this mental connection:

> My responsibility during the time that someone submits to me is to ensure their well-being, both mental and physical. . . . I have to decide everything for them. You know, make sure nothing bad happens to them. You have to be here for every second that they're here.

In summary, pro-dommes report strong interpersonal connections with clients. While making these connections with clients is demanding, pro-dommes find it personally satisfying to provide a safe environment for people to explore stigmatized desires. Though not explored in detail here, forming relationships with other pro-dommes while working in houses also greatly enhances satisfaction.[18] Classism and racism affect interactions with clients, though not always in expected ways. Elle, white and in her early twenties, feels her college education is a turn-on for submissives because they are being dominated by a "woman who is intellectually superior or at least an intellectual equal." Sasha advertised her college education and ability to speak multiple languages on her website. Rather than hurting her potential earnings as it does for other sex workers,[19] Miss Troy Orleans reports getting more clients because she was one of only two Black pro-dommes working in houses when she started, though she benefits in scenes with clients by drawing from an educated, middle-class conversational style. On the other hand, Marcela, a Latina dominatrix in her thirties, reports playing up her "street style" to intimidate her white male clients. Both women benefit from adhering to traditional feminine standards of beauty.

Conclusion: Skill and Job Satisfaction

Interviews, memoirs, and blogs by dominatrices reveal high levels of job satisfaction. While pay and control over working conditions are important, all sources of data link satisfaction to opportunities to exercise technical, creative, and interpersonal skills. Though not explored in detail here, pro-dommes report other skills such as the use of financial software and web designing skills. Elle's skilled background in stocks and financial software makes her an effective financial dominatrix, or "findom." By studying sex work as we would any other occupation, we can hopefully mitigate some of that stigma and present fuller pictures of sex workers' lives and contribute to discussions regarding sex workers' rights.[20]

Despite stories of high job satisfaction, stigma and criminalization of commercial eroticism make it difficult for researchers of work to understand why someone might choose sex work, particularly how a person can find the work personally satisfying and pleasurable. As noted, stigma is greater with pro-domme work because of negative attitudes toward BDSM. Laws against commercial BDSM are vague and vary by state.[21] This ambiguity of commercial BDSM under the law protects pro-dommes from the more harmful aspects of sex work compared to prostitutes who engage in sex with clients. Though most pro-dommes do not engage in vaginal or oral sex, scenes involving anal play, such as fisting and dildo training, constitute "sexual acts" and are illegal in New York City. Though one of the pro-dommes I interviewed was arrested during a police raid of a house, she was released without charge. None of the pro-dommes I talked to are concerned about their physical safety when alone with clients. In fact, there was greater concern for the safety of their clients.

Typically, jobs that require this level of skill and complexity are seen as having the potential for high personal satisfaction. It is unlikely, however, with current stigma and criminalization, that the dominatrix would score high on a measure like occupational prestige since this evaluates how other people rank a job. Such stigma is apparent when we consider that tasks performed by pro-dommes are considered valuable in other contexts, such as acting, providing therapy, and performing medical procedures. For example, a nurse administering an enema to relieve physical pain is considered valuable while a dominatrix administering an enema for physical pleasure is stigmatized and criminalized.

Projects addressing stigma and satisfaction in sex work must consider the class, race, and gender privilege of pro-dommes and how these characteristics promote or decrease worker choice, autonomy, and satisfaction. My current research focuses on BIPOC and gender-expansive dominatrices to tease apart the effects of race, class, and gender on their work experiences.[22] For example, while racism may adversely affect wages for some, a Black dominatrix in my interview sample feels her race increased her and other Black pro-dommes' earnings because there were not many Black dominatrices and plenty of white clients wanted to be dominated by a Black woman. My research also suggests that middle-class conversational styles influence interpersonal skills, such as the ability to convincingly dominate clients, though race-ethnicity influences the types of improvisational narratives available to pro-dommes, as previously explored when a Latina dominatrix invoked a client's whiteness in a humiliation scene.

I am hopeful that stigma reduction directed toward dominatrix and other sex work occupations is ongoing. Because my research spans two decades, I see that over time the dominatrix has become more visible on social media, in mainstream online pornography, and in television shows that are not specifically about sex work or BDSM, such as Showtime's *Billions*. This lessening stigma might explain my finding that women interviewed since 2020 seem less concerned than women from earlier waves about people discovering their work as dominatrices. However, the attitude that dominatrix work is still unworthy is illustrated in Mistress Snow's recent experience in academia. Her mentor abandoned her after learning about her work as a dominatrix, asking, "Was it worth it?"[23] This experience shows why academics might prefer to work as low-paid adjuncts rather than as well-paid dominatrices.

The Internet may prove to have the most influence on the destigmatization of the profession. Dominatrices can advertise on social media, and they report greater ease at working independently and outside of major cities like New York and San Francisco. Though my interviewees all learned their skills in person, YouTube and other BDSM websites provide extensive how-to videos for technical tasks such as rope suspension, allowing people with no connections to houses or other pro-dommes to "learn the ropes." While Mistress Vena had her leather garments and props made by a slave, now "fetish" clothing and items such as floggers and restraints can be purchased on the Internet. Pro-dommes also worked remotely during the COVID-19 pandemic. Findoms, for instance, can easily work remotely because they can control clients' bank accounts by installing financial software on their computers. It is my hope that growing visibility and increased opportunities for pro-dommes, coupled with research and activism on sex workers' rights, will continue to lessen the stigma around commercial dominance.

NOTES

1 The vast majority of pro-dommes identify as women, as demonstrated by dominatrix directories such as maxfisch.com, ddimag.com, and dominaguide.com and confirmed by Lindemann's extensive research (2012). This research includes pro-dommes who identify as women, trans women, and queer.

2 For a review of sociological theories of skill, see Attewell 1990.

3 Stasz 2001.

4 Lindemann 2012.

5 Most clients are men who want to be dominated by women, though there needs to be more research on trans and queer pro-dommes.

6 Brewis and Linstead 2000; Chapkis 1997; Pheterson 1993; Sanders 2005b.

7 Some pro-dommes are also lifestyle dominants, meaning they have dominant-submissive relationships in their personal lives.

8 Levey and Pinsky 2015.

9 Levey and Pinsky 2015; Pinsky and Levey 2015.

10 The client was left alone during the session and almost suffocated. Afterwards, law enforcement closed several New York City houses.

11 Barton 2002.

12 Sounding is the insertion of metal probes into the urethra.

13 Bernstein 2007b; Sanders 2005a.

14 Pinsky and Levey 2015; Lindemann 2012.

15 Renaissance Diva 2006, par. 1.

16 Subspace is usually described as a euphoric feeling of floating that submissives experience during a scene.

17 Spider 2006, 107.

18 Barton (2017, chapter 6) finds that meaningful relationships with other exotic dancers greatly enhances happiness.

19 Jones 2015.

20 Global Network of Sex Work Projects n.d.
21 For a detailed discussion of the legal contexts for commercial domination in New York City and San Francisco, see Lindemann 2012, appendix B.
22 Levey 2024.
23 Mistress Snow 2019.

15

Not a Client, Not a Sex Worker

Dismantling the "Pimp" Stereotype

ZOEY JONES, STACEY HANNEM, AND CHRIS BRUCKERT

Like any industry, the sex industry relies on networks of people who facilitate work and provide resources and support for workers. Often disparaged as pimps, traffickers, and profiteers,[1] third parties in the sex industry are stereotyped as evil, assumed to be men (and particularly men of color) who manipulate or coerce naïve women into sexual labor.[2] In these imaginings, sex workers are envisioned as hapless women—passive objects upon whom sexual violence is enacted—rather than as individuals with agency, making choices within a context of structural and social constraints. This pervasive sociocultural framing is used to legitimate laws that criminalize those who profit from another's sex work.[3]

In this essay we draw on interviews with third parties and focus groups with sex workers in Canada to dismantle the stereotype of the "pimp" and offer a more nuanced understanding of the varied relationships between sex workers and third parties. Our research finds that many third parties are women supporting sex workers in a variety of roles and, moreover, that a significant number of third parties also (or did previously) engage in sex work themselves. We show that laws criminalizing third parties operate against sex workers' interests by impeding clear communication and preventing workers from accessing important protections and supports, while increasing their vulnerability to harm, violence, and exploitation in myriad ways.

The data that informs this chapter was collected as part of the Management Project, which endeavored to provide rigorous empirical research about individuals in the sex work exchange who are neither clients nor sex workers. The project was led by a bilingual interdisciplinary academic team of Canadian scholars. A Community Advisory Committee of four sex worker organizations provided valuable insights for project design and implementation.

When the data was collected in 2011–2012, Canada's laws prohibited "living on the avails" of another person's prostitution, "keeping" (or being found in) a "common bawdy house," procuring or transporting a person for the purposes of prostitution, and "communicating for the purposes of prostitution." The living-on-the-avails, bawdy-house, and communicating provisions were successfully challenged in 2013 on the grounds that they violated sex workers' rights under the Canadian Charter of Rights and Freedoms. However, the Conservative government at the time opposed the decriminalization of sex work and introduced new laws that largely reproduced the same criminalized conditions. In 2014, the Protection of Communities and Exploited Persons Act came into effect, criminalizing the purchase of sexual services and reproducing the criminalization of third parties by making it illegal to procure, to receive a financial or material benefit from, or to advertise another person's sexual services.[4]

The Management Project conducted fifty in-depth face-to-face interviews with individuals who work(ed) as third parties in the in-call and/or out-call sectors of the sex industry in Eastern Canada between 2000 and 2010/2011.[5] We defined a third party as an individual who for direct or indirect financial compensation or benefit supervised, controlled, facilitated, and/or coordinated the labor process (what they do, when, and where) and/or the labor practices (how they work) of an adult sex worker(s). The project also conducted focus group interviews with twenty-seven in-call/out-call sex workers who had worked for and/or with third parties in the same time frame. All the third parties interviewed were at risk of criminalization for violating Canada's prostitution laws. While this research was conducted more than a decade ago, the effects of criminalization that we describe below can be found in Canada today, as well as in other countries, such as the United States and the United Kingdom, where third parties continue to be subject to various forms of criminalization; in some areas, penalties are becoming even stiffer.

Who Are (These) Third Parties?

Counter to stereotypes, third-party work in the in-call/out-call sectors is largely "women's work." Of the fifty third parties interviewed, forty (80 percent) were women (including two trans women). The majority (thirty-nine) identified as white, four identified as Black, two as Asian, four as biracial, and one participant identified simply as "a woman of color." Ages ranged from twenty-four to sixty-two years old, and third-party experience ranged from three months to forty years. While we cannot know if our interview sample reflects the diversity of third parties in Canada generally or is the result of a self-selection bias, the fact that most of the participants were white, cisgender women highlights how the intersection of racialization and police visibility plays out in representations of sex work. The stereotyped image of the Black man as "pimp" obscures the prevalence of third parties who occupy more privileged social locations.

Similarly contrary to the normative framing, we see that the line between sex worker and third party is porous, with roles frequently overlapping and alternating; twenty-nine respondents (including two men) were engaged in sex work and working as third parties and thirteen were former sex workers. As in other labor-market sectors, sex work experience often led to third-party work. Workers leveraged expertise and experience to move into non–service provision roles (e.g., receptionist) or to start their own businesses. These career trajectories also speak to the restricted options available to sex workers given gaps in resumes, stigma and social judgment, the failure of mainstream businesses to recognize transferable skills,[6] and the lingering impacts of criminalization (e.g., criminal records, travel restrictions).[7]

The Varieties and Value of Third-Party Relationships in the Sex Industry

I think the biggest stereotype is probably that I'm exploiting the person who works with me, that I'm making money at the expense of hurting her or damaging her in some way. I think there's also the stereotype that she works for me. . . . In my opinion, I work for her by providing a space and providing

supplies, and she compensates me for that. . . . She's my client.
(Lilith, sex worker and in-call workplace provider)

As in the mainstream business world, third parties in the sex industry provide services that allow individuals to access skills and competencies they do not possess, avoid tasks they do not wish to undertake, free up time for other activities, and/or connect with individuals/businesses with whom they do not normally have contact. These relationships can be typologized in three ways:

1. The For Relationship. Sex workers may work *for* a commercial sex business (individual or agency) where managers (or the business owners) organize service transactions between clients and sex workers. In exchange for a percentage of client fees, third-party managers provide a range of services, including marketing, advertising, booking clients, arranging transportation, or maintaining service-provision spaces. Managers of agencies attempted to minimize the risk of criminal charges by presenting their business publicly, via advertising and signage, for example, in a way that obscures the sexual nature of the services provided. In-call establishments labeled themselves "massage parlors," and out-call agencies presented the fiction that they are escort agencies organizing companionship.

2. The With Relationship. Some sex workers collaborate or work *with* third parties who operate in various capacities to facilitate the sex worker's business in a mutually beneficial arrangement. Commonly, these relationships emerge out of the third party's other business ventures (often sex work) and are a sideline and secondary source of income. The Management Project identified five types of associate relationships in the in-call/out-call sector: agents,[8] mentors, workspace providers, event planners, and collectives.

3. The Hired-By Relationship. Third parties may be *hired by* sex workers (or other third parties) as contractors who are compensated on a fee-for-service basis. Services may include personal assistant/receptionist duties, transportation, security, or website and promotion support. Arrangements vary according to the sex workers' needs. For example, a driver's principal task is to transport sex workers to appointments. However, drivers may also operate as

a form of security and serve as an emergency contact. Some also hold funds during the call. Contractors exercise little or no control over sex workers' labor. Rather, sex workers usually have considerable authority to define when and how these third parties perform their tasks.

Each type of third-party relationship—characterized by decreasing levels of control or authority over the sex worker's labor—can be critical to how sex workers manage their labor. Criminalization has implications for the dynamics of each of these arrangements.

The Impacts of Third-Party Criminalization

Laws pertaining to third parties in the sex industry are often based on assumptions that all individuals who manage, coordinate, or facilitate sex workers' labor are abusive and exploitative. Though the issue is not without controversy,[9] sex worker–rights organizations increasingly advocate decriminalizing third parties, arguing that "the criminalization of third parties increases sex workers' vulnerability."[10] Indeed, our research found that third parties engage in strategies that they believe will reduce their risk of coming to the attention of police and being charged. Many of these strategies have the unintended consequence of rendering sex workers more vulnerable to violence and harms.

Criminalization Limits Communication

Several of the strategies that third parties employ center on carefully censoring communications about themselves and the nature of their work. Criminalization disincentivizes third parties from providing clear and legally enforceable employment contracts and from communicating openly about services. It also creates a situation where they are distrustful of sex workers who might be in a position to report them to police.

I've had issues with one girl in the past. My biggest fear was the fact that because of the laws, she could have reported me and then I would be screwed. And all the girls who are working with me would be screwed. (Brenda, sex worker and cooperative in-call agency manager)

Moreover, when procuring or encouraging others to sell sexual services is illegal, third parties are often vague or indirect during the hiring process. This results in misunderstandings about the exact nature of the work, the services to be provided, and the responsibilities of the third party. It is also in the managers' interests to withhold personal information from the sex workers with whom they work, including in some cases their real names or identifying information. Combined with the fact that employment agreements must be verbal, sex workers have little recourse to hold managers accountable if they experienced harm or if the third party is negligent.

Individuals entering the sex industry need to acquire knowledge and skills to work safely—effective screening procedures, safer sex practices, and crisis management are all vital. In the face of procuring laws, experienced sex workers hesitate to share information (e.g., via a mentor-like relationship), and some third parties are reluctant to train or offer advice to new workers. By contrast, in decriminalized contexts, like Aotearoa New Zealand, support, training, and information are understood as critical for occupational health and safety. The NZPC Aotearoa New Zealand Sex Worker Collective can educate and support new sex workers and openly communicate about sex work practice, unconstrained by threat of criminalization.[11]

One key service managers provide is communicating with clients to arrange the exchange of sexual services. However, we found that third parties in a criminalized context often use veiled or coded language to interact with clients or to establish terms and conditions. Not all clients understand the euphemisms; sex workers described having to explain services and costs and impose boundaries that the client was not anticipating. This resulted in, at best, challenging encounters with frustrated clients that could have been avoided had the manager communicated clearly and directly with the client at the time of booking. At worst, these kinds of situations result in violence and harm to sex workers.

Criminalization Constrains Workplace Safety and Well-Being.

I hate worrying that I'm going to get busted. I hate coming in the front door and having the feeling like the concierge notices the times I'm coming and leaving. I hate coming and leaving the space dressed as a hooker and feeling like people are judging me or know what I'm doing. I hate how I have to hide from most people that I have this business and this space because I'm actually really proud of it. (Rhonda, sex worker and in-call workplace provider)

The third parties in our research made decisions about how they operated their businesses to avoid coming to the attention of police. To reduce traffic at their in-call establishment and be less conspicuous, some avoid hiring in-house or on-call security or installing visible security devices like cameras; some prohibit workers from leaving the establishment during work hours (e.g., to pick up food); and some limit external hires like cleaning services. Some managers opt not to provide safer-sex supplies to avoid such materials being seen and collected as evidence by police.[12] "High-end" in-call/out-call establishments that operate discreetly, whose clientele are middle- and upper-class men, and whose predominantly white workers appear unexceptional in a "nice" middle-class neighborhood are less likely to be the target of law enforcement raids than more noticeable establishments (and particularly Asian massage parlors). As a result, some agencies limit the number of BIPOC workers, reducing racialized workers' options for safe work.[13] These decisions have negative effects on sex workers' working conditions and safety.

Further, while many of the third parties the Management Project spoke with were prepared to call law enforcement in an emergency or crisis (e.g., a sex worker being attacked), they were not willing to retroactively report acts of aggression, theft, or harassment. Some third parties also discouraged sex workers from reporting victimization to police for fear that they would be charged with prostitution-related offenses. As a result, predatory violence is often not brought to the attention of police, allowing aggressors to victimize with impunity.

The risks are with bad tricks and then not being able to report it to the police, because we don't want to be charged a second time. The risks are mostly with the police and the law. (Mielle, sex worker and out-call agency owner/operator)

Criminalization Prevents Sex Workers from Accessing Labor Protections and Establishing Collectives

Unfortunately, with this kind of workplace situation, there is no union or guidelines that they have to follow. So, it's really hard because sometimes you get the short end of the stick. (Leda, out-call sex worker)

In any industry, third parties provide useful services but can also exploit workers. Sex workers report that some managers impose unfair expectations regarding appearance (including body weight) and availability or demand excessive percentages. Some impose fees or fines for violations of house rules, or verbally abuse, sexually harass, or otherwise act inappropriately toward workers. However, unlike workers in mainstream labor sectors, sex workers have no recourse to labor legislation to resolve workplace conflicts. Workers cannot report workplace health and safety violations or access workplace insurance coverage if they are injured at work; nor do they have recourse when they are wrongfully dismissed or subject to discrimination. This renders BIPOC sex workers particularly vulnerable to racial discrimination in their earnings and working conditions. Conversely, criminalization prevents even good managers who do not abuse workers from establishing a legitimate business that could offer their workers access to such protections and benefits.

A labor collective is another means of creating supported working conditions. Membership in a collective provides workers with community as well as a mechanism to share advertising and clerical duties, secure workspace, and distribute the labor and costs associated with operating a business. In criminalized contexts, like Canada and the United States, all sex workers who assume managerial, organizational, financial, or administrative responsibilities (e.g., website maintenance, scheduling) are vulnerable to being charged as third parties, particularly if they are legally associated via a lease, bank account, or website ownership. Even in decriminalized or legalized contexts, the establishment of collectives may be impeded by licensing requirements, laws that restrict who can register a sex work business (e.g., individuals with criminal records may be prohibited from registering or operating a collective), and municipal zoning laws. For example, although the Australian province of New South Wales has nearly full decriminalization of adult sex work, brothels that do not receive zoning approval from municipal councils are still considered illegal.

Conclusion: Nuancing Third Parties

I don't want to get busted. I don't want to go to jail for this.
It's so ridiculous. I mean, we don't really make anybody
do this. . . . I don't want what's not mine. I'm willing to
work for every dollar I make. Thirty dollars is not a lot for
a driver—to go pick up someone and drive them and sit
outside at 4:30 in the morning for an hour in a car and then
drive them back home and then come back out six hours
later, do the same thing. This is a hard job. For everybody
involved. (Justine, out-call agency manager)

Laws criminalizing third parties in the sex industry imagine a firm line between sex workers and third parties that does not in actuality exist. The Management Project found that sex workers move in and out of third-party work and may inhabit both roles simultaneously. The broad scope of laws aimed at third parties criminalizes sex workers who assume managerial or organizational responsibilities. In addition, sex workers who provide assistance to an agency manager (e.g., answering the phone and booking calls for an escort agency, locking up at the end of a night in a massage parlor) or who help another sex worker, with or without compensation (e.g., sharing a service provision call, providing information to a novice, allowing their home to be used as a workplace, using their credit card for hotel bookings) are potentially subject to criminalization. Moreover, when a third party is charged, further harms accrued to associated sex workers who lose their workplace, their clients, and their collegial relationships; some find themselves entangled in court cases and potentially flagged as sex workers in police databanks.[14] Sex workers may also be threatened with charges, including contempt charges, should they refuse to provide evidence.[15]

The problems created by criminalizing third parties are exacerbated by the intersection of class, gender, and racial stereotypes. Because sex work third parties are stereotyped as racialized men, women who work as third parties (and particularly white, cisgender women) are less likely to draw the attention of police or to be suspect, meaning that criminalization disproportionately harms BIPOC and socially/economically marginalized individuals working in the sex industry.

> I've seen what happens to folks who don't present like I do, I've seen what happens to people of color and to visibly poor people, and to people living in the margins or outside the margins. It's horrendous, it's horrific, it's horrible, and I just know that I haven't been caught, and I don't know why that is, but I have to think that some of it is because I walk with privilege. And I can't help but think of it in any other way—I'm treated differently by law enforcement. (Lisa, sex worker and in-call agency owner/operator)

The arrangements between sex workers and third parties are more complex and, at times, more beneficial than criminal laws assume. Politicians and anti–sex work advocates claim that the laws that criminalize third parties protect sex workers and prevent sex trafficking (as with Canada's "end demand" model). However, as we have demonstrated, criminalizing important supports and services risks rendering sex workers more vulnerable to harm. These laws are deeply steeped in moralizing narratives and stereotyped beliefs about the inherent harms of sex work—including the racist trope of the "pimp"—and even couched as routing out the "evil" of sex work itself. Such narratives are most often drastically disconnected from the everyday working lives of both sex workers and third parties. Research consistently demonstrates that decriminalized contexts are the safest for sex workers and that criminalizing third parties reduces sex workers' access to protective services while offering no corresponding benefit. Decriminalizing sex work—including the work of third parties—is essential to securing labor rights and safer working conditions for sex workers.

NOTES

1 Bruckert and Parent 2018.
2 Hannem and Bruckert 2016.
3 Hannem and Bruckert 2016.
4 The bawdy house provisions were repealed, and existing case law was codified to clarify that a dependent family member of a sex worker (e.g., parent or child) would not be charged for materially benefiting.

5 The Management Project also interviewed street-based and strip-club third parties and sex workers; this chapter focuses only on the in-call/out-call sectors.

6 See, for example, Swer 2020.

7 See, for example, Michaels 2017.

8 Agents fulfill many of the same roles as managers, and so these individuals' roles (and the consequences of criminalization) overlap. However, rather than "hiring" workers, agents provide customized services to one or more independent sex workers.

9 Some sex worker–led organizations adopt a Marxist-feminist framing that views any profit from another's labor as a form of exploitation, inevitable in a capitalist context.

10 NSWP 2017, 10; see also the Canadian Alliance for Sex Work Law Reform 2015.

11 See Armstrong and Abel 2020.

12 Also see Anderson et al. 2016.

13 Quotas that operate against BIPOC sex workers also exist in relation to stereotypes about "demand" and evidence deeply embedded racist tropes that reify whiteness as a standard of beauty and sexual attractiveness.

14 Sayers 2014.

15 See Roots 2018.

16

Masturbating to Capitalism

How Findom Challenges and Reinforces Patriarchal and Capitalist Relations

JESSICA VAN MEIR AND HOLLIE ANISE

Money: Power at its most liquid.
—Mason Cooley

Mia is an American woman in her early twenties. Maybe she's a Latina college student working for minimum wage to pay tuition or a white new mom in a nine-to-five office job that barely covers childcare. One day, she comes across a *Cosmopolitan* article titled, "How I Get Men to Give Me Money for No Reason as a Financial Dominatrix."[1] The article describes a fetish, financial domination (or "findom"), in which men get off sexually from sending money to women. Incredulous, Mia searches and finds Twitter accounts of women making money from seemingly little more than posting a few photos of themselves and hurling insults towards submissive men ("subs").

She creates a pseudonymous Twitter profile, posting a selfie with a caption she has seen others use: "Fuck you, pay me." At first, she gets no responses. But after a week of posting photos, interacting with other findom profiles, and opening a Cash App and PayPal account, she receives her first "tribute," twenty dollars. Her heart pounds as she demands more, and like magic, it appears in her account. This is real.

For the following months, Mia spends hours scrolling Twitter, researching unfamiliar terms like "CBT" (cock-and-ball torture) and "CEI" (cum-eating instruction). She expands her knowledge of BDSM ethics, mandating that all activities must be consensual and emphasizing the importance of setting limits, establishing safe words, and administering "aftercare." After falling victim to a few "timewasters"—who convince her to dominate them on false promises of payment—she develops her instinct to distinguish genuine subs from scammers. With practice, she learns how to run a domination session by text or video call and gains confidence in her abilities.

As her skills improve, her earnings grow. But her PayPal account soon gets shut down for violation of its terms against adult services, leaving her unable to withdraw her thousand-dollar balance for months. Seeking new payment methods, she opens an OnlyFans account to post photos to subscribers and creates video clips for sale on adult sites like IWantClips, which take a 20–40 percent cut of her earnings. She must be on her phone constantly and spends over twenty hours per week answering messages and posting content, leaving her often sleep-deprived and burnt out. She sometimes faces online harassment—maybe racial abuse, body shaming, or unwanted dick pics—and fears someone could hack her account and "dox" her (expose her identity or share her account with her family or employer). She learns to take safety measures. She also develops genuine relationships with some of her subs and fellow Dommes and feels she belongs to a unique community. Despite findom's challenges, she feels it is worth it; after two years, she is earning enough to quit her other job entirely.

Though far from representative of all FinDommes' experiences, this fictional account represents an increasingly common story of women's entry into this practice at the intersections of sex work and BDSM.[2] In the past decade, findom has gained prominence in pop culture, frequently the subject of sensationalized press articles, TV shows, and social media.[3] Once an obscure practice limited mainly to the domain of professional dominatrices ("ProDommes"), findom has become a cultural fascination and common portal into sex work.

In this article, we introduce findom and examine its proliferation. Despite rising public interest in findom, few academic studies on the practice exist.[4] We examine findom as a product of late capitalism—the postindustrial period characterized by globalization, financialization, developments in financial technology and communications, extreme wealth inequality, and the increasing commoditization of all aspects of life.[5] These economic changes, we propose, have created both the social conditions motivating individuals' participation in findom and the technology that facilitates it. We further argue that findom simultaneously challenges, subverts, and reinforces patriarchy and capitalism.

Our research is based on informal conversations with individuals in the findom community, public social media posts, and further sources such as blogs, media articles, and published interviews.[6] One of the authors, Hollie, is an online FinDomme with over five years' experience, and our analysis is informed by her personal experience. The other author, Jessica, is a scholar researching sex work and cofounder of a content platform used by many FinDommes. Both of us are white cisgender women in our twenties.

What Is Financial Domination?

Financial domination is the consensual exchange of financial power for sexual purposes. Submissives, or finsubs,[7] obtain sexual gratification from giving money to a dominant or giving the dominant control of their finances. The dominant may also obtain sexual pleasure from the receipt of a sub's money.[8] Women dominants are referred to as Fin-Dommes and men dominants as FinDoms or Cashmasters. Although payment without expecting anything in return may seem irrational to nonpractitioners, the sacrifice of power that money represents is itself the sub's reward. In one finsub's words, "BDSM role-play with whips, chains, bondage is one thing, but at the end of the day those are just games which focus around male fantasy. But handing over your hard-earned money to a beautiful woman while being denied any sexual and/or romantic reciprocation is about as real as female domination gets."[9] Nonetheless, findom practitioners also incorporate other kinks into the D/s (Dominance/submission) exchange, such as humiliation, foot fetish, chastity, or cuckolding.

Findom can be practiced online or in person, as a form of sex work or within "lifestyle" D/s relationships. Many FinDom(me)s operate exclusively online, while others additionally offer "cashmeets" (where the sub hands over cash in a public place) or other in-person domination sessions.[10] Many others are ProDommes who incorporate findom into their in-person practice, later expanding to online work.

Here, we focus primarily on online heterosexual findom, a type of female domination ("femdom"). While the findom community spans the full spectrum of gender and sexual identities, and there is a significant gay male findom community,[11] the majority of online FinDom(me)s are young women, and the vast majority of subs are male. We explore how this gender dynamic both destabilizes and reinforces patriarchy. Language barriers limit our analysis to English-speaking findom communities, though they include many nationalities.[12]

The Rise of Findom

Financial control in D/s relationships likely predates the coinage of the term "financial domination" and has historical roots in other paid erotic practices. However, colloquial knowledge among the findom community suggests that the term arose in the 1990s as ProDommes incorporated control of their clients' finances into their practices and promoted financial servitude on Internet chat rooms.[13] With the emergence of social media and evolutions in financial technology, enabling pseudonymous peer-to-peer (P2P) money transfers through apps like Cash App and Google Pay, findom began to reach a wide audience. Google searches for "findom" steadily rose beginning in 2013, the advent of mobile payment apps in the United States.[14] The increased popularization of sugar dating with the launch of SeekingArrangement.com in 2006 may also have laid the groundwork for findom to gain traction; findom involves similar financial exchanges from men to women as sugaring but a reversal of the power dynamics.

Major economic events have also facilitated the spread of financial fetishism. Sex advice columnist Dan Savage draws a parallel between economic crisis and financial kink, commenting on Twitter in 2021,

> Our erotic imaginations seize on broad cultural events/traumas and the 2008 crisis combined with growing awareness of economic inequality—IMO—was the spark that set the Findom on fire. The [COVID-19] pandemic just poured a whole lot of gasoline on it.[15]

During the 2020 pandemic, many young women entered findom and other forms of online sex work as sex workers could no longer meet clients face-to-face, people who lost their jobs sought alternative income, and the global population spent more time online.[16] Google searches for "findom" reached an all-time peak in September 2020.[17]

"Fuck You," Patriarchy?

The rise in young women earning money from men for humiliating them online has radical implications for gender relations. Like many other forms of sex work, upon becoming FinDommes, women find that the sexual labor they already perform has significant economic worth. Young women, especially, may already engage in activities similar to those required in online sex work, for instance by posting selfies on social media to gain followers, obtain social capital and affirmation, or express themselves. The creation of these images can entail substantial time and effort, including doing makeup and nails, practicing poses, and editing photos.[18] When these practices become a source of income, how are young women's subjectivities transformed?

Many women describe how findom increases their sense of self-worth and raises their expectations from men. For instance, Cult Clare, a twenty-five-year-old Asian American TikTok influencer, explains, "It's empowering, particularly as women, because we're taught to constantly undervalue ourselves. Findom really gives you a space to say, 'No, I'm worth this much, and if you can't pay that, then get away.'"[19] Another white American college student asks in a September 2020 TikTok with 7.8 million views, "Y'all still talking to men for free?? get ur bag queens," followed by screenshots of payments she has received from finsubs. Findom challenges patriarchal power relations by not only requiring payment for sexual labor typically expected from women for free but additionally insisting that women deserve payment simply for existing and owe men nothing in return.

Yet paradoxically, while findom seems on the surface to challenge male hegemony, it simultaneously reinforces patriarchal relations. By asserting that men must pay women, heterosexual findom perpetuates norms of men as financial providers for women. Though FinDommes exercise considerable control in their work, often setting high standards for their subs, they must still ultimately cater to male desire. For instance, online Dommes must post sexualized photos to attract new subs and must adjust their behavior with each sub based on his kinks. One ProDomme, Nic Buxom, explains, "If you just stop at 'Put the money in my palm' you're going to fail because there's no reward for the guy.

There's a misconception that dom[me]s do whatever they want to men. But really, you're fulfilling his need, you're doing what he wants."[20] While findom challenges patriarchy by redistributing wealth from men to women and celebrating female dominance, it also reinforces it through furthering women's financial reliance on men, catering to the male gaze, and often upholding the gender binary.[21]

Online findom can also exacerbate inequalities between women. As in other sex work sectors,[22] FinDommes of color, particularly Black Dommes, must typically work harder to achieve the same level of success as white Dommes, often dealing with racist comments or undesired fetishization. The findom community often perpetuates white, fatphobic beauty standards and places high erotic value on symbols of class status and wealth. Dommes receive attention for demonstrations of extravagant spending on items like designer handbags and shoes, luxury vacations, or expensive meals. Indications of low-class status, such as asking for money to cover rent, may be ridiculed and garner a Domme fewer tributes.[23] Clients' fetishization of wealth reproduces class and racial inequalities among Dommes, as wealthier Dommes can more easily demonstrate lavish expenditures and invest in props such as lingerie or lighting equipment.[24] Still, findom can serve "as a mode of socioeconomic mobility" outside of wage labor.[25] Findom concurrently eroticizes and entrenches class inequality and combats it through wealth redistribution.

Masturbating to Broke: Findom as a Late Capitalist Sexuality

Just as findom challenges and reproduces hegemonic gender relations, it also glorifies and undermines capitalism by sexualizing it. While FinDommes' motivations seem straightforward, more challenging is disentangling why finsubs desire to give their money away. Findom epitomizes capitalist sexuality; not only is sexuality monetized, but for some, the transfer of money itself becomes their sexuality. Capital has become sex, and sex capital.

Within D/s play, submission can provide relief from stress and social pressures. One finsub remarks, "Findom is merely another form of escapism for people who struggle with everyday life in this bizarre cash- and self-obsessed modern society."[26] Submission may be liberating or stress relieving in its facilitation of the relinquishing of responsibility and power. If submission is willingly giving up power, then in a capitalistic world, giving up financial control may be the ultimate form of submission. Canadian FinDomme Goddess Macha writes, "What one thing gives a person the most power in this world? The answer is easy. Money."[27] Money both *obtains* (material comfort for the possessor) and *signifies* (social status and success). By allowing her to control his money, a finsub symbolically and materially increases her power at the expense of his own.

Findom also involves a sacrifice of patriarchal power, as money symbolizes masculinity. Goddess Ambrosia, a twenty-four-year-old nonbinary FinDomme in Utah, explains, "In the capitalist world we live in, money is so fetishized, especially by men. Men are taught from a young age that they need to be breadwinners and they need to provide for women, for their families."[28] In transferring control of their money, male finsubs give up both financial power and masculinity. Some find this humiliating, eroticizing the feeling of doing something "dumb." Others find relief from the burdens of conforming to restrictive ideas of masculinity. Still others view their tributes as a form of respect and worship of their "Goddess," obtaining a kind of altruistic pleasure from knowing they are making her life materially better.

In some cases, findom even adopts a quasi–"social justice" purpose as individual-level wealth redistribution. In their viral social media campaign #GiveYourMoneytoWomen, dominatrices Bardot Smith and Yeoshin Lourdes and feminist educator Lauren Chief Elk-Young Bear argued for men to transfer money to women as retribution for sexism and in recognition of women's unpaid emotional and sexual labor.[29] This conceptualization of tributes as gender justice resembles the racial "reparations" discourse employed by many Black Dommes. In an April 2021 *New York Times* interview, New York–based FinDomme Mistress Marley explains, "For me, especially as a Black woman, I see my financial gains as reparations." On Twitter, posts by Black Dommes instructing "white slaves" to send reparations abound. This discourse suggests that at least in some cases, subs may use tributes as a form of "recompense" for their male and/or white privilege, though the extent to which subs are motivated by social purpose versus fetishization of Dommes' identities is not always clear.

In providing subs a sense of purpose or escape from their daily lives, findom may also serve as a way of coping with capitalist alienation. For individuals whose earnings are a social marker of success, yet who feel that their work has little social purpose, dedicating their "hard-earned money" to a Domme repurposes every hour they work into an hour serving her. Not only does the sub get off on the waste of his work but sending can give his work new meaning. Bettering his Domme's life may provide renewed motivation for dealing with the mundanity, stress, and alienation of daily working life. Simultaneously, eroticizing the exploitation inherent to labor under capitalism makes it more tolerable.

Findom transfers the object of erotic desire from sex or commodities to the financial exchange itself. Only through the technological tools of late capitalism—fintech and social media—has findom been able to develop into active and accessible communities.[30] Without Cash App, for example, one could not know the heart-racing sexual excitement of tapping the green "Pay" button or the Pavlovian arousal response produced by the "ding" of a cash notification. These neurochemical responses, nel yang argues, are intentional results of capitalist planning; User Experience designers go to great lengths to make the use of their applications pleasurable and addicting, part of the broader "aestheticization of finance."[31]

Yet, in laying bare the importance of money as a source of power and erotic potential, findom also subverts capitalism, revealing financial exchange as potentially unproductive, exploitative, or even ludicrous. At times, findom parodies itself, poking fun at our culture's obsession with money, for instance through Dommes sharing photo-shopped images of themselves lying on piles of cash. Findom further challenges capitalism by providing an avenue for resisting wage labor—though it remains a precarious and stigmatized source of income.[32] Findom's relationship to capitalism and class inequality, like its simultaneous rejection and re-enactment of patriarchy, is dialectic, exposing its absurdity while also reveling in it.[33]

Conclusion and Areas for Further Research

We have examined how findom is a product of late capitalism that operates in tension with patriarchal, racial, and capitalistic power relations.

The analysis of this little-studied form of sex work expands on prior research on how technological advancements are changing the sex industry and contributes to understanding the economy's influences on sexuality.[34] It also highlights a new common entryway into sex work, particularly for young women. Further interview and survey data could better illuminate FinDom(me)s' and finsubs' subjectivities and how findom impacts their relationships to sexuality and work. Historical research into findom's relative novelty or whether similar practices have existed across cultures and time periods would further uncover its relationship with developments in capitalism.

Findom's reliance on fintech and social media also highlights the need to combat sex workers' exclusion from financial services and online spaces. Though we do not explore these challenges fully here, FinDom(me)s, like other online sex workers, frequently have their payment and social media accounts shut down or "shadow-banned," which limits the reach of their posts.[35] This discrimination limits FinDom(me)s' income and makes them reliant on adult platforms that take substantial cuts of their earnings. What could be a model of autonomous sex work is made insecure by these limitations on their ability to operate independently. In FinDommes' battle with capitalist modes of exploitation and patriarchal control of women's sexuality, the latter still have the upper hand.

NOTES

1 Ducatti 2015.
2 Margot Weiss defines BDSM as the "consensual exchange of power" and D/s as "primarily about symbolic power." M. Weiss 2015, 1.
3 Ducatti 2015; Hosie 2021; A. Weiss 2021. Also see Hummel 2019; Coady 2020.
4 A few exceptions: yang 2022; Yang 2018; McCracken and Brooks-Gordon 2021; Cameron 2016; Durkin 2007.
5 Mandel 1975; Jameson 1984; Hennessy 2017; Lowrey 2017.
6 We also obtained feedback on earlier drafts of this article from a cis male finsub, a cis male finswitch (who dabbles as both a FinDom and finsub), and a cis female FinDomme.
7 Finsubs are also referred to in online communities as paypigs, human ATMs, moneyslaves, cashslaves, or cashfags (in gay male findom), though some of these terms have fallen out of fashion.
8 We know of at least one Domme who claims to be a "timophiliac," or someone who is aroused primarily by gold or wealth. Many Dommes report finding their

"drains" of subs' money arousing, and those for whom domination is a part of their sexual identity may get sexual gratification from exerting control or administering pain more generally.

9 Ellin 2015.

10 Some Dommes also allow subs to visit their homes to perform chores, even having live-in "slaves" who pay to live in their home and serve them.

11 Yang 2018; yang 2022; @Master_Updates n.d.

12 The countries where online findom is practiced are largely dependent on ease of access to international financial transactions, and subs tend to come from countries where people are more likely to have disposable income, though cultural factors likely play a role as well. Participants tend to be from North America, Western Europe, the Middle East, Australia, and sometimes East or South Asia.

13 Informal conversation with a finsub who claims to have been involved in findom prior to its arrival online; Urban Dictionary 2017; Findom Princess Sierra n.d.; Bauer 2018; @Master_Updates n.d.; yang 2022, 142.

14 Google Trends n.d.

15 Savage 2021a, 2021b.

16 Drolet and O'Neill 2020; Friedman 2021.

17 Google Trends n.d.

18 Dobson suggests that these media practices by young women, including sexual self-representations on social network sites and sexting, "can be seen as 'cultural modes of 'survival' and 'getting by' (Berlant, 2008, 27)" in a postfeminist world. Dobson 2016, 2.

19 Weiss 2021, 5.

20 Ellin 2015.

21 Danielle Lindemann makes similar observations on the simultaneous destabilization and duplication of gender norms in her study of ProDommes in New York and San Francisco. Lindemann 2012, 3, 153–54, 162.

22 For example, see Brooks 2010b; Jones 2015; Miller-Young 2013, 2014; Weinberg, Shaver, and Williams 1999.

23 According to FinDomme Cleo Tantra, "Most slaves are turned off if they think the dom needs their money, and paying a bill for her may appear that way" (Chester 2013).

24 It is important not to take Dommes' demonstrations of wealth at face value, however, as many are well aware of this fetishization of class status and use it as a marketing tactic, for instance by buying designer items to take photos with and then returning them afterwards.

25 yang 2022, 175.

26 Hosie 2021.

27 Goddess Macha 2018.

28 A. Weiss 2021, 3.

29 Chief Elk-Young Bear, Lourdes, and Smith 2015; Schaffer 2015.

30 Margot Weiss similarly argues that BDSM itself is a product of advanced capitalism. M. Weiss 2011.

31 yang 2022, 8, 16.

32 The porn performers in Heather Berg's fieldwork similarly frame their work as a mode of resistance to "regular" wage jobs. Berg 2021.

33 For similar arguments on BDSM's ambivalent relationship to social inequalities, see Cruz 2016; M. Weiss 2011.

34 Sanders et al. 2018; Campbell et al. 2019; Dewey, Crowhurst, and Izugbara 2018b; Walby 2012; Hennessy 2017; Berg 2021; Brents and Hausbeck 2007.

35 Are 2021; Blunt et al. 2020.

17

Gifts of Desire

The Erotics of Gift Exchange and Sex Worker Mutual Aid

KASSANDRA SPARKS AND LENA CHEN

An eight-hundred-euro gold lighter. A jiu jitsu *gi*. A set of Meissen porcelain plates. These objects share a common origin story: each was given as a gift by a client to a sex worker. Today, they exist within *Objects of Desire*, a digital archive and physical exhibition series presenting stories of sex workers through objects. Curated by a collective of artists, anthropologists, and sex workers in London and Berlin, the collection includes expected tools of the trade (lingerie, sex toys, purses) alongside a variety of gifts—objects unique to the experience of sex work that transgress typical limits of intimacy and compensation. *Objects of Desire* declares the gifts to be a prevalent, if not constitutive, feature of sex work.

Drawing from Chen's research on *Objects of Desire*'s artistic representations of sex work and Sparks's ethnographic fieldwork observing sessions with New York City professional dominatrixes (Pro-Dommes), this paper considers the role of the gift in the sex industry. In the first part of the paper, we explore the circulations of gifts between sex workers and clients. Gifts abound in the sex industry, where they reinforce fantasies of authenticity and intimacy. By gifting to their provider, clients attempt to distance their relationship from the transactional or economic.[1] The gift articulates (and produces) their fantasy of their relationship with their sex worker—a fantasy that is always gendered, racialized, and classed.[2] This fantasy always genders material effects. Because the gift demands reciprocity, it establishes a social bond between the client and sex worker that not only appears to deny a commodity relation, but actually does so.[3] In the second part of this paper, we examine how sex workers respond to gift demands through the widespread practice of gift giving and mutual aid among sex worker communities. Here, the

Figure 17.1. Installation view of the exhibition *Objects of Desire* at Schwules Museum, Berlin, 2019. Courtesy of *Objects of Desire*.

very features of the gift that attract clients are leveraged in the service of building community.

Gifts Exhibited: Background on *Objects of Desire*

Created against the backdrop of impending legal regulations on sex work in the UK and Germany, *Objects of Desire* combines a material anthropology approach with more traditional curating to create an archive of stories and objects collected from participants. Though the curators were predominantly white, British/European citizens who could afford to organize the project with limited compensation, they attempted to reflect a broad range of identities when seeking out and interviewing over sixty sex workers who ranged from migrant street-based workers to higher-income escorts.

Artistic and ethnographic representations of sex workers often emphasize narratives of pain and oppression.[4] The *Objects of Desire* archive—which focuses on telling stories through objects—refuses such a singular narrative of sex work and does not explicitly identify the owners according to markers such as gender, race, class, sexuality, ability, or nationality. Contextual clues within the story, however, may hint at a worker's identity and experience. According to cocurator Rori, "Stories of diverse sex workers could appear without being tokenized or set apart from each other." Such a framework "counters the gaze of the viewer who wants to know if someone is a trans worker or a disabled worker. Those details are in the story if the owner deems them relevant."[5] In this chapter, we follow *Object of Desire*'s refusal to categorize workers to elucidate a more general analysis of gifts in commercial intimacy. Where necessary, we situate our analysis in specific segments of the industry and in racialized, gendered, and sexual realities; but we also intentionally speak in broad terms.

Gifts of Desire

Gifts are constitutive of commercial sex relationships, where the object of exchange is not an act but rather a fantasy. In *Object of Desire*'s 2016 London show, the installation *Eve's Mound* featured a haphazard stack of items given by a single client to a sex worker named Eve. The sheer quantity testified to a relation that could not be contained within the bounds of a simple contract, let alone "professional" relationship. The curators observe, "The physicality of the objects, their bulky and enduring presence . . . were more than a representational presence of the client, they demanded engagement."[6] As with much of the emotional labor required of sex work, gifts may encroach upon the worker's nonprofessional space, demand an emotional response or performance, and create a condition of indebtedness. Take, for example, this object from the archive, the Pearl Thong:

> [Jon] was going through a very difficult time when we first met. His wife had Alzheimer's and aggressive, unremitting cancer. . . . As a new escort it was unnerving as he barely touched me. He was a true gentleman and "courted me" with gifts, dinners, and surprise money added to my account. He started to call me by a totally new name, which got confusing. He told me that being with me was like stepping back in time as my resemblance to his wife was uncanny. He started to tell me

more about her. She was a model and had legs that went on for days. Jon treated me like a princess. He never had sex with me, and I think that is why the pearl panties came into play. . . . He believed somehow that just by wearing them I would be getting off on them rubbing against my bare lips. Or perhaps he felt he was being loyal to his wife by not having sex with me.[7]

Gifts have an erotic charge. For all of us, the gift participates in our fantasy of a relationship and draws the other towards us. When clients

Figure 17.2. *Eve's Mound*, courtesy of *Objects of Desire*.

give gifts to sex workers, they assert that the relationship is one deserving of a gift, enacting what Katherine Frank calls "realness," a fantasy of
reality that matters not "so much for its details or truth value, but more
for its ability to 'compel belief' in the entire interaction, and in the man's
fantasized identities."[8] Clients like Jon give gifts in order to believe the
worker is who they desire the worker to be.

While gifts may be fantasies, fantasies have tangible effects. Gifts support our illusion of who the other is, but they also impose an ethical obligation that tethers the gift's recipient to its giver.[9] Because we use them
to weave intimacy and relationships, gifts can transform the experience
of commercial sex for both clients and sex workers. Gifts can make a sex
worker feel held and cared for, with "good clients" proactively offering
support in moments of need. In her study of migrant ex-hostesses in
Japan who have married their patrons, Lieba Faier writes,

> Love was part of both the emotional labor women performed in these
> bars and the pride and the pleasures they found in their employment.
> In this sense, love was more than a strategic display of emotion (Bren-
> nan 2004) or a form of "deep acting" . . . for these women. Love was
> also a term for claiming selfhood and asserting belonging in a modern,
> global world.[10]

Just as Jon's gift demanded that his provider act as a surrogate for his
wife, many Pro-Dommes' relationships with clients are structured by
complex factors that can, and often do, include emotional intimacy.[11]

While realness and authenticity are at stake in all provider-client relationships, the nature of that realness is racialized and classed. Gifts can
confirm the sex worker's (often fictitious) claim to a certain class or life
experience, thereby participating in the client's fantasy of the encounter. In higher income brackets of the sex industry, clients prioritize gifts
with little to no resale value, such as flowers, wine, and lingerie.[12] The
less useful and fungible the gift, the less transactional and, therefore,
more intimate. While this can frustrate sex workers who have less use
for lingerie than for cash, home appliances, or technology, these useless
gifts confirm the "realness" of a relationship and the client's fantasy of
the sex worker.[13] Since higher-earning sex workers perform luxury, gifts
must always appear to pale in comparison to what the worker already

Figure 17.3. *800 Euro Lighter*, courtesy of *Objects of Desire*.

has or could have,[14] a situation that can be destabilizing when work-ers find themselves struggling financially.[15] For example, when Mistress Smoke, a white, queer, high-price-point Pro-Domme and kinky escort, asked her client for help with paying rent at the start of the COVID-19 pandemic, he instead sent her a pair of designer boots nearly equivalent in value.

For lower-income sex workers, on the other hand, the utility of the gift can actually bolster the client's erotic fantasy by enabling a nar-rative of white colonial masculinity in which the erotic value of the gift is derived from its capacity to "save" someone in need.[16] Anthro-pologist Kimberly Kay Hoang observes that among white backpackers engaging with lower-income Vietnamese sex workers, such clients often do not even have physical intercourse—the financial exchange alone satisfies their desire.[17] Sparks's research demonstrates likewise: a lower-income Asian ex-stripper expressed that her clientele were most invested when she needed them to survive. As soon as her situation stabilized, they would disappear. By feigning disaster to earn sympathy gifts, she even convinced herself of her inability to independently survive.

Not all gifts are good gifts, as *Objects of Desire*'s *Birthday Package from Splenda Daddy* illustrates:

> For my birthday he gave me a jar of marmalade, some chocolates, and a card. On the card he had drawn a portrait of me, just a quick pen drawing, almost a cartoon. It was of a photograph of me that I knew he would not have been able to see had he not known my real name and found my Facebook. So, there was this thing of having to sustain a performance of thanking him for the gift while on the inside thinking, "Jesus, how the hell did he get this?" It was a tough space to navigate, trying to keep the booking normal after that.

The card gifted by Splenda Daddy contained a threat to the worker's safety that the worker needed to manage to continue working. Precisely because gifts are so intimate and tether the recipient to the giver in a relation of obligation, malicious gifts can be challenging to accept. When sex workers receive gifts through troubling, upsetting, or even violent experiences with clients—or when clients give gifts maliciously as a form of control—they must find ways to cleanse themselves of that gift or cleanse the gift of its memory. In a conversation about such gifts, Mistress Smoke recounted to Sparks how an old client who routinely pushed her boundaries recently tried to reconnect with her by sending her one hundred dollars on PayPal. Her immediate reaction was, "Ew! I need this money out of my account now!" Another Domme describes such gifts as "ghosts" that need to be "exorcised." Frequently, Dommes perform these "exorcisms" by recirculating bad gifts as quickly as possible, often by treating other sex workers or donating to mutual aid funds. Indeed, Mistress Smoke sent that hundred dollars to a sex worker raising funds for housing.

Recirculated Gifts

As Mistress Smoke demonstrates, gifts demand to be paid forward, propelled by a drive for endless circulation.[18] Since gifts can only be reciprocated if one gives to someone else, gift giving weaves communities through relations of indebtedness. As the recipients of such frequent gifting, sex workers build community through gift exchange. The very features of the gift that attract clients—its capacity to establish intimacy, its demand to be repaid, the relationships it weaves—also enable it to strengthen ties among sex workers. Despite the limited literature on this topic, anecdotal evidence suggests that sex worker gifting exists across many sectors of the sex industry in different places around the world. Pro-Dommes in New York City frequently participate in wardrobe swaps, circulate gifts and cash, and share client resources. While not a form of mutual aid per se, *Objects of Desire* is a platform that not only offers sex workers the opportunity to share their stories but also leverages institutional resources to pay sex workers for sharing them.

Mutual aid networks have a long history in the sex workers' rights movement,[19] most recently serving as lifelines for sex workers in the United States who were excluded from COVID-19 relief packages.[20] Dozens of US sex worker initiatives provide housing, healthcare, childcare, and unemployment support in the absence of institutional support. In her discussion of Black strippers in the United States, sociologist Siobhan Brooks writes, "The criminalization of desire industries, along with intersections of racism, classism, and geographic location, adds to isolation of people and the disruption of communities."[21] Defying state control and discrimination, sex workers create community and foster solidarity in the face of continued marginalization and erasure. By recirculating gifts from clients and giving them new life in community relationships, sex worker mutual aid "materially disrupt[s] the hegemonically gendered economy."[22]

Though mutual aid is common within marginalized communities, sex worker mutual aid is unique in its prioritization of pleasure. Fundraising efforts and activist events often serve the dual function of redistributing funds and creating beautiful and often erotically charged spaces for community. Sex worker activist groups like Kink Out, VOW, and GLITS (Gays & Lesbians Living in a Transgender Society) host play parties, drag shows, and memorials that locate the act of giving within a vibrant libidinal and sociosexual economy. In the wake of the Atlanta massage parlor shootings in March 2021, Red Canary Song, a grassroots organization of Asian and Asian American sex workers fighting for migrant worker justice in Queens, New York, responded by gifting cash to sex workers for the purpose of booking generously tipped massages with Asian migrant massage parlor workers. By delivering resources to the sex workers most in need, while also providing sex worker solidarity and care for sex workers' bodies, this effort celebrated the pleasure in both giving and receiving—in the exchange itself. Rooted in the erotic and intimate nature of sex work, sex worker mutual aid efforts strive not only to redistribute cash but to create a world in which sex workers live well, beautifully, and in community together.

It is important to qualify this vision. While sex worker mutual aid may very well disrupt a gendered economy, it is nevertheless structured by inequalities and differences in wealth and privilege. Mutual aid is at best only "mutual" in the long run. And sex workers may constitute a "community" through the shared experience of erotic labor, but otherwise sharply diverge from one another. Our research suggests that sex workers—themselves familiar with navigating these hierarchies with their clients—often leverage their relative privilege as an opportunity for solidarity and as an obligation to those with less. "Our marginalization is [due to] how we monetize our lives," notes Fera Lorde, a sex worker and organizer. "It's a little easier to say, 'Well, I have these resources, so I'm gonna share that wealth and redistribute this income that came as part of the privileges I have.'"[23] For Lorde, the power differentials endemic to sex work are what animate the drive to give.

Objects of Desire similarly addresses marginalization and power differentials through the curatorial process. Though sex workers donating objects possessed varying degrees of privilege and disparities in lived experience, such differences were assets to the mutual project of "foregrounding sex workers' voices and stories and creating a living record of their artifacts."[24] Rori notes, "Between all of us, we could create a kind of consensus over how to present this information. Working collectively and having different people from different positions in the industry was really important." Rori continues, "We saw the project as a community-building opportunity, because even the people who were doing the

Figure 17.4. Installation view of the exhibition *Objects of Desire* at Schwules Museum, Berlin, 2019, courtesy of *Objects of Desire*.

carpentry or painting were sex workers. It was almost more important to have the money, time, and space to work on something together and strengthen our relationships than to actually show something at the end of the day." In this way, the exhibition—originally sparked by the relationship of the sex worker to the object of the gift—functioned as an informal avenue for gift exchange in the form of resource redistribution. Reinforcing social bonds at each exchange, the objects were transformed as they moved from client to sex worker to exhibition. At the project's conclusion, the objects that returned to their respective owners were no longer the same objects, having incurred new meaning through their journey.

The Gift of Freedom

Sex workers' networks of gift exchange and mutual aid recall the 1970s Italian feminist Milan Women's Bookstore Collective (MWBC)'s notion of *affidamento*, or entrustment.[25] Departing from the sisterhood approaches to feminist action popular at the time, MWBC proposed seeing power differences among their members as obligations: those with more have the responsibility to share with those with less.[26] "When the hierarchies of power threaten us, or tend to be reproduced among us, we oppose them neither with the ideal nor with the practice of equality, but rather with the practice of disparity in its given forms."[27] *Objects of Desire* was created through a network of entrustment: diverse sex workers contributing what they could, acknowledging the hierarchies and obligations that structured their relations, and creating regimes of value, meaning, and friendship through those differences. While prioritizing diverse representation through outreach efforts, the project's object-oriented approach foregrounds the circulations and relations that bind sex workers together. These circulations and relations among sex workers take form alongside adjacent communities. For example, Black women,[28] disabled people,[29] and the leather community (among many others) have their own long histories of vibrant community care networks, both inclusive and independent of sex workers.[30] Supporting this, Sparks finds that Pro-Dommes establish care networks for sex workers who share their intersecting backgrounds, and also leverage sex worker ethics when participating in their adjacent communal networks.

For MWBC, freedom is not inherent, nor something possessed or bestowed, but is rather a gift that must be continually gifted by one's community. "We bind ourselves in a pact of freedom with our sisters, and through them with the world."[31] It is through the "binds" and "pacts" established in gift exchange that we give each other rights and, therefore, freedom.[32] While sex workers also demand rights from the state,[33] they simultaneously gift each other their own rights at the level of community. The sex worker practice of gifting—as an always-unequal resource redistribution—points to difference, exchange, and intimacy as constitutive of solidarity.

NOTES

1 Zelizer 2005.
2 Ramberg 2014.
3 Mauss 2006; Bataille 1991; Baudrillard 2017.
4 Dewey and Zheng 2013; Tuck and Yang 2014.
5 Rori (*Objects of Desire* cocurator) in discussion with the author, May 2021.
6 Jeevendrampillai, Burton, and Sanglante 2020.

7 All quotations attributed to *Objects of Desire* can be found at the project archive. *Objects of Desire* n.d.

8 Frank 1998, 191.

9 Baudrillard 2017; Mauss 2006.

10 Faier 2007, 154.

11 For further research on informal "gift-for-sex" relationships, see Swader et al 2013.

12 Frank 2002.

13 While sex work often involves elements of fantasy and performance, this does not mean the experiences and emotions shared in this context are any less real.

14 Many Pro-Dommes resell gifts for cash after taking photos, buy luxury items second-hand but charge clients the full price, and share and swap items among themselves.

15 Hoang 2015.

16 Brennan 2004.

17 Hoang 2015.

18 Mauss 2006.

19 Mac and Smith 2018.

20 Herrera 2020; Hamilton and Webber 2020.

21 Brooks 2010b.

22 Hankins 1998.

23 Herrera 2020.

24 "*Objects of Desire* PR 2016," *Objects of Desire*, August 2016, www.projectofdesire.co
.uk.

25 Milan Women's Bookstore Collective 1990.

26 It is important to note that MWBC intends the practice of entrustment to be specific to women—implicitly, cisgendered white women. Moreover, while there is little documented on the MWBC's stance on sex work, given their commitment to a widespread rejection of women's complicity in masculine symbolic orders, it is likely they would have been skeptical of a feminist political project emerging from the sex economy. We acknowledge this legacy while also exploring how MWBC's insights might be generative in situations they either did not account for or even, perhaps, opposed.

27 Milan Women's Bookstore Collective 1990, 133.

28 Nash 2011.

29 Piepzna-Samarasinha 2018.

30 Thompson 2001; Califia-Rice and Sweeney 2000; Cunt 2021.

31 Milan Women's Bookstore Collective 1990, 145.

32 Milan Women's Bookstore Collective 1990, 147.

33 For a comprehensive review of contemporary sex worker activism, see Mac and Smith 2018.

PART IV

The State and Criminalization

18

"Beat 'Em at Their Game"

The Strategic Deployment of "Victimhood" as Resistance

LILLIAN TAYLOR JUNGLEIB

I never ever, ever looked at myself as a victim. I looked at
myself as somebody who there's a war upon.
—Alyssa (Black, twenties)

Tiana (Black, fifties) hushes everyone as she joins us on the old couches
and begins to read from the Return to Grace program's facilitator handbook.[1] The topic of today's court-ordered session, she announces, is
"Dealing with Stigma." The goal, she reads aloud, is to "discuss the importance of when to disclose our past in prostitution, and when not
to, . . . and how to deal with it while transitioning to mainstream work.
[It is] extremely important not to disclose our past when applying for
mainstream employment . . ." Tiana stops reading abruptly and looks up at
me and the five program clients in the room, who are facing misdemeanor
prostitution-related charges. As part of a new criminal diversion program
in partnership with the San Nicholas District Attorney's Office, they are
completing these sessions to avoid conviction and, in some cases, jail.
"You hear what it says, though?" Tiana asks, "It says not to disclose our
past when applying for mainstream employment!" She chuckles and sets
the book face down in her lap, indicating her intention to go off-script.

This diversion program is ostensibly designed to "rescue" women
from prostitution through a process of arrest and rehabilitation at Return to Grace.[2] However, program clients overwhelmingly experience
this carceral feminist intervention as unwelcome, ineffective, and harmful writ large.[3] The heart of the program is compulsory support-group-
style sessions designed to "empower" women to leave sex work. In an
interview, Return to Grace client Brandy (multiracial, twenties) critiques

the approach: "They're stupid," she says. "Obviously we out there for a reason. It's either because we like what we're doing, or we need to do what we gotta do to get what we got to." Most clients of Return to Grace do not want to leave sex work, and for those doing "what we gotta do," arrest and group therapy do nothing to help change the structural realities constraining workers' choices.

Tiana, though, is a rare Return to Grace "success" story. After Tiana completed the program herself, the program's director hired her to facilitate sessions. Clients respect and genuinely connect with Tiana, who is jovial, warm, and gives tough love. After placing the handbook in her lap, Tiana proudly shares her story of securing a job in the formal economy. Following repeated unsuccessful job applications, she explains, "I didn't want my past to keep kicking me in the ass," and so against the advice of the Return to Grace handbook, she disclosed her criminal record at a job interview—and then some. She throws her hands up now, mocking a helpless stance. "[I was] like, 'I was human sex trafficked! I was forced to be out there!'" Everyone in the room laughs, aware that Tiana was not trafficked. Rather, she worked independently, in mostly street-based prostitution. They understand that Tiana is mocking not "sex trafficking" itself but the way "civilians" (laypeople) think about sex work. Tiana repeats, "I let all of them know about my past, but I put a little bit on it . . . but to where they won't say, 'Okay, you lied to us, so you're going to get fired.'"

Tiana's experiences are impacted not only by the stigma of her criminal record but by her social locations as a poor Black single mother who does not have a high school diploma. Tiana is keenly aware of the cultural discourses surrounding her life experiences; claiming victim status allows her to subvert these limiting structures temporarily. This strategy worked; it was the first job in the formal economy she had secured in decades, aside from her part-time work at Return to Grace. "My whole job just feels sorry for me now," she laughs. "[Even my manager:] she's like, 'Oh, you poor baby!'" Tiana, of course, was not looking for pity; she was looking for a job.

I refer to Tiana's survival strategy here, which I will discuss throughout this chapter, as *strategically deploying victim identity*. Through this savvy mobilization of the victim frames, sex workers in the carceral-therapeutic system can sometimes overcome their circumstances to gain access to otherwise inaccessible support and resources. As Tiana summed up later, she "beat 'em at their game." A victim-centered framing of her sex work experience, by definition, denies Tiana's agency, and, arguably, therefore, her humanity. But ironically, by playing to this construction of a helpless trafficking victim, Tiana reclaims her agency and uses the label as a form of capital. Amid widespread cultural and carceral reframing of prostitution not only as sin, or work, but now also violence, Tiana can use the ascribed victim status in ways likely not envisioned by those outside "the life" who originally argued for its use.

Most sex workers overwhelmingly reject being classified as victims or survivors.[4] This designation is disempowering, infantilizing, and simply inaccurate for most sex workers from across a wide spectrum of experiences, who continue to make their own best choices, sometimes under constraining circumstances. In this chapter, I specifically explore how sex workers in the carceral-therapeutic system can maintain a fluid relationship to their socially and criminally ascribed victimhood, moving in and out of both agentic and victim/survivor roles.

These findings do *not* suggest that victim-centered policies and the increased criminalization of commercial sex are in any way beneficial to sex workers; rather, these findings highlight the degree of social and criminal constraint to which sex workers are subject under victim-centered public understanding and criminal-legal policies, as well as the resilience of individuals and communities who continue to adapt in the face of chronically unjust and continually shifting social and state practices. Through attending to the times when sex workers deploy victimhood strategically, I argue that doing so is one way sex workers adapt, survive, and navigate changing and chronically unjust conditions, "refusing" what historian George Lipsitz calls the "unlivable destinies" otherwise imposed on the most marginalized citizens.[5]

An Ethnography of Diversion Programs

These data come from a larger project exploring the nature and impact of prostitution-diversion programs and their effects on sex workers and their communities.[6] I completed eighteen months of ethnographic fieldwork at the Return to Grace diversion program, including volunteering at the organization and regularly attending diversion classes as a participant-observer. I also conducted fifty-two audio-recorded interviews with program clients, staff, and related experts, along with countless additional informal conversations. Additionally, I analyzed the program's comprehensive database of client records (n=504).

During my fieldwork, I actively participated in diversion group sessions. All of the participants were fully aware of my role as a researcher, participated in individual interviews strictly on a volunteer basis, and were given the option to decline to have their contributions to group sessions included in this research. However, overwhelmingly, participants welcomed the opportunity to have their perspectives included in this project. I balanced minimizing my level of participation and influence on the conversation with contributing authentically and open-heartedly. I routinely shared openly about my own life experiences, particularly surrounding labor and sexuality, with Return to Grace clients and staff. Although I sought to remain conscious of my status as a researcher, sharing openly about topics related to the program helped me and the participants in this research to build rapport, mutual trust, and genuine relationships.

The Rise of "Victim-Centered" Carceral-Therapeutic Interventions

The contemporary anti–sex trafficking movement has gained and maintained staggering momentum in the twenty-first century, resulting in the increased criminalization of sex work. "Sex trafficking" has a precise legal definition: compelling an adult into prostitution through "force, fraud, or coercion," or compelling a child by any means.[7] However, in practice, the mainstream anti–sex trafficking movement has expanded the term to refer to all prostitution. This construction frames prostitution as inherently violent to women and children, with the goal of abolition.[8] While sex trafficking is a real issue worthy of public concern and intervention, this conflation runs counter to a substantial body of research demonstrating a wide range of experiences in prostitution.[9] The classification of all sex workers as victims also runs counter to the voices of the vast majority of sex workers themselves, who call for "rights, not rescue."[10]

Victim status, and corresponding "victim-centered" policies, are now at the heart of a growing carceral-therapeutic alliance ostensibly designed to "rescue" women from prostitution. Feminist anthropologist Susan Dewey and legal scholar Tonia St. Germain identify a "punitive-therapeutic confederation" of law enforcement and nonprofit social-service entities that serve people in (primarily street-based) prostitution.[11] The Return to Grace diversion program is a quintessential example of this alliance. This strategy ultimately harms the population it purports to serve. It is rooted in core beliefs that (particularly street-based) prostitution is inherently harmful and that women in prostitution require "sociolegal intervention" through arrest, incarceration, and/or court-mandated treatment. The resulting interventions enforce the idea that the "problems" associated with prostitution stem from individual poor choices, rather than from mutually coconstitutive systems of criminalization, economic inequality, gender inequality, and white supremacy. This framing leads to a "solution" that focuses recovery on individual women and their choices instead of the broader structural and socioeconomic context that constrains these choices. And so, necessarily, sex worker resistance has come to be defined by resistance not just to designations of sin or vice but also now to victimhood. Sex workers have a long history of collective organizing to push for decriminalization,[12] establishing prostitution as a form of legitimate labor, and workplace protections. They continue to fight back. Tiana's story is just one small example of the myriad ways sex workers adapt to, resist, and continue to survive this new reality.

Strategically Deploying Victimhood

Sex workers like Tiana who adopt the victim/survivor identity can be understood as resisting, rather than acquiescing to, the dominant victim narrative; it is a means of surviving the very conditions of increased criminalization and violence that the antitrafficking movement has created. Due to discriminatory patterns of policing, which disproportionately target women in street-based and lower-end prostitution, as well as to stratification within the sex industry resulting in marginalized people being overrepresented in these hypercriminalized segments of the industry, women arrested for prostitution are especially likely to experience social marginalization and exclusion. This includes women occupying multiple intersecting identities as women of color, particularly Black women, transfeminine people, people who are poor or working-class, queer people, mothers, and people structurally excluded from work in the formal economy on the basis of formal educational attainment and criminal record. Therefore, women subjected to the carceral-therapeutic alliance are, by the design of the state, structurally excluded from access to financial and social resources. Accordingly, sex workers are forced to create strategies for getting by within the carceral-therapeutic system to which they find themselves involuntarily subjected.

Ana's Story

Ana (Latina, forties) followed her husband to the United States with her children. When she arrived, the conditions were far worse than he had suggested, and he was emotionally abusive. She started working in prostitution secretly until she saved up enough to rent a room in a relative's house for herself and her kids. She initially worked in street-based prostitution, and now also does in-call work out of a motel. Ana is undocumented, has limited help with childcare, is unable to read or write, and is a monolingual Spanish speaker—all of which make finding employment in the formal economy almost impossible, much less being able to earn a living wage.

When Ana enrolled in Return to Grace, a volunteer translator without much experience completed her intake assessment. After hearing her story, the volunteer was horrified, and characterized Ana's husband as her "trafficker." The volunteer then contacted Project Dawn, another human-trafficking organization with more resources, serving mostly transnational "victims," and convinced them to meet with Ana. She enrolled in a transitional housing program through this avenue and received a modest grocery stipend. Project Dawn also gave Ana information about a free legal clinic for trafficking victims to pursue legal status, though she does not plan on pursuing it because, as she puts it, "I wasn't trafficked, exactly."[13] "Me obligó," she says. "I mean, he made me a prostitute. Even if he didn't say, 'Okay, now you have to prostitute.' No. But his actions got me to the same place."

Faced with limited opportunities and few resources, especially given her immigration status and language abilities, Ana pursued the one course of support available to her—allowing herself to be categorized as a transnational trafficking survivor. She knows her circumstances do not meet the legal definition of trafficking, but she sees herself as equally in need of, and entitled to, this form of help. Ana says, "I did what I had to do [prostitution]. What else could I have done?" Ana understands herself not as the victim of interpersonal force per se but as forced to make choices under severely constrained circumstances. Therefore she feels comfortable, as Tiana put it, "putting a little bit on it," and strategically deploying the trafficking label to receive resources through Project Dawn.

Destiny's Story

Destiny (white, thirties) also used her experience in sex work and subjection to the carceral-therapeutic alliance to launch a career speaking at antitrafficking-movement events. The mainstream movement is led almost entirely by conscious adherents, or "allies," ostensibly working on behalf of people in prostitution. Sex workers and even trafficking survivors are largely excluded from the movement and typically only invited to share their traumatic stories to lend legitimacy to the movement, especially during fundraising events. Thus, trauma stories shape the dominant narrative of sex work by presenting the extreme experiences of workplace violence and harm as normative, obscuring the experiences of the vast majority of sex workers, and using this skewed representation to legitimate further criminalization of prostitution in the name of abolition and rescue. Anthropologists Joan Kleinman and Arthur Kleinman argue that these victim stories "transform" a person into "an image of innocence and passivity, someone who cannot represent [them]self, who must be represented."[14] Despite the exclusionary structure imposed by the antitrafficking movement, as I have detailed elsewhere,[15] sex workers and survivors nevertheless find ways to influence movement practices and goals from within.

Destiny insists upon "represent[ing]" herself. She had primarily worked as a stripper and in amateur porn, and also did some out-call prostitution work. "Call me a 'sex worker,' call me a 'survivor,' they can call me whatever they want," she tells me in an interview. "Some days were incredible—I'd be rolling in money. But other days were bad. Sometimes really bad." Destiny chuckles: "On those days, I was a survivor!"

Her laughter references our mutual insider understanding that the anti-trafficking movement generally, and Return to Grace specifically, intend "survivor" as an all-encompassing identity label, and that there is something irreverent about using the term to apply only to a specific day or experience.

After completing the Return to Grace program, Destiny was asked to speak on a panel of "survivors" at a human-trafficking symposium put on by a law school. Afterwards, she started getting invited to speak at additional events, eventually charging a speaker's fee. "When I was arrested, I saw the cops and the judge, and everyone else just thought we were all these helpless girls. They won't listen." Destiny alludes to a central tenet of the Return to Grace philosophy, which program staff call "unrecognized victimization":[16] the belief that women's rejection of the victim label is actually further evidence of victimization. As the executive director of the diversion program puts it, women who reject victim status are "so victimized they have been convinced they are willing participants in their own victimization." Destiny shares, "I do the best I can to tell them how it really is out there. What it's really like. What they should be doing if they actually want to help us." Despite her frustrations, Destiny enjoys working within the anti–sex trafficking movement: "I like showing them we actually have a voice. Whether they're gonna listen or not!" She continues, "By calling myself what they want to call us, I get in the door. If I called myself anything else, they'd all just act like I was still brainwashed." She stops and chuckles, rolling her eyes.

Destiny must fight to have her voice heard, but less so than many other women at Return to Grace. As a white woman who grew up poor but now easily passes for middle-class (in large part due to her sex work earnings), she blends more easily on panels and in rooms with politicians, activists, and members of law enforcement. Further, she was able to move up through the industry quickly, aided by her racial privilege and her conventionally attractive appearance, which comprise what sociologist Siobhan Brooks calls "erotic capital."[17] Those who speak on "high-end" segments of the sex industry allow organizers to further their claim that *all* prostitution is inherently harmful, not just street-based sex work. In other words, Destiny's experiences not only highlight a "trauma tale" of prostitution, but symbolically her white, seemingly middle-class presence also legitimizes the idea that "anyone can be a victim." This is a rallying cry of the antitrafficking movement to heighten public panic and concern, and also obscure structural factors, including poverty, white supremacy, patriarchy, and cisgenderism, that result in marginalized people disproportionately experiencing low wages, coercion, criminalization, and violence in sex work.

I went with Destiny to deliver a paid speech at a "human-trafficking awareness" event at a large evangelical church in San Nicholas. Organizers pitched her traumatic story as the capstone of the day. She did share her story, including experiences of violence. But she also used the opportunity to bring nuance and perspective to how "survivors" had been presented by the other speakers, members of law enforcement, and social-service organizations. By strategically deploying the survivor label, Destiny transforms the identity assigned to her. Her expert status can hopefully influence the movement from within and allow her to financially support herself now that she has transitioned out of sex work.

In conclusion, Tiana's, Ana's, and Destiny's stories provide three examples of women subjected to the carceral-therapeutic alliance who strategically deploy their ascribed victimhood as a mechanism for refusing unlivable destinies. As I have shown, sex workers use this strategy to help overcome stigma, criminalization, and other structural barriers, and to access resources. It allows workers to reclaim power in a system that infantilizes and diminishes women's choices.

Not everyone subjected to the carceral-therapeutic alliance can use victim identity in this way. In some cases, as with Ana, the opportunity is a matter of chance. Additionally, since the emergence of panics over so-called white slavery at the turn of the twenty-first century, antiprostitution efforts have been grounded in tropes of the white innocent female victim. Then, as now, this trope relies heavily on a racist and patriarchal construction of the "ideal victim." The further one's identity and experiences are located from that "ideal," the harder one must work to claim victim status, and for some, including especially Black women, trans women, and street-based sex workers, it may never be truly achievable.

Achieving recognition of one's victimhood by institutions creates another obstacle. In her work with survivors of domestic violence, sociologist Paige Sweet demonstrates that women have to work to accomplish a very specific version of victimhood to be legible to institutions and access services.[18] She finds that survivors are subject to a "paradox of legibility" wherein they are forced both to display their helplessness and to be self-efficacious. For many sex workers, adopting a static identity label to define one's experiences in sex work simply is not beneficial or necessary to trying to live one's best life within intersecting structures of criminalization, marginalization, and social exclusion. As Tiana puts it, "That whole trafficking debate thing is a luxury I don't have—I'm just living my life." Sex workers like Tiana, Ana, and Destiny maintain a transitory and multidirectional relationship to labels such as "survivor" and strategically deploy these terms not as identities but as opportunities to *minimize disadvantage* within a context of a severely restrictive carceral-therapeutic system. This example of everyday resistance is one small piece of a legacy of sex worker resistance, resilience, and radical joy in the face of increasingly criminalized labor conditions that promote structural and interpersonal violence.

NOTES

1 All names are pseudonyms, including of research participants, the organization, and the city in which it is located.

2 Although Return to Grace de jure serves people of all genders, in practice over 99 percent of program clients overall, and 100 percent during the course of this research, identify as cis or trans women.

3 "Carceral feminism" refers to the use of the criminal-legal system to achieve "feminist" goals. For more information, see: Bernstein 2010.

4 There are people who do understand their experiences in prostitution as fundamentally harmful and victimizing, who relate to and find comfort in a definition of their experiences as a form of violence perpetrated against them, and/or who come to firmly identify as survivors of trafficking or commercial sexual exploitation. These experiences are important and worthy of further discussion, though they fall outside of the scope of this chapter.

5 Lipsitz 2020.

6 For a detailed description of methodology, see Jungleib 2019a.

7 Victim of Trafficking and Violence Prevention Act of 2000, Pub. L. No. 106–386, 114 Stat. 1464.

8 While there are sex workers of all genders and ages, these public discourses are grounded in long-standing gendered notions of the helplessness of women and children, which continue to dominate cultural understandings of prostitution and resulting policy responses.

9 See, for example: Weitzer 2009a.

10 For more information, see Chateauvert 2014.

11 Dewey and St Germain 2017; Dewey and St Germain refer to this as the "criminal justice–social services alliance."

12 The decriminalization of sex work means removing legal penalties for sex workers, clients, and helpers. For more information about decriminalization, legalization, and the difference between the two, see: "Amnesty International Policy on State Obligations to Respect, Protect, and Fulfill the Human Rights of Sex Workers," Amnesty International, 2016.

13 Conversation translated from Spanish to English by author.

14 Kleinman and Kleinman 1996, 10.

15 Jungleib 2019b.

16 In my field notes, "unrecognized victimization" was a common phrase used by the staff and is a widely used among antitrafficking activists.

17 Brooks 2010 a, 2010b.

18 Sweet 2019.

19

The Harms of Helping

An Indigenous Perspective on the Industrial Rescue Complex

DANIELLA ROBINSON

In 2018, 2019, and 2020, the Canadian federal and Ontario provincial governments collectively pledged over $300 million to combat human trafficking in Canada.[1] Numerous agencies across Canada successfully applied for anti–human trafficking funding, leading to more antitrafficking support services for various communities. Antitrafficking support services in Toronto, Ontario, now include case management, clinical mental health support, group homes, crisis beds, and specialized support for survivors under sixteen. In 2021, the Ontario government funded an additional project that unites child welfare agencies and specially trained police units to better support children at risk of exploitation and street-entrenched youth.[2]

I consider this massive network of supports part of an industrial rescue complex, where indiscriminately "rescuing" agentic sex workers, survivors of sexual exploitation, and those considered at risk of experiencing exploitation has become its own money-generating industry.[3] My understanding of the industrial rescue complex builds on the important work of Laura María Agustín, who has conducted participatory, ethnographic research and has written about the rescue industry, pro- and anti–sex work arguments, exploitation narratives, sex workers, trafficking survivors, and support workers themselves.[4] Agustín's work critiques how many helping professions perpetuate anti–sex work perspectives, such as the conflation of agentic sex work with labor and sex trafficking. The rescue industry generates large sums of money from public and private donors, who direct how the money is used. The money is rarely given directly to the survivors and sex workers, who struggle to navigate systemic barriers, including lack of access to safe housing. Agustín argues that despite their public outcry over the harms of sex work and trafficking, helping professionals fail to make material changes in the lives of those they support.

I have a complicated relationship with Canada's industrial rescue complex because I work in the sector. I supervise a team that supports Indigenous community members considered "at risk" for experiences of exploitation,[5] survivors of sexual exploitation and other forms of sexual trauma, and agentic sex workers. I believe in the work that my team and I do—our services are voluntary,[6] and we operate from holistic, Indigenous perspectives to support community members to find balance in ways that are meaningful to them. However, I also recognize that we are one small part of a massive, heterogeneous entity of supports—the industrial rescue complex—that reifies colonialism, capitalism, white supremacy, ableism, and toxic benevolence.[7]

Building on Agustín's work, I define the industrial rescue complex as multiple helping industries (i.e., government, social work, policing, supportive housing), with different priorities, agency mandates, and funding expectations, collaborating to "rescue" survivors from "harm." Like Agustín, I do not intend to moralize individual motivations.[8] The rescue complex and helping professionals within it perpetuate systemic barriers by overemphasizing individual support while under-addressing systemic issues, including housing crises, poverty, concurrent struggles, and community desperation. The industrial rescue complex exemplifies how harmful the helping sector can be.

In this essay, using autoethnography,[9] I draw data from my experiences working in the sector to argue that the "rescue" agenda creates paradoxical, often violent, support experiences for Indigenous survivors and sex workers by erasing their agency and lived experiences. I explore how the rhetoric of worthiness impacts perceptions of sex work, sexual exploitation, and "rescuing" within Canada's industrial rescue complex. The chapter ends with recommendations for better helping-sector practices that holistically consider the need for individual and structural change.

Sex Work and Sexual Exploitation in Canada

The industrial rescue complex hyperfocuses on extracting people from dangerous situations. To determine whether a person needs "rescuing," helping professionals assess choice, coercion, and context.[10] The Canadian government defines trafficking as involving coercion or control of people for gain, especially financial gain.[11] The federal government is anti–sex work, which is reflected in the federal legal framework that informs sex work and trafficking legislation. Canadian sex work legislation makes it difficult for sex workers to work safely (i.e., difficultly vetting potential clients) because these criminalized activities must happen "underground."[12] Maggie's Toronto, a Toronto-based organization run by and for sex workers, argues that sex workers should lead legislative changes that affect sex workers.[13] When the industrial rescue complex presumes that all sex work is exploitative and only affects women and girls, it perpetuates systemic challenges that create more dangers and desperation for all citizens.

Indigenous People and Canada's Industrial Rescue Complex

Canada's industrial rescue complex is deeply interconnected with colonial rescuing and conquering narratives. In fact, "rescuing" people against their will is foundational to Canada's history as a country.[14] The belief that Indigenous people are undeserving of self-determination leads to horrific acts of Canadian nation-state sanctioned violence against Indigenous people, to "rescue" us from ourselves and "rescue" society from us. For example, "uncivilized" Indigenous children were forcibly "rescued" from their families and put into residential schools and/or forcibly adopted into white families.[15] The schools were rife with illness and all forms of abuse, including sexual abuse done to the children by the priests and nuns who were running the schools. At the time of this writing, unmarked graves are still being discovered. Eugenics-driven, colonial "rescuing" narratives are ongoing with the continued forcible sterilization of Indigenous women,[16] disrespect and violence towards Indigenous sex workers and high rates of sexual exploitation,[17] and overrepresentation of incarcerated Indigenous people. Colonial violence is inextricably linked to economic precarity, intergenerational trauma, and systemic racism, making Indigenous community members extremely vulnerable to experiences of exploitation.[18] I see this every day in the work that I do.

The Dangers of Rescuing

The kind of "rescuing" that is at the heart of the industrial rescue complex is problematic and can be dangerous for the people being "rescued,"
especially if the folx meaning to "rescue" ignore situational nuances, systemic barriers, and the need for wraparound supports. "Rescuing" is
grounded in ableism, distance from situational nuance, and a superiority complex. The industrial rescue complex presumes a lack of agency in
the people it means to rescue. While some people want the support, not
everyone who is rescued wants to be rescued. Sex worker Gabrielle Shirley describes how empowering sex work is for them and their clients.[19]
Rescuing folx against their will can be understood as a form of forced
engagement, which reflects the forced engagement survivors of sexual
exploitation endure.

Relationships between traffickers and survivors are complex. Survivor
Karly Church describes how traffickers identify the community member's most basic needs (i.e., food, love, affection), meet their needs, and
then create confusion by mixing intermittent reinforcement and abuse.[20]
When they are coerced into working, the exploitation is a natural extension of their relationship. The relational complexities make it difficult to
imagine ending trafficking/exploitation outright. A survivor may also
financially or emotionally depend on their trafficker. When they are
rescued from this relationship, the survivor loses their primary source
of financial stability and their source of emotional support. Sometimes,
survivors experience a trauma-bond with their trafficker.[21] When a rescue forcibly disrupts whatever relationships are present, it can be extremely distressing to the survivor or sex worker. I know many folx who
developed a trauma bond with their abuser, causing them to experience
suicide ideation after their rescue because of losing their partner and
stability (life, food security, etc.). I also know children who were sexually exploited by adults; they believed the relationships were consensual,
so their rescue was deeply confusing and distressing.[22] The industrial
rescue complex focuses on saving people from harm but does not always
attend to the aftermath.

Another problem with the rescue narrative is its focus on saviorism. I have heard countless conversations about workers wanting

to save the people they work with. The savior complex promotes a sense of superiority, encourages learned helplessness in the supported community members,[23] and can result in compassion fatigue for the helping professional. Saviorism also overemphasizes the power of individual action. To properly support community, equal attention must be paid to the systemic issues that create difficulties for so many people. For example, trafficking sometimes happens within families because they believe it is the only way to survive.[24] All adult survivors I have met say that accessing basic necessities (i.e., safe housing, food, mental health services) is extremely difficult, leading to desperation and eventual exploitation. Alaya Mcivor speaks about their experience of exploitation, which was connected to experiences with the welfare system, culture shock (after moving to a large Canadian city from her small community), and online luring. Similar to experiences shared by other survivors, there are also themes of trauma, isolation, and poor self-esteem.[25] Many survivors have let me know how worthless they feel—like no one cares about them and they are alone in the world. Each issue—lack of access to resources, exposure to systematic racism, family disruption, intergenerational trauma, and low self-esteem—increases vulnerability to exploitation. Saviorism does not adequately address these issues.

Rescuing Narratives and Rhetorics of Worthiness

In the industrial rescue complex, rhetorics of worthiness determine who is worth listening to and who is deemed worthy of support. I define *rhetorics of worthiness* as discursive categories connected to perceptions of value. Values are assigned to all people within the rescue industry, including sex workers, social workers, boards of directors, managers, survivors, and community consultants. These values reflect the same white-supremacist, ableist, and sexist issues that are foundational to the rescue industry. Some voices and bodies are perceived as being more valuable than others, and, therefore, have more to offer the rescue industry (i.e., feedback on how funding should be spent) or are considered more worth saving.

Worth Listening To

I am an Indigenous professional and am considered a well-educated PhD candidate. In the industrial rescue complex, my voice has value—I am invited to speak on many panels and advisory committees, where people listen to my advocacy as "the" Indigenous representative.[26] I am often one of the only Indigenous people in the room. In spaces where I am asked to speak on how I support Indigenous survivors of sexual exploitation, I notice there are rarely survivors or sex workers who speak about what it is like to receive services within the rescue industry. Survivors and sex workers have expressed frustration regarding their exclusion.[27] A few survivors have shared with me that helping professionals sometimes make them feel judged for being too emotional. Sex worker Lady Emmy writes that she finds it disturbing when her negative experiences in sex work are tokenized to justify anti–sex work rhetoric, while positive experiences are ignored.[28]

I once attended an anti–human trafficking–focused event that featured some of the most disrespectful organizers and panelists I have ever met. During the first day of the event, an Indigenous trafficking survivor (who had previously acknowledged themself as a survivor) wanted to share something or ask a question as a speaker concluded their talk. A conference organizer approached them and said there was no time for questions. Shortly after, a white academic raised his hand to ask a question. The conference organizer walked up and gave him a microphone. After a few similar instances throughout the event, the survivor left the event early and did not return.

Later in the event, two academics presented their grant-funded sex-trafficking research. They created a visual presentation to supplement their talk; they began with a slide that used cartoon images to illustrate demographics affected by trafficking. The cartoon images featured a woman with a feather in her hair and a short dress to represent Indigenous women, a woman with lines for eyes wearing a kimono to represent Asian and migrant women, a young white girl to illustrate children, and a young boy in a wheelchair wearing a cast on his foot to represent folx with disabilities. The researchers described trafficking as a terrifying epidemic and said that survivors "prostitute themselves," "put themselves into [bad] situations," and are usually "drug abusers." They made no differentiation between sex work and sex trafficking. During the question-answer period, I offered feedback. I shared that from my perspective as an Indigenous woman and front-line worker in the anti–human trafficking sector, their images and language were offensive and misrepresentative of the demographics they were trying to depict. I encouraged compassion for the vast range of survivor experiences and to include Black women in their analysis. One researcher laughed, and the other commented on my lack of understanding regarding the research process. I said I was completing my doctoral research, which also informed my feedback. The first researcher stopped laughing, while the second said they respected my opinion as a researcher and implied a future collaboration opportunity.

Overall, the presentation was offensive, violent, and inaccurate. The visual aids were racist and tokenizing; their language was violent towards sex workers, survivors, and folx who use substances. When they claimed trafficking survivors choose to work, they conflated sex work and sexual exploitation. Survivors of exploitation have been coerced—it is not their consensual, agentic choice to engage in sex work. Additionally, the term drug "abusers" denotes a negative perception of the person using substances. Survivors have shared with me that they hate it when people judge them for their substance use, as it helps them cope with their traumatic experiences. The presenters were disrespectful to me when I was "just" a community member; they valued my opinion only when I was recognized as a fellow academic. The event showed me how easy it is for some to access industrial-rescue-complex funding, regardless of how disrespectful and violent they are towards the marginalized groups they hope to study.

Worth Supporting

It is part of my job to network with other service providers to make appropriate referrals when needed. Unfortunately, I often meet service providers in the anti–human trafficking sector who know little about sex work, trafficking, or trauma. The ignorance is sometimes connected to a lack of empathy and situational understanding, which leads to service-provision gatekeeping.[29] One sex worker shared her frustrations regarding a helping professional who insisted it was impossible for the sex worker to work safely and refused to support any additional referrals unless they stopped working. In another story, an Indigenous survivor was advised to stop lying about a consensual experience with a well-respected member of the community. Her requests for support were denied, and the survivor stopped asking. These stories demonstrate how helping professionals can paradoxically create violent experiences by erasing community members' lived experiences and disregarding their agency.

I had an experience with an organization known for its barriers to service.[30] This organization's website highlights how "survivor-centered" it is and how its members work from a holistic perspective to meet community members "where they are at"—a phrase that is used to describe when a helper or their affiliated organization is willing to be flexible to meet the needs of the community members they serve.[31] Staff working there admitted to knowing little about trafficking, despite working directly with survivors. I recently learned that the staff members at another agency responsible for reviewing survivor applications do not have any training regarding the subject matter outlined in the applications. Ultimately, ignorance about how trauma functions, anti–sex work beliefs, racism, and ableist attitudes influence perceptions of who is worth supporting.

New Directions

It is irrevocably accurate to say that exploitation happens, often to the most marginalized people. The potential for harm is amplified when the industrial rescue complex has historically negative relationships with the community members it means to support.[32] When neo-abolitionists co-opt anti–sex trafficking arguments, they ultimately position ending all forms of sexual commerce as more important than creating a safer, more equitable community for all. Community support should be holistic and empowering.[33] In Ontario, providing genuinely holistic support means a systemic overhaul of poor housing infrastructure, food insecurity, inaccessible mental health supports, and inaccessible treatment facilities.[34] Appropriate services must be accessible to all community members, regardless of age. As systemic inequities increase vulnerability to exploitation,[35] the hyperfocus on individual service provision is counterproductive.

While structural changes are made, many helping professionals in the industrial rescue complex should also overhaul their practices. My perspectives are inspired by Indigenous epistemologies, which focus on holism and wraparound approaches to support: balance, relationships, connections, and emotional well-being. For helping professionals to be more effective in their work, they must see the community they serve as more than singular narratives. Regardless of role, all staff should be trained with different support models to broaden their perspectives.[36] They should also be supported by well-trained senior leadership because burnout rates in the social-service sector are high.[37] Support services should be comprehensively evaluated, and guided by both research and the unique needs of the populations they mean to serve.

For me, relationship building is the most important part of imagining any new directions. We are all so much more than our labels and more than what other people have done to us. Agustín writes, "People who desire to travel, see the world, make money and accept whatever jobs along the way do not fall into neat categories: 'victims of trafficking,' 'migrant sex workers,' 'forced immigrants,' 'prostituted women.' Their lives are far more interesting—and complex—than such labels imply."[38] New directions are made possible when we can honor this message and honor all the vulnerabilities, relationships, and complexities that come with being human.

NOTES

1 Taekema 2020.
2 Ontario.CA 2021.
3 The anti–sex trafficking industrial rescue complex ensnares everyone, with little attention to nuance.
4 Agustín 2007.
5 My mentors taught me that we support community members, not clients. We honor the communities we are all a part of and the relationships that sustain the communities. "At-risk" is highly subjective and broadly defined; in the antitrafficking sector, "at-risk" often refers to minoritized (i.e., Black, Indigenous, person of color, member of the queer community, etc.) community members, children and youth, those lacking access to social determinants of health, those who have intergenerational trauma, those who have witnessed or experienced violence,

those with developmental disabilities, those with substance use, those who grew up in foster care, those who have experienced discrimination, and those with mental health struggles.

6 I recognize that it is complicated to say that community members want my team's support. Usually, it is desperation that drives community members to access the kinds of social supports my team offers, especially when the person is in danger. Subsequently, though our services are voluntary, I recognize that many would prefer to not need our services at all.

7 I work alongside some truly incredible people in the sector, many of whom have had their own experiences with exploitation. I believe in the work I do, and I honor the teachings that guide the paths I choose in this work. My frustrations are with the overall rescue industry and the issues that sustain it—but more on this later.

8 Agustín 2007, 396.

9 To protect the anonymity of community members, colleagues, and organizations: all included stories are amalgamations of different stories shared directly and/or indirectly with me or are situations I was personally involved in.

10 Boyd 2017.

11 Public Safety Canada 2021.

12 Argento et al. 2020.

13 For more information about Maggie's Toronto's work, see, www.maggiesto.org/.

14 Joseph 2018.

15 Joseph 2018.

16 Pinkesz 2020.

17 Women's Legal Education and Action Plan 2020; Women and Gender Equality Canada 2020.

18 Olson-Pitawanakwat and Baskin 2021.

19 Shirley n.d.

20 Church 2020.

21 Church 2020.

22 To support survivors and sex workers of all ages and genders, it is important to take a humanistic, holistic approach that considers their complicated traumas and resiliencies.

23 Learned helplessness can result in ongoing self-victimization, where community members perceive a total lack of control in their lives and project feelings of success and failure onto those around them.

24 Murphy 2014.

25 Mcivor 2017.

26 I am Bigstone Cree and Italian and fair-skinned, which I'm sure makes my advocacy more palatable to some.

27 Van Der Linde 2014.

28 Lady Emmy 2014.

29 Agustín 2007.
30 The process is lengthy and asks invasive questions, which are retraumatizing to applicants. The organization requires applicants to relay detailed information already presented to them in other formats.
31 This non-Indigenous agency also coopted Indigenous teachings, despite having no Indigenous staff and being quite disrespectful towards Indigenous people.
32 Crosby and Monaghan 2018.
33 For me, empowering means gaining access to pleasure, joy, healing, safety, and culture. Empowerment is different for everyone, of course, but access is crucial.
34 Service inaccessibility has been amplified during the ongoing COVID-19 crisis.
35 Traffickers take advantage of struggles caused by systemic inequality. For example, traffickers will target young Indigenous girls in foster care, with promises of love, money, and caretaking because they know that youth is likely lacking those things.
36 Trainings could include sex worker perspectives, deescalation, substance use, harm reduction, case management, DBT and CBT basics trainings, trauma-informed healing work, and Indigenous histories.
37 Wacek 2017.
38 Agustín 1998, 12.

20

"The Police Don't Protect Us!"

Why Sex Workers Don't Trust the Police

KAYTLIN BAILEY

When I was twenty, I was a junior in college. My recent ex-boyfriend, who was thirty-eight at the time, tried to rape me. I had understood instinctively that I was in danger, suddenly alone with a man trying to reestablish possession of my body against my will. He was not trying to connect with me. He was trying to hurt me. And he did. I grabbed a kitchen knife, which startled him, and so I was able to flee.

I called the police almost immediately. Despite our history together, this man did not have the right to hold me down and shove his fingers into me while I said, and then screamed, "Stop that!" and "No!" I had written papers articulating my hard-won right to decide with whom, and for what reasons, I had sex. I knew, for example, that marital rape in this country had been illegal in all states since 1993. This assault was not my fault, and reporting it to law enforcement was the first step I should take to pursue justice. I felt confident that the law was on my side.

Part of my confidence came from the fact that I am a white, cis citizen of the United States. I come from a comfortable middle-class family. I was raised to believe that the police were there to protect me.

I was wrong.

Two cops arrived at the cheap apartment I shared with five other people in downtown Charleston, South Carolina, and took a statement from me. A detective arrived the next morning. I repeated my statement. I confirmed the details: "Yes, he put his fingers inside me." "Yes, I told him to stop." "Yes, we had been intimate before." The detective took some notes, but he wasn't anything like the D.A.R.E. officer who had come to my school in the fifth grade, or the cops on the TV show *Law & Order*. He said, "Look, if you really want to do this—I can go pick this guy up right now. But in my experience, these 'he said, she said' situations, they never get prosecuted."

I kept expecting this detective to have more options for me. But there were only two—insist on having my ex arrested, handcuffed, and prosecuted for criminal rape or pretend that nothing happened. Hold his secret and make it mine. I decided not to prosecute. Nothing I have learned about our criminal legal system in the last decade has led me to believe that I should have.

* * *

Drawing on my past personal experience as an escort, conversations with current and former sex workers, experts, extensive research, an intimate focus group, and interviews with sex worker advocates across the country, this essay discusses sex workers' experiences with policing, some of the reasons why policing cannot address violence, and alternatives that can help.

Despite lip service about trying to protect sex workers through antitrafficking policies, evidence consistently shows that sex workers face daily harassment and violence from the police, including blackmail, beatings, and rape, as well as being denied access to justice.[1] Far from being an exception, sex workers are just one subculture within a wide range of people whom the police fail to protect. The criminal legal system in the United States is organized to protect those in power. The first professional police officers in the United States were hired to protect property, not people. Merchants in the rapidly industrializing Northeast in the early 1800s hired security to protect their cargo while it sat in ports. Starting in the 1830s, state-funded police departments continued this work. In the South, the first police officers hunted enslaved people who were running away, repressed uprisings, and later enforced segregation.[2] Publicly funded police departments were sold to the American people as a public service, "to protect and serve." But the criminal legal system was designed not to help communities thrive but rather to control poor people and to protect the property of those in power.

The first antiprostitution law in this country was also its first anti-immigration law. The Page Act of 1875 barred Chinese women from immigrating to the United States for "immoral purposes." Community leaders at the time feared that these women would "infect" cities both morally and literally. Racist anxieties that recently emancipated Black men and immigrant men were forcing white women into sexual slavery culminated in the 1910 Mann Act, also known as the White Slave Act. This national law made it a felony to transport women across state lines for "immoral purposes." Both laws targeted women's "morality" as a way to police minority and immigrant communities. Over the next century, authorities aggressively policed prostitution and interracial couples while ignoring domestic violence, acquaintance rape, and the rampant sexual violence that white men perpetuated against vulnerable and unprotected women. These laws do not protect vulnerable people; they protect perpetrators.

Today, one-third of all US adults are under some form of criminal justice supervision, through current or prior felony offenses, misdemeanors, arrests, parole, or supervision by specialty courts or alternative treatment programs, and a disproportionate number of these people are from minority groups. Funding for all sorts of health, economic, and social-support programs is now funneled into institutions designed for "crime control," disproportionately impacting poor neighborhoods and people of color.[3] Across the country, defending "law and order" means repressing marginalized communities; Black, immigrant, indigenous, LGBTQ+, and "notorious" women. These racist, paternalistic ideas have permeated police departments since their inception, hindered their ability to protect those in need, and continue to inform policing practices today. And this is why sex workers, and most vulnerable groups, do not go to the police for help.

* * *

I worked as a full-service hourly escort in Raleigh, North Carolina, from 2004 to 2005 and returned to sex work ten years later to supplement my sporadic income as a writer and performer in New York City. Other than the interaction when I was twenty, I had no further experience with police. I started talking about my experiences in the sex industry when I was working as a stand-up comic, and that is how I met Ceyenne Doroshow. We were booked on the same show back in 2016. Ceyenne is also an activist, organizer, community-based researcher, and public figure in the trans and sex worker–rights movements. As the founder and executive director of Gays and Lesbians in a Transgender Society (G.L.I.T.S.), she provides holistic care to LGBTQ sex workers while serving on the following boards: Sex Worker Outreach Project (SWOP-USA), Caribbean Equality Project, Sharmus Outlaw Advocacy and Rights (SOAR) Institute, and New York Transgender Advocacy Group (NYTAG). She works with Decriminalize Sex Work (DSW), a national advocacy organization.

Ceyenne introduced me to a network of organizers who were working to change laws to protect sex workers and their communities from police violence. They inspired my own activism. In 2017, I started *The Oldest Profession Podcast*, where each episode tells the story of a different sex worker from the past. I developed an appreciation for our history of multigenerational resistance. I transitioned from telling my own story in comedy clubs to sharing at conferences and public hearings. I became the director of communications for Decriminalize Sex Work, and eventually founded Old Pros in 2020, a nonprofit media organization creating conditions to change the status of sex workers in society.

The Network of Sex Work Projects (NSWP), a global organization of national sex worker–based research projects,[4] hired me to write a report about sex workers' access to justice in the United States. This is why, on July 30, 2019, Ceyenne, three other sex workers, and I sat around Ceyenne's kitchen table in Queens to record a conversation about the police, the criminal legal system, and victims' services in the United States of America for this report. In addition to these conversations, I also spoke to over forty US sex worker activists at the 2019 Woodhull's Foundation's Summit for Sexual Freedom.[5] All forty shared a pervasive, paralyzing fear of the police and their accomplices that left them with few resources to deal with sexual violence and indeed made them more vulnerable to that outcome.

The five of us who sat around Ceyenne's kitchen table that night had all worked in different parts of the industry. I introduced myself as a thirty-two-year-old, white, cis woman. When I worked as an escort, I saw clients primarily in hotel rooms and occasionally at their homes. Ceyenne is a Black trans woman in her midfifties. When asked about the details of her work, she replies simply, "I am a whore." Madeline, twenty-three, who is white and identifies as nonbinary with no sexual preference, works primarily as a "camgirl" from their home. Scout, thirty-one, is white, gender-nonconforming, and identifies as queer. They primarily do out-calls. Danielle, forty-four, is a straight Black cis woman. She identifies not as a sex worker but as an entrepreneur. She also identifies as "a proud Black girl from the inner city who worked her way up." She continues, "I am the child of slaves. My great-grandmother was the first free slave in my family."

Everyone in the room knew someone who had been raped or robbed by a law enforcement officer. Danielle felt that most of her interactions with cops were "just the way poor, Black people are policed." At any given moment, she has five or six friends or family members incarcerated, which makes dealing with the criminal legal system a daily ordeal. Scout and Madeline piped in, guessing that they know someone, a friend, family member, or acquaintance, who gets arrested about three times a month. "It's a culture," explained Danielle. Scout, Ceyenne, and Danielle all reported unnecessarily rough treatment, tight handcuffs, and name calling during their arrests.

It was these traumatic experiences that reinforced the belief that law enforcement, and many forms of institutional government assistance, perpetuate more violence than they prevent. Almost everyone had been a victim—assaulted, raped, or robbed outside of sex work. Anyone who did call the police regretted that choice. They all echoed the sentiment that no matter what was happening to them, the police would make it worse.

Ceyenne described a violent assault by an ex-boyfriend that occurred in her own home. Her neighbors called the police and when they arrived, Ceyenne was arrested and they called her "that thing." She spent seventeen hours shackled, alone at the police station, with shards of glass in her head and body. She attributed this treatment to her race, gender identity, and known status as a sex worker. Her ex-boyfriend got to go home.

After hearing her story, I asked, "Is this . . . a common experience?" All four immediately nodded yes. "We could be 100 percent right. The justice system is not designed to take care of us," Ceyenne explained.

While Scout was attempting to report a sexual assault, the police began grilling them about a separate Child Protective Services (CPS) report showing up on their screen that mentioned sex work and an incident of being a victim of sexual assault from their childhood that they had then chosen to withdraw. Surprised that this old information was still available, Scout understood immediately that now the police saw them as an unreliable witness to their own rape. Police never investigated or processed the rape kit. Scout never again reached out to law enforcement, even after suffering further assaults. The suspect in their rape was later arrested for an unrelated attempted murder.

In a 2003 study conducted by the Sex Workers Project at the Urban Justice Center, 80 percent of sex workers interviewed had experienced or been threatened with violence, the overwhelming majority of whom would not report that violence to the police. The police themselves had victimized 27 percent of the sex workers interviewed. "Sex worker, queer, Black, Black woman, all of our communities have told us our whole lives 'don't trust the police.' And they were right," explained Scout.

We shifted our discussion to victims' services, which generally include social and financial services for victims of violent crimes including rape, trafficking, and domestic violence. Despite their intentions, many of these services perpetuate the same racism and violence as police. Even when social-service providers do not hand over their clients to the police, they often mimic their tactics and attitudes.

In the United States, sex work is often linked to human trafficking, with sex workers being portrayed as victims needing rescue. But sexual and labor exploitation is rarely a simple story of victims and villains. While intended to help those coerced to sell sex, this approach shifts services toward punishing offenders rather than assisting sex workers and those who are coerced, and in the end reduces their agency, autonomy, and ability to advocate. Mirroring nineteenth-century "white slavery" panics, the current trafficking hysteria justifies violent policing of minority communities to "protect" white women. Nonprofits see arresting "helpless" sex workers as necessary to ensure that they exit the industry. Some services require a victim to cooperate with prosecutors and depend on labeling arrested workers as "victims" to keep their funding. This interdependence between social services and law enforcement creates a widespread fear of institutional authority among sex workers.

I asked the group at the table, "Do sex workers who have been raped, trafficked, or experienced domestic violence have access to victims' services?" In unison, everyone said, "No." The most often reported reason is that doing so would put them in contact with police. Even if not affiliated with police, many services are financially inaccessible despite sliding-scale pricing. Ceyenne and Scout observed that victim services frequently shame sex workers.

Many jurisdictions across the United States have created human trafficking diversion courts intended as alternatives to incarceration, sentencing an offender to programs and classes. These courts only address prostitution, ignoring other forms of coerced labor in agriculture, domestic labor, hospitality, and construction. These services are being funded by law enforcement; police are gatekeepers to them. A Yale University and Sex Workers Project analysis found that these courts rarely addressed sex workers' structural needs. Programs monitor personal relationships, prioritize quitting sex work over basic needs like housing and healthcare, and often require free labor or involvement in religious organizations that operate like gay conversion camps.[6] For example, a single mother had to drop out of college to attend "classes" shaming her for doing sex work to support her family. Participants I spoke with felt more like prisoners than clients. These punitive approaches hurt the very people that services claim they want to help.

The best example of this dichotomy is the Fight Online Sex Trafficking Act (FOSTA) and the Stop Enabling Sex Trafficking Act (SESTA). Framed as an anti–sex trafficking effort, this 2018 law holds platforms criminally and civilly liable for user posts seen as promoting sex trafficking. As a result, online services broadly began to censor all sexual content, fearing it might be misconstrued as supporting trafficking. The online spaces that sex workers used to use to connect with clients and with each other immediately disappeared. These laws destabilized sex workers, exacerbated antitrafficking hysteria, and further empowered criminal legal systems, immigration detention centers, and an increasingly militarized police force. In every community I visited, all over the country, sex workers are scared.

Everyone at Ceyenne's table believed that labor conditions have worsened, and that violence and deaths have increased after FOSTA/SESTA. Ceyenne said, "You haven't seen numbers like this in a generation. But after FOSTA/SESTA, the rapists, the pimps, and predators came back out. Trans deaths large, rapes large, abuse large, domestic violence large." She feels everything is getting worse for every marginalized community all at once: sex workers, immigrants, indigenous people, racial and religious minorities, women, and the LGBTQ+ community. Everyone.

The sex worker-rights movement today exists in large part because of SESTA/FOSTA and the coalition building that happened in its wake.

Nevada is the one state in the nation with a limited number of legal licensed brothels operating in a few rural counties. The brothels are mostly owned by men, workers must register with the local sheriff for a permit, and they must follow a confusing combination of state, county, and house rules that can leave workers feeling disempowered and exploited.

I questioned sex worker activists from Nevada about whether they felt women working in legal brothels had more access to justice, and they all simply said, "No." One young legal brothel worker said management discouraged her from reporting a client who sexually assaulted her to law enforcement or discussing it with her colleagues. A lack of rights for independent contractors of any type, coupled with whorephobia, the relative power of brothel owners, and the prejudice of law enforcement all conspire to keep sex workers from reporting crimes, whether the crime be domestic violence, a predatory manager, or an abusive client. Because dense urban areas, including Las Vegas and Reno, still criminalize prostitution, the state has the highest arrest rate per capita for prostitution in the United States,[7] and independent sex workers suffer.

Another model known as "end demand" criminalizes paying for and managing sex workers within the paradigm that all sex workers are victims, and that all others involved are "pimps and predators."[8] More and more people who support sex workers are labeled "traffickers" and are receiving hefty prison sentences. Like the diversion courts and FOSTA/SESTA, these laws have bad outcomes for sex workers and victims of violence. Everywhere "end demand" laws have been implemented, violence against sex workers has increased as it becomes more difficult to screen clients for safety.

Imagining solutions to systemic problems is sometimes impossible. But the way we police communities is our choice. We can translate our values and priorities into better laws. I aspire to live in a healthy, free society where everyone has access to rights and opportunities to determine their own future. I seek the full decriminalization of sex work, where individuals are not arrested and cannot be evicted, fired, or lose custody of their children because of their participation in sex work. All people, whether they have ever participated in sex work or not, should have access to services and support to avoid exploitation, stay safe, and make choices about their own lives. Sex workers have a right to unencumbered access to the building blocks we all need to move our lives forward. This includes access to banking and investment services, healthcare, education, legal assistance, relevant government programs, and technology platforms. I imagine a society that values their most vulnerable, where police officers help people resolve disputes, deescalate conflict, and connect people to well-funded resources. I imagine that a police force focused on connecting to the community, instead of punishing it, could be trusted to protect and serve. The first step is decriminalizing prostitution.

Instead of reaching out to the formal criminal legal system to resolve conflicts, everyone I spoke to in the United States depended on informal social networks to share information and resources, and to resolve disputes. But that is not the case for sex workers in Aotearoa New Zealand.

In 2003, Aotearoa New Zealand decriminalized all forms of adult, consensual prostitution. Sex workers can solicit online or on the street. They can practice their trade in their homes, hotels, or any private location. Only people working together in groups of four or more had to register as a brothel and be subjected to small-business laws.

The results have been incredible. Street prostitution decreased dramatically as more people preferred to work indoors. There was no overall increase in prostitution or trafficking. In fact, there was a marked decrease in violence and STI cases as sex workers felt more comfortable advocating for their safety and health.[9] In one instance, a young woman working by herself had a client who refused to pay after their appointment. She called the police, who explained to the client that he could either pay the young woman or face charges himself.

Sex workers spend a significant amount of time negotiating sexual boundaries with strangers. We are adept at sensing malicious intent and sexual and physical threats. Our lives depend on it. If we are free to advocate for our own safety and health, we will. That is the future sex workers want. We want to create a culture where the police can and do protect everyone. When I was assaulted by my ex-boyfriend, I knew that what had happened to me was wrong, and I also knew that law enforcement could not help me. I was lucky that I was only met with indifference instead of hostility, but hundreds of thousands of people who do this work cannot report crimes committed against them while at work or at home and cannot advocate for their own safety because they fear arrest and punishment. If we want to work towards a less violent and more just future, then we have to stop criminalizing people for engaging in the oldest profession.

NOTES

1 Platt et al. 2018; Sanders et al. 2021; Dewey and St. Germain 2014; Deering et al. 2014.
2 Potter 2013.
3 The Sentencing Project 2023.
4 Global Network of Sex Work Projects (NSWP) 2020.
5 In 2019, sex worker activists took over the Woodhull conference because the Desiree Alliance conference, a long-standing organizing conference for sex worker activists, was canceled due to concerns about FOSTA/SESTA.
6 Global Health Justice Partnership 2018.
7 Britannica ProCon 2018.
8 Also referred to as the "Nordic Model," "Entrapment Model," "Feminist Model," and "Partial Decriminalization."
9 Abel 2014.

21

Raids and Rescues

The Effects of Prostitution-Diversion Programs on Asian Women Massage Parlor Workers

MOSHOULA CAPOUS-DESYLLAS AND AMIE CARR

He looks at the sign in the window of a strip mall building that says, "Thai Massage Here," and he opens the door, very well knowing that he isn't really there for the massage. He lies down on the massage table, as a woman who appears to be from Thailand and in her late forties, enters the room to administer the massage. After the Thai massage, the man hands her sixty dollars; the woman looks at it with confusion on her face and shakes her head. The sixty dollars is well over any normal tip range. The man then points to his genital region and continues to hand her the money. The woman continues to shake her head, but the man is insistent on her taking the money. At a loss for what to do and unable to communicate in English, she takes the money but leaves the room. She stalls for time by going to get more towels. Upon her return, the man is no longer alone and accompanied by uniformed police officers. They talk to her in a language she doesn't understand and administer a ticket she cannot read but is forced to sign. It is a night she will always remember and long to forget.

Law enforcement officials trying to "crack down" on sex work and sex trafficking in California have led to increased police stings and raids of massage parlors, and the subsequent ticketing and arrest of immigrant Asian women. Asian migrants (along with Latina trans women) are overrepresented in police-led trafficking interventions across the globe.[1] In Los Angeles, city officials contend that policing the sex trade is one of the best methods for rescuing trafficking victims and giving sex workers a way out, if they want one.[2] Much of this "rescuing" takes the form of court-mandated prostitution-diversion programs (PDPs) that partner with local social-work organizations that fight sex trafficking. Prostitution-diversion programs are designed to "educate" individuals about the social, health, and legal ramifications of engaging in the act of or the solicitation of prostitution.

In this chapter, we examine one social-service organization in Southern California that works with law enforcement to ticket and arrest sex workers and mandate their involvement in criminal legal systems through prostitution-diversion programs. Through our observations as feminist social workers and sex work activists, we detail our experiences interacting with the organization Save Our Sisters (SOS).[3] Save Our Sisters takes an antiprostitution rescue approach to its services, conflating sex work with sex trafficking as a form of violence against women. As we will show, collaborating with law enforcement in antitrafficking efforts to "identify" and "fight" human trafficking targets Asian communities in ways that perpetuate racist stereotypes about helpless, subservient, powerless immigrant Asian women. These efforts build on the stigma and racism against Asian communities that were recently exacerbated during the coronavirus pandemic. We find that these approaches police immigrant Asian women's lives in ways that do not improve well-being, often retraumatize women, and fail to address the underlying structural inequalities.

Locating Ourselves in Our Work

We are two cisgender women with US citizenship privilege and extensive experience working with individuals involved in the sex trades within the field of social work. The first author identifies as a woman of color feminist academic and activist who has engaged in participatory, arts-based research with sex workers for the past fourteen years from a decriminalization standpoint. The second author identifies as a white, feminist social worker who has spent the last two years working with survivors of sex trafficking within a harm-reduction approach. We have extensive experience facilitating prostitution-diversion groups and classes for immigrant Asian women ticketed for prostitution in massage parlors. We acknowledge that working in the sex industry can be empowering as well as a means of survival, and some individuals lack choice, and experience exploitation and coercion. Here we focus on the negative effects of criminalization in sex-trade workers' lives.[4]

Testimonio Methodological Approach

Grounded in a collective history of resistance, we use *testimonio*, a methodological approach used by nondominant groups to challenge oppression and bring attention to and transform injustice by centering marginalized voices.[5] Latinx critical race theorist Lindsay Pérez Huber describes *testimonio* as a "verbal journey of a witness who speaks to reveal the racial, classed, gendered, and nativist injustices they have suffered as a means of healing, empowerment, and advocacy for a more humane present and future."[6] Methodologically, *testimonio* departs from Eurocentric traditional research because it is guided by an antiracist and antihierarchical agenda. It builds on the lived experiences of marginalized people to document and theorize their oppression. The power of this methodological approach is that it acknowledges and draws from foundations of knowledge that exist outside of academia and that reside within marginalized communities.[7]

Prostitution Diversion and SOS

The social-service organization Save Our Sisters, in Southern California, informed our experience in the field. The organization's roots are faith-based, as it was originally founded and headed by a reverend of a local church and informed by a neo-abolitionist approach to the sex industry that sees prostitution as violence against women and seeks to abolish the sex industry. This organization's mission assists "victims" of sex work to leave "the life" of abuse and violence they are believed to be in and help women in the sex trades reach their full potential. Services include law enforcement crisis response, clinical counseling, group counseling, direct street outreach, community education and training, food, clothing, as well as linking victims to resources such as emergency housing, legal referrals, tattoo removals, and job training.

Social workers from Save Our Sisters regularly work with law enforcement officials to "combat" sex trafficking. Once police arrest and ticket individuals in the sex trades, they are routed to human trafficking intervention courts (HTIC). These courts are intended to divert "victim-defendants" from jail to social services via prostitution diversion programs (PDPs). Save Our Sisters provides one of these PDPs. The PDP aims to provide treatment, reduce crime, and change behavior rather than administer punishment through incarceration. Participation in PDPs can include, but is not limited to, group therapy, life skills workshops, trauma-based therapy, art therapy, and yoga. Other course topics include presentations on health issues related to sexually transmitted diseases, HIV/AIDS prevention and education, legal concerns, psychological aspects related to "Johns" and the effects on the local community.

PDPs may seem like an appropriate approach, but as we observed, the criminal legal system has little understanding of key structural issues and regularly dismisses the clients' perspectives and lived experiences. Most of those we observed in the PDPs were immigrant Asian women who worked at massage parlors. These are the easiest available jobs given a language barrier and immigration status. Yet police deem immigrant Asian women most likely to be "at risk" of trafficking, and so these groups disproportionately experience raid-and-rescue interventions that threaten deportation and heighten state surveillance.

Court-ordered mandatory PDPs also enforce more sessions than those the state requires for sex workers. Typically, within California, when someone is arrested for prostitution, the court orders eight one-hour group classes; however, in some cities or counties, the ticket for prostitution can require more classes. I have seen someone mandated to attend up to twenty-five required PDP classes. Social-service workers at Save Our Sisters also spend time "training" law enforcement officers in how to "spot" trafficking. These trainings also perpetuate racist stereotypes of helpless, subservient, powerless Asian woman needing to be saved. The raid-and-rescue efforts of law enforcement serve to justify the policing of and continuing racism against immigrant Asian women's bodies.

As I reflect back, what originally drew me (Amie) to work for this organization, Save Our Sisters, was its fight against trafficking in the sex industry. I was drawn to the staff's passion; they genuinely want to help survivors of sex trafficking and are out there on the streets trying to make a positive difference in these women's lives. What eventually led me astray from this organization was its blurring of the concepts of sex trafficking (sexual exploitation through force, fraud, or coercion) and sex work (choosing to engage in sex work openly).[8] With its faith-based origin, Save Our Sisters' religious ideals of women's sexual modesty and the need to protect women's virtue inform its approach to the population it serves. As is typical of many social-work organizations partnering with law enforcement, the staff of SOS consistently and openly shared that they believed that no person openly chooses "the life," and that all individuals who are involved in the sex industry are oppressed by men and exploited as commodities, and that all they need is rescuing.

I was also disillusioned with their alliance with law enforcement. The executive director of SOS was a former police department law enforcement officer in Southern California. Save Our Sisters continues to align with the police, despite the multiple accounts of abuse the organization's clientele (individuals in the sex trades) reported during intakes at the hands of the police during their arrest. Caseworkers acknowledged and empathized with the clientele during the intake, but then ignored this as soon as the intake was done. The caseworkers that I talked to believed that the women deserved this treatment for engaging in prostitution in the first place.

Caseworkers at Save Our Sisters often accompany police officers on sex-trafficking stings or when police encounter sex traffickers in the field. They also hold educational trainings and engage in outreach together. I (Amie) did not personally work with law enforcement during my time there. However, as we document shortly, I heard troubling stories from the women I worked with, particularly the immigrant Asian women who were ticketed in massage parlors for prostitution. These women often were given no other alternative but to access services and PDPs at this organization.

Raids and Rescues of Asian Massage Parlors

When I (Amie) worked at Save Our Sisters, it served mostly immigrant Asian women who were ticketed in sting operations, and due to the cultural and language barriers, they expressed heightened fear, confusion, and lack of understanding. I also started to notice a pattern during my intakes when working with this specific population. The majority were first-time offenders and over thirty-five years old. The women would break down crying or express their frustration with not understanding how they came to be where they were. They would share their stories of what happened the night of the ticket and arrest, and all the stories sounded very much like the vignette shared above. Thus, such antitrafficking efforts punish and control the very people they aim to protect, revealing paternalistic and punitive dimensions of carceral-oriented antitrafficking efforts.[9] Raids and rescues, facilitated under the rhetoric of victimhood, prohibit immigrant Asian women from speaking out against and defending their lived experiences.[10]

The PDP classes that Save Our Sisters administers revolve around educating immigrant Asian women about the definitions of prostitution, sex trafficking, and domestic violence; how to exit "the life"; and how to better themselves (often without considering their perspectives, circumstances, or life situations). The classes are shaped by and impose Western values and individualistic belief systems while paying little attention to the clients' cultural perspectives. The courses focus on an individual's responsibility for her values, decisions, and actions, rather than considering that Asian women come from cultures where collective decision making is based on community values. They also retraumatize participants by constantly reminding them of the night they were ticketed for prostitution, without considering that with a more collectivist value system comes a greater burden of shame. PDPs do not address how the perception of shame negatively impacts the lives of immigrant Asian women and their families and communities.

As the case manager facilitating the group discussions in the PDP, I (Amie) was accompanied by multiple interpreters. The classes were not divided by language but were combined. There were many times when I facilitated a group with up to three interpreters (Mandarin, Korean, and Thai) present, with the possibility of even more, if needed. As one can imagine, this creates a slow-moving group process, and hinders interactions between the members. From my experience, typical best practices include being culturally competent, which should entail creating groups based on the different languages spoken. Since this was not an option at the agency, for reasons unknown, and despite the slow process of the group due to the use of multiple interpreters, I implemented group discussions instead of a lecture. I also felt that a lecture based on the PDP curriculum generated by the organization could sound preachy or paternalistic, and infantilize the women.

Without permission from the directors of the Save Our Sisters, I also altered the organization's agenda, using a harm-reduction approach with cultural humility. While the facilitators at the organization do not formally have this freedom, nor did the directors know that I was altering the PDP curriculum, it was important for me to take the risk to maintain an ethical approach to working with the clients. The PDP curriculum was developed from a moralistic, paternalistic approach, with its rigid topics such as educating on what prostitution is and why one should not engage in it. The curriculum ignored structural reasons as to why some women have no other options for supporting their families and for making ends meet, especially when they are undocumented. In contrast, I took a harm-reduction approach, which requires starting where the client is and acknowledging the trauma in the client's life associated with the ticketing and arrest, while providing support services in a way that is accessible and appropriate without retraumatizing the client.[11] Approaching the groups from a stance of cultural humility means being open to the other person in relation to aspects of cultural identity that are most important to the person while engaging in a commitment to self-reflection.[12] Working from these standpoints, I did not make any assumptions about their beliefs and the struggles they were going through, which I find critical for social workers to implement when working with this population. I allowed time and a safe space for everyone to share their perspectives, values, and beliefs on the topics discussed.

When I followed the course outline just described, immigrant Asian women working in massage parlors were more willing to speak if we discussed topics on self-care or current barriers and issues, rather than sex-industry terminology. I found ways to talk about the required PDP topics rather than just applying the themes to prostitution as a form of violence against women. For example, one class topic revolved around stigma. I invited the immigrant Asian women to discuss what stigma meant to them, where they had experienced it, how it felt, and how to navigate stigma, rather than reinforcing the stigma surrounding the act of prostitution itself.

Implications for an Anticarceral Approach

Various scholars have documented the adverse and detrimental effects of ticketing and arrest for prostitution on the lives of immigrant Asian women. Recent studies, such as one by Selvey and colleagues,[13] document how criminal laws, racism, isolation, poor English skills, and stigma increase the vulnerability of immigrant Asian women working in massage parlors. The participants in these research studies experienced poor mental and physical health, increased assault by police, and a fear of their legal standing. Another research study by Capous-Desyllas, Payne, and Panichelli highlights how incarceration harmed the physical and mental health, economic security, opportunities for growth and education, and sense of autonomy and freedom of individuals working in the sex trades in Los Angeles.[14] Research also reveals that such policing practices disrupted work environments, diminished support networks and compromised safety and risk-reduction strategies, and limited access to health services and justice.[15] US politicians and police forces continue to expand antitrafficking initiatives by amplifying police surveillance and crackdowns on Asian massage businesses while offering civilian and incorrect, racist trainings on "how to spot human trafficking." This perpetuates racist cultural imagery and stereotypes.[16] New racial anxieties around the coronavirus as an Asian disease have mobilized the state to further justify policing Asian immigrant women's health, migration, and sexual labor.[17]

We propose an anticarceral feminist approach to working with individuals in the sex trades.[18] An anticarceral feminist approach moves from criminalization of immigrant Asian women toward mutual aid, community accountability, decriminalization of illegal sex trades, drugs, and citizenship status, harm-reduction tools, and linkages to the self-identified needs of people in the sex trades.[19] Antitrafficking and sex worker–led organizations focusing on harm-reduction approaches can improve sex-trade workers' access to justice by advocating for these reforms.[20]

Finally, we found that the biggest problem with most current sex-trafficking policies, like the ones used in Save Our Sisters, is that authorities do not consult sex workers and self-identified victims of trafficking in the drafting or passing of laws and the implementation of them.[21]

Practice and policy efforts to address sex work and sex trafficking need to be community-led, grassroots initiatives designed by marginalized migrants and sex workers of color most impacted by criminalization of the sex trades. We stand by the slogan used by sex worker-rights activists, "Nothing about Us without Us!" Therefore, all practice and policy efforts need to include the voices and expertise of sex workers themselves without involving law enforcement and carceral approaches that negatively impact people.

NOTES

1 Mai et al. 2021.
2 Booker 2002.
3 To maintain confidentiality and anonymity, we are using the pseudonym "Save Our Sisters" to refer to the organization where Amie worked.
4 Capous-Desyllas, Payne, and Panicelli 2020; Capous-Desyllas and Loy 2020.
5 Booker 2002.
6 Huber 2009.
7 Delamont and Jones 2012.
8 Sawicki et al. 2019.
9 Musto 2016.
10 Hoefinger et al. 2020.
11 Rekart 2005.
12 Hook et al. 2013.
13 Selvey et al. 2018.
14 Capous-Desyllas, Payne, and Panichelli 2020.
15 Platt et al. 2018.
16 Lam et al. 2021.
17 Lam et al. 2021.
18 Bernstein 2010.
19 Capous-Desyllas, Payne, and Panichelli 2020.
20 Lutnick 2019.
21 Hoefinger et al. 2020.

22

Disability at the Revolving Door

Perspectives on Mental Illness and Predatory Policing

SUMMER LOPEZ COLORADO

"We know what you trannies are doing out there," the police call to a Black trans woman, the client of lawyer and author Andrea Ritchie. In her recent book, *Invisible No More*, Ritchie recalls the night her client received a ticket for "loitering for the purpose of prostitution" while standing outside a convenience store after buying a snack with friends. "When she went into the local precinct to complain, she was violently tackled to the ground by four officers, arrested, handcuffed to a railing for eight hours, subjected to transphobic slurs, and taken for a psychiatric examination—to the bewilderment of the examining doctor, who told the police there was absolutely nothing wrong with Ryhanna that they themselves hadn't inflicted."[1] This story demonstrates the well-documented excessive arrest and use of force that police inflict upon trans women. Simultaneously, it demonstrates the way in which mental illness is handled and projected upon people who work in or are suspected of being involved in the sex trade. However, we are just beginning to hear the voices of those who are themselves disabled, and more specifically, those with mental illnesses, and how they are implicated in this multilayered system of control.

In this chapter I present a primarily quantitative analysis—supplemented by quotations—of a study on participants' experiences with predatory police.[2] I first briefly take a look at how sex work functions as a safety net for disabled individuals, then turn to analyzing prevalence of predatory policing experiences across sex workers and take a deeper dive into the mean counts of arrest by disability, race/ethnicity, and gender.[3] Using responses from over three hundred individuals in the sex trade, I find that sex workers with mental illnesses are caught in the predatory cycle of police intervention—a revolving door of arrest, harassment, and rearrest—in a way that sustains their marginalization. In my analysis of frequencies of arrest, I find that police are more likely to repeatedly criminalize cis and trans Black and Latinx sex workers with mental illnesses, demonstrating what law professor Camile A. Nelson terms the "disabling of race and racing of disability."[4]

This study draws on a secondary analysis of a mixed-methods survey collected by researchers White and colleagues at the Center for Court Innovation.[5] The larger survey sought to provide evidence-based foundations for the development of suitable policies and interventions for adults in the sex trade. Surveys were collected between 2015 and 2017 from participants living in New York City who traded sex for money, housing, food, or other things they needed. Using respondent-driven sampling, the researchers were able to access a population otherwise difficult to reach due to its association with stigmatized behavior.[6] Grounded in a participatory approach, the research team consisted of individuals who had their own experiences in the sex trade.[7]

During survey collection, respondents were asked if they had ever received a mental health diagnosis. Approximately 55 percent of the entire sample reported being given a mental health diagnosis.[8] For the purposes of this study, "mental health disability" and "mental illness" are used interchangeably. Prevalence of a mental health diagnosis is an imperfect measure of mental health disability, but it is a good start in the effort to understand and address patterns of inequality that emerge in the experience of sex work.

Sex Work as Safety Net

> Where else can I make an income that will allow me to survive, me and my partner to survive, where I can make my own hours, or on a day that I can't get out of bed because I'm so sore I can barely move, or I can't face people because I'm having a bad mental illness day and I don't have to work? But on the days that I can, I can be super productive and make up that money? There is no other way to survive in this world. (Biracial trans woman, forty-seven)[9]

Respondents provided several reasons for disabled individuals to enter sex work. When asked if they liked anything about sex work, individuals with mental illness highlighted flexible hours that allowed them to plan their schedule around potential flareups and limitations and said that the pay was better than in any other potential avenues of employment. One fifty-one-year-old Black cis woman directly pointed to the lack of support from federal and state subsidies to sustain livelihood with a disability:

> I try to supplement that because it's so hard to work with one check a month. SSI [Supplemental Security Income] don't get it. You got three kids. You got rent. You get a certain amount. That's what you work with, so I have to supplement.[10]

When all respondents were asked if they had a disability, chronic illness, or other medical or mental health condition related to their participation in sex work, 35 percent responded yes, although it is unclear from the wording of this question whether they were stating that this relationship is a product of their participation rather than a motivator for entry.

Documenting Predatory Policing

Table 22.1 tells a story about sex worker interactions with the police and the unequal distribution of predatory police encounters for respondents with a mental health disability.

Surveillance in the form of stopping, questioning, and checking bags and pockets was highly prevalent for all respondents. While there was not a significant difference in ever getting stopped by the police, the content of those stops—questioning and the checking of bags and pockets— was different for those with mental health disabilities and those without. Seventy-three percent of respondents with mental illness and 63 percent of sex workers without a mental illness experienced being stopped by the police and questioned about where they were going or what they were doing in a certain neighborhood. When these numbers are broken down by gender and race, Black cis women with a mental illness

TABLE 22.1: Patterns of Predatory Policing Measures, Center for Court Innovation, 2018

Predatory Policing Variables	Diagnosed with a mental illness?	
	No	Yes
Police stopped them on the street but they were not arrested	63%	73%
Police questioned where they were going or what they were doing in a certain neighborhood**	56%	72%
Police asked to check bag or pockets*	56%	69%
Police threatened verbal, physical, or sexual violence**	21%	36%
Police did not arrest in exchange for sex**	8%	19%
Police officer otherwise pressured or forced sexual contact*	5%	11%
(Sample size)	(131)	(161)

*p<.05, **p<.01, ***p<.001

had the highest rates of questioning, with 80 percent being questioned about where they were going or what they were doing in a certain neighborhood.[11]

Thirty-six percent of sex workers with mental illness say that they were threatened by the police with verbal, physical, or sexual violence. This type of harassment is 14 percent lower for those without diagnosed mental illnesses. These discrepancies are likely in part facilitated by the higher precarity of working conditions—sex workers with mental illness more commonly were currently active in street sex work (45 percent). Working on the street provides more opportunities for contact, and a system of profiling that leads law enforcement to disproportionately surveil through stops and questioning, which can lead to threats or exploitation by police officers. This exploitation is punctuated with sexual coercion and sex in exchange for freedom, which were both significantly higher for sex workers with mental illness.

When these statistics are broken down further, I find that 42 percent of Black and Latina women (including both trans and cis women) with diagnosed mental illness had experienced being threatened with verbal, physical, or sexual violence as compared to only 13 percent of Black and Latina women without a mental illness.

Quotations from the respondents in the White et al. report elaborate on the nature of these threats and sexual violence. Experiences of violence and harassment due to profiling and gender presentation for trans women frequently include more physical and sexual forms of harassment:

> One time a cop, he thought I had a wig on but I had a sew-in and he pulled my head back. He pulled my head back and put a gun in my face and threw me on the fence and kicked my legs apart. I had a skirt on. He was basically trying to humiliate me. (Black trans woman, twenty-three)[12]

This experience, along with experiences of sexual coercion, expose the common culture of derision police express towards sex workers that result in humiliation, fear, and trauma.

Table 22.2 depicts a system of repeated carceral contact that materializes into a revolving door of arrest and rearrest. Arrest is frequent for sex workers—just over three-quarters had been arrested at least once. Most arrests were for nonviolent offenses other than prostitution (which approximately 30 percent were charged with),[13] including jumping the turnstile, petty theft, trespassing, and having an open container of alcohol. Most respondents had less than three arrests; however, a small group had extreme rates of recidivism—10 percent of the sample reporting over twenty counts of arrest. Of those with a mental illness disability, the average counts of arrest were over twice the average in comparison to respondents without a mental health diagnosis.

Bringing the Margins to the Center

Following principles of disability justice and Black feminist scholarship, I shift the scope of my research on predatory policing from "the margins to the center,"[14] focusing on complex and intersectional cases. The data here suggest notable inequalities in the frequency of arrests between cis women, cis men, and trans women across margins. Cis men and trans women had nearly three times the average number of arrests in comparison to cis women. However, these averages suggest that some of the largest inequalities were not between these groups, but rather within

TABLE 22.2: Mean Counts of Lifetime Arrests by Mental Illness Disability, Race/Ethnicity, and Gender, Center for Court Innovation, 2018

	Diagnosed with a Mental Illness?		
	No	Yes	N
Total	5.4	10.6	303
Gender			
Cis Women	2.4	9.8	138
Cis Men	7.6	11.8	93
Trans Women	6.6	14.4	54
Race/Ethnicity			
Black	5.6	12.0	152
Latinx	5.8	11.5	90
White	5.1	7.3	42

each racial and gender group. Cis women with a mental health diagnosis had four times the average of arrests in comparison to nondisabled cis women. In addition to the pattern of higher rates of arrest for respondents with mental illness, men and trans women with a mental illness had higher rates of arrest than cis women diagnosed with a mental illness. Cis men participating in sex work, although often not considered in political discourse regarding the sex trade, had a substantially higher average number of arrests with and without mental illness when compared to cis women. However, trans women with mental illnesses had by far the highest average number of arrests, averaging at about fourteen arrests.

Racial inequalities only become clear in the differences between respondents with mental health diagnoses. Black and Latinx respondents with mental illness had on average at least four more arrests than white respondents with mental illness. This unique intersection further solidifies the linkage between carceral logics that utilize ableism in conjunction with racism to justify arrest. Mental illness is a factor that bolsters racial inequalities, despite similar rates of arrest between sex workers with and without a mental health disability.

It is difficult to discern whether my findings are due to increased surveillance or profiling of those with mental illness or whether mental illness is an outcome of increased contact with the criminal legal system. The reality is that it is most likely explained to some extent by both. As disability lawyer and activist Katie Tastrom writes, "We don't talk about this enough, but trauma is disabling. As criminalization makes sex work disproportionately traumatic compared to other professions (and yes, sex work is a profession), even if people are not disabled when they start sex work, they may become disabled from the trauma imposed upon them."[15] The harassment and coercion that sex workers experience in their interactions with police are disabling in themselves and may explain high correlations among police harassment, arrest, and disability.

The methods police use to profile and respond to people with mental health conditions contribute to these high rates of arrest and violence. In legal scholar Camile Nelson's analysis of criminal cases of street-level police encounters, she finds that in cases where police receive information on a person having a mental illness, or they suspect a mental health condition, they often escalate the use of force to contain and incarcerate the individual—especially when the individual is a person of color. People with mental health conditions can respond in ways that are seen as noncompliant because of their conditions, which police use to further rationalize the use of force. Through these characterizations by police, mental illness and race are mutually constitutive factors in surveillance, mistreatment, and incarceration. While Nelson does not directly look at the experiences of sex workers, these findings promote further research into cases involving sex workers, mental illness, and police discretion.

Decriminalizing Survival: Policies and Considerations

A focus on mental health disabilities exposes caveats and concerns with how we can get to full decriminalization—a long-term goal of sex worker communities globally. As policies shift, we need to be vigilant in preventing the extension of carceral logics into our proposed reforms. For example, legalized systems, such as restrictive licensing, worker registrations, and brothel ownership, might help some sex workers, but many of these systems hinge on restricting autonomy through the force of the criminal legal system and are embedded with policies and practices towards queer folks, men, individuals with long-standing health conditions, and workers of color that exclude them from the benefits of regulation.[16] These types of reforms do little to change the threats of law enforcement encounters for those who cannot work legally or find suitable employment due to mental health concerns.

These findings also highlight the problems with antitrafficking policies that increase criminalization, expand the definition of trafficking, raise penalties, and criminalize clients of sex workers. One particularly controversial package of legislation—FOSTA/SESTA—has gotten critical attention from researchers. Sex worker advocates and researchers Wolfe and Blunt have found that these policies have closed off safe avenues for screening and alerting colleagues about dangerous clients, as sex workers lost popular blacklisting sites that they used to communicate with one another about clients who were potentially violent.[17] Sins Invalid organizer Cyreé Jarelle Johnson has documented testimonials from disabled sex workers on the disproportionate impact of the loss of these Internet advertising sites and forums—many disabled sex workers who had begun using Internet service to access safer and more steady income were forced to move back to street sex work and take on riskier clients. One worker interviewed explicitly addressed the increased paranoia that developed as a result of this legislation: "I am more afraid than ever of being caught or killed by a cop that poses as a john, or a john that wants to blackmail me with these new laws. I started taking chances when FOSTA/SESTA were passed."[18]

Disability is a central axis for concern about how these legislative efforts are implemented due to the already precarious economic conditions of disabled persons,[19] and to the point of this paper, their common experiences of abuse by law enforcement. Predatory policing is built as a system of repression that both traumatizes and limits opportunities for growth due to arrest. While legislation targeting forced sexual exploitation may bring justice for a few select people, it also increases the ability for actors of the state (i.e., law enforcement) to reify hard divisions of deserving and undeserving and expand surveillance technologies around the sex trade.[20] Authorities have even criticized the legislation for making it more difficult to identify and rescue survivors of trafficking and inflicting increased trauma from police raids and sting operations.[21]

Ultimately, any policy propositions must challenge the use of policing logics that persist in pathologizing sex work and perpetuate the economic precarity of individuals in the sex trade. Movements that rely on the criminal legal system do not change the culture of disability-based discrimination or the predatory carceral environments that prevent individuals from meeting their basic needs. Finally, policies must address the transphobia and racism intertwined with disability that plague job opportunities and safety in the United States. Working under the table to make ends meet is often the most viable option for disabled individuals to make a living.

Disability-justice movements, sex worker–activist communities, and racial- and gender-justice communities that seek to abolish the prison industrial complex have much to gain by working alongside one another to reach collective liberation. The future of policy must look towards new systems of crisis response and harm reduction, and work towards developing community-based systems of care to support sex workers who wish to stay in the sex trade and those who seek opportunities to leave.

These findings bring to the forefront the disparate impact of "tough on crime" approaches to stigmatized behavior. I demonstrate that legal enforcement and policing of low-level misdemeanors have contributed to the surveillance and harm of sex workers, particularly those with mental illness and those who are Black, Latinx, and/or trans. These points of contact have resulted in the disproportionate and continuous harm of sex workers through the carceral system. Predatory policing highlights a driving force in the US prison industrial complex, which relies on a steady flow of prison labor, fines, and civil asset seizures that can reliably generate profits.[22] This is a systemic issue and one that comes along with the historical legacy of policing in this country. On a practical level, my research creates a further understanding of the relationships between law enforcement and sex workers with mental illnesses that previous studies have not had the data to document. Predatory policing practices are contingent on the marking of individuals as unworthy of care, deviant, and in need of containment. Intersectional disability scholarship pushes us to propose solutions that fundamentally change our conception of that which is "other," so that we can develop systems of care that aid structurally deprived populations to live with dignity and autonomy.

NOTES

1 Ritchie 2017.
2 I understand the web of encounters within the criminal legal system as constitutive of "predatory policing"—a term coined by legal scholar Devon Carbado to describe the carceral plight of Black Americans. Predatory policing identifies the ways in which police profile, reprimand, and traumatize individuals deemed as deviant and potentially criminal, and exploit them through a web of civil asset forfeiture, cash bail, and incarceration.
3 The respondents who fell into the Asian and American Indian/Alaskan Native categories were not included in the tables as the sample sizes fell below twenty cases. This is also the case for those who identified as two-spirit, gender-nonconforming, trans men, etc.
4 Nelson 2022.
5 Data originally presented in White et al. 2017.
6 Heckathorn 2002.
7 Although many of the individuals in the study identified their sex trade as "sex work" or simply "work," not every person in the sex trade self-defines as a sex worker and may even resist such a label. I use the term here as a nonstigmatizing alternative to "prostitute," which fails to encompass the range of types of exchanges in the sex trade.
8 There are limitations to using this measure due to the problematic and racialized nature of psychiatric diagnosis; however, over 90 percent of the respondents reported that they agreed with their mental health diagnosis. The category of disabled is socially constructed with boundaries that are constantly in flux—although medical discourses portray these boundaries as rigid.
9 White et al. 2017.
10 White et al. 2017, 16.
11 Additional statistics by race and gender not included in this paper, but available upon request.
12 White et al. 2017, 28.
13 However, trans women were more likely to be arrested on prostitution charges than any other group, at twice the rates of cis women and nearly six times the rates of cis men.
14 Berne et al. 2018; hooks 1989.
15 Tastrom 2019b.
16 Weitzer 2012.
17 Blunt and Wolf 2020.
18 Johnson 2018.
19 Disabled people experience poverty and job discrimination at uniquely high rates—in 2018, 26 percent of noninstitutionalized disabled adults were living below the poverty line, as opposed to 11.7 percent of the US adult population overall. Moreover, many who apply for disability benefits are ultimately denied or are

expected to live on subminimum wages to cover rising medical costs. Those who can gain federal benefits such as Supplemental Security Income are expected to receive benefits at a maximum of ten thousand dollars a year, capping outside income to approximately sixty-five dollars a month before the government reduces their benefits. Erickson, Lee, and von Schrader 2021.

20 Kulig and Butler 2019; Bernstein 2018.

21 Blunt and Wolf 2020.

22 Carbado 2016.

PART V

Sex Worker Activism

23

After Decriminalization

A Labor-Rights Agenda for the Sex Industry

KATE D'ADAMO

The question of liberation for sex workers has never had a single answer.

The sex workers–rights movement in the United States is multi-faceted, with goals addressing everything from policing to housing to stigma. Both domestically and abroad, decriminalization has been a central fight. Measures to remove criminal penalties for consensually trading sex have been introduced from San Francisco to DC,[1] Louisiana to New York.[2] Sex work decriminalization is the inevitable next goalpost in the fight to improve sex worker health and safety. Decriminalization of the sex trade removes criminal penalties for participation in the sex industry without the high-barrier requirements imposed under legalization. The delineation between decriminalization and legalization is not the presence of regulations—every industry has some form of regulation, even if it's minimum wages—but treating the sex trade like other workplaces, and centering workers.

But what is next? As sex work is not a uniform experience and advocates are not a single-minded group, what happens after decriminalization will look different according to where it occurs and who is leading the work. Some campaigns have begun looking ahead. The DC Sex Workers and Advocates Coalition included a needs assessment in their decriminalization campaign to inform future services and outreach. DecrimNY's proposed legislation includes provisions for criminal records expungement.[3] Decriminalization of the sex trades is not the end of advocacy but the beginning of a new chapter. This essay leans into sex work as work by proposing a labor-rights agenda for a decriminalized industry.

While labor-rights frameworks have elements of regulation, this chapter rejects a legalization framework, and supports decriminalization.

Legalization regulates how, where, and when sex work can take place, with unnecessarily stricter regulation for the sex industry than for other industries. Workers operating outside of those regulations still face penalties, especially marginalized workers like migrants. These schemes benefit management and regulatory enforcement bodies over workers. Nevada is an example of a legalization, or regulation, scheme, where the exchange of sex for resources legally takes place within highly regulated brothels in specific counties. Sex workers who work outside of the brothel system can face up to six months in jail and up to a thousand-dollar fine. Regulations such as this continue to invest in the state violence of criminalization and offer outsized control of workers by brothel owners and managers. Legalization also represented a unique moment in time—many of these regimes were passed in Europe as discussions of the European Union were growing, and intercontinental migration was about to shift dramatically. Sex work has always provided an opportunity for migrant workers without documentation. While countries often concretized existing practices like red light districts, these schemes also created new barriers and exposure for migrant sex workers.

Sex Worker Organizing and Atrophied American Labor Rights

Sex worker organizing does not draw a clear line between community and labor organizing. As sex worker organizers, we are just as likely to run workshops on criminalization and dating stigma as we are to share strategies for increasing income and filing taxes. For independent workers, community building is central to the information sharing and interdependence that make work safer and better. For criminalized workers, for whom law enforcement is one of the most significant factors determining working conditions and income opportunity, collective action for decriminalization is labor organizing. For others operating in a grey area online, companies like Mastercard and OnlyFans function as exploitative managers, making unilateral decisions to the detriment of workers.

Sex worker movements have overlapped with formal labor organizing. In the 1940s the American Guild of Variety Artists began organizing dancers and clubs. This action was gutted by the 1973 ruling that dancers were independent contractors, not employees, and not entitled to the benefits of collective organizing.[4] Undeterred, in the 1990s two strip clubs in California, Pacer's in San Diego and the Lusty Lady in San Francisco, formally unionized, in the new context of a sex workers– rights movement.

Internationally, sex worker unionization has offered significant support for health and safety. In India, the Karnataka Sex Workers Union hosts programming, engages in policy advocacy, and is affiliated with a national trade union network, like the AFL-CIO in the United States.[5] In Aotearoa New Zealand, the main bargaining body for decriminalization was the NZPC Aotearoa New Zealand Sex Worker Collective. In an industry where most workers will continue to operate independently, union-model organizing provides new ways for collective action.

The last several decades, though, have seen workers' rights declining in the United States. When the federal government passed the 1938 Fair Labor Standards Act (FLSA), establishing a baseline for worker protections, the landscape of work looked radically different than today. FLSA's protections centered formal employees in a central workplace like a factory. While these recognitions were important, racial and gender discrimination were baked into the structure. Agricultural and domestic workers were excluded from the new federal protections, including child labor restrictions, to continue oppressing Black workers in a post– chattel slavery society reliant on an exploitable workforce.[6] Worker protections have been further eroded by court decisions like *Lamps Plus v. Varela*, which attacked the right of workers to collectively fight against an employer.

These disintegrating labor structures have also not kept up with changes in the labor force. Nontraditional labor is increasingly important to people trying to make ends meet. Self-employed workers, who are not employees and do not receive benefits, made up 11 percent of the workforce in February 2022.[7] Independent contractors and gig workers have almost no worker protections.[8] As traditional jobs have not kept pace with inflation (disproportionately impacting Black individuals),[9] one in three people supplement their income with a "side hustle."[10] For workers in illicit trades like sex work, labor rights are further inaccessible. Nontraditional work is more likely to support communities of color, queer people, and other marginalized people. Black and Hispanic workers are far more likely to be involved in gig labor than white workers.[11]

Globally, women dominate the informal labor market.[12] Ninety percent of respondents to the Transgender Discrimination survey reported harassment, mistreatment, or discrimination in the workplace, with such experiences compounded for respondents of color.[13] American labor protections are being dismantled for traditional workers and are insufficient for the needs of an evolving workforce, with marginalized workers facing the brunt of the harm.

While sex work is not new, it has many of the characteristics of these new forms of labor. Sex work can be informal labor, gig work, intimate labor, emotional labor, or own-account work, among a range of other categorizations. Sex work, with low barriers to entry, is available to people who are criminalized, undocumented, or have other barriers to living-wage jobs. For sex workers, traditional American labor movements are inadequate to handle a profession at the cutting edge of possibility. Below are descriptions of labor-rights efforts offering new ideas for making sex work great work.

Collective Power, Independent Worker

Collective bargaining, in which workers have common demands of management, is a cornerstone of labor organizing. The independent workforce builds collective power without management to collectively bargain against.

One campaign that took on this challenge was the World Class Cities for All Campaign,[14] which launched in cities across South Africa ahead of the 2010 World Cup. As with the Olympics, countries compete to host the games, promising large-scale projects to transform the location. South Africa's bid was no different, and in reaching an agreement with the international soccer organization FIFA, host cities were to undergo a series of "beautification" projects.[15] These beautification projects, though, led to human- and labor-rights abuses, especially against poor and homeless residents.[16] For street economies in the area, increased licensing and policing mean that many people lose access to buyers.[17] This is not unlike gentrification, which targets the sex trade through street-sweeps of strolls and zoning ordinances that displace strip clubs and massage parlors.

Almost immediately, workers began to feel the pressures of beautification. Durban alone removed twenty-five thousand street vendors and established a district where no more than five hundred vendors could return to work. Under the leadership of StreetNet, a workers' rights conversation began to form among similarly situated laborers that evolved the concept of collective bargaining. Each city formed a coalition of local own-account, or self-employed, workers, including sex workers and waste pickers, and social-justice organizations. Antipolicing critiques were also squarely grounded in a gender-justice framework, pointing out the disparity in impact among street vendors as police crackdowns "[result] in pitched battles, which often militarizes the struggles of street vendors, giving prominence to militant militaristic male leadership figures, and the women literally disappear from the public profile, even if they were prominent before—as all the development issues disappear." Without a company to organize against, collective bargaining can feel illogical, but StreetNet saw collective action as wider than street vendors. "What all these groups have in common is that they are part of the poor and marginalized classes. . . . They are not seen as forming part of the host population which anticipates benefitting from hosting a high-profile international event."[18]

Each local organizing body brought unique goals to local municipal bodies. All local groups sought more representation in the planning process leading up to the World Cup, and some formed local bargaining units for workers. The campaign also aligned with a national and international media campaign highlighting issues with the event and built international solidarity. This campaign plants seeds for what collective organizing could look like for independent industries like sex work, redefining workplace organizing to reflect their situation. The city became the workplace, and the diverse forms of informal labor within it became colleagues, regardless of what they sold. The campaign also changed the concept of workplace management to one of spatial management. The policymakers who control city spaces were the target of collective bargaining. Instead of negotiating with a management team, the campaigns focused on governments and FIFA, who controlled the contract stipulations. Instead of wage and hour negotiations, workers negotiated access to space and permits. When a similar campaign launched in India ahead of the Commonwealth Games, demands included participating in municipal planning, accessing low-interest loans, and curbing policing.[19] StreetNet's strategy for collective bargaining also drew attention from global human rights leaders, who called on FIFA to meet with the organizers.[20] While the campaign in South Africa was not successful in having the cities meet the demands of street-based workers, the campaign offered strategies and insights that could be re-created in India and Brazil.

Intimate Labor: Beyond Minimum Wage

Another consideration stemming from the informal nature of sex work is not simply how to organize but what labor rights to ask for. For example, while one of the biggest federal labor campaigns is the fight for a fifteen-dollar minimum wage, many workers, including sex workers, are not engaged in work arrangements that would be served by this lift. When it comes to envisioning labor rights, other industries have begun to expand how we think about what is offered at work.

One workforce facing similar challenges is that of domestic workers, a field heavily populated by women of color, especially migrant women. Sex work and domestic work are unique forms of intimate care labor that require unique health and safety standards. Domestic work also happens in a clients' home, outside of a workplace setting where health and safety standards can be made consistent. And importantly, labor-rights movements in the United States have marginalized domestic workers due to misogynoir.[21] Sex workers, just like domestic workers, will have to fight for labor rights in a way that honors histories of stigma and discrimination. One organization taking this on is the Domestic Workers Alliance (DWA) through the Domestic Workers' Bill of Rights. The campaign seeks to include domestic workers in existing labor standards, including paid time off, guaranteed meal and rest breaks, and protection against unfair wage deductions. In these ways, domestic workers are asking for inclusion in an existing labor framework, and the ability to access what many other workers take for granted.

Beyond these asks is a recognition that domestic work has its own unique dynamics of work that must be recognized alongside traditional issues. For example, the Bill of Rights included demands such as the right of live-in employees to use the client's home Internet at no charge. The protections are rooted in direct organizing asks of domestic workers, as opposed to adopting protections from other workplaces. Workers can demand what is necessary, instead of asking to fit inside atrophied molds. This approach also took labor-based goals and put them into a human rights trope—the Bill of Rights. Taking workplace goals and placing them in a different discourse helps reframe the conversation for an audience who may be hostile to workers' rights language. Ten states have passed domestic worker protections, and federal legislation has been introduced. While sex workers can seek some existing protections, the sex trade is a unique enough industry to have to renavigate what those rights entail. Questions like condom use, safety cameras, and contract refusals do not have clear answers. DWA utilized an existing framework to create meaningful protections, and sex workers can use this model to see how policy beyond decriminalization can continue to advance sex workers' rights.

Who Is a Worker?

A long-standing issue for noncriminalized sex work is worker categorization.[22] In the United States there are two categories of formal employment—employee and independent contractor. Employee status provides protections like the right to minimum wage and record keeping. While FLSA remains vague about the definition of an employee under the law, typically this means someone hired by a company for employment paid by that company in a permanent relationship. Increasingly, laborers find themselves far outside of that structure and classified as independent contractors who do a specific job and move from company to company, or client to client, independent from a single, permanent employer. While independent contractors supposedly have more flexibility, they also do not receive workplace benefits or protections and have a more precarious working life. Increasingly, forms of work such as gig labor, wherein someone relies on a third-party service to connect to paying clients, struggle to fit into either category. Many workers are miscategorized.

This issue has been most prominent for strippers, whose status changed from employee to independent contractors after a 1973 court case that "clarified" the delineation of employee and contractor. There have been numerous state-based debates on whether dancers are employees or independent contractors, with policy moving the recategorization back to employee.[23] For most sex workers, there is no one model of employment, even for sex workers in legal work such as porn. For example, a cam performer who works exclusively on one platform because of the website's outsized market share is not an employee of the platform and must still be paid by clients, but the lack of other options means the performer lacks the independence of a true contractor.

In October 2018 the International Conference on Labor Statistics adopted a third categorization of worker, the dependent contractor, and resolved to include more information on this group.[24] Dependent contractors are similar to independent contractors in the nature of their work but depend on a single company for their income, for example, as just noted, a cam model, whose income is almost exclusively from one platform. As the criminalization of websites that support the sex trade has gotten more aggressive, there has been more consolidation of platforms, compromising the ability of workers to move independently. This new category of dependent contractor potentially covers workers ranging from a hair stylist who rents a chair to a gig worker who delivers for UberEats. Proposed protections vary, but workers would retain some independence while also acknowledging that these business models, such as porn and streaming websites, are profiting from the labor of workers and hold some responsibilities as employers. "Sex work" is a broad umbrella, and decriminalization will cover a range of working experiences, but many will not fit into the employee/independent contractor dichotomy. Sex workers could lead the charge to create a new category of worker that is responsive to evolving work models and help usher in a new way of seeing independent laborers as deserving of protections.

Beyond Work

The United States is at a critical moment for workers' rights. As the existing protections are being dismantled, the shifting dynamics of work should make us question whether they are worth saving. With structures built on exclusion and protections that do not serve many workers, the sex trade could be at the forefront of redefining workers' rights. To be meaningfully transformative, sex worker organizing will have to learn from and repair the same histories of racial exclusion as other mainstream labor histories. When the Lusty Lady sought unionization and collective legal action against club owners, wage and hour claims were prioritized over racial-discrimination claims (club restrictions limited the number of Black dancers on the most lucrative shifts and banned workers from swapping shifts with a darker-skinned dancer).[25] Racism on advertising platforms, cis supremacy, xenophobia, and stigma against substance users are workplace problems as well as structural violence.

As we consider enforcement of rights, it is imperative to build mechanisms that do not utilize the tools of surveillance and state violence that are being dismantled in anticriminalization efforts. A transformative labor-rights agenda requires centering workers currently relegated to the margins—workers who are Black and racialized, disabled, undocumented, parenting, formerly incarcerated, First Nation and indigenous, and other workers who suffer exclusion in accessing resources. But the beauty of organizing at the edges is that it can be as fluid and responsive as the people driving it. As Sydney-based worker Edie Lau put it, "The industry itself is a moving, living structural being. You support people (POC or not) by uplifting them, giving them real opportunities and being accountable for when you do fuck up."[26]

Labor rights will have to wrangle with the tension that under capitalism, all work is exploitation and good work is only possible in a world where no one is dependent upon work for survival. It is valid to wonder whether a workers' rights frame is reformist or an incremental step towards liberation from capitalism, and many sex workers are asking whether we should be fighting for sex work as work at all.[27] As we imagine what liberation can be, we can learn from other workers' efforts, and find solidarity in shared innovation. We can redefine the workplace and management to find new collaborators with aligned goals. From domestic workers, we can define workplace protections that are relevant to lived experience instead of imposed top down. From international labor-rights discourse, we can explore what it means to be a worker and create definitions that align with the reality of how people are working. Sex work has always been a story of resilience. In the face of poverty, sex workers work. In the face of marginalization, sex workers organize.

NOTES

1 Ballotpedia n.d.; HIPS n.d.
2 Paterson 2021; DecrimNY n.d., "Home."
3 DecrimNY n.d., "Advocacy."
4 Wilmet 1999, 465–98.
5 Karnataka Sex Workers Union 2018.
6 Hendersen 2020; Dixon 2021.
7 Gregory, Harding, and Steinberg 2022.
8 Molla 2021.
9 Harvard T.H. Chan School of Public Health 2022.
10 Gabrielle 2021.
11 Gelles-Watnick and Anderson 2021.
12 UN Women 2019.
13 Grant et al. 2011, 3.
14 StreetNet International n.d., "World Class Cities for All: Background."
15 Lindell, Hedman, and Nathan-Verboomen 2010.
16 Wyatt 2010.
17 Hummel 2018.
18 StreetNet International n.d., "Progress Report on World Class Cities for All."
19 StreetNet International n.d., "Progress Report on World Class Cities for All."
20 StreetNet International n.d., "Progress Report on World Class Cities for All."
21 Henderson 2020.
22 While sex workers such as dancers or porn performers are not directly criminalized for their labor, many still face the issues of being part of, or very close to, a criminalized industry.
23 Mersol 2019.
24 Mehrotra 2019.
25 Query, Funari, and Plumb 2001.
26 Hunt 2022.
27 Babylon et al. n.d.

24

It's Time to Sue for What We Want

The New Legal Tools for Strippers

CAITY GWIN

Stripping is a job and strippers are workers. This should not be a controversial notion. Yet strippers often cannot access workplace protections. We have often thought that because we are classified as independent contractors, we do not have the rights and resources available to employees. We cannot access workers' compensation, we do not accrue Social Security benefits, we will never qualify for company health insurance or retirement plans, and, as we used to think, we have no legal recourse if we are discriminated against or sexually harassed at work, and we cannot unionize. Despite this, the job's flexibility and high earning potential makes this trade-off tolerable, even preferable, for many strippers.[1] As independent contractors, we have the flexibility to work when we want, jump from club to club, choose our customers, and earn significant cash income in a relatively short amount of time. Sacrificing employee benefits like healthcare or unionization rights for flexible access to fast cash seems a tolerable trade-off for most strippers.

However, in recent years, racial discrimination, exploitation and harassment from management, and general lack of workplace safety have become intolerable for some dancers. We have marched in the streets, picketed our clubs, organized, and spoken out. Much to our surprise, we have found that when strippers bring legal action against their clubs for wage theft, unionization rights, and racial discrimination (suits that have been historically reserved for employees, not independent contractors), strippers win. The amount of control that our bosses exert over us means that we are entitled to certain employee rights without being legally labeled employees. In other words, strippers may already be able to access the rights that we have been marching for. The myth of the flexibility-for-rights trade-off has kept us in golden handcuffs. Unemployment benefits or company healthcare might still be inaccessible, but when we fight for the things we really care about—discrimination, harassment, and safety—the courts and other judicial bodies support us. In this chapter, I will explain the activism, legal arguments, and wins and losses that represent this new terrain in stripper law. It is time to dispel the myth of the trade-off and sue for what we want.

What We Want: Equality, Safety, Fair Dealings

Although stripper-led activism is not new, there was an increase in organizing in the late 2010s. In 2018 Congress passed antitrafficking bills SESTA/FOSTA, making the lives of sex workers more dangerous, and inadvertently sparking a new generation of sex work activists. Strippers, working both in tandem with, and as part of, the larger sex-working community, joined the movement. The Black Lives Matter movement was also gaining momentum, and the intersection of these two causes led to the first national conversation about strippers' rights since the unionization of San Francisco's Lusty Lady in the '90s.

One of the first, and perhaps most widely publicized of these recent movements was the 2018 #NYCStripperStrike, which addressed racial inequity and discriminatory hiring practices in New York City strip clubs. Led by Gizelle Marie and other Black dancers, the movement began as a response to a new promotional scheme that pitted guest model bartenders ("startenders") against the house strippers. Because of the club's layout, the startenders danced between the customers and the stage, which meant startenders were tipped generously while strippers were relegated to second-class. The startenders did not have to pay house fees or tip-outs and were almost exclusively light-skinned and/or not Black, while many of the strippers were dark-skinned Black women. Strippers saw their income cut dramatically and were understandably upset. The club ignored their complaints.[2]

Gizelle, and others, went public with their grievances and took to social media with the hashtag #NYCStripperStrike. What began as frustration against the startender problem expanded into a larger conversation about racism in strip clubs. Strippers chastised Manhattan clubs for their pattern of hiring very few Black and brown dancers. Strippers outside of

New York spoke out against the racism and colorism that they too had experienced. The movement attracted widespread national media and inspired marches and protests. As the movement grew, the conversation expanded beyond racism. Strippers shared their experiences of sexual assault in the clubs, stigma, and violence against strippers outside of work. Strippers collectively shared complaints about high house fees, mandatory tip-outs, and lack of healthcare or basic workplace protections. Dancers' anger, resentment, and hope for justice had been boiling for years, and Gizelle's complaints opened the floodgates.

Inspired by, or simply in tandem with the NYCStripperStrike, stripper-led movements emerged across the country. In 2019 Minneapolis stripper Andi Seymor and her coworkers crafted, lobbied for, and eventually got passed a city ordinance that required clubs to maintain certain safety standards and prohibited required tip-outs.[3] During the 2020 COVID-19 shutdowns in Portland, Oregon, Cat Hollis launched the Haymarket Pole Collective to end racially discriminatory hiring practices and offer cultural-sensitivity training to offending clubs.[4] Also in 2020, Philadelphia dancers' rights organization Stilettos, Inc., held a rally calling for "equal employment opportunity and representation for BIPOC dancers, safer working conditions and properly installed equipment, and protection from sexual violations in the workplace."[5] Behind these widespread calls for reform, the myth of the independent contractor trade-off loomed. Strippers were fed up with their exploitative and racist work conditions, yet they were at a loss for what actions they could take. They feared losing their jobs. Lawsuits seemed off the table, since strippers understandably believed that as independent contractors, they were without employment protections.

Our Main Legal Weapon: The Misclassification Lawsuit

Strippers were, however, familiar with one form of lawsuit against clubs. In the decade leading up to the blossoming activism in the late 2010s, the most popular and widespread form of stripper-based legal action was the misclassification class-action lawsuit. Here is how it works: attorneys representing a group of strippers prove we have been misclassified as independent contractors and then sue the club for unpaid back wages that we should have been paid as employees. Generally, this means challenging our employment status under the Fair Labor Standards Act or analogous state laws. These laws designate whether a worker should be classified as an employee or an independent contractor based on the amount of control that her employer has over her work conditions. The courts will look at factors like whether workers have required hours, pay for their own supplies, set their own fees, and are essential to the main business. A good example is *Doe v. La Fuente*, a 2021 Nevada case that determined that strippers at Cheetah's Lounge Las Vegas (yes, the one from *Showgirls*) were misclassified as independent contractors when their conditions were more analogous to those of employees. In *La Fuente*, the Nevada Supreme Court applied the federal economic realities test to the dancers' working conditions to determine whether they should have been classified as employees. This test consists of six factors, all of which the court found to favor employee status. Finding the dancers had been misclassified, they were able to sue Cheetah's for the unpaid minimum wage that was owed to them. The named plaintiff dancers (the ones who initiated the lawsuit and served as representatives for the rest of the group) got handsome settlement checks, and all the dancers who signed on got smaller payouts. The outcome in *La Fuente* is similar to the result of almost all stripper misclassification lawsuits. Across the board, strippers' work conditions are more similar to those of employees than those of independent contractors, and clubs pay.[6]

These lawsuits have been an effective tool for getting large settlements into the pockets of strippers, and signaling that clubs are not immune from lawsuits. Clubs cannot simply evade legal responsibility by classifying strippers as independent contractors. Judges see through this and continue to side with strippers. Importantly, strippers do not need to become employees to win these lawsuits. The mere fact that we have been misclassified in the past is enough to warrant a legal victory or settlement in our favor. One of the main critiques of wage-theft misclassification lawsuits is that the current strippers' rights movement is less concerned about unpaid back wages. While we are not completely disinterested in fair dealings when it comes to our earnings, what we have been marching in the streets about is racial equity, safety, and an end to coercive business dealings.

Excitingly, though, recent lawsuits have used the same logic of the misclassification wage-theft lawsuit to fight for racial equity and lay a groundwork for safety through unionization. The misclassification of strippers as independent contractors is not limited to wage-theft law. Both the Equal Employment Opportunity Commission (EEOC) and the National Labor Relations Board (NLRB) have held that strippers are entitled to rights that have traditionally been reserved for employees only.

Discrimination: The EEOC

Years before the mainstream calls for racial justice in the #NYCStripperStrike, Ashley Williams and four other Black dancers in Jackson, Mississippi, brought a claim of racial discrimination against their club, Danny's Downtown Cabaret, in 2013.[7] Danny's limited the number of Black women who could work any given shift by instituting a "Black dancer quota."[8] Black strippers were also required to work an additional shift at an affiliated club, Black Diamonds, where they were physically and sexually harassed, and forced to deal with drug use, cigarette smoke, and other safety and cleanliness concerns. They did not experience these problems at Danny's; however, if they wanted to work at Danny's they either had to endure a shift at Black Diamonds or pay a one-hundred-dollar fee every shift. White dancers did not have this same requirement. Williams and the other dancers brought their complaint to the Mississippi branch of the Equal Employment Opportunity Commission. After an initial investigation, the EEOC brought a lawsuit against the club and the case made its way through the system, eventually landing at federal court. In 2019, the five dancers won a $3.3-million lawsuit. The club's main defense? The strippers were independent contractors, not employees, so they had no ability to bring a case through the EEOC. In an argument that echoed the misclassification wage-theft suits, the court found that the degree of control the club had over the strippers' work life meant they had been misclassified. This fact, when paired with the blatant racial discrimination, meant they were entitled to relief.

Unionization: The NLRB

Historically, workers have fought workplace exploitation through the labor rights granted in the National Labor Relations Act (NLRA). Introduced in 1935, the NLRA allowed workers to unionize and protected them from retaliation from their bosses. Strippers have unionized in the past, most famously at the Lusty Lady in San Francisco in 1992. One of the reasons the union was possible was that Lusty was a peepshow, with a smaller number of dancers who worked in an enclosed space where they could communicate and build comradery more easily than in a traditional strip club. The Lusty dancers agreed to become employees to unionize.[9] They made the trade-off from being independent contractors because it was understood to be the only path to unionization. Although other stripper unions were attempted in the 1990s, they either failed or were quickly disbanded after pressure from management. Strip-club unions and other labor activities were virtually nonexistent after the 1990s.

However, in 2020 the National Labor Relations Board (NLRB, the government entity responsible for enforcing the NLRA) was faced with a now familiar question: Can strippers, as independent contractors, enjoy the benefits of the NLRA even though these protections are statutorily reserved for employees? The NLRA, like the EEOC, and numerous judges before them, said yes. Strippers were treated like employees, even though they had been misclassified as independent contractors. Brandi Campbell, a dancer in Ohio, was fired from Centerfolds Club after threatening to file an unfair-labor-practice complaint against the club. An unfair labor practice (ULP) is an action performed by a business that would discourage unionization or other worker organization. ULPs are prohibited by the NLRA. In *Nolan Enterprises, Inc. d/b/a Centerfolds Club and Brandi Campbell* the administrative law judge determined that, because Centerfolds exerted a "significant degree of control over the dancers' opportunities for economic gain," the dancers should be considered employees. Because Campbell had been misclassified, she was entitled to protection under the NLRA, and her firing was illegal. As a result of the board's ruling in *Nolan*, Centerfolds was ordered to stop discriminating against workers wishing to file ULPs, offer Campbell her job back, and compensate her lost earnings. Additionally, Centerfolds was required to post copies of a notice from the board explaining dancers' rights under the NLRA, including their ability to form or join a union.

Brandi Campbell's fight against Centerfolds laid the groundwork for the first stripper union in almost thirty years. In May 2023, dancers at

Star Garden, a strip club in North Hollywood, California, became the nation's only unionized strippers after months of picketing and legal challenges from the club. While working at Star Garden, dancers faced abuses including wage theft, retaliatory firings, racially discriminatory hiring practices, and a security guard policy that put the dancers in harm's way. They brought their concerns to management, who responded by firing them.[10] The strippers went on strike.

On March 18, 2022, dancers from Star Garden began picketing. Dancers protested nearly every evening with signs and often in themed costumes, requesting that customers not patronize the club. Dancers issued a list of demands, filed three ULPs, and submitted a petition for unionization with Region 31 of the National Labor Relations Board. The NLRB granted them an election, and eighteen dancers cast ballots. The club challenged the ballots' validity, arguing, unsurprisingly, that the independent-contractor dancers were not protected by the NLRA. In December 2022, the NLRB determined that Star Garden had indeed violated labor law by firing and locking out dancers when they originally complained.[11] The NLRB's favorable ruling, despite the dancers' independent-contractor status, is consistent with the decision it made in Brandi Campbell's case. Once again, strippers can access a protection previously reserved for employees only. In labor law, like wage and employment law, the trade-off does not apply.

Rights We Must Leave Behind: The Real Trade-Off

Legal action initiated by strippers shows that despite being independent contractors, the clubs we work at cannot violate wage laws, employment discrimination laws, or labor laws. The amount of control that clubs exert over our work life means that regardless of how they do their paperwork and taxes, clubs cannot continue to perform such blatant workplace abuses without consequence. Additionally, strippers do not need to give up the autonomy, flexibility, and earning potential that make this job so attractive. In the abovementioned cases, the myth of the trade-off is truly a myth.

How far could strippers push this argument? Could we use misclassification to access unemployment insurance, workers' compensation, or health insurance? Theoretically, the argument could translate. However, pushing for resources like these, which require clubs to pay additional taxes and fees into external, government systems, may have detrimental consequences for strippers. When it comes to government benefits, rather than legal protections, strippers may face a true trade-off. Accessing these benefits might require strippers to truly reclassify as employees, and recent events in California indicate that this will lead to unintended, detrimental consequences.

In 2019, the state of California showed strippers what can happen when we are reclassified as employees. The result was catastrophic. Strippers, as it turns out, are not the only misclassified workers. The rise of the tech-industry-built gig economy has ushered in an influx of independent contractors. Like strippers, gig workers such as ride-share drivers, delivery people, and other workers in the app economy were also denied basic employment rights like minimum wage, workers' compensation, and unemployment insurance. Like strippers, they brought a lawsuit to reclaim their stolen wages. In *Dynamex Operations W. v. Superior Court* (2018), the California Supreme Court found that delivery drivers, like strippers, had been misclassified and were legally employees for the sake of employment and tax purposes. After the ruling, the state of California attempted to protect these workers through new legislation—AB5, which codified the *Dynamex* decision into law. Any worker who had been similarly misclassified must be reclassified as an employee and covered under the California wage orders.[12] Thus, California strip clubs too were forced to reclassify their dancers.

Reclassification meant that clubs not only would have to pay their dancers minimum wage but also were responsible for paying into unemployment insurance, workers' compensation, health insurance marketplaces, payroll taxes, and other government programs.[13] Instead of taking these payments out of their own profits, California strip clubs found a way to take it from the strippers. Clubs began paying dancers minimum wage, but in return demanded that strippers turn over a huge portion of their tips to the club. Strippers' income was slashed overnight, with some dancers reporting up to a 90 percent decrease in income. For example, in one club, dancers earned sixty dollars of a four-hundred-dollar private dance, when previously they had taken home much more.[14]

Strippers who spoke up against the new terms were fired; those who wished to stay were forced to pay bribes. Many quit. Managers blamed dancers, claiming dancers had wanted employee status and should now be happy they had it. Clubs also cut dancers' hours to keep them part-time employees and thus not eligible for benefits. They fired dancers en masse, with undocumented dancers and dancers of color being the first to go. Strippers found their lives upended and many were forced to get second jobs. "There is nothing sadder than being a stripper with a second job," mused one California dancer regarding her post-AB5 plight at a 2022 National Lawyers Guild student chapter panel at the William S. Boyd School of Law at the University of Nevada, Las Vegas. This outcome is to be avoided at all costs. The ability to collect unemployment insurance is not a logical trade for a 90 percent drop in income and loss of workplace freedom. It makes sense for ride-side drivers, but for high-earning strippers it is a destabilizing loss. Unlike our right to sue for discrimination or to unionize for our safety, when it comes to government-sponsored benefits, strippers are faced with a true trade-off, and it is one most of us will accept.

Conclusion

Strippers, like many workers in the gig economy, are wedged in a legal space somewhere between employee and independent contractor. Currently, we are carving out a sweet spot where we can be protected from blatant abuses and discrimination, while still maintaining our autonomy, flexibility, and earning potential. Courts and other judicial bodies agree that we are entitled to these protections and are willing to compensate us when our club violates the law. Lawsuits, though, are expensive, time consuming, and not an option for everyone. Dancers who bring these lawsuits are compensated for the abuses they experienced, but it is easy to wonder if a lengthy and draining lawsuit is worth it. For Ashley Williams and the other dancers at Danny's, their entire EEOC case took nearly a decade. Given the attorney's fees, split among five women over a seven-year period, it is not a stretch to say that the strippers here could have earned the same amount of money, if not more, had they simply been treated like their white counterparts. And did anything really change for the other strippers in Jackson? In 2021, the EEOC performed a follow-up assessment and found that the "Black dancer quota" still existed. Looking forward, we need to ask, How can we move beyond compensatory payouts and move into actual change? After the settlements and legal successes, clubs often return to their same discretions. For now, litigation offers a viable, yet slow-moving option to pressure clubs into ceasing their most egregious violations. We can hope that if they are forced to continue to pay for their abuses, their offenses will eventually become economically unsustainable. Perhaps selectively changing aspects of labor and employment laws to cover independent contractors would offer long-term protection and avoid relitigating the issue. We do not, however, want to push so far as to cause clubs to reclassify us as employees and have total control over our work lives. We exist in this sweet spot, accepting the trade-offs we must, while slowly accessing the protections that are rightfully ours.

NOTES

1 Piper 2019; Sepic 2019.
2 Setaro 2017.
3 Seymour 2019.
4 Riski 2020.
5 Decriminalize Sex Work 2022.
6 LeRoy, 2017, 260–62.
7 WLBT 2019.
8 U.S. Equal Employment Opportunity Commission n.d.
9 Alemzadeh 2013, 354; Chun 1999, 248; Rutman 1999, 555.
10 Moreno 2022.
11 Hussain 2022.
12 Chavez 2020, 147.
13 Waxmann 2022.
14 Waxmann 2022.

25

Taking Our Words Right out of Our Mouths

The Appropriation of Sex Worker–Rights Language

CRYSTAL A. JACKSON

Who would not want laws against slavery?! Federal legislation since the turn of the century, like the Trafficking Victims Protection Act of 2000 and the Fight Online Sex Trafficking Act of 2018 (FOSTA), alongside mainstream anti–sex trafficking advocates, refer to sex trafficking and sexual labor as "modern-day slavery" that needs to be abolished.[1] When I teach my classes, all my students agree that sexual slavery is horrible. Yet they find it difficult to understand the differences between nonconsensual sex trafficking and consensual sexual labor. They find it especially difficult to articulate ways to end violence against sex workers without calling for the eradication of the sale of sex—even when learning what sex workers themselves demand. Among my peers, whether at a gathering of academics or at a party meeting new people, when someone finds out I am a professor they often ask me what I study, and I say something along the lines of "I study sex worker–rights activism in the US because most people don't know that sex workers can and do advocate for themselves." And the response is invariably something like, "Oh wow, that's great, sex trafficking is a huge problem; it's so sad." I then take a breath and try to determine how I can educate this person in a welcoming, nonpatronizing way with just another sentence or two. This is how it has been for me for over fifteen years.

This chapter focuses on how and why anti–sex trafficking policies and advocates are appropriating social-justice language, specifically, "abolitionism" and "decriminalization," to undermine sex worker–rights activism in the United States today. By the end of this chapter, readers, much as I wish for partygoers, you will learn to apply a critical eye to what appear to be dueling frameworks. What is very powerful about sex worker–rights activism is not only that sex workers' demands are being heard by larger numbers of people since the turn of the century, including at the United Nations, but that their activism reveals that anti–sex trafficking "modern-day slavery" narratives are racist, transphobic, sexist, and anti-immigrant. But the increased visibility of sex worker–rights efforts in the United States may be the very reason why antiprostitution and anti–sex trafficking advocates are, quite literally, taking these words right out of sex workers' mouths.

Dueling Intents: Abolitionism and Decriminalization

Most people in the United States are familiar with the term "abolitionism" in reference to antislavery abolitionism in the past, and today's #BlackLivesMatter demands to defund, disrupt, and dismantle the mass incarceration industrial complex of policing, courts, jails, and prison, including undocumented-immigrant detention centers and Immigration and Customs Enforcement (ICE), and to decarcerate our prisons and jails. In this context, abolition means undertaking a radical change to a powerful, imposing structure that shapes the lives of many families and communities in the United States: the criminal legal system. Black feminist legal scholar Michelle Alexander argues that the criminal legal system is inherently racist because of its historical growth and focus after the federal government outlawed slavery. Alexander identifies mass incarceration as the contemporary form of racialized social control: literally removing Black people and other people of color from their families and communities.

Abolitionism is a process; it takes time. Respected racial-justice abolitionist organizer and educator Mariame Kaba offers concrete actions to take on the way to abolition: "dramatic decreases of police budgets and redirecting those funds to other social goods," "ending cash bail," "abolishing police unions," and "disarming the police."[2] Abolition means more than erasure and removal; it provides the foundation to build something new and different to meet community needs for safety and accountability.

In discussions of racism and immigration, abolition connotes a progressive set of ideals that would, if enacted, improve the lives of people. However, anti–sexual slavery advocates want to abolish sex work and sex trafficking, not reform the laws policing sex work. "Prostitution abolitionism" refers to the goal of abolishing the sale of sex itself in the name of protecting women and girls from what anti–sex trafficking advocates call "modern-day slavery."[3] Ignoring police brutality and the inherent racism of the criminal legal system, prostitution neo-abolitionists advocate for more sex-trafficking laws with increased penalties. They believe that the existing criminal legal system is a source of protection despite decades of data showing this is not true for Black people, Indigenous people, and other people of color who disproportionately fill US jails and prisons in a country that carries the distinction of having the highest incarceration rate at the world.

Thus, the word "abolition" confuses people because prostitution neo-abolitionists have opposite goals as #BlackLivesMatter advocates. Again, the historical use of "abolitionism" refers to the freedom movement of enslaved Black people, while the current, related use of "abolitionism" refers to prison abolitionism and the defunding of law enforcement to keep Black communities and other communities of color safe. Consider what it means, then, for prostitution neo-abolitionists to use historical antislavery language to push for legislation to support growth of the criminal legal system. Consider that contemporary prison abolitionists, including researchers and activists, want to end the criminal legal system as we know it because it is an inherently violent, racist, sexist, transphobic, and homophobic system. Thus, calling for more policing and more punishing laws to "save women and girls" while Black women and girls, and Black boys, men, and nonbinary people are calling for the abolition of police is not only counterproductive; it is violent.[4]

In addition to appropriating the word "abolition" and twisting it from its racial-justice roots, prostitution abolitionists have also appropriated "decriminalization." Sex workers have long demanded decriminalization of all sexual labors as step number one to mitigate violence that sex workers experience and reduce stigma. Decriminalization, broadly speaking, refers to the removal of all criminal code for an activity. With respect to sex work, decriminalization means that police would not surveil, harass, hurt, or arrest sex workers anymore—or at the very least, police would not be able to do so under the justification of policing prostitution. It means that sex-working parents would not lose their children to Child Protective Services simply for engaging in erotic labor.

Importantly, decriminalization could also assert sex workers' right to self-determination, and to work without fear of arrest—which in and of itself is a form of violence that can beget other violence. Decriminalization further makes it easier for sex workers to report violence that they do experience, especially at the hands of the state, as when police stalk, physically assault, sexually assault, and verbally abuse sex workers and people assumed to be sex workers or insist on a quid-pro-quo exchange of sexual services to avoid arrest.[5]

However, decriminalization can vary in its visioning and implementation. Plus, there are other legal models: "criminalization," whereby policies declare an action illegal, and "legalization," which regulates an action or industry. Legal sex work industries in the United States include adult pornography, Nevada's legal brothels, and strip clubs, and are heavily regulated. For example, county or city strip-club regulations across the United States engage in verbal acrobatics to define the "lap" of lap dance or what constitutes a nipple.[6]

These three legal models (decriminalization, criminalization, and legalization) are spectrums that can run the gamut from maintaining a status quo to challenging sociolegal norms, from calling for reforms that leave systems in place to radical models that dismantle violent systems like the criminal legal system. Activists and scholars like feminist sexualities scholar Siobhan Brooks (2021), who also worked at a peep show in San Francisco, warn that "binary framings of debates about sex work focusing on decriminalization versus criminalization, innocence versus guilt, or choice versus forced sex work do not address the actual needs or political desires of sex workers, especially Black women." Brooks goes on to affirm,

> In fact, these binary framings do sex workers a political disservice. One way feminists can think more productively about issues of sex work and the debates surrounding them is to apply an intersectional analysis as opposed to a single-issue one. This can move feminists beyond the good/ bad dichotomy and allow them to explore multiple ways of addressing the harms and inequality that can be associated with sex work.[7]

As you will read shortly, what sex workers mean by "decriminalization" is very different from what prostitution neo-abolitionists mean by "decriminalization." In fact, "decriminalization" was a word prostitution abolitionists did not use until it gained popularity in sex worker–rights circles. Yet their methods and goals are the exact opposite of racial-justice abolitionism and of sex worker–rights activism.

Appropriating Sex Worker–Rights Language

You may ask yourself, "How can a call to end modern-day slavery be at odds with prison abolitionism?!" On the surface, this seems unlikely. Fascinatingly, rising prostitution abolitionists are embracing the term "decriminalization" as a synonym for the "Nordic model" or the "Swedish model." In 1999, Sweden was the first country in the world to implement a policy model that criminalizes the customer but not the sex worker. You may also hear this approach referred to as "end demand," as in, end the client's demands for this service by criminalizing it.

On the surface, this may seem like a win. However, sex workers themselves are not supportive of this model because it criminalizes their source of income, making the end demand model a form of economic violence.[8] This policy may also lead to clients being more demanding because they do not want to be arrested (e.g., pressuring a worker to forgo a condom for time's sake). And if police are looking to arrest clients, then sex workers are still exposed to police interactions—the very police who are often violent with sex workers. I argue that referring to "end demand" as "partial decriminalization" or "decriminalization" is a prime example of appropriation: taking something created by a less powerful group and using it in a disrespectful or exploitative way.

For example, DemandAbolition.Org (a neo-abolitionist group) has an article titled "Why Prostitution Should Not Be Fully Decriminalized." This is a shift in language for prostitution abolitionists as they did not have this vocabulary in the early 2000s. This article's title is also an exercise in linguistic acrobatics: it is meant to differentiate Demand Abolition activists from sex worker–rights activists. To be clear, to "not be fully decriminalized" means it is not decriminalized. To "not be fully decriminalized" indicates reform, perhaps a legalization model. Prostitution abolitionists only want to stop the sale of sex and are unconcerned with reforming existing state systems and institutions that facilitate abuse and oppression, nor eradicating the racism, sexism, and heteronormativity inherent in the criminal legal system. Thus, some prostitution neo-abolitionists have successfully co-opted abolitionist language and sex worker–rights language. One key piece of evidence of this is that no state in the United States is entertaining a prison-abolition or law-enforcement-abolition bill. States are not working to radically defund and dismantle the criminal legal system. Yet anti–sex trafficking policies and advocacy efforts continue to grow in number and in funding at state and federal levels.

US Sex Worker–Rights Activists Go to the United Nations

Much sex worker–rights activism since the turn of the century has contended with the impact of prostitution-abolitionist policies and anti–sex work advocacy that patronizingly categorize most sex workers as trafficking victims who do not know what is best for themselves. But, US sex workers will not be silenced! Sex workers have crafted a submission to the United Nations (UN) four times in an international effort to hold the United States government accountable for "human rights violations against people who engage in sexual labor, and people assumed to be engaging in sexual labor."[9] Their 2020 submission to the UN Universal Periodic Review enumerated twenty-nine points calling out violent racist policing, violent transphobic policing, and the federal government's failure to act on previous agreements to protect the well-being of sex workers. In particular, sex worker–rights organizations note the federal government's refusal to consider the advice of respected, established global organizations that have argued again and again that the best path toward equity and justice for sex workers is the removal of punitive laws—in other words, decriminalization—from the World Health Organization to the United Nations Development Program and the United Nations Program on HIV/AIDS. The international nongovernmental agency Amnesty International has also adopted this stance.

The statement further calls out the sexist racism of local law enforcement. For example, the section headed "Equal Rights to Protect under the Law" starts with the authors' seventh point:

> 7. Law enforcement disproportionately hyper-police sex workers of color in the United States for arrest because of profiling minority status. People

of color from the lowest income communities who do sex work in public spaces to meet their needs are relentlessly and disproportionately targeted by the police. Statutes and policies mandating the "banishment" of
people from certain areas or eroding the reasonable suspicion standard
for arrest and conviction violate due process rights. Law enforcement officials routinely invoke such concepts to threaten people they profile as
sex workers, subjecting them to degrading and violent treatment such as
removal of wigs or clothing, confiscation or destruction of property, and
verbal abuse including homophobic, anti-transgender, and racist slurs
and sexual harassment.

Sex worker–rights activists and organizations have very strong antiviolence platforms, evident in their continued submissions to the UN
Universal Periodic Review of the United States, and in their own efforts
to change laws in their home cities and states.

I share this specific example of sex worker–rights activism within an
established, respected arena of the UN for two reasons. First, it is very
easy to create dichotomies when it comes to activism. Sex workers are
obviously antitrafficking. Yet prostitution abolitionists argue that sex
worker–rights efforts are misguided and misplaced. Appropriating the
word "decriminalization" is a powerful strategy to invalidate and undermine what sex workers themselves are advocating for. Second, people
often disagree on the best path toward equality and equity. In such moments, it is often the most well-funded, the most normatively organized
(e.g., incorporating as nonprofits with politically powerful, rich board
members), and the most politically normative (e.g., cisgender, middle-
class white people with no criminal record) who are heard and supported by local, state, and federal policymakers.

As a sex worker–rights scholar-activist myself, I want this chapter to
act as a call to support historically situated abolition and decriminalization efforts. My hope is that this chapter clarifies the racial-justice
roots of abolitionism so that you, readers, have key information needed
to make informed decisions. Sex worker–rights activism is just one of
many facets of racial-justice abolitionism.[10] To that end, many US sex
worker–rights organizations align with prison-abolition efforts. Indeed,
some sex worker–rights activists come from a background in prison-
abolition work or engage in prison-abolition work as well, like Sex

Worker Outreach Project's Behind Bars initiative, which provides direct support for currently and formerly incarcerated sex workers.

Sex worker–rights organizations in the United States advocate for decriminalization as the best path forward for sex workers—the first step on a long path toward bodily autonomy and freedom from violence.[11] However, most sex worker–rights wins since the turn of the century are reforms: changes to the existing structure without any radical overhaul to that structure.[12] And that's fine! The wins reflect what is possible within the current system. We desperately need these stopgaps for immediate relief. That does not preclude us from having a vision of an abolitionist future. The laws, policies, and policing at the intersection of carceral feminism, paternalistic sexism, and a racist criminal legal system will not be edited out of society overnight. I leave you with a popular US sex worker–rights slogan: *Be nice to sex workers.*

NOTES

1 Victims of Trafficking and Violence Prevention Act of 2000, Pub. L. No. 106-368, 114 Stat. (October 28, 2000), accessed December 12, 2023, www.govinfo.gov.

2 Kaba 2021, 13.

3 Jackson, Reed, and Brents 2017. Also see Lee 2021.

4 Brooks 2021.

5 See Albright and D'Adamo 2017. See also Begum and Bibi 2022.

6 Jackson 2011.

7 Brooks 2021, 13.

8 For more on economic violence, see Allard 2016.

9 Human Rights Council 2020.

10 Schulte 2020.

11 There are dozens of organizations across the country. These include local chapters of the national Sex Workers Outreach Project (SWOP), and SWOP's Behind Bars initiative, alongside the national Desiree Alliance, and the Sex Workers Project's legal services in New York State. GLITS (Gays & Lesbians Living in a Transgender Society), whose mission is to "approach the health and rights crises faced by transgender sex workers," and HIPS in DC ("HIPS" formerly stood for Helping Individual Prostitutes Survive; now it stands for Honoring Individual Power and Strength) prioritize sex workers of color. Organizations may explicitly center racial justice, such as the Black Sex Workers Collective, New York City's Red Canary Song, by and for Asian and Asian migrant sex workers, Women With a Vision in New Orleans, and Black Trans Nation, "a non-profit organization dedicated to serving the black transgender community and survival sex workers."

12 Jackson 2016.

26

"May There Be Evidence of My Life at My Disposal"

Israeli Sex Workers Dismantling the "Whore" Stigma

YEELA LAHAV-RAZ AND AYELLET BEN NER

Since the late 1990s and early 2000s, international antitrafficking organizations, state actors, NGOs, and journalists have led an extensive struggle against Israel's booming sex industry. This struggle culminated on December 31, 2018, when Israel changed its sex work policy to the end demand approach, criminalizing clients of sex workers. The Israeli end demand policy resulted from the determined efforts of both radical, neo-abolitionist and conservative, religious parliamentarians who leveraged Israel's values as a Jewish and democratic state linking gender equality with the protection of women's modesty and family purity.

Based on arguments that allowing the sex industry to exist freely abuses human rights, harms women, and contradicts Jewish values, on July 10, 2020, the Prohibition on Consumption of Prostitution law came into force. Similarly to what we are witnessing worldwide, coalitions between the religious Right and abolitionist feminists in Israel used a prostitution-as-harm narrative to frame their arguments about the realities faced by sex workers and appropriate policies to address them.[1] As was mentioned by Levy-Aronovic and colleagues,[2] these two parties have become strange bedfellows seeking to protect Israeli sex workers by framing the issues within a paradigm of oppression. In this chapter, we aim to show how Israeli sex workers have been active since the early 2000s in various arenas to confront these framings and policy changes, fighting a harmful "whore stigma,"[3] which portrays them as perpetual victims and sexual objects, ignoring their autonomy. Despite lacking political power and the difficulty of speaking publicly as sex workers, especially in a conservative state like Israel, sex workers used online platforms like blogs, erotic magazines, and social media to assert their perspectives and experiences. Fighting against mainstream media or aid organizations that try to speak on their behalf, Israeli sex workers have effectively presented a more nuanced perspective on the sex work experience.

As we will show, Israeli sex workers' online writing developed as a re-action against the public discourse and legislative procedures that began in the early 2000s, which they felt denied their voice, excluded them from the political discussions, and increased their stigmatization. De-spite the existence of a global sex work movement,[4] Israel has, until 2019, lacked sex worker organizations.[5] Since involvement in the sex industry is so stigmatized, using online platforms where one can remain anony-mous assisted both the online and offline worlds of sex work activism. Thus, online media have become an important alternative channel for building Israeli sex workers' organizations.

This chapter examines how sex workers' public writings became "speech-as-action." Katriel explains that "speech-as-action" means that words themselves can become powerful forms of activism in volatile contexts of political and cultural dissent.[6] Because many societies still view sex work as one of the most reprehensible forms of deviance for women,[7] openly sharing personal experiences in writing can reclaim "whore stigma" and become a way of validating one's own experiences. Analyzing historical examples of sex workers' public writing on online platforms, we found that as the legislative process progressed, their writ-ing became more political and activist oriented, often motivating offline actions like protests. Although the characteristics of their writing dif-fered between time periods and online platforms, the prevailing theme was sex workers' attempts to deal with the stigma directed towards them. We conclude that while not all sex workers' actions were successful on the legislative level, writing in public online spaces held transformative potential by generating solidarity and class consciousness. This ground-work created the infrastructure for establishing ARGAMAN—the first Israeli sex workers organization.

The Study

To describe the development of Israeli sex workers' public writing for this short chapter, we analyzed texts that have been published since the early 2000s on various online platforms such as independent blogs, online magazines, and social media networks. The data included forty posts published in the first two decades of the 2000s, mainly on independent blogs, and fifty posts published between 2017 and 2021 on Facebook. We selected texts that met the following criteria: published on open and public platforms; self-definition of the author as a "prostitute," "sex worker," or "escort girl" appears within the written text; and the text revolves around the experience of stigmatization resulting from being a sex worker. The texts were written in Hebrew and were translated by the authors. All efforts were made to remain faithful to the writers' original meaning.

Cracking the Silence

As was mentioned, while the struggle to eradicate the Israeli sex industry began in the early 2000s, until 2019, Israel lacked any sex work organization. The victim narrative and the "whore stigma" that dominated the Israeli feminist "rescue industry,"[8] as well as the conservative nature of the country, prevented sex workers from coming out in public. Israeli sex workers found independent blogs, which were highly popular at the beginning of the millennium, as an alternative channel through which to take back ownership of their identity since one can remain anonymous, use pseudonyms, and control the data published:

> To write, just to write and get everything out . . . just to write. Not necessarily for everyone. I usually write for myself. To remember, so that there will be evidence of my life at my disposal. In this life, I have the words. (Whore 1 Pedotan)

Following Shaw's assumption that the question of who can speak and whose words are recognized is the very basis of the political,[9] we argue that writing against the dominant victim narrative held revolutionary potential. This quotation from "Whore 1 Pedotan" reflects the common theme among sex workers who shared their stories on public blogs— using the writing to confront the feeling of having their identity and life story erased and commodified by others. Many of the texts along those years expressed how the volatile context of the "whore stigma" created an immense sense of solitude and a compelling urge to write out of it. For example, "Escort Girl" posted on her blog a post titled "Loneliness in a Crowd":

> I can't tell my mother how I live; I can't reveal my secret to my sister. I have many friends and relatives, and no one knows what I'm doing and where. My life is completely built on fantasies that I invent and tell skillfully. So, if in life I can't open up to almost anyone, I'll do it here.

"Escort Girl" expresses how the stigma involved in being a sex worker results in hiding or lying about one's identity, which may result in stress, anxiety, and exhaustion.[10] The fear of public condemnation prevents sex workers from sharing their varied work experiences and inevitably flattens their ability to express a nuanced perspective to others, making blogs an alternative arena for stigma reappropriation. Furthermore, writing became an active strategy to deal with the state's stigma towards sex workers in enforcing laws that increase stigmatization:

> The stigma surrounding the sex industry must be stopped! . . . Feminists, lobbies, and MKs [elected members of Knesset, the Israeli legislative body] are pushing delusional laws under the guise of saving the soul and body of the poor woman. . . . But the naked truth is that most of the sex workers I've met want to work in the industry. Some enjoy the work, and some enjoy the liberation and economic independence that the occupation gives. . . . Most of us are not dumb or helpless. (The "Happy Hooker")

The "Happy Hooker" published her stories in an independent blog, where she reclaimed her experience as a prostitute by calling herself a "happy hooker" who enjoys the work while pointing to the prevailing stigma toward sex workers in a relatively conservative country. Scholars have argued that policy decisions are influenced by the stigma toward sex workers, often portraying them as a homogeneous group who are oppressed, enslaved, and need rescue.[11] However, as our analysis shows, what sex workers testify that they need is not rescue but rather validation and acknowledgment of their perspectives and experience. When their voices go unheard, they become victims not of the "whore stigma" but of the victim narrative.

The examples presented thus far demonstrate the first time Israeli sex workers addressed whore stigma in Israeli society. They articulated their work and nonwork lives and the variety of ways they understand and experience the work they do. However, during the first two decades of the 2000s, the use of writing to establish and develop themselves as subjects facing "whore stigma" was more of an individual-level resistance.[12] The blogs were created by different writers who were not necessarily familiar with each other, each sharing their individual experience without forming collective political action. This reality started to change in 2014.

Cracking the Narrative

While sex workers' blogs remained, in some sense, niche, since 2014, the growing online arena has enabled activists to make visible the once highly private experiences of sex workers' lives. It began in 2014 when neo-abolitionist activists opened several Facebook pages to influence political and public discourse around sex work and sex work policy. They aimed to promote the end demand policy by using activities such as online campaigns against sex-industry consumers and grassroots activism such as demonstrating in front of strip clubs and brothels. Their actions were successful. Their posts strengthened public awareness of the prostitution-as-harm narrative and were used by politicians to promote various laws against the sex industry.[13]

Neo-abolitionists' organizing successes also propelled a counterforce, this time of sex workers. In 2017, four women with experience in the sex industry, including Ayellet, the second author of this chapter, opened a new Facebook page titled "When She Works" (WSW) to oppose the Israeli legislative progress toward the end demand policy. Like other sex worker organizations around the world, these women claimed that policymakers prevent those involved in the industry from expressing their opinions about the policies that affect them. The creation of WSW was no less than a revolution in Israel's online public discourse. While cyberspace and conventional media focused mainly on the humiliating, exploitative, and harmful aspects of the sex industry, WSW tried to create a safe space for Israeli sex workers to advocate for ending criminalization and reducing the stigma.

Our analysis of various posts reveals how writing in a shared space dedicated to sex workers fostered a community that, in light of how legislation was progressing, also motivated activist actions. In its first year, the writing on WSW revolved around describing a nuanced life experience that transcends simplistic dichotomies, the desire to be heard without mediators who claim to speak on your behalf, as well as the attempt to dismantle the stigma:

> The shame that society imposes on you, the violence you cannot legally defend against, and the isolation from society—it kills you. The inability to ask for and receive mental help kills, but prostitution doesn't kill. You, those who completely ignore anything that causes a person to commit suicide or die from various diseases that have nothing to do with sex, kill prostitutes. (Anonimus, November 17, 2017)

In 2018, the State Prosecutor's Office issued a new directive to consider lap dances with customers at strip clubs an act of prostitution and thus a criminal offense. This "Lap-Dance" law closed all strip clubs in Israel. Sex workers on WSW then organized a "strippers' protest" in Tel Aviv on May 3, 2018. In a kind of chain reaction, the protest received media coverage, which inspired sex workers' writing, which then became more militant, political, and activist. Furthermore, strippers began using the Facebook page to write to fight back. Fassi notes how lawmakers prioritize ostensibly expert knowledge as meaningful sources of information above the claims, experiences, knowledge, and needs of sex workers.[14] As legislative efforts progressed, in response, sex workers' public activist writing became more professional and strategic. It also turned into grassroots activism such as organized meetings where people could meet sex workers and listen to their experiences. Thus, sex workers' writings about their experience in the sex industry can generate knowledge independent from the hegemonic discourse promoted by state actors and neo-abolitionist activists.

Another example occurred in 2019, when the shuttered Pussycat, formerly one of Tel-Aviv's leading strip clubs, was taken over by a project called "The Social Space." A sign explaining the project's purpose was hung at the entrance of the building, saying, "In the past few years, the building housed a notorious strip club, eventually becoming a focal point in the campaign against the objectification of women and their abuse." The current building's investors decided to

> dedicate it instead to social activism and Jewish culture. . . . We have taken upon ourselves to make amends ("Tikun"): from a place of darkness to a source of enlightenment. We shall turn this building into a center of social empowerment, a flagship for good doing in the city of Tel-Aviv.

The developers decided to turn the building into a museum that displays the club's life by leaving some of the decor and placing high heels, a mattress, and a sofa scattered throughout the club. The museum finances itself by conducting guided tours where the tourers can listen, through recorded voice guidance, to descriptions of the "horrible" lives of the strippers at the club.

The tours drew massive criticism from sex workers, and some even compared the displayed props to the shoe display in the Holocaust extermination camps. Furthermore, during the last four years that the tour has been taking place, many sex workers have referred to it in their writings and have objected to how touring the strip club legitimizes the stigma towards them:

> They presented it as a stage show. Like it's a fucking scene from a theatre show as if all the girls who worked here were part of a set. But I'm not an actress, and none of the strippers here is an actress but rather a real woman with a real life and true desires. We are neither a show nor a set for you. (Ariel, December 19, 2019)

> Instead of talking about how stigma destroys sex workers' lives and trying to dismantle it for both sex workers and their clients—the tour intensifies whore stigma. It shows the strippers as poor victims who desperately wanted money and time on stage and the customers as people who must hide their terrible secrets. (Gali, December 10, 2021)

Concluding Remarks

Sex work cannot be separated from its historical and social context. Israel's struggle over the last two decades to foster an end demand policy, despite evidence worldwide that a victim narrative deprives sex workers of their agency,[15] has profoundly affected Israeli sex workers' lives. Their continued exclusion from public debate and legislative procedures, and the hostility they faced when they tried to talk about their experiences in feminist communities,[16] have turned the online arena into an alternative platform where they have voiced their perspective and reclaimed ownership of their agency and subjective narrative.

Beginning with writing publicly on blogs and later using social media through the WSW Facebook page, Israeli sex workers used their writing to confront two decades of "victimized prostitute" narratives perpetuated by the Israeli feminist rescue industry and state actors. Israeli sex workers realized that, within the volatile contexts of sex work dissent, their voice and narrative were being privatized, leaving them struggling to articulate their nuanced experiences of the sex industry. Nonetheless, they used online spaces to highlight the failures of the end demand policy and how it stigmatized the most marginalized, excluded minorities, and forced them to go further underground.

Although Israel's decision to adopt the end demand policy can be viewed as a failure of Israeli sex workers, one cannot ignore how despite the thick stigma of sex work, they also managed to use their public writing for political action. What started as an individual-level resistance grew into grassroots activism through protests, demonstrations, gatherings, and, more importantly, the establishment of ARGAMAN—the first Israeli sex workers organization. Furthermore, ARGAMAN's establishment sparked the formation of two other organizations: ISU (Israeli Strippers Union) and Trans.Israel. These organizations, along with other veteran LGBTQ organizations, are working unremittingly to improve the lives of marginalized communities, especially as they did during the precarious COVID-19 pandemic. The Israeli case study demonstrates sex workers' ability to protest governmentality by building bottom-up solidarity and developing political-class consciousness.

NOTES

1 Lahav-Raz 2020.
2 Levy-Aronovic, Lahav-Raz, and Raz 2021.
3 Benoit et al. 2020; Stardust et al. 2021.
4 Anasti 2017.

5 Two previous attempts have failed. The first was in 2002 by the organization We Are Equal, and the second was in 2011 by the Association for the Regulation of Prostitution. Both organizations no longer exist.

6 Katriel 2021.

7 Armstrong 2019; Sanders 2005a.

8 Agustin 2007.

9 Shaw 2012.

10 Tomura 2009.

11 Benoit, Jansson, and Flagg 2018; Armstrong 2019.

12 Weitzer 2018.

13 Lahav-Raz 2020; Levy-Aronovic, Lahav-Raz, and Raz 2021.

14 Fassi 2015.

15 Pitcher 2019.

16 Lahav-Raz 2020.

PART VI

New Directions and Perspectives

27

The Field of Sex Work Studies

Past, Present, and Future

RONALD WEITZER

In one of the earliest sociological commentaries on prostitution, published in 1937, Kingsley Davis asserted two core arguments: that prostitution serves positive functions for society (including keeping marriages intact) and that transactional sex is strictly utilitarian, with no affective dimension.[1] We don't know how this article was greeted at the time, but it took another forty years before sex work would become a field of study in its own right. Only in the mid-1970s did we begin to see a few solid studies of strip clubs, illicit massage parlors, and prostitution. Sex work was generally not discussed in graduate school (and certainly not the topic of an entire course), and only a few students wrote theses on the topic. Social scientists apparently considered the topic either too marginal or "settled" and not worth exploring further. Things began to change, slowly, after the appearance of sex worker–rights campaigns in the 1970s, including the founding of COYOTE in San Francisco in 1973 and similar organizations internationally.[2] But it would not be until the twenty-first century that the field would truly blossom.

What did the nascent arena of sex work studies look like in 1980? What terminology was conventional? What kinds of actors were focused on? And what, if any, larger social structures were implicated in sexual commerce?

- The terms "prostitute," "john," "pimp," "punter," and "stripper" were standard fare. Today, more neutral occupational language is common: "sex worker," "performer," "provider," "webcammer," "dancer," "customer," "client," "third party," and "manager." The term "sex work" came into vogue only in the late 1980s.

- The focus was on the individual worker—not customers, managers, or other third parties.
- Only one type of worker attracted attention: cisgender women far more than men, while transgender providers were entirely invisible in the literature.
- What about customers? In the 1970s, a few studies of strip club customers appeared, but sex buyers were almost entirely ignored. Real-world consumers of pornography were jettisoned in favor of experimental lab studies of small samples of college students—hardly representative of the population of consumers.
- Structural conditions were largely neglected. While family breakdown, drug addiction, homelessness, and poverty were described as push factors, other arrangements were ignored for the most part, including state and local policies and law enforcement practices.
- Race and ethnicity may have been mentioned but were not core variables. It was rare to find a study that systematically compared sex workers, demographically or experientially, from two or more racial groups.[3]
- Regarding prostitution, the focus was on street markets.[4] Research on indoor settings—generally safer and more pleasant work environments—was scarce.
- There were absolutely no studies of porn performers. Instead, we have a few content analyses of magazine photos and videos, but nothing on the actors' lives, work, and the meanings they attached to pornography. It was not until 2000 that the first study of that kind was published.[5]
- Aside from magazine pictorials (in *Playboy*, *Penthouse*, *Hustler*, etc.), pornography was consumed in movie theaters or peep shows. Home viewing began in earnest only in the mid-1980s, thanks to the advent of VCRs.
- News and entertainment media were saturated with negative representations, and still are for the most part. The first sex work–positive documentary that I recall seeing was the A&E Network's excellent *Red-Light Districts* in 1996.
- Regarding prostitution in particular, researchers appeared to assume the immutability of the laws. Alternative policies, such as decriminalization, were almost never discussed, except in a few law review articles.

1980 to 2000

Three major developments appeared between 1980 and 2000. First, institutional review boards were in their infancy in 1980, when they began to produce regulations governing researchers' treatment of human subjects. Previously, procedures for gaining consent and minimizing risks were not codified and enforced by an ethics board at a university or research institute. It goes without saying that such oversight is important, but many of the boards imposed steeper requirements on sexuality scholars than on other researchers, creating a higher bar for approval.[6] Second, a major antiporn campaign was launched. In 1984, the Reagan administration created a commission to investigate the content and effects of exposure to pornography, headed by Attorney General Edwin Meese. The final report was full of anecdotal testimony by self-described victims of porn and antiporn activists. The report was widely regarded as biased, yet it resulted in increased funding for the Justice Department's obscenity unit as well as the successful prosecution of many of the largest producers of pornography by 1990.[7] The commission concluded that pornography was conducive to violence against women, despite an earlier national commission reaching the opposite verdict.[8] Third, the late 1990s saw the construction of human trafficking as a "new" social problem and one that has been conflated with sex work. Unlike 1970 or even 1990, when sex work is debated today it is almost inevitable that trafficking is invoked. The law generally makes a distinction between voluntary sex work and labor that occurs under conditions of "force, fraud, or coercion" (the key offenses under the US Trafficking Victims Protection Act, 2000), yet this has not stopped anti–sex work activists from pressing to expand the law to cover consensual transactions as well. These activists have attempted to tie trafficking not only to prostitution but also to pornography, strip clubs, and commercial webcamming.[9]

A final trend pertains to the post-2000 years: targeting customers, whom prohibitionists consider the root cause of commercial sex. In 1999, Sweden became the first country to criminalize clients exclusively, in order to attack "the demand" and thus reduce prostitution overall. Since then, a similar model has been adopted in Norway, Iceland, France, Ireland, Northern Ireland, and the state of Maine in the United States. Outlawing only one of the parties to a contractual agreement affects the other party as well, as both are forced to operate in a clandestine and potentially precarious manner—yet does not seem to reduce prostitution as intended.[10]

The 2000s

Fast forward to today. Compared to past decades, both academia and civil society have seen progress in several areas: (1) a large and growing group of scholars studying the sex industry, (2) a more mixed depiction of sex work in the media, including television series and films that normalize or routinize aspects of this work, or at least complicate the messages previously attached to it, (3) changes in public opinion, with a slim majority in Britain, Canada, and the United States favoring legal reform, and (4) several US states seriously considering bills to decriminalize prostitution.[11]

Over the past two decades, we have witnessed an explosion of research, helping to fill in some of the gaps mentioned above. Faculty and graduate students around the world are increasingly interested in the topic; conferences centering on sex work have been held; an academic journal devoted to pornography research, *Porn Studies*, was founded in 2014; and since 1998, Las Vegas has been home to the AVN Adult Entertainment Expo, a trade show attended by thousands of fans every year (similar conventions are held in other nations). The knowledge base has expanded greatly, especially regarding indoor prostitution, cisgender men providers, and customers.[12] And the state has been increasingly implicated in its impact on participants and alternatives to criminalization policies. Recent research has examined places where prostitution has been decriminalized and legalized, although much more is needed to document the ways in which these models work in the real world.[13]

One sector has been very well researched: strip clubs. Reflecting the continuing lopsidedness of scholarly work on the sex industry, it can be argued that we have more than a critical mass of studies of these clubs and the dancers who work there, many of which repeat the same findings: that the work involves both exploitative and agentic dimensions, that the intimacy expressed between dancers and customers is feigned, and that the type of club makes a difference.[14] And this literature tends to focus on the most prevalent type of strip club: where cis women perform largely for cis men. We have a handful of studies of gay clubs and venues where men dance for audiences of women, and such studies have been important in documenting both similarities to and differences from the conventional clubs—but much more investigation of alternative clubs is needed to appreciate the ways in which gender matters in this sector. In short, the strip club sector needs to be refreshed by moving away from rehashing the same themes and researching only heterosexual clubs.

Research Gaps Today

More broadly, is the field still lopsided in the types of actors and topics studied? Has the nature of the research questions changed? Regarding the latter, most twentieth-century research centered on demographic factors, occupational risks, health outcomes (condom use, HIV, STIs), and abuse. Today, while these themes remain a priority to public health scholars, social scientists increasingly devote their attention to actors' experiences, meanings, and interpersonal relationships. There has also been a slight shift away from viewing sex work exclusively as a problem to recognizing that it can be a potential opportunity for many of those involved. Yet we still know relatively little about (1) transgender workers, (2) women customers, (3) escorts, (4) commercial webcammers, (5) pornography performers and producers, (6) contemporary brothels, (7) the owners and managers of erotic businesses, and (8) sex work outside the Global North.[15]

Two explanations can be offered as to why certain actors/topics/ dimensions, and not others, have been researched. First, a fixation on cisgender women sex workers seems to have jettisoned other genders as well as customers, managers, and profiteers. For those working in prostitution and commercial stripping, the classic research question often boiled down to "Why do they do it?," prompting inquiry into their backgrounds and decision making. Yet the same question was not asked (until the 2000s) of customers or third parties. The opposite was the case in pornography: researchers lacked access to porn performers and producers, so they focused instead on the viewers—usually college men involved in laboratory experiments under artificial conditions that had no resonance with how porn is consumed in the real world. Many of these experiments were grounded in the hypothesis that viewing pornography increased the odds of attitudinal or behavioral problems, especially in men's relations with women. A meta-analysis of such experimental studies published from the 1970s to 2020 found that nonviolent porn was not associated with aggression and that violent images were only "weakly correlated with sexual aggression."[16] Only recently have consumers in the real world been interviewed regarding their engagement with porn and how they believe it has affected them. These studies point to considerable variation in viewers' preferences and the effects of exposure on their lives.[17]

In addition to a narrow focus on certain types of actors, scholars prior to the 2000s tended to categorize sex work as deviant, which shaped the kinds of research questions they explored and what they ignored: (1) a focus on pathologies such as deficient upbringing, mental health deficits, drug use, victimization, and risky health practices; and (2) insufficient inquiry into workers' everyday work lives: their occupational practices, aspirations, and interactions with customers, managers, other sex workers, and the authorities. Research on the latter has grown over the past decade.

The second standard answer as to why some issues and sectors have been studied thoroughly and others rarely is *access*. Can the investigator gain entry to the population or setting of interest, and what roles are open to those who do get such access—researcher, confidant, health worker, simple observer, participant?

Access is especially difficult in remote areas, such as agricultural and mining sites, where the researcher-as-stranger would be regarded with suspicion. In the only agricultural-based study I know of, conducted in Florida, the working women reduced risk "by building a clientele of regular customers, refusing risky transactions and referrals, and creating a local infrastructure of sanctuary."[18] Those who work near mining camps have been studied only historically. Traditionally, prostitution played a significant role in such areas: "as a way for women to make money, as a way to encourage male labor, as a social problem, and as a corporate concern."[19] An important finding has to do with worker agency: "Nowhere is the idea of prostitution as a resistance strategy more discussed than in accounts of women selling sex in mining regions, because prostitution seemed to be directly connected to the exclusion of women from the licit profits of the mining enterprise," leaving the sale of sex as either the only or the most lucrative means of earning a living.[20]

Access would also be a hurdle if one wanted to research contemporary truck-stop prostitution, a sector that scholars have neglected entirely. Sex sellers solicit customers at gas stations, truck stops, and highway rest areas, and conduct their business inside the truck. These work sites present some of the same risks to providers as urban street prostitution, but the fact that they solicit in areas that are typically remote and far from home makes them especially vulnerable to assault and murder. Truck stops provide easy entry and exit, which means that a trucker can be long gone by the time a person is declared missing, if discovered at all. Of the 459 people who died along American highways under suspicious circumstances between 1970 and 2010, "at least 234 victims were prostitutes," according to the FBI. As of 2010, the authorities were investigating 200 suspects nationwide, and "almost all are long-haul truck drivers"; by 2016, the number of suspicious deaths had increased to more than 750.[21]

Unknown to most scholars, a *subculture* has emerged in the truck-stop sector. Like many street sellers in urban areas, the workers fraternize and look out for each other, and truckers discuss the trade and their experiences on their CB radios. Opponents have responded with campaigns to end the practice, including one organized by Truckers Against Trafficking. And some gas stations and truck stops have made efforts to discourage such liaisons. While challenging, it would not be impossible to study one of these sites, provided that the researcher is able to gain the permission and confidence of others present.

Other underresearched venues are not so remote. Three types of businesses stand out. Few contemporary studies center on erotic massage parlors or brothels, especially in comparison to the many historical studies of brothels. (Notable exceptions are recent studies of Polish and German brothels and Asian American massage parlors.)[22] Similarly underresearched are *escort agencies*. We have a few studies of individual escorts and their advertising techniques but almost nothing on the agencies that some of them work for. How do these agencies recruit providers? What kind of training (if any) do they undergo? What are the standard business models for minimizing risk? How are client complaints handled? The most comprehensive and insightful study examined a gay agency in the United States. It employed thirty-two men, five of whom lived on the premises. The benefits of working for this agency included job training and social support from peers and managers.[23] Women also employ the services of escorts, including for threesomes and erotic exploration with same-sex providers. But we lack studies of this population.[24] Finally, as far as I know, no one has researched casinos, where sex workers solicit prospective customers on the gaming floor and then retire to a hotel room. Some casinos are more worker friendly than others, but we have no data on the frequency or magnitude of transactional sex initiated in gaming casinos.

Regarding the field more generally, as research has multiplied, so has resistance from some prominent scholar-activists who seek to jettison mainstream studies and replace them with their ideologically based agenda, what I call "the Oppression Paradigm."[25] Ignoring well-documented variation in structural and experiential dimensions of sex work, oppression writers traffic in simplistic images and tropes, all of which paint sex work as universally exploitative, immiserating, violent, demeaning, and reflective of men's supremacy. It is claimed that these are constants, not variables, and as such, apply to all types of sex work everywhere and across time periods. These writers pay little attention to the canons of scientific research, and some of them have staged incidents at conferences, denouncing speakers who do not share their views. In print as well, they have sometimes denigrated mainstream scholars, accusing them of being "apologists" for pimps and traffickers. We do not see such ad hominem attacks in any other area of inquiry in the social sciences. And some of these actors have been in the vanguard of efforts to pass laws that have the effect, if not the intent, of further stigmatizing and marginalizing sex workers and their customers, just as they routinely lobby against reforms intended to empower workers. Doing the latter would interfere with the grand goal of eliminating all forms of erotic commerce.

Going forward, oppression theorists and prohibitionists will remain a force to be reckoned with, but mainstream scholars have roundly discredited their claims, and, in some ways, the field has moved on. As it has expanded, there appears to be less and less room for simplistic, monolithic thinking and the propaganda spread by oppression writers. The good news is that the field has explored many new directions over the past two decades, and many scholars are amenable to challenging policies that infringe on workers' rights and well-being. I expect these trends to continue.

NOTES

1 Davis 1937.
2 Weitzer 1991. "COYOTE" stands for "Call Off Your Old Tired Ethics."
3 An example of such comparative research at the street level is Porter and Bonilla 2010.
4 Cohen 1980; Silbert and Pines 1981.
5 Abbott 2000.
6 In her analysis of IRB handling of proposals to study sexuality, Janice Irvine found that "sexuality has been a 'special case'": "among a few topics automatically deemed 'sensitive' and therefore generally subject to enhanced scrutiny in IRB deliberations." In cases of disapproval, the result is "simultaneously constraining sexual knowledge while reinforcing sexual stigma" (Irvine 2012, 29).
7 Attorney General 1986.
8 Commission on Obscenity and Pornography 1970.
9 Weitzer 2007, 2011.
10 Kohn 2017.
11 In recent polls, the number supporting decriminalization has varied between 52 percent and 54 percent. Examples are television shows like *The Deuce*, *Secret Diary of a Call Girl*, and *The Girlfriend Experience*, and the documentaries *Prostitution* (National Geographic), *Dirty Money: The Business of High-End Prostitution* (CNBC), and *Sex for Sale: The Untold Story* (A&E).
12 For an overview of research on customers, see Monto and Milrod 2023.
13 Abel, Fitzgerald, and Healy 2010; Brents, Jackson, and Hausbeck 2010; Weitzer 2012, 2023a.
14 Bradley-Engen (2009) draws sharp contrasts between what she calls "social clubs," "hustle clubs," and "show clubs."
15 Exceptions include Abbott 2000; Berg, Molin, and Nanavati 2020; Jones 2020a; Meehan 2021; Pilcher 2012; Weitzer 2023c.
16 Ferguson and Hartley 2022, 278.
17 For a review of this research, see Weitzer 2015.
18 Bletzer 2003, 251.
19 Laite 2009, 744.
20 Laite 2009, 745. See also Goldman 1981.
21 Morrison 2010; FBI 2016.
22 Ślęzak 2019; Staiger 2022; Chin and Takahashi 2023.
23 Smith, Grov, and Seal 2009.
24 Goldhill 2015.
25 Weitzer 2023b.

28

Were the Feminist Sex Wars Inevitable?

Smashing the Binary

BERNADETTE BARTON AND BREANNE FAHS

The feminist sex wars of the 1980s garnered a sizeable amount of scholarly attention partly because they marked a historic split between groups of feminists into sex-positive and radical feminists. Sexist attacks on Andrea Dworkin, a key radical feminist, the activities of the Meese Commission (a committee established by the Reagan administration to study the effects of pornography on society), tension between attendees of the 1982 Barnard Conference on Sexuality, disagreements over censorship, liberal interventions in the construction of both sex-positive and radical feminism, and the failure of either group to fully incorporate the theoretical contributions of third world feminism fostered divisions.[1] Each group also had different priorities on sexuality, pornography, and concepts of sexual freedom,[2] with sex-positive feminists favoring the "freedom to" do what we want, and radical feminists fighting for "freedom from" doing what we do not want to do.

To illustrate, sex-positive feminists focus on the freedom to express diverse genders and sexualities, access comprehensive sex education, and support sex workers' rights while radical feminists concentrate on freedom from rape, domestic violence, harmful depictions of women in pornography, enforced sexual labor within the home, and compulsory forms of sexuality.[3] Thus, as sex-positive feminists wrestled sexuality away from religious and puritanical cultural beliefs of sex as "sinful" and "bad," radical feminists worked to free women from unwanted sex or sexual representation while also sounding the alarm on oppressive and gender-conservative sexual practices that harmed or disadvantaged women.[4] While the tendency to identify oneself as more compatible with a sex-positive *or* a radical-feminist perspective persists in the sex-work literature, personal attitudes, and feminist belief systems, some scholars of the sex industry have rejected the "sex wars" binary framework in favor of the "polymorphous paradigm," a theory sensitive to the complexity of occupational arrangements and power relationships within the sex industry.[5]

We argue here that while there is substantive variance between radical and sex-positive feminists, too much feminist writing over the decades has emphasized differences and conflict between the positions rather than points of alignment, what scholar Lorna Bracewell calls the "catfight narrative."[6] In doing so, some feminists have, in their writing and ideologies, engaged in horizontal hostility,[7] perpetuating a divisive patriarchal framework of competing and incompatible beliefs that minimizes our accomplishments. This "catfight" narrative masks the significance of mid- to late-twentieth-century feminist theorizing on sexuality and sex work. As Bracewell and other scholars underline in their work,[8] this was an immensely fertile and generative time in feminism as second wave feminists of all stripes—radical, sex positive, Marxist, antipornography, intersectional, and third world—articulated rich critiques of patriarchy and advocated radical changes in sexual expression and gender roles.

In this chapter we honor the contributions of second wave feminists by dismantling the "catfight" story. Here we show how systems of domination—primarily patriarchy, neoliberal capitalism, and white supremacy—co-opted and perverted the language of sex positivity (that is, the perspective that sexual freedom and lack of censorship are key priorities of sexual politics). We explore this through analysis of discourses of raunch culture and sex work as empowering, hosting sites like OnlyFans, the popularity of "sugar relationships," heterosexuality as a chore, compulsory bisexuality, and compulsory sexual behavior to develop two areas of thought: (1) aspects of women's sexuality that have been obscured, understudied, silenced, and ignored; and (2) possibilities of what could happen within the studies of sex work and sexuality if we shift our paradigm from division to alignment by better attending to the theoretical work of intersectional feminists.

Sex Positivity Gone Wild

The hegemonic takeover of the narrative of sex positivity began soon after the sexual revolution and other fights for equality in the 1960s, slowly gathering steam in the 1970s and 1980s, becoming more widespread with the development of the world wide web. Mainstream messaging devolved the language of sex positivity from an ecosystem of consent, pleasure, safety, and respect to the single expectation that women who are "empowered" are sexy and hot. This turn is especially visible in raunch culture, the hypersexualization of culture dating from the mid-1990s.[9] At this time, as more and more people used the Internet for work, socializing, and shopping, the content of Internet porn began to influence mainstream culture so that behaviors, gear, and attitudes once the exclusive purview of the sex industry filtered into mainstream culture. Raunch culture, or pornification, objectifies women not only as impossibly beautiful but also as sexy and hot, "like a porn star." Being sexy like a stripper or porn star might mean wearing push-up bras and thongs, getting Brazilian waxes, engaging in hookup sex, and taking pole-dancing classes for exercise.

We argue, provocatively, that raunch culture *is* culture in the West in the 2020s. Its presence is seen everywhere: in social media, television shows, movies, billboards, conversations, storylines, clothing, malls, and comedy material. Pornification sells itself to girls and women using the rhetoric of sex positivity and empowerment, i.e., "Look how free you are to express your inner porn star and be sexy." This narrative falsely equates freedom with the freedom to be objectified in a particular kind of commodified sexualization, thus funneling women's choices into pornification and upending the more diverse aspects of sex positivity. Moreover, not only does pornification socialize Westerners into a formulaic, heteronormative, cis-centered, uncomfortable, and reductive *performance* of sexuality drawn from popular images of sex work; it does so in societies lacking freedom from sexism and racism.

To elaborate, laws disproportionately punish Black and Hispanic men for real and invented abuses of sex workers, while sex workers of color face harsher sanctions than their white peers.[10] Western legal systems also do little to alleviate the many burdens sex workers suffer, including theft, rape, assault, criminalization, penalization, and exploitation.

Thus, we argue that the freedom to "be like a stripper" means little in a culture that still stigmatizes sex workers, while continuing to blame all women for the assaults they endure. In raunch culture, the sex worker is a symbol, not a person.[11] Finally, pornification does not diminish whore stigma nor weaken the double day, wage gap, rape myths, sexual violence, and domestic abuse, just as it also does not provide well-paying occupational alternatives to sex work. Instead, pornification manipulates women into giving men free sex work and to perceive doing so as "empowering." In our opinion, pornification is a patriarchal scam framed as sex positivity.

OnlyFans

OnlyFans is a hosting site that emerged in 2016 and currently has 210 million users. OnlyFans allow members to create and share their own porn content, charge a fee via a subscription model to customers, and earn money directly rather than through a commercial tube site like Porn Hub. On hosting sites like OnlyFans and JustForFans, a site run and created by sex workers, users can control their own content (rather than following the dictates of a director) and individualize it for specific viewers. We perceive the paid erotic content on such hosting sites as an improvement over the pornography found on a site like Porn Hub because there is more worker control of the material and fewer parties take a cut of the money. However, OnlyFans is an inadequate solution to institutional problems of neoliberal capitalism like deindustrialization and income inequality because it naturalizes individuals shouldering burdens better addressed through policy changes, not personal choices. Content creators are free to do gig work promoting their own images, but they are not free from the whims of a precarious economy, not eligible for unemployment benefits should they need them, and do not have healthcare benefits. Like many similar "gig" jobs, they lack the safety net that could lead to economic stability and long-term sustainability.

Gig work—or work in general—does not empower us, but neoliberal renderings of sex-positive narratives often encourage us to think it does. In the case of sex workers (the original gig workers), Molly Smith and Juno Mac observe in *Revolting Prostitutes: The Fight for Sex Workers' Rights* that the sex-positive "happy hooker" narrative blurs the lines between paid and recreational sex, suggesting that sex workers are "hot" for their customers, and "creates the illusion that worker and client are united in their interests."[12] Further, unlike gym trainers and celebrities on hosting sites, sex workers also negotiate whore stigma on- and offline. Thus, neoliberal rhetoric emphasizing the "freedom to" do what we want without a foundation in "freedom from" state-sanctioned sexism, racism, and worker exploitation perpetuates oppression, especially when sex itself is assumed to be liberating. In other words, framing sex work as empowering, liberated, done by choice, and "freeing" without an acknowledgment of the inequities and harms stemming from institutional inequality conflates sexual behavior with sex work, obscures how work itself is often disempowering under conditions of neoliberal capitalism, and maintains systems of gender inequality and white supremacy. Further, our critique of sex work as empowering also allows for a broader critique of framing work as empowering; under the terms of capitalism, we cannot get our emotional needs met from work. At best, we argue that we should view work as a utilitarian practice that serves our survival needs.

Sugar Relationships

While some on hosting sites explicitly engage in sex work, those who are sugar dating mask their transactional exchange as a romantic relationship largely to avoid the stigma of sex work. A sugar relationship usually occurs between a young, attractive woman (sugar baby) and an older, wealthy man (sugar daddy), though there are also sugar mamas and male babies, and gay sugar daddies and babies. In a sugar relationship, the younger party offers youth and beauty in exchange for expensive meals, designer items, trips, and (hopefully) money. Sugar babies who conform to conventional beauty norms, display middle-class manners, and either have a degree or are enrolled in a university are most desirable. Sugar websites like Seeking Arrangements, for example, advertise to college students by offering those who sign up with a university email (.edu) an automatic upgrade to a premium profile.

Sugar dating, especially between male sugar daddies and female sugar babies, reinscribes traditional gender roles with a twist. A wealthy man pays a young, beautiful woman to charm, soothe, flatter, entertain, flirt, and maybe have sex with him, absent expectations of continuity or fidelity. As some have noted,[13] sugar babies often engage in far more emotional and aesthetic labor than sex workers, and for less compensation. Hegemonic messaging focused on how babies benefit from sugar dating—fancy meals, travel, college tuition, a mentor, mature conversation, access to a social network—camouflage significant inequalities and beg a number of questions. For example, we question, Why is college priced so high that young people pivot to quasi sex work to pay their tuition? Also, what does it reveal about heterosexual dating practices that women would choose to simulate attraction to men to acquire meals and travel, as well as meet their basic living expenses? What does sugar dating reveal about the persistence of traditional gender norms?

Heterosex as a Chore

An emerging body of work is grappling with problems inherent to heterosexuality, or "heterosex." Feminist scholar Jane Ward argues in her book *The Tragedy of Heterosexuality* that heterosexuality is plagued by mutual disdain, sexual and emotional labor, and an often futile struggle to reconcile power differentials between women and men.[14] Australian queer theorist Annamarie Jagose argues that the fake orgasm represents the epitome of heterosex, exposing heterosexuality as a farce as penile-vaginal intercourse ultimately fails to deliver pleasure in any reliable way.[15] Jagose and Ward theorize that heterosexual sexual practices often feel more like labor than pleasure or sexual freedom, a claim supported by numerous studies finding heterosexual women engaging in sexual compliance, minimizing sexual pain, and focusing on *men's* sexual pleasure rather than their own orgasms.[16] Ultimately, radical feminist critiques of sexual liberation and the sexual revolution—namely, that women would be subjected to an "orgasm frenzy" and would end up engaging in more rather than less sexual labor[17]—have been obscured by shaky assumptions that traditional heterosexual sexual practices are reliably pleasurable and empowering for women. There is no easy, simple, or singular path to sexual liberation or empowerment.

Framing heterosex as compulsory or required began with Adrienne Rich's famous 1980 essay "Compulsory Heterosexuality and the Lesbian Existence,"[18] in which she theorized that heterosexuality was not a choice per se but something enforced, policed, and pushed onto people through coercion and fear. Building on this, numerous scholars have argued that other forms of sexuality have themselves become compulsory, suggesting that distinctions between paid and unpaid sex work are difficult to discern. For example, pornification promotes compulsory bisexuality where (mostly) heterosexual-identified women make out with one another at parties or in social settings *in front of* men in order to please, titillate, or satisfy them.[19] There are also increasing reports of "unicorn hunting" in online dating, whereby heterosexual couples pursue women for a threesome under the guise of women seeking other women to date, making it harder for women to date lesbian or bisexual women (without lusty boyfriends in tow).[20] Building on this, queer feminist scholar Ela Przybylo has argued that sex itself has become compulsory, making the path harder for those who identify as asexual, as well as those who abstain from sex either temporarily or permanently, or do not engage in sex for personal or political reasons.[21] Consequently, in the post–sexual revolution age, heterosexuality, bisexuality, and now sexuality itself have all become compulsory aspects of women's sexual experiences, further limiting their "freedom from" having to be sexual in particular ways.

Again, these examples highlight the importance of critiquing the ways in which hegemonic discourses have co-opted, poisoned, and perverted rhetorics of sex positivity. We argue for a feminist reclaiming of sex positivity that includes the freedom to have sex the way one likes, to not have sex at all, or to engage in sex work, and freedom from sexual abuse, reproductive control, economic exploitation, and stigma—in short, for real, life-enhancing choices. In this work we need not reinvent the wheel. Intersectional feminists have long attended to the complexities of multiple systems of oppression, noting that freedom to is contingent on freedom from.[22]

Smashing the Sex Wars Binary

Ultimately, we contend that radical and sex-positive feminism are not opposites, but partners intimately intertwined in the politics of women's sexuality and sex work. Smashing the sex wars binary involves critiquing the one-dimensional, watered-down version of sex positivity advanced in raunch culture, acknowledging the institutional sexism of most sex work while fighting against carceral attacks on sex workers and customers, and carefully attending to intersectionality in our analyses. Many possibilities emerge when we do this. First, feminists could better focus our attention on social contexts, groups, organizations, and institutions that more severely harm women and other lower-status groups (e.g., BIPOC communities, sexual minorities, poor and working-class people, etc.). In particular, we support feminist critiques of religious conservative rescue groups that enforce traditional gender roles and require compulsory Christianity of residents. Such feminist analyses need not position themselves in a binary manner: for example, as allies either of pornification *or* of conservative religiosity. For example, a union of sex-positive and radical-feminist analysis reframes purity culture (the expectation that girls remain virginal until marriage to a male head of the household) and pornification not as opposites but as two sides of the same coin, each defining how girls and women should present themselves—modest or hot—to best follow men's rules and patriarchal practices.[23]

Second, by reclaiming and aligning sex positivity with intersectional feminism, we better account for and support those whose version of sexual freedom deviates from a "one size fits all" model of sexual liberation. For example, those who have been sexually traumatized may not have as much interest in expanding their sexual expression, and instead want more support for social scripts of sexuality that allow for long pauses in sexual activity, better mental health support from practitioners, the fundamental right for women to refuse sex any time they choose to, and consciousness-raising groups that advocate against domestic violence and sexual assault. Others may want to fight for pleasure-centered sex education, militate against censorship, or advocate for better support for those on the margins of sexuality (e.g., sex workers, fetish communities, disabled people, adolescents seeking birth control, etc.), to dismantle repressive systems that overvalue "purity" and "chastity" at the expense of sexual expression. Still others may channel their energies into thinking about the needs of a particular group that is understudied or underserved, such as trans and nonbinary people, fat women, indigenous women, and others. Like sex workers, activists, and authors Juno Mac and Molly Smith, we do not stake a claim as sex positive or sex negative but advocate for the rights of people to be "sex-ambivalent":[24] to assert *both* the right to have the freedom to have the sexual expression they want, and the freedom from having to be sexual in ways they do not want.[25]

For the study of sex work, smashing the binary means speaking a feminist language of sex positivity that grounds radical and sex-positive theories in intersectionality. We see an illustration of this in the voices of sex workers naming their experiences of workplace harassment and violence in the groundbreaking anthology *We Too: Essays on Sex Work and Survival*. Thus, the feminist union we advocate supports the following goals: consideration of structural constraints related not only to sex but also to race, class, gender, ability, and sexual orientation; the understanding that those working in the sex industry are best able to tell the stories of their own lives and best know what they need; destigmatization and decriminalization of sex work; critiquing the hypocrisy of a culture that encourages girls and women to be "like porn stars and strippers" while demonizing and criminalizing actual sex workers; job training attentive to systemic inequality; universal healthcare, free higher education, state-subsidized child care, and a universal basic income allowing people to make real choices about their occupations; and freedom from unwanted pregnancies, rape, sexual coercion, sexual compliance, and sexual assault. By recognizing the ways that the "freedom to" and the "freedom from" are interrelated and operate in tandem toward the overarching project of human liberation, we see feminists working together toward common goals and against common enemies.

NOTES

1 Bracewell 2021.
2 Brents 2008.
3 Queen and Comella 2008.
4 Echols 1989, 2016.
5 Weitzer 2010b.
6 Bracewell 2021.
7 Pharr 1996.
8 Fahs 2020.
9 Barton 2021.
10 Sankofa 2016; Dewey and St. Germain 2015, 211–34; Brooks 2021; Nelson 1993.
11 Smith and Mac 2020.
12 Smith and Mac 2020, 32.
13 Kavita Nayar Jablonka, in this volume.

14 Ward 2020.
15 Jagose 2003.
16 McClelland 2011; Fahs 2019; Impett and Peplau 2003.
17 Fahs 2018.
18 Rich 1980.
19 Fahs 2009.
20 Beggan 2020.
21 Przybylo 2019.
22 Bracewell 2021.
23 Barton 2021.
24 Smith and Mac 2020, 22.
25 Fahs 2014.

29

Following the Money

Kenyan Sex Workers' Strategies during Crisis

PENINAH MWANGI AND EGLĖ ČESNULYTĖ

The Kenyan Ministry of Health confirmed the first case of COVID-19 in Nairobi in March 2020. One year later, in March 2021, the Bar Hostesses Empowerment and Support Program (BHESP)[1] did a survey with 825 sex workers who had been enrolled in the BHESP Mowlem clinic of Nairobi Eastlands at the beginning of the pandemic.[2] Of the women who were registered with the clinic in 2020, 473 could not be traced at the primary addresses and mobile phone numbers that they registered with. BHESP contacted listed next of kin to learn that out of these 473 women, 30 percent (141) had gone back to live with their relatives in rural areas as they could not afford to live in the city anymore. During the pandemic, nearly 60 percent (282) indicated that they changed the way they work, as we will discuss below. Many sex workers surveyed indicated that they started doing other types of work—part-time hairdressing, market vending, laundry services, and other, similar jobs—to support themselves. The data gathered in this survey offer a unique opportunity to see systemic changes in sex work during crisis and form the basis for this paper.

The changes in Nairobi's sex work during the pandemic reflect challenges experienced across society. Increasing insecurity and violence accompanied many Kenyan women during the pandemic, with UN Women counting one in five Kenyan women feeling unsafe in their homes during the first six months of the pandemic.[3] Just like most women employed in the informal sectors of the economy globally,[4] Kenyan women selling sex started experiencing more economic difficulties, resulting in even more fragile livelihoods. However, sex workers' actions during the pandemic also reveal the importance of *localization* as a strategy used to sustain livelihoods during crises. Sex workers react to crisis by changing their work patterns to fit with local conditions. As we will discuss in this paper, strategies of localization, such as moving away from globalized markets to rural or peri-urban areas, blending into residential areas, or changing location and type of work form an important part of contemporary sex work, all of which impact marginalized workers more severely. In all these strategies, workers use their knowledge of local dynamics and mobilize local networks to ensure continued financial success and even basic survival during times of crisis.

This chapter will explore the first year of the COVID-19 pandemic in Nairobi to show how Kenyan sex workers adapted to changing conditions in a globalized economy and redirected their efforts through strategies of localization. It is important to study such strategies of adaptation, as the crises resulting from climate change and the instability of global capitalism are likely to become more frequent, and thus people living in the informal sectors of the majority world—like Kenyan sex workers—will need to be supported to survive.

Globalization, Localization, and Sex Work Research

The relationship among globalization, migration, and sex work is well studied and researched. Scholarship spans from investigations of sex tourism to migrant sex workers to international trafficking to livelihood making in new urban or economic centers.[5] In the Kenyan context, sex workers tend to be portrayed as responding to new opportunities that come with global economic and social shifts and changes—from moving to colonial cities to relocating to emerging economic centers to targeting tourists on Kenyan beaches.[6] Individuals selling sex are highly mobile and respond to socioeconomic developments by moving to places where money circulates, and in the Kenyan context, that is often linked to international processes.

However, while globalization is definitely an important factor in the way sex work functions, the other trend—the localization of sex work—is less explored. We use the term "localization" to refer to a variety of strategies focusing on local dynamics used by sex workers when global processes and connections are unreliable. In some cases, these situations can be cyclical and predictable—for example, in the off-season months when international tourists are not coming. However, often such strategies are needed unexpectedly, and are related to global and local crises slowing money flows, such as global economic crises, terror attacks, international travel disruptions/bans, climate change events, and global pandemics. In other words, we need research about uncertain times when the forces of globalization turn sour, and well-paying clients who are linked to the international domain (tourism and related industries, for example) are difficult to meet in the usual venues. This reversal of orientation of sex worker strategies—from global to local processes—is what we call "localization strategies."

The COVID-19 pandemic and the Kenyan state's response had enormous effects on sex worker livelihoods. The curfew (no movement allowed between dusk and dawn), and bar and entertainment closures meant that sex workers could no longer work at night, nor in the usual locations. Furthermore, the initial COVID-19 response—requiring social distancing—meant that many individuals who usually complemented their sex work income by providing services in the informal economy (such as vending, laundry services, and the like) lost both streams of income. However, while COVID-19 undoubtedly pushed sex workers to strategies of localization, this was not the first time in the recent past when such strategies were needed. The 2002 Mombasa terrorist attacks disrupted Kenyan tourism significantly, as did the Al-Shabaab attacks and kidnapping of tourists in 2012–2013, both events having a disproportionate effect on sex worker populations and their livelihoods.[7] The postelection violence affected sex workers as it did other Kenyans in 2007–2008.[8] Climate change–related events such as ongoing droughts that leave millions of Kenyans food insecure or the swarms of locusts that invaded rural farms in 2019–2020 and decimated harvests all affected sex workers working in these regions.[9] So, while we use COVID-19 as an example to explore sex worker strategies of localization, such decisions are not uncommon. With climate change–related disasters becoming more frequent and severe in their impact, understanding strategies of localization will soon become even more important.

Localization Strategies as Determined by Sex Workers' Livelihoods

Kenyan sex workers are diverse and positioned in different ways in society. Sex workers are women and men, cisgender and transgender people. Some earn substantial amounts of money and establish other businesses; many are barely surviving. Some have families and kin to rely on; others are on their own; and many have children and other dependents to take care of. Some are very young; others are older. Some are healthy; others have health conditions, including HIV/AIDS. Some rely solely on sex work income; some have other jobs as well. Most of the women are Kenyans from a variety of ethnic and religious communities; some are migrants or refugees. All this diversity means that different groups of sex workers have different work strategies, and so in difficult times their localization strategies vary. Here we use the lens of intersectionality to attend to these intersecting differences when discussing workers' localization strategies.[10] We focus our discussion on woman-presenting sex workers as that is the main client group of BHESP, and it is on this group's localization strategies we can comment with confidence.

Moving to Residential Complexes

Women who are financially successful in their sex work and have disposable income became the center of a moral panic in Nairobi during the COVID-19 pandemic. With closure of many upscale urban entertainment venues (bars, clubs, restaurants, hotels, and the like), many sex workers were now renting apartments and working from Nairobi's middle-class residential complexes. The arrival of sex workers in middle-class spaces previously seen as "a perfect place to raise a family" were perceived as facilitating criminality and unsocial behavior.[11] Part of the problem, as seen from a middle-class perspective, was that some of the women blended in and onlookers could not tell who was and who was not a sex worker.

This moral panic was caused by higher-end sex workers' strategy of localization. Women who worked with wealthy or middle-class clients needed to find new venues to operate from. Before the pandemic, this group of women found their clients in the leisure and entertainment areas for the upper strata of Nairobi society—upscale coffee shops, hotels, restaurants, and bars. In these more centralized spaces clients could be found and screened and sexual transactions arranged, before moving to private rooms or hotels for sex. With the onset of the pandemic, most such venues closed. Renting rooms in middle-class residential neighborhoods was an attractive alternative as it allowed discreet and safe places for clients to enter, especially considering the policing of the public spaces and movement restrictions in the city.

Of course, this strategy was available only to women who could pay rent up front. While upscale middle-class residential complexes dominated newspaper stories, the BHESP survey indicates that sex workers moved to work from private rooms in all different parts of the city representing housing in different price ranges. Many women had no choice but to start working from their own homes as well.

Moving to private rooms in their own homes or rentals in residential areas also meant that sex workers were giving up some of their security—before the pandemic, to ensure their safety, many women relied on collaborations with other sex workers and with staff employed in the entertainment districts and connected to hotels or lodges renting hourly rooms. Tipping a barman might ensure that he would point out men purchasing expensive drinks; maintaining relationships with other sex workers meant that information about abusive clients was shared; giving tips to people working in the venues that rent hourly rooms or having close friends work together in private spaces ensured that there was someone to check on sex workers if they did not return soon enough. After the pandemic, the closing of entertainment districts and restrictions on nighttime movement meant that women had to work alone in private rooms, sacrificing their cultivated safety networks. Moreover, the risk of abuse behind closed doors increased, as it was harder to call for help in residential areas where one is attempting to "blend in." This was a special concern for many women who started using online tools to find new clients and thus were inviting strangers to their rooms. The BHESP survey indicated that safety concerns and experiences of violence dominate the narratives of sex workers operating from private accommodation.

Operating from private rooms in residential areas also meant that women had to reduce the number of clients that they saw. First, there were practical limitations of balancing the need to blend in and not antagonize the neighbors of the residential estates with work concerns. Upper-class clients need a discreet place to see sex workers, and thus an open conflict with the neighbors would deter them. Similarly, to stay on good terms with the neighbors and avoid daily complaints, harassment, or eviction meant that the number of men coming and going had to be limited. Furthermore, due to the curfew, which limited their clients' mobility, a client often had to stay the night with the woman if he came after dark. Second, finding new clients became more complicated and entailed engaging with online tools and platforms or word of mouth in a context where everyone suddenly became more wary about spending money and mixing with people outside their households. To make up for the lost income linked to fewer clients, many sex workers started offering extra services such as meals, massages, and drinks and charged for them. Still, many sex workers surveyed by BHESP reported earning less money.

Sex workers who move to private apartments or rooms mimic strategies of offering the "comforts of home" of colonial Nairobi *Malaya* sex work, providing services such as meals, baths, and tea in addition to sex;[12] as in colonial Nairobi, this strategy implies that a woman already has a disposable income and a capacity to attract enough well-paying clients, which is not an option for the majority of sex workers. Similarly, not all women can begin operating from their home because of caring responsibilities and the stigma attached to this occupation, which is especially important for those who hide their sex work from their families.

Following the (Local) Money

Another localization strategy that sex workers employ is moving away from higher-end globalized zones to places where money can be found in the local economy. This strategy is available only to those who can afford the travel costs, and who either have no caring responsibilities or can arrange for that care to be performed by someone else (family, kin, friends). Considering that most sex workers have children and often support their families,[13] it is not an easy feat to relocate. This option is also not available for visibly queer sex workers or male sex workers whose nonconforming gender identities or sexualities would stand out in often conservative peri-urban or rural contexts and whose work venues are more restricted geographically even in noncrisis periods.

The strategy of moving in search of money is common. For example, many women frequented tourist areas during high seasons and shifted to places where Kenyan middle-class men can be found in the off-season. It is not uncommon for women to move their client search to different neighborhoods and entertainment venues in response to this seasonality. Others go further and move to other cities or peri-urban areas where they know that residents are making money from farming, mining, or other enterprises. For example, around the time when tea farmers in Bomet and Kericho counties receive their bonus payments,[14] both areas see an influx of sex workers, many traveling from as far as Mombasa. Similarly, Narok County sees arrivals of sex workers to service wheat farmers at the time of harvest.

During COVID-19, these strategies of localization remained prominent. BHESP records indicate that at least thirty sex workers surveyed have moved to Kericho after the announcement that tea bonus payments would be made despite the pandemic. Others have moved to Narok, where income from owning livestock was not affected by pandemic restrictions, and where cattle farmers can spend money on entertainment while living expenses are much lower than in the capital. A significant number of sex workers who could not be reached by BHESP one year into the pandemic were women who moved to smaller towns or peri-urban areas while searching for local men with some financial capacity.

Moving Away from Sex Work (for Now)

The final localization strategy was to (temporarily) give up sex work or to move into survival sex work. Despite proclamations about the moral character of women selling sex in the public domain, the truth remains that sex work is better-paid work than other available alternatives, and many women do it to supplement other income or for limited periods of time.

Historically, a significant number of sex workers in Nairobi come from rural areas, and their income supports not only themselves but also their farming families, especially when harvests fail. Luise White has documented waves of women coming to colonial Nairobi in times of droughts affecting Kenyan farmers.[15] Eglė Česnulytė also found that a majority of women in her sample were supporting their families in rural Kenya.[16] Many of these women have strong family links and, in times of crisis, can rely on them to wait out the crisis or to reinsert themselves in different economic and possibly lower-paid activities, such as farming. The BHESP survey indicates this trend clearly in the context of COVID-19: 30 percent of sex workers contacted a year into the pandemic were back with their families in rural areas. It is possible that the majority of those who could not be reached did the same.

While moving back with families in rural areas is a good strategy for many, the BHESP survey also indicates the dark sides of this shift. First, some women made the decision to return to abusive husbands, or to violent homes from which sex work provided an escape. Second, some women had no choice but to send their children to live either with their children's fathers or with grandparents while they remained in the city. This put an enormous strain on women's and children's mental health, well-being, and quality of life as these women may have trouble seeing their children in the future. Third, both women and their children who come back to rural areas report a lot of experiences of stigmatization. Stigma not only affects their everyday lives but also can make it difficult to access healthcare, including HIV/AIDS treatment and support. Healthcare facilities are sparse in rural settings, and women often must travel long distances to get specialized help. Finally, this strategy is not available to those who severed their links with rural families because of violence, because of the type of work they do, or because of their sexuality or gender identity.

Most sex workers do other types of work as well—the Kenyan National AIDS Control Council has determined that 95 percent of sex workers have another source of income apart from the sex trade.[17] For many, sex work helps to supplement other poorly paid work in the informal and formal sectors, such as working as a secretary, maid, cleaner, guard, and other, similar occupations. For these sex workers, periods of crisis mean lower living standards and more precarity. Many sex workers associated with the BHESP report have moved into more crowded accommodation to be able to stay in the city. The limited space means that some women must (temporarily) give up selling sex and survive on other sources of income. For some, this also means a move to transactional sex. For example, the BHESP survey found that many women moved to fishing communities to exchange sex for fish to eat. Similar dynamics prevail in urban areas, where women might forgo payments in cash in exchange for food or transportation services.

Conclusion

Using the pandemic of COVID-19 and the response to it in Kenya as a case study, this chapter has discussed how strategies of localization, such as moving away from globalized markets to rural or peri-urban areas, blending into residential areas, or changing geography and type of work form an important part of contemporary sex work. Sex workers employ such strategies during global uncertainty and economic downturns or crises. Considering the increasing frequency of climate- and capitalism-related crises, understanding strategies of localization offers guidance in public-policy considerations and advocacy efforts.

We want to emphasize several key areas that are important to policy interventions during periods of uncertainty in Kenya. First, the experiences of sex workers during the first year of the COVID-19 pandemic demonstrate the consequences of the government's exclusionary protection schemes. As sex workers could not access government aid, their livelihoods became even more fragile. Many moved within the city or within the country, and this meant that many lost their access to specialized support (healthcare, education, or other support provided by the NGO sector, for example), while others made difficult choices to come back to violent or abusive homes, or to work in less secure conditions. Policy interventions supporting vulnerable populations in the informal economies should expand their remit by providing housing support, healthcare, and monetary aid to ensure that these populations do not suffer disproportionate consequences in times of crisis. This is especially the case for those who cannot rely on mobility solutions, because the urban spaces where they created their lives are the only safe spaces for them—people whose sexualities or gender identities are not in line with heterosexual patriarchal norms dominating much of the country, but also vulnerable individuals who are survivors of violence or people who require specialized medical care available only in big cities.

Second, while big urban centers like Nairobi or Mombasa have some infrastructure for vulnerable populations to use (specialized health clinics and peer support groups, for instance), such facilities are rarely available in rural areas, which means that if vulnerable individuals return to their rural homes, the risks of gender-based violence, dropping out of HIV/AIDS treatments, and mental health issues increase. Thus, expanding support in rural territories is important not only for the returning urban migrants but for rural vulnerable populations. Third, gender-based violence grew exponentially with COVID-19. Unless systemic efforts are employed to start addressing gender-based violence, the next crisis will again cost women's lives, health, and well-being.

Sex workers often experience societal crises in harsher or more profound ways because of the nature of their work; however, the issues that affect them are also relevant to other groups of women and queer populations working in informal economies of the majority world. Here we call to expand social security networks. More support for individuals in informal economies, often on the margins of society, would make adapting to potential future crises easier for everyone.

NOTES

1 BHESP is an organization for and by sex workers, women having sex with women, women using drugs, and bar hostesses in Kenya. BHESP was founded in the year 1998 by a group of these vulnerable women as a "loose" association to advocate for their rights and recognition. Most of the women associated with the BHESP are bar workers in low-income settings, and many are part-time sex workers. While the majority of women are Kenyan, some are from neighboring countries or are refugees. Also, while the majority of women are cis women, some are transwomen. BHESP also works closely with HOYMAS (an organization that serves queer and male sex worker communities), and this partnership ensures that people get the most appropriate support from either of the organizations regardless of their gender identity and sexuality.

2 This paper focuses on women who self-identify as sex workers, as that is the main group of clients at BHESP as well as the key group of interlocutors in Česnulytė's research. We expect that some of the localization strategies will be similar among men and queer sex workers (for example, shifting the focus from tourist groups to local clients in down times), while some strategies will differ significantly (moving to work in semi-urban or rural areas might not be an option for those who are visibly queer and work in niche sections of urban sex work, for instance). However, since we do not have data on the strategies of sex workers who are not

women, we cannot comment on the similarities or differences with confidence, and therefore in this paper focus on women sex workers only.

3 UN Women 2021.

4 WIEGO 2022.

5 See for instance Kempadoo and Doezema 1998; Agustin 1998; Česnulytė 2019.

6 White 1990; Omondi and Ryan 2017.

7 See for example Kamau 2006 on the context of the 2002 attacks; Onuoha 2013 for the Westgate attacks; Humphrey 2011 on tourist kidnapping.

8 See United Nations: High Commissioner for Human Rights 2008 for its report on Kenya's 2007–2008 postelection violence.

9 See Carleton 2021 on the impact of 2019–2020 locust swarms in Kenya.

10 See Crenshaw 2017 on intersectionality.

11 See for example Thatiah 2022, 4. Sex work occupies a grey area in Kenya. Legally, sex work is not criminalized, but the surrounding activities, such as soliciting and "living off the earnings of prostitution," are criminal offenses. Sex workers, however, are often arrested on different grounds, such as loitering with intent to commit crime, being vagabonds, or public disorder and drunkenness. People selling sex also suffer from stigma and discrimination surrounding this work.

12 See White 1990.

13 National AIDS Control Council 2011.

14 Small-hold tea farmers affiliated with the Kenya Tea Development Agency receive their pay in monthly installments plus annual bonus payment, which depends on how well tea is doing in the international markets that year.

15 White 1990.

16 Česnulytė 2019.

17 National AIDS Control Council 2011.

30

"I'll Take What I Can Get"

Transmasculine and Nonbinary Sex Workers, Sexual Capital, and Trans Joy

ELLIOT CHUDYK AND ANGELA JONES

As transmasculine (Elliot) and nonbinary (Angela) community-engaged researchers with ties to sex worker communities, we noticed extant sex work research fetishizing and pathologizing transfeminine sex workers and, at the same time, ignoring transmasculine and nonbinary sex workers. Angela began researching transmasculine and nonbinary sex workers after completing their study on the camming industry and noting that most cam sites have options for cisgender women and men only, and ones with spaces for trans people have spaces for trans women only. It was clear that there were undoubtedly transmasculine and non-binary people working in these industries but that the cissexist design of the sites was forcing them to work in gender categories that did not fit. Elliot's journey into this work was even more personal.

Upon starting their PhD program, Elliot received gut-wrenching news that their friend had died. During their last meeting, Elliot's friend had spent the afternoon discussing his recent struggle to find clients as a transmasculine full-service sex worker. That conversation echoed in Elliot's head each time they were asked to solidify a research question and became much louder during various local sex work support and advocacy meetings and groups. Elliot could not help but notice how the specific concerns of the transmasculine and nonbinary sex workers in the space were constantly sidelined, erased, and negated as too niche to be prioritized. This same pattern that Elliot noticed plays out in academia, particularly from scholars who have spent their careers studying sex work. So, while this research fills a much-needed gap, for us, it also does something more: it is an homage to the many trans and nonbinary sex workers in our lives whose stories have gone untold both within and outside the academy.

In this essay, first, we provide a brief background on the existing research on transgender sex workers. Then, we present critical, descriptive data from our studies with transmasculine and nonbinary sex workers. We provide an overview of worker demographics, the industry segments they work in, and their wages, alongside participants' discussions of how transitioning affects their labor and how sex work for some is a pathway to self-affirmation and trans joy. Finally, we pinpoint new directions for future lines of inquiry.

The Problem with Existing Research on Trans Sex Workers

The existing research on transgender sex workers focuses almost exclusively (until recently) on transfeminine sex workers, with extant studies largely ignoring trans men and other gender-nonconforming people.[1] Cissexism and sexism converge in studies of sex work, and transmisogyny and the fetishization of trans women in cultures worldwide shape research. The fields of public health and criminology dominate the studies on transgender sex workers. Given the intellectual focus of these fields, studies tend to primarily center on disease and trauma—almost exclusively on HIV.[2] Given that trans women have significantly higher rates of HIV than trans men, public health researchers do not see trans men's sexual behaviors as a public health threat—or, in other words, worthy of study. Unfortunately, instead of treating trans women sex workers as humans with needs, who labor and live under necropolitical systems that harm them and do not support them, existing research tends to treat transfeminine sex workers as a public health problem to be solved.

The centering of trans women in full-service sex work ignores both transmasculine and nonbinary people. Many researchers still rely on binary systems of sex, gender, and sexuality to collect data. When they do collect data on trans people, they deploy a trans/cis binary, ignoring nonbinary and other gender-nonconforming people. Newer studies that have captured data on nonbinary sex workers often exclude them due to small sample sizes.[3] The pathologization of transfeminine sex workers and the intentional exclusion of transmasculine and nonbinary people from existing studies exemplify how transmisogyny and cisgenderism and its by-product, cissexism, shape research, which has adverse implications for policy, resource allocation, and direct services.

Our Interviews with Transmasculine and Nonbinary Sex Workers

This chapter is based on our individual research projects with sex workers on the transmasculine spectrum. Taken together, we interviewed fifty transmasculine and nonbinary sex workers. In both of our studies, for workers' own sense of identity and the nuanced language they used to self-define to remain intact, participants defined their demographic characteristics using open measures. The sex workers in the studies come from Australia, Belgium, Canada, Germany, Norway, Thailand, the United Kingdom, and the United States of America. However, despite Angela's recruitment of participants outside of the US, the sample population is overwhelmingly from the United States of America.

Regarding gender, the samples included twenty-four nonbinary AFAB individuals and twenty-six transmasculine individuals.[4] Among the nonbinary participants, four identified as enbie men/boys,[5] three as genderqueer, three as agender, one as bigender, and another as genderfluid. Among the transmasculine people, twelve identified as trans men, eight as men, two as transexual, and two as genderfluid and trans. Next, respondents' ages ranged from eighteen to forty-two years old. Interestingly, in both our samples, no one identified as straight; fourteen identified as pansexual, twelve as queer, eleven as gay, nine as bisexual, two as other, one as homoflexible, and another as asexual.

Finally, regarding race, 36 percent of the sample (n=18) are Black, Indigenous, or people of color (BIPOC), and 64 percent (n=32) are white. Of the BIPOC respondents, three participants identified as Black, two as Chicano, two as Hispanic,[6] one as South Asian, one as Asian, and six as multiracial. Of the multiracial respondents, two are white and Native American (USA); one is Black, white, and Indigenous; one is white and South Asian; one is white and Indigenous (Yorta Yorta) (Australia); and another, Indigenous (Algonquin Métis) and white (Canada). This racial composition is critical because many sociological studies fail to capture Indigenous people's experiences. Huyser,

Sakamoto, and Takei noted, "Although Native Americans continue to be enumerated as a distinct demographic group, recent research has tended to neglect them."[7] Whiteness often goes unacknowledged within trans and nonbinary scholarship;[8] white trans people's experiences are often generalized as representative of those of all trans and nonbinary people. To avoid further reproductions of the invisibility of whiteness, racialization must be central to analyses of trans sex workers' labor experiences.

Transnational capitalism and economic precarity cause working-class people to hustle and find multiple income streams in gig economies. Participants described moving between different forms of sex work or expanding the kind of sex work they do in response to material need, personal life shifts, and safety concerns (including FOSTA). Thus, while some participants engaged in only one kind of sex work, participants often transitioned from one kind to another or did multiple kinds of sex work simultaneously. In our collective samples, participants had experience working in full-service work, studio porn and online porn content creation, camming, pro-domme work, phone sex, and sugaring. Finally, ten respondents spoke directly about working in street-based sex work and "survival sex work," or trading sex for basic needs such as housing, food, and medicines.

Market segment and worker subjectivity and embodiment shaped their wages. Data suggests that transmasculine full-service providers have the lowest market rates among escorts advertising online.[9] In Angela's sample, escorts' minimum advertised rates varied from $50 to $450 per hour, averaging $200. Nonbinary escorts averaged $218, and transmasculine escorts $182. A 2020 study looking at the rates of women independent online escorts in the United States (n=839) documented the following mean hourly advertised rates: for all women, $420, and for Asian escorts $426, Black $350, Latina $398, multiracial $470, and white $423. Transfeminine escorts average $300, and Black transfeminine escorts $205. Documented rates for cisgender men are $200/hour. In sex markets, men and nonbinary people have lower sexual capital than women (both trans and cis), due to lower market demand because of their nonfemme and/or nonnormative embodiment(s). A commonality among our participants discussing precarity was how cissexism and racism mean that they cannot charge anywhere near what their cis women peers do, especially white ones.[10] One worker suggested that when things were tight, they were forced more into an "I'll take what I can get mentality." Some workers discussed using sliding scales in the interest of social justice, which is yet another undocumented theme in the extant literature.

Across our studies, workers were more comfortable with their bodies and sexual labor post-transition (physical and social), with lower dysphoria for those who experienced it and increased gender euphoria and trans joy (more on that shortly). Still, workers indicated that they had difficulty finding clients. For transmasculine workers, this often meant reducing wages and working in more niche markets, and for nonbinary workers, this meant concealing their identities at work. Coen is a twenty-two-year-old, nonbinary, white-presenting Indigenous Australian (Yorta Yorta People) and has worked in the industry for four years. Discussing transitioning and wages, they said,

> Most cis women in the area charge anywhere from three hundred to six hundred an hour. So, I was charging three hundred, and then, as I started to work as a trans guy, my clients dropped massively because there's way less demand. So, I went down to charging two hundred just so I could get bookings, especially with disability stuff, trying to afford all the costs related to being disabled. So, easy preparation meals, air conditioning, 'cause I'm quite heat-sensitive, transport because I wouldn't be able to walk to the bus . . . little things people don't realize. So, I had to drop [my rates] to get any work. And a lot of my clients were men who wanted to see someone with a vagina, a hole to fuck, basically, but didn't want to pay money to see cis women because their rates were higher. . . . But it's been pretty bad all year here, actually, since FOSTA/SESTA. It's really impacted international sex work. . . . I'm thinking about reducing my rates again 'cause I've had one booking in the past fortnight, and he shortchanged me.

Coen's story is instructive. Transitioning in a cisgendered market post-FOSTA put Coen in a particularly precarious position not only as a transmasculine nonbinary person but as someone with disabilities.

When transmasculine and nonbinary escorts had access to clients, working as themselves, they discussed engaging in unique and understudied forms of *gendered labor*. Alx is a twenty-five-year-old, white, trans man from the United States who has been working as an escort for several years. Alx shared that he often had to engage in gendered labor that ran contrary to his transmasculine identity. He remarks that the following was a very typical booking for him:

> A client I was seeing used to book me for his frat. I would go over, and we would role play that they were all forcing me to detransition. . . . During the scene, they would talk about how I was going to be forced to carry their children, that kind of shit you know? We all got off on it. But when the scene was done, I would put my sweatpants on, and Chase [one of his clients] would crack open a beer, and we'd shoot the shit and play video games and stuff. When the scene was done, they just treated me like they would any other frat brother.

Alx shared that the demarcation between his treatment "in scene" and "out of scene" helped him compartmentalize this kind of gendered labor. In scene, his trans identity was eroticized by clients through role play around forced detransition and insemination, which served to bolster the clients' masculinity; however, he shared that this ends the moment the scene is done, and then he is treated like "just one of the guys."[11] Therefore, Alx was able to see the gendered dynamics as part of the erotic exchange, rather than indicative of transphobia from his clients. Consequently, many trans and nonbinary workers deploy complex management strategies to cope with the complex demands the market makes on them.[12]

Sex work offered the trans and nonbinary people in our sample genuine avenues to gender euphoria and trans joy. The paradigm shift to trans joy highlights how many trans people's lives are characterized by authenticity, pride, and community,[13] not just deficit, violence, and struggle. Here we utilize the concept of trans joy and euphoria, not as a "naive optimism" but as a "conscious, purposeful" resistance strategy against a "world that has insisted upon cishet norms."[14] Using this frame highlighted that sex work not only was a place where workers could experiment with gender, and solidify meaning making around their own identities, but also offered avenues to subversive resistance, pleasure, and job satisfaction. For example, Gabe, a twenty-seven-year-old white, transmasculine escort and cammer, explained,

> [Sex work] has affected my gender and sexuality too, in ways that are profound and in ways I don't think I imagined before getting into it. It helped me figure out the ways my desires are both wrapped up in my gayness and transness. I think, in a lot of ways, the work I do has helped shape who I am . . . and allowed me to explore my femininity and masculinity, and the place that exists in between.

Despite sometimes being asked to engage in gendered practices of feminized erotic labor and kink, these spaces offered distance to separate embodiment from identity. This not only helped workers solidify a sense of stability in their own masculinity and gendered disposition, but it also helped some workers reincorporate femininity separate from womanhood into their own understanding of their gender.

Chey is a twenty-three-year-old, Black, nonbinary street worker who recalled,

> I started to identify as nonbinary after working with a bunch of white clients and seeing how they would treat me. . . . Even when I was working as a cis girl, I was still seen as more masc. It got me thinking about gender. Gender isn't just about *gender* . . . it's colonial, it's political, . . . and more about race than people want to admit.

Chey highlighted the inherent racialization implicit in the gendered ways clients respond to them. These workers were then able to reflect back that this kind of gendered and racialized fetishization and the masculinizing of their Blackness by others was not unique to sex work but, in many ways, did shape the way they understood their gender— indicating that their transness was both constructed in resistance and imposed by a colonial structure of gender. Workers discussed how, in addition to allowing for gender play and challenging hegemonic gender systems, performing sex work as their authentic selves produced job satisfaction and joy.

Merritt, a twenty-six-year-old, white, nonbinary escort from Australia, discussed how performing femininity in the brothel felt after identifying as nonbinary.

> I felt like work was really contributing to the dysphoria that I was
> experiencing—that I felt like I was having so much sex as a woman and
> being touched as a woman. . . . Yeah, it just grated on me quite a bit. It
> was just things like when a client would be going down on me. I almost
> wouldn't feel anything. It was like just really numb. That took a while
> to get better. I think when I moved to independent work, I was able to
> build more of a brand that I chose, I suppose, and a brand that I felt more
> comfortable with, and I suppose, got more clients who knew that I was
> nonbinary. . . . And now, like fingers crossed, all of that, like tension and
> dysphoria, is behind me.

As Merritt highlighted, brothels forced them to perform embodied
femininity. Merritt underscored that such performances were stress-
ful, exacerbating their dysphoria, and they disassociated to manage the
psychological tolls of these encounters. Critically, full-service providers must avoid a wide range of issues, from stealthing (nonconsensual
removal of a condom) to violence. Therefore, if they disassociate or go
"numb," as Merritt remarked, it compromises their safety and mental
health. Still, as Merritt discussed, when they moved to independent
work and began advertising as nonbinary and as their authentic self and
clients accepted them, eventually, working as their authentic self, they
no longer experienced dysphoria. Merritt continued to unpack the connections between cisgendered workspaces, working as one's authentic
self, and the capacity for trans joy. They noted, "I've made a choice to be
pretty open about my gender identity . . . and that's where I find workplace satisfaction. I like bringing in my gender fluidity and everything
like that; that's something that gives me real joy at work."

Scholarship on trans people often heavily leans on narratives of danger and despair, which too often erases agency, resiliency, joy, and pleasure.[15] Conversely, others critique the contemporary shift of scholarship
focused on trans joy, fearing that it may present too rosy a picture and
sometimes does not adequately capture the material conditions of trans
people's lives.[16] However, what we find is that often, these are part and

parcel—trans joy and gender euphoria emerge in resistance to the oppressive conditions and structures that press upon trans people's lives.

New Directions

Street-Based and Survival Sex Work

Research and cultural imagery regarding street-based sex workers suggest that only cisgender women work in them. In our samples, ten participants indicated that at one time, they had engaged in street work, but we still know too little about transmasculine and nonbinary sex workers' experiences with street-based work. Further, many participants indicated that at some point in their lives, they had engaged in "survival sex work." People use sex in instrumental ways all the time but may not identify as sex workers. If a trans person trades blowjobs for couch surfing, is this not sex work? How does survival sex figure into current definitions and understandings of what constitutes sex work? By only studying people who self-identify as sex workers, researchers are failing to capture the experiences of a wide range of people who trade sex.

Wages

We still know very little about the wages of sex workers. Scholars do not always ask about wages, and when they do, small samples in qualitative research are not generalizable to all sex workers. Further, when studies purport to document the wages of full-service providers, these numbers are based on advertised rates, not actual earnings, and often oversample escorts in the "high end" of the market. As Victoria Bee has written, when researchers extract data from sex worker websites, "well-meaning researchers frequently produce research which takes at face value information which needs decoding by a secretive and hard to reach community."[17] Sex workers construct "manufactured identities" as part of harm-reduction strategies, which means everything from posted identity categories (e.g., age, race, nationality, gender, sexuality) to rates may not be accurate measures. Further, any attempts to conduct large-scale quantitative research about earnings must also contend with the influx of fraud in online surveys.

Clients

Much of what we know about clients comes from the insights of sex workers themselves. However, much less research is focused on the clientele of sex workers.[18] We suspect that researchers themselves prefer studying workers, whom they see as sympathetic victims or comrades (depending on one's political and feminist orientation), but clients, who are assumed to be privileged, straight, cishet men, do need research conducted about them. In our research, workers talked about providing sliding scales to clients who are women, trans, disabled, or other providers. So, even if full-service providers primarily see cisgender men, we know clients are diverse; researchers just aren't studying them. There is no existing research on sex workers providing services to other sex workers. Given the heteropatriarchal underpinnings of perceptions of sex industries, there is little focus on gay men or other queer clients. We encourage more research about clients and especially studies that disrupt common assumptions.

Identities

Identity shapes individuals' experiences of sex work. However, more research is needed using intersectional and transnational frames to accurately integrate individuals' various social and political identities. Researchers can apply such frames to document better the experiences of disabled sex workers, gay men, lesbians, people on the Ace spectrum, Indigenous and Black workers, and workers throughout the Global South. For example, we do not know enough about the correlations between disability and sex work.[19] As one of our respondents noted, "Every trans disabled person I know has done sex work. It's a massive thing in the community, especially if you're disabled." Additionally, there is still little research on nonbinary sex workers, and to our knowledge, there have been no studies focusing on nonbinary people who were assigned male at birth. Additionally, while our work has focused on trans men, the research on all men in sex industries remains thin. Relatedly, future research is needed to explore sexual fluidity among sex workers.

Minors

While several of our respondents shared that they had begun sex work prior to being eighteen, we were only able to document their experiences retroactively. Laws worldwide make any engagement in sex work under the age of eighteen illegal. Take the Trafficking Victims Protection Act (TVPA) in the United States of America, for example, which indicates that anyone under eighteen cannot consensually choose sex work. However, our conversation with sex workers who worked as minors tells a different story. From this, we know that consent and coercion exist on a continuum. Additionally, we know that getting past institutional review boards with adult sex workers is hard enough, so researchers may shy away from studying sex workers under eighteen. However, we know that LGBTQIA+ sex workers often engage in sex work as a means of survival, particularly when also facing housing insecurity, lack of familial safety nets, and overall material precarity.[20] Minors engaged in sex work have unique labor demands that are still poorly documented.[21]

In conclusion, we pinpoint new directions for conducting research *with* transgender sex workers. First, researchers must adopt fluid measures for collecting demographic data on gender and sexuality and not ignore disability.[22] Second, small samples do not legitimate the exclusion of people from critical research, which often informs policy and social services. Using qualitative methods and conducting interviews are critical in research with such populations. Third, researchers must stop treating people as "human subjects" and more like partners in research. We believe studies about any demographic of sex workers must be community engaged and involve sex workers.

NOTES
1 For exceptions see, Jones 2022b; Chudyk 2023.
2 Jones 2019.
3 Clark et al. 2017.
4 AFAB: Assigned female at birth. "AFAB" was the most accurate and inclusive term with respect to people who identify outside femme and masc labels, but for whom sex assigned at birth is relevant within this context.
5 Enbie is a nonbinary identity category people use when their gender is outside of the gender binary. It is synonymous with nonbinary.

6 Generally, Angela uses "Latinx," but their respondents used "Hispanic." When we report demographic information herein, we use participants' language.

7 Huyser, Sakamoto, and Takei 2010, 542.

8 Vidal-Ortiz 2014; Moussawi and Vidal-Ortiz 2020.

9 Jones 2023a, 2023b.

10 Jones 2023b.

11 Schilt 2010.

12 Chudyk 2023.

13 shuster and Westbrook 2022.

14 Branstetter 2022; Joseph 2021.

15 shuster and Westbrook 2022; Chudyk 2023; Jones 2020a, 2023a.

16 Pechey 2022.

17 Bee 2021.

18 Sanders, Brents, and Wakefield 2020; Scott, Callander, and Minichiello 2014; Kingston, Hammond, and Redman 2020.

19 See, the 2022 *Disability Studies Quarterly* special issue (vol. 42, no. 2) on Disability and Sex Work. Accessed December 13, 2023. https://dsq-sds.org.

20 See Robinson 2020 for a brief discussion of LGBTQ youth experiencing homelessness doing survival sex work.

21 Showden and Majic 2018.

22 Jones 2022c.

31

Cybrothel

The World's First A.I. Sex Worker

KENNETH R. HANSON AND ALEXIS SMILEY SMITH

They [sex workers] share some of the same fears of other
workers—that technology developments may put them
completely out of business. All the peepshows now sell
substitutes—dolls to have sex with, vibrators, plastic vaginas, and penises—and as one woman groused in New York,
"It won't be long before customers can buy a robot from the
drug store and they won't need us at all."[1]

Using "sex robots" for sex work used to be science fiction, but technological gains are forging a new frontier in digital sex work. Companies
such as Orient Industry and Abyss Creations have developed thousands
of hyperrealistic silicone and thermoplastic elastomer (TPE) love and
sex dolls costing upwards of six thousand dollars. The success of these
companies has spurred both fascination from scholars who view dolls
as a benign extension of sex toys,[2] and scrutiny from those who criticize
their hyperfeminine (and hypermasculine) construction.[3] Moreover,
journalists reporting on the burgeoning "doll brothel" industry have
brought attention to dolls being used in sex work today.[4] Doll brothels
across Europe, North America, and Asia rent inanimate dolls for private
use in hotel rooms or at established locations to clients looking for fu-
turistic sexual experiences.

A few scholars have noted the legal and moral quandaries doll
brothels pose. One argument in favor of doll brothels advanced by
David Levy, a prominent futurist and scholar of human-robot interactions, is that doll brothels might "save" people (read: women) from
sex work and provide clients (read: men) with safer, more readily

available, more physically flexible, less morally tainted, and more customizable sexual services.[5] Some even suggest this will be the last form of sex work and will replace human sex workers entirely. Other scholars are more critical of the sexual objectification they see in a future with sex robots and dolls. Prominent anti-doll scholar-activist Kathleen Richardson argues that the normalization of dolls as legitimate sexual partners will perpetuate patriarchy and misogyny, given that the industry primarily caters to heterosexual cisgender men.[6] And yet, despite these debates, media psychologist Nicola Döring and colleagues noted in their review of scholarship on dolls and doll brothels, "We have not yet seen data collected from sex workers' perspectives on the issue."[7]

In this chapter, we introduce some of the first empirical data and analysis of doll brothels. We analyze the experiences of Alexis, a former escort and current co-owner of Cybrothel, a doll brothel in Germany where clients interact with dolls animated with the remote voice of an unseen sex worker. This experiential data is supplemented by digital ethnographic data from Kenneth's study of the love-and-sex-doll industry. We show how this new form of sex tech exists in and expands sex work markets while reflecting on how it may potentially reproduce an unequal society. In our case study of Cybrothel, we use the autoethnographic reflections of this chapter's coauthor, Alexis Smiley Smith, who is the voice and creator of Kokeshi (the lead doll persona at Cybrothel), to explore the promise and pitfalls of doll brothels. Alexis's experiences in this form of disembodied sex work have shown her the potential for dolls to promote sex positivity and feminist ideals. However, we also analyze trends in the industry that, left unchecked, will reproduce social inequality by reinforcing racialized fetishes, racialized capitalism, white supremacy, and fatphobia. Finally, we discuss both the potential and limits of dolls' "object-ness." For example, clients can use dolls to explore sexual desires they are uncomfortable exploring with a human partner, but we argue that there is a limit to these experiences because of dolls' lack of interactional and emotional spontaneity. Our analysis of Cybrothel challenges our ideas of where sexual pleasure and intimacy with the human body, sex toys, and consciousness begin and end.

The Case: Cybrothel, Kokeshi, and Analog A.I.

Although Kokeshi is an inanimate love/sex doll, Alexis has crafted a persona for her and designed the Cybrothel apartment as a sexual and sensual playground. When clients first enter the room, they find Kokeshi basking in a heater to warm her silicone skin, wearing a curly blue wig and clear plastic skirt, with her galactic blue eyes fixed on a bowl of condoms dangling above the bed. After Alexis places Kokeshi on the bed, she leaves the room. Then, speaking as Kokeshi from an external control room, Alexis welcomes clients into the room. Strategically placed cameras and microphones allow Alexis to view and hear the client (or clients) as they interact with Kokeshi. Importantly, clients never see Alexis during the interaction. Instead, a speaker inside Kokeshi's head allows Alexis to bring Kokeshi to life, digitally, in what Cybrothel calls the "Analog A.I." experience.

> When Cybrothel opened, it seemed a natural fit for me to be the voice of Kokeshi, as I am technically her "maker" and a former sex worker. My offsite room is a literal closet packed with doll clothes, wigs, a small table with monitors, a headset, an audio mixer, and a laptop. The equipment is outdated, so it looks like something out of the early 1990s. I created a ritual to get into character before clients arrive—a small finger of brandy, a glass of water, and meditative breaths. I arrive early to practice Kokeshi's voice, which is slightly robotic, but also soothing and sexy with a blended British-American accent. (Alexis)

Cybrothel offers a cutting-edge sexual service for clients who want to explore the liminal tech space between subject and object. Rather than offer what other doll brothels provide (a doll and a room), Alexis and her business partners decided to integrate digital interactions into having sex with dolls. In a way, this is phone sex with a shared physical medium. Although these experiences are limited because Kokeshi cannot move herself, the digital interactions are more engaging for clients because Alexis has more control over how Kokeshi's persona affects the experience.

> With Cybrothel/Kokeshi, my business partners and I saw an opportunity for a sex doll to become a developed character with human consciousness.

However, I had never interacted with a silicone doll before and imagined incel-type men, simply labeled "doll fuckers," coming to her flat and having creepy sex with her. At the same time, I was smitten with the idea of writing a fully developed character for Kokeshi, a blue-haired galactic sex doll with a heart of gold. I wanted to queer her a bit, instead of offering up the standard hyperfeminized form of perfect-tits perfect-ass kind of woman with no agency. I refused to cater to the heteronormative male gaze. However, her body was built in the hyperfeminine ideal, so my queering of Kokeshi was in her personification. I gave her a mission with three main tenets: to spread pleasure consciousness, to teach consent, and to promote the shame-free enjoyment of one's fetishes and desires. I also bought her an attachable penis and insisted she identify as a postgender being. (Alexis)

In addition to analog A.I., Cybrothel allows clients to request having pornography play overhead on a projector, ask for specific music to play over the flat's speakers, and/or have Kokeshi dressed in fetish attire. Another benefit of robotic sex work that David Levy noted is its unending and customizable variety.[8] And so, alongside Kokeshi, Cybrothel offers digitally interactive sessions with Paris, a hyperfeminine girl next door, Guy Rider, a sultry bisexual male doll, Mistress Oxana, a German dominatrix, and, coming soon, Hito, a pixie-esque Manga doll with pointy ears, as well as a blue-skinned alien doll. Welcome to the future of sex work.

This Is Sex Work, after All

As a cutting-edge business, Cybrothel has attracted the attention of journalists and academics interested in the technology behind analog A.I. Yet by focusing on the dolls, few recognize the cognitive, physical, and emotional labor that goes into making Cybrothel possible. Alexis finds that personifying Kokeshi requires labor like other forms of sex work such as catering to clients' emotions, developing a connection, and encouraging consensual interactions all while asserting her feminist ideals.

People often ask if I feel removed from the clients because of the distance. Certainly, the physical separation between me and Kokeshi's flat makes the work feel different, but I still develop an intimate connection with clients. The cameras and intensity of the interactions cause me to develop a hyper awareness of the client's voice and movements, which translate into a specific type of intimacy with the client. Often, I find myself taking control by directing the client to get undressed, to come sit on the bed next to me (Kokeshi), to touch my arms, the little dip of my collar bone, or to smell my hair. I mention lube is important and say, "Yes, you can touch me there, thank you for asking." I reward consent and make it a point to bring up how important consent is, even in this context. When clients want to watch porn, I avoid commercialized productions, preferring Erika Lust and other feminist pornographers.

And yes, I simulate orgasms, moan, and say names. This is a form of sex work, after all. In one case, a client had difficulty getting hard, so I led him through a meditation session to try and relax. We decided against penetrative sex. Instead, we watched underwater relaxation videos as he sat naked next to Kokeshi, just breathing. (Alexis)

As noted in *Revolting Prostitutes* by Juno Mac and Molly Smith, the emotional and physical labor involved in sex work is often devalued by its association with "women's work."[9] In some instances, clients have tried to control the interaction and speak directly to Alexis, thus refusing to engage in the analog A.I. experience. In these moments, the service Alexis is providing is drawn into question as a legitimate professional experience. Moreover, she provides familiar sex work services by sexualizing her voice, making sexual sounds, and comforting men. Throughout these interactions, Alexis consciously promotes a feminist agenda by rewarding consent and choosing feminist pornography despite the clients who devalue the labor she puts into creating Cybrothel.

In a sense, I am a madam and a sex worker at the same time. The dolls are not actually sex workers, they are more like a medium through which an exchange occurs. In interviews and discussions with people about my work as Kokeshi, people tend to focus on my relationship with the character of Kokeshi. This is lovely for discourse about the performative aspects of my work, but this reduces the service to the persona. I have to remind people that this is sex work. Not only am I sexualizing the tone of my voice and spontaneously interacting with clients, but the upkeep of

Kokeshi's body is work, too. After every client, I take her into the shower and douche her, disinfect her, dry and oil her body. I have overhead costs on lube, dildos, wigs, and over time, replacement doll bodies. Kokeshi's electric heater and her flat all cost money. I am not doing this merely because I am a happy hooker who loves the concept of dolls and sex so much that, because of my sex positivity, I would do this for free.[10] And of course, I am a specific kind of sex worker in that I am white, privileged, working out of choice rather than survival, and live in a country where sex work is legal. When people focus on the negatives of sex work, they seem to forget or ignore that those negatives are due to structural issues that fail to treat sex work as paid labor. My position gives me the vision and opportunity to make money and create a new form of sexual and sensual services. (Alexis)

The Business of Doll Brothels

The fact that dolls are objects, rather than people, raises questions about how they may change the economics of sex work. Since dolls do not collect a paycheck, they seem potentially more profitable for brothel owners than human workers. One of the earliest doll brothels, Doru No Mori in Japan, claimed in 2004 to have made a return on its investment within the first month of opening. Additionally, as human-robot-interaction scholar David Levy points out, dolls do not have to worry about fines, imprisonment, STIs, or physical and sexual abuse.[11] That said, these "human" limitations are outcomes of structural barriers and stigma against sex workers. While it may be tempting to argue that dolls can "save" humans from sex work, sex workers often need and want the work. Not only can sex work provide a living wage; when coupled with digital technologies, it can be flexible, autonomous, and in some cases pleasurable.[12]

However, as a business enterprise, doll manufacturing is tethered to capitalism in ways that undermine efforts to use dolls in radical ways and instead reproduce androcentrism, fatphobia, racial fetishism, and white supremacy. Content analysis of Sexy Real Sex Dolls, an online third-party doll vendor, reveals that of the more than seven hundred dolls available for purchase on the site, 96 percent of them are female-sexed, which is unsurprising given that most doll owners are heterosexual cisgender men. Because they are the largest consumer demographic, dolls are often designed with the heteromale gaze in mind. So not only are most dolls female-sexed, but many share the familiarly unattainable form—a young face with large breasts, a small waist, flat stomach, wide hips, and slender limbs.

Dolls are also designed according to sexualized racial hierarchies. Most female-sexed dolls on Sexy Real Sex Dolls are white (73 percent) and Asian (15.5 percent).[13] These racialized products capitalize on the perceived femininity and hyperfemininity of white and Asian women. The mass manufacturing of white and Asian dolls, with the production of few Black (6 percent) or Indigenous (<1 percent) dolls, means the modes of femininity that perpetuate racialized gender inequality are, literally, reproduced.[14] Further, since many dolls share the same skin tone, companies use fetishized language to advertise the same few skin tones as an array of racial and ethnic categories. Two dolls with the same "dark skin tone" are sold in one ad as "Ebony," and in another ad as "Big Black Bubble Butt with Huge Tits Coco. Imani has a big fat ass and massive boobs. If you were looking for a big black love doll. This is the one!" In other ads, the assumed heteromale customer is racialized in ways that reinforce the privilege of white femininity. One white doll ad reads, "This Big Booty Jude Love Doll is equipped with large titties and huge ass, this sex doll is truly a black man's kryptonite." These racialized discourses play off tropes found in mainstream pornography and work to reinforce patriarchal white supremacy, and Cybrothel is not immune to this discursive environment.

Marketing Cybrothel

While Cybrothel's owners hope to create a queer utopic play space where sex, technology, and intimacy unite in ways that allow people to explore kink, play, and more, Cybrothel still exists at the intersection of capitalism, racism, and heteropatriarchy. For example, to widen Cybrothel's market viability, Kokeshi is advertised in ways that increasingly conform to pornographic tropes.

> Do you crave anonymous uncomplicated sex? Maybe a one-night stand with a wet and loving sex doll? I am Kokeshi, a female sex doll who lives

at Cybrothel Berlin. You can rent me by the hour in a private room where your hottest fantasies and fetishes are my true delight. When you visit me, you will find my silicone body soft to touch and penetrate. You will feel welcome and safe in a shame free environment to live out your sexual and sensual desires. (Cybrothel website)

At times I feel I have to fight for not becoming too base and simplified. Is there a happy medium where I can use hypersexualized images and content to get clients in the door and expose them to my feminist narrative? (Alexis)

Cybrothel is preparing to offer sessions with Hito, a Manga-inspired Asian cosplay doll who loves gaming and hard-core pornography. Bringing Hito to Cybrothel is a direct appeal to white men who enjoy gaming and desire hyperfeminine Asian dolls. Personifying an Asian doll to capture this market raises new questions for Alexis. Given that she is a white woman, doing the digital work that would bring nonwhite dolls to life for clients is like a form of digital blackface that exposes a tension with her feminist commitments. Although Cybrothel needs to attract business, the profit motive works against the intersectional feminist ideals that were central to the conception of Kokeshi.

We're at the point where we must hire new employees. For now, I call the women "voice queens." The training sessions, the writing of manuals and scripts—this is all solidifying our business work structures. I am solidifying my role as a madam, somewhat, as I am becoming a manager whose responsibility is making a safe workplace with fair wages and support. I also bear the responsibility of casting the dolls in ways that align with our mission and brand. Hito, the Manga doll who loves hardcore pornography and gaming, is not available yet. She needs to have her own agency despite the stereotypes she plays into. As a white woman, I cannot write her persona myself. (Alexis)

Selling Connection

All the work that goes into marketing Kokeshi and the other dolls at Cybrothel hinges on the success of analog A.I. Fortunately, Alexis has found that analog A.I. adds something to the experience beyond the novelty of having sex with a doll. For example, Kokeshi has clients who desire sexual experiences they are too shy to try with human partners and opt for visiting Cybrothel instead.

> I had clients where, the wife in a heterosexual relationship wanted a threesome and was more sexually adventurous than her husband, but he was open and supportive. They made a date with Kokeshi. When they entered, the wife immediately popped open a bottle of champagne and took off her shirt, the husband slouched in a chair in the corner. Sensing the room, I was able to use Kokeshi, with my voice, to soften the mood and take some pressure off the couple. Kokeshi was just sitting on the bed, cross-legged, but my voice made it her room. And it dawned on me, as a sex worker, I sell more than sex, I sell connection. I can laugh at the champagne cork hitting the ceiling, ask meaningful questions, banter, and sort of, fuck. I am certain dolls will never replace human sex workers, much like how the dildo has yet to replace the cock, but the question is, where will their place be? (Alexis)

Rather than reproducing idealized forms of gender normativity and heterosexuality, we suggest that doll brothels have the unique opportunity to facilitate the exploration of different sexual pleasures that expand our understanding of "human" sexuality. As a doll, its objectness may help some clients feel safer to explore themselves sexually or emotionally. Still, though, there is *something* about spontaneous human connection that people desire, perhaps more than sex itself. The allure of a doll that can hold any sexual position indefinitely is one thing, but having someone who encourages you to try new positions is something altogether different. Analog A.I. merges both worlds by bringing together the novelty and advantages of an inanimate doll with some of the interactive pleasures that come from sex with a human. Moreover, through these experiences, Alexis has come to better understand the people who have sex with dolls and found that many defied her expectation of "incel-type" men.

> After the first several clients, I began to change my views on both those who fuck dolls and the dolls themselves. The doll is a source of novelty

and curiosity, as well as a conduit to explore a new fetish, try a new position, or play with gender a bit. There is no need for clients to provide an explanation or backstory; Cybrothel is anonymous and very "come as you are," pun intended. I began to think, as a girl, I often played with dolls. I projected private and public social behaviors onto them by imagining various roles and situations. I enjoyed exploring the realities that my dolls inhabited. It is interesting to enter a doll reality again, but with adult needs, traumas, desires, and fantasies. All of these realities enter into a human sex worker's experience, so why not with dolls? (Alexis)

In "The Future of Sex Report," scholars estimate that by 2045, one in ten young adults will have had a sexual encounter with a humanoid robot.[15] That said, exactly what role doll brothels will play in future sex tech enterprises is uncertain. Like much sex work, the industry operates under constant threat from authorities. Even though dolls are not humans, their application to sex work has led to several legislative crackdowns. Numerous doll brothels have been shut down, or preemptively shuttered, in North America, Europe, and Asia. But in Berlin, the market is thriving, if only in its infant state. It is unclear what direction doll brothels will take. Some may adopt a strictly for-profit model that capitalizes on racial fetishes and the affordability of dolls, while others may harness the potential of their objectness, in ways similar to Cybrothel, to challenge our ideas around where sexual pleasure begins and ends with the human body, toys, and consciousness. As a leader in this industry, Cybrothel reveals how sex workers can use dolls in ways that may redefine sex work in the twenty-first century.

NOTES
1 Weatherby 1983.
2 Döring and Pöschl 2018.
3 Cassidy 2016.
4 Breslin 2018.
5 Levy 2012.
6 Richardson 2017.
7 Döring, Mohseni, and Walter 2020.
8 Levy 2012.
9 Mac and Smith 2018.
10 Mac and Smith 2018.

11 Levy 2012.
12 Jones 2020a.
13 All male-sexed dolls at the time of this study were white.
14 Zhou and Paul 2016.
15 Owsianik and Dawson 2016.

ACKNOWLEDGMENTS

Bernadette, Barb, and Angela began work on *Sex Work Today* in the fall of 2020, which was, as we all know, a tumultuous and confusing time. Amid the challenges of the COVID-19 pandemic, this project became a refuge from the isolation, connecting us to one another and to the authors in this book. After three years of working together, we found that we make a good team. Each of us wants to thank the others' kindness, generosity, skills, perseverance, encouragement, and hard work through all our ups and downs.

At the same time, this project laid bare our privileges as tenured academics, allowing us to continue our teaching, research, and writing remotely with minimal impact on our livelihoods. In stark contrast, many of the sex-working authors in this book and sex workers worldwide were not given these privileges and received none of the paltry stimulus support offered in some nations. Instead, sex workers crafted mutual aid funds to support one another, hustling across market segments to survive, putting themselves at risk and ramping up political organizing.

Therefore, our first and most heartfelt acknowledgment goes out to all the sex workers whose lives are documented in this book.

We want to thank everyone whose hard work helped make this book possible. We want to extend a huge thanks to all the authors whose work appears in this volume. They also experienced the pandemic in varying ways, and they persevered and delivered amazing, perceptive, insightful, and well-written chapters.

We also express our appreciation for everyone who submitted abstracts, even if their work did not find a place within this particular volume.

The book is better thanks to the invaluable feedback of two sets of anonymous reviewers who offered thoughtful insights on the organization and content—thank you!

We are grateful for the publishing home of NYU Press and its excellent, meticulous, responsive staff. A special thanks to our editor, Ilene Kalish, for her interest in, encouragement of, and engagement with the project.

Many colleagues, friends, and family supported the creation of *Sex Work Today*. We thank our families for their support in all our endeavors, and especially through the pandemic: Anna Blanton, Mike, Sydney, Abby, and Greta Pawlak. We give a heartfelt thanks to Mary Underwood Hood, who helped us throughout the project, from keeping track of our initial abstracts to formatting the bibliography.

Thank you all for helping to make this project a reality. It is our hope that this book helps foster the understanding and knowledge we need to chart a path to a better future for sex workers.

BIBLIOGRAPHY

Abbott, Sharon. 2000. "Motivations for Pursuing an Acting Career in Pornography." Pp. 17–34 in *Sex for Sale*, ed. Ronald Weitzer. New York: Routledge.

Abel, Gillian M. 2014. "A Decade of Decriminalization: Sex Work 'Down Under' but Not Underground." *Criminology & Criminal Justice* 14, no. 5: 580–92.

Abel, Gillian, Lisa Fitzgerald, and Catherine Healy, eds. 2010. *Taking the Crime out of Sex Work: New Zealand Sex Workers' Fight for Discrimination*. Bristol, UK: Policy Press.

Acceptance Matters. 2021. "Today We Demand Real Acceptance." Acceptance Matters. Accessed October 7, 2022. www.acceptancematters.org.

Agustín, Laura M. 1998. *Sex at the Margins: Migration, Labor Markets, and the Rescue Industry*. London: Zed Books.

———. 2007. *Sex at the Margins: Migration, Labor Markets, and the Rescue Industry*. London: Zed Books.

Ahearne, Gemma. 2015. "Between the Sex Industry and Academia: Navigating Stigma and Disgust." *Graduate Journal of Social Science* 11, no. 2: 28–37.

Ahmed, Sara. 2014. *The Cultural Politics of Emotion*, 2nd ed. Edinburgh, Scotland: Edinburgh University Press.

Albert, Kendra. 2021. Enough about FOSTA's "Unintended Consequences." *Kendra Albert* (blog), July 28, https://kendraalbert.com.

Albright, Erin, and Kate D'Adamo. 2017. "Decreasing Human Trafficking through Sex Work Decriminalization." *AMA Journal of Ethics* 19, no. 1: 122–26.

Alemzadeh, Sheerine. 2013. "Baring Inequality: Revisiting the Legalization Debate through the Lens of Strippers' Rights." *Michigan Journal of Gender and the Law* 19: 339.

Alexander, Michelle. 2010. *The New Jim Crow: Mass Incarceration in the Age of Color-blindness*. New York: New Press.

Allard, Patricia. 2016. "Crime, Punishment, and Economic Violence." Pp. 157–263 in *Color of Violence: The INCITE! Anthology*, ed. INCITE! Women of Color Against Violence. Durham, NC: Duke University Press. https://doi.org/10.1215/9780822373445-019.

Aloni, Ronit, Ohayon Keren, and S. Katz. 2007. "Sex Therapy Surrogate Partners for Individuals with Very Limited Functional Ability Following Traumatic Brain Injury." *Sexuality and Disability* 25, no. 3 (2007): 125–34.

Anasti, Theresa. 2017. "Radical Professionals? Sex Worker Rights Activists and Collaboration with Human Service Nonprofits." *Human Service Organizations: Management, Leadership & Governance* 41, no. 4: 416–37.

Anderson, Solanna, Kate Shannon, J. Li, Y. Lee, J. Chettiar, S. Goldenberg, and A. Krüsi. 2016. "Condoms and Sexual Health Education as Evidence: Impact of Criminalization of In-Call Venues and Managers on Migrant Sex Workers' Access to HIV/STI Prevention in a Canadian Setting." *BMC International Health and Human Rights* 16, no. 30: 1–10.

Are, Carolina. 2021. "The Shadowban Cycle: An Autoethnography of Pole Dancing, Nudity, and Censorship on Instagram." *Feminist Media Studies* 22, no. 8: 2002–19. https://doi.org/10.1080/14680777.2021.1928259.

Are, Carolina, and Susanna Paasonen. 2021. "Sex in the Shadows of Celebrity." *Porn Studies* 8, no. 4: 411–19.

Argento, Elena, Shira Goldenberg, Melissa Braschel, Sylvia Machat, Steffanie A. Strathdee, and Kate Shannon. 2020. "The Impact of End-Demand Legislation on Sex Workers' Access to Health and Sex Worker–Led Services: A Community-Based Prospective Cohort Study in Canada." *PloS One* 15, no. 4: 1–18.

Armstrong, Lynzi. 2014. "Diverse Risks, Diverse Perpetrators: Perceptions of Risk and Experiences of Violence amongst Street-Based Sex Workers in New Zealand." *International Journal for Crime, Justice and Social Democracy* 3, no. 3: 40–54.

———. 2019. "Stigma, Decriminalization, and Violence against Street-Based Sex Workers: Changing the Narrative." *Sexualities* 22, no. 7–8: 1288–1308.

Armstrong, Lynzi, and Gillian Abel, eds. 2020. *Sex Work and the New Zealand Model: Decriminalization and Social Change.* Bristol, UK: University of Bristol Press.

Arner, Douglas W., Janos Barberis, and Ross P. Buckley. 2015. "The Evolution of Fin-Tech: A New Post-Crisis Paradigm." *Georgetown Journal of International Law* 47, no. 4: 1271–1320.

Arvidsson, A. 2006. *Brands: Meaning and Value in Media Culture.* New York: Routledge.

Attewell, Paul. 1990. "What Is Skill." *Work and Occupations* 17, no. 4: 422–48.

Attorney at Bruckheim & Patel. 2020. "Is Sugar Dating Prostitution?" Bruckheim & Patel. Accessed May 3, 2024. www.brucklaw.com.

Attorney General. 1986. *Final Report of the Attorney General's Commission on Pornography.* Nashville, TN: Rutledge Hill Press.

Attwood, Feona. 2010. *Porn.Com: Making Sense of Online Pornography.* New York: Peter Lang.

———. 2017. *Sex Media.* Cambridge, UK: Polity Books.

AVN. N.d. "BBW Fan Category Added to 2018 AVN Awards." *AVN.* Accessed October 14, 2022. https://avn.com.

Babylon, Femi, Madeline Marlowe, Kitty Milford, and Lorelei Lee, panelists. N.d. "Work and Anti-Work: What Are People in the Sex Trades Fighting For?" Video. Hacking//Hustling. Accessed October 14, 2022. https://hackinghustling.org.

Bacchi, Carol. 2012. "Introducing the 'What's the Problem Represented to Be?' Approach." Pp. 21–24 in *Engaging with Carol Bacchi,* ed. Angelique Bletsas and Chris Beasley. Adelaide: University of Adelaide Press.

Ballard, Finn Jackson. 2014. "Transcendental Gazes: Pornographic Images of Trans-masculinity." In *Sensational Pleasures in Cinema, Literature, and Visual Culture*, ed. Glad Padva and Nurit Buchweitz. London: Palgrave Macmillan.

Ballotpedia. N.d. "San Francisco City and County, California Ballot Measures. 2008." Ballotpedia. Accessed October 14, 2022. https://ballotpedia.org.

Banks, Ingrid. 2000. *Hair Matters: Beauty, Power, and Black Women's Consciousness.* New York: New York University Press.

Barman, Jean. 2004. "Encounters with Sexuality: The Management of Inappropriate Body Behaviour in Late-Nineteenth-Century British Columbia Schools." *Historical Studies in Education* 16, no. 1: 85–114.

Bartky, Sandra Lee. 2003. "Foucault, Femininity, and the Modernization of Patriarchal Power." Pp. 25–45 in *The Politics of Women's Bodies*, 2nd ed., ed. R. Weitz. New York: Oxford University Press.

Barton, Bernadette. 2002. "Dancing on the Möbius Strip: Challenging the Sex War Paradigm." *Gender and Society* 16, no. 5: 585–602.

———. 2017. *Stripped: More Stories from Exotic Dancers.* New York: New York University Press.

———. 2021. *The Pornification of America: How Raunch Culture Is Ruining Our Society.* New York: New York University Press.

Baskin, Cyndy, Carol Strike, and Bela McPherson. 2015. "Long Time Overdue: An Examination of the Destructive Impacts of Policy and Legislation on Pregnant and Parenting Aboriginal Women and Their Children." *International Indigenous Policy Journal* 6, no. 1: 1–17. https://doi.org/10.18584/iipj.2015.6.1.5.

Bataille, Georges. 1991 [1949]. *The Accursed Share: An Essay on General Economy.* Vol. 1, *Consumption.* Translated by Robert Hurley. Brooklyn, NY: Zone Books.

Baudrillard, Jean. 2017. *Symbolic Exchange and Death*, 2nd ed. Translated by Mike Gane. London: Sage Publications.

Bauer, Kiara. 2018. "Kiara's Corner: What Is Findom Anyway?" *YNOT CAM* (blog), May 24. www.ynotcam.com.

Baumeister, Roy F. 1988. "Masochism as Escape from Self." *Journal of Sex Research* 25, no. 1: 28–59. https://doi.org/10.1080/00224498809551444.

Bee, Victoria. 2021. "Vital Statistics." Forged Intimacies, May 31. https://forgedintimacies.com.

Beggan, James K. 2020. "Monomyth or Monogamyth? Polyamory's Conceptual Challenges to the Hero's Journey." *Heroism Science* 5, no. 2: article 3: 1–46.

Begum, Raani. 2020. "Whorephobia and Whorearchy." *Ko-Ji* (blog), March 3, 2020, https://ko-fi.com.

Begum, Raani, and Sultana Bibi. 2022. "Destigmatize, Decriminalize, Decarcerate: A Racial Justice Lens on Sex Worker Rights and Harm Reduction." Philadelphia Red Umbrella Alliance (blog), July. www.phillyrua.com.

Bembe, Lina. 2021. "Demystifying Porn, for Pornographers." In *We Too: Essays on Sex Work and Survival*, ed. Natalie West. New York: Feminist Press.

Benoit, Cecilia, Mikael Jansson, and Jackson Flagg. 2018. "Prostitution Stigma and Its Effect on the Working Conditions, Personal Lives, and Health of Sex Workers." *Journal of Sex Research* 55, no. 4–5: 457–71.

Benoit, Cecilia, Renay Maurice, Gillian Abel, Michaela Smith, Mikael Jansson, Priscilla Healey, and Douglas Magnuson. 2020. "'I Dodged the Stigma Bullet': Canadian Sex Workers' Situated Responses to Occupational Stigma." *Culture, Health & Sexuality* 22, no. 1: 81–95.

Benoit, Cecilia, and Leah Shumka. 2021. "Sex Work in Canada." Understanding Sex Work project, Canadian Institute for Substance Use Research, University of Victoria. Accessed July 19, 2022. www.uvi.ca.

Ben-Zeév, Aaron. 2020. "Why Sugar-Daddy Relationships Are on the Rise." *Psychology Today*, June 18, 2020.

Berg, Heather. 2014. "An Honest Day's Wage for a Dishonest Day's Work: (Re) Productivism and Refusal." *Women's Studies Quarterly* 42, no. 1/2: 171.

———. 2016. "'A Scene Is Just a Marketing Tool': Alternative Income Streams in Porn's Gig Economy." *Porn Studies* 3, no. 2: 160–74. https://doi.org/10.1080/23268743.2016.1184478.

———. 2017. "Porn Work, Feminist Critique, and the Market for Authenticity." *Signs: Journal of Women in Culture and Society* 42, no. 3: 669–92. https//doi.org/10.1086/689633.

———. 2021. *Porn Work: Sex, Labor, and Late Capitalism*. Chapel Hill: University of North Carolina Press.

Berg, Rigmor, Sol-Britt Molin, and Julie Nanavati. 2020. "Women Who Trade Sexual Services from Men: A Systematic Mapping Review." *Journal of Sex Research* 57: 104–18.

Berlant, Lauren. 2008. *The Female Complaint*. Durham, NC: Duke University Press.

Berne, Patricia, Aurora Levins Morales, David Langstaff, and Sins Invalid. 2018. "Ten Principles of Disability Justice." *WSQ: Women's Studies Quarterly* 46, no. 1: 227–30.

Bernstein, Elizabeth. 1999. "What's Wrong with Prostitution? What's Right with Sex Work? Comparing Sexual Markets in Female Sexual Labor." *Hastings Women's Law Journal* 10, no. 1: 91–117.

———. 2007a. "A Note on Methodology." In *Temporarily Yours: Intimacy, Authenticity, and the Commerce of Sex*, 189–202. Chicago: University of Chicago Press.

———. 2007b. *Temporarily Yours: Intimacy, Authenticity, and the Commerce of Sex*. Chicago: University of Chicago Press.

———. 2010. "Militarized Humanitarianism Meets Carceral Feminism: The Politics of Sex, Rights, and Freedom in Contemporary Antitrafficking Campaigns." *Signs: Journal of Women in Culture and Society* 36, no. 1: 45–71.

———. 2018. "The Sexual Politics of Carceral Feminism." Pp. 34–67 in *Brokered Subjects: Sex, Trafficking, and the Politics of Freedom*. Chicago: University of Chicago Press.

Bimbi, David S. 2007. "Male Prostitution: Pathology, Paradigms, and Progress in Research." *Journal of Homosexuality* 53, no. 1–2: 7–35.

Bletzer, Keith. 2003. "Risk and Danger among Women-Who-Prostitute in Areas Where Farmworkers Predominate." *Medical Anthropology Quarterly* 17: 251–78.

Blewett, Lindsay. 2022. "The Criminalization of Sex Work: Creating Conditions for Disability." In *Disability Injustice: Confronting Criminalization in Canada*, ed. Kelly Fritsch, Emily van der Meulen, and Jeffrey Monaghan. Vancouver: University of British Columbia Press.

Blewett, Lindsay, and Tuulia Law. 2018. "Sex Work and Allyship: Examining Femme-, Bi- and Whorephobia in Queer Communities." *Feral Feminisms*, no. 7: 58–65.

Blue, Violet. 2015. "PayPal, Square, and Big Banking's War on the Sex Industry." Engadget, December 2. Accessed October 7, 2022. www.engadget.com.

Blunt, Danielle, Emily Coombes, Shanelle Mullin, and Ariel Wolf. 2020. "Posting into the Void: Studying the Impact of Shadowbanning on Sex Workers and Activists." Hacking//Hustling, September. Accessed October 7, 2022. https://hackinghustling.org.

Blunt, Danielle, and Zahra Stardust. 2021. "Automating Whorephobia: Sex, Technology, and the Violence of Deplatforming." *Porn Studies* 8, no. 4: 350–66.

Blunt, Danielle, and Ariel Wolf. 2020. "Erased: The Impact of FOSTA-SESTA and the Removal of Backpage on Sex Workers." *Anti-Trafficking Review* 14: 117–21.

Booker, Marja. 2002. "Stories of Violence: Use of Testimony in a Support Group for Latin American Battered Women." Pp. 307–20 in *Charting a New Course for Feminist Psychology*, ed. L. H. Collins, M. R. Dunlap, and J. C. Chrisler. Westport, CT: Praeger.

Bordo, Susan, 2003. *Unbearable Weight: Feminism, Western Culture, and the Body*. Berkeley: University of California Press.

Boris, Eileen, and Rhacel Salazar Parreñas, eds. 2010. *Intimate Labors: Cultures, Technologies, and the Politics of Care*. Stanford, CA: Stanford University Press.

Bourdieu, Pierre. 1978. "Sport and Social Class." *Social Science Information* 17, no. 6: 819–40.

Bowen, Raven. 2013. "They Walk among Us: Sex Work Exiting, Re-entry, and Duality." M.A. thesis, Simon Fraser University, Burnaby, British Columbia, Canada. Accessed October 7, 2022. https://summit.sfu.ca.

———. 2021. *Work, Money, and Duality: Trading Sex as a Side Hustle*. Bristol, UK: Policy Press.

Boyd, Danah. 2017. "What Anti-Trafficking Advocates Can Learn from Sex Workers: The Dynamics of Choice, Circumstance, and Coercion." *Huffpost*, December 6. www.huffpost.com.

Bracewell, Lorna N. 2021. *Why We Lost the Sex Wars: Sexual Freedom in the #Metoo Era* Minneapolis: University of Minnesota Press.

Bradley-Engen, Mindy. 2009. *Naked Lives: Inside the Worlds of Exotic Dance*. Albany: State University of New York Press.

Branstetter, Gillian. 2022. "Trans Joy Is Most Necessary When It Feels the Most Impossible." ACLU, June 17. Accessed December 13, 2023. www.aclu.org.

Brennan, Denise. 2004. *What's Love Got to Do with It?* Durham, NC: Duke University Press.

Brents, Barbara G. 2008. "Sexual Politics from Barnard to Las Vegas." *Communication Review* 11, no. 3: 237–46.

Brents, Barbara G., and Kathryn Hausbeck. 2007. "Marketing Sex: US Legal Brothels and Late Capitalist Consumption." *Sexualities* 10, no. 4: 425–39. https://doi.org/10 .1177/1363460707080976.

Brents, Barbara G., Crystal A. Jackson, and Kathryn Hausbeck. 2010. *The State of Sex: Tourism, Sex, and Sin in the New American Heartland*. New York: Routledge.

Brents, Barbara G., and Teela Sanders. 2010. "Mainstreaming the Sex Industry: Economic Inclusion and Social Ambivalence." *Journal of Law and Society* 37, no. 1: 40–60.

Breslin, Susannah. 2018. "Why Sex Doll Brothels Won't Replace Real Brothels Anytime Soon." *Forbes*, July 26. Accessed October 7, 2022. www.forbes.com.

Brewis, Joanna, and Stephen Linstead. 2000. "'The Worst Thing Is the Screwing': Consumption and the Management of Identity in Sex Work." *Gender, Work, and Organization* 7, no. 2: 84–97.

Brittanica ProCon.Org. 2018. "US and State Prostitution Arrests, 2016." Britannica ProCon.Org. Accessed October 12, 2022. https://prostitution.procon.org.

Bronstein, Carolyn. 2021. "Deplatforming Sexual Speech in the Age of FOSTA/SESTA." *Porn Studies* 8, no. 4: 367–80. https//doi.org/10.1080/23268743.2021.1993972.

Brooks, Ellis. 2021. "How Sex Work Saved Me from Academia." *Human Parts*, August 24. Accessed October 7, 2022. humanparts.medium.com.

Brooks, Siobhan. 2010a. "Hypersexualization and the Dark Body: Race and Inequality among Black and Latina Women in the Exotic Dance Industry." *Sexuality Research and Social Policy* 7, no. 2: 70–80.

———. 2010b. *Unequal Desires: Race and Erotic Capital in the Stripping Industry*. Albany: State University of New York Press.

———. 2021. "Innocent White Victims and Fallen Black Girls: Race, Sex Work, and the Limits of Anti–Sex Trafficking Laws." *Signs: Journal of Women in Culture and Society* 46, no. 2: 513–21.

Brown, Jane D., and Kelly L. L'Engle. 2009. "X-rated: Sexual Attitudes and Behaviors Associated with US Early Adolescents' Exposure to Sexually Explicit Media." *Communication Research* 36, no. 1: 129–51.

Bruckert, Christine. 2014. "Activist Academic Whore: Negotiating the Fractured Otherness Abyss." In *Demarginalizing Voices: Commitment, Emotion, and Action in Qualitative Research*, ed. Sheryl C. Fabian, Maritza Felices-Luna, and Jennifer Kilty. Vancouver: University of British Columbia Press.

Bruckert, Chris, and Colette Parent. 2018. *Getting Past "The Pimp."* Toronto: University of Toronto Press.

Bujold, Christine. 2021. "Ontario Protecting Children at Risk of Sex Trafficking" *Ontario: Newsroom*, July 29. Accessed July 29, 2021. https://news.ontario.ca.

Bungay, Vicky, Adrian Guta, Colleen Varcoe, Allie Slemon, Eli Manning, Scott Comber, and Melissa Perri. 2021. "Gaps in Health Research Related to Sex Work:

An Analysis of Canadian Health Research Funding." *Critical Public Health* 33, no. 1: 72–82. https://doi.org/10.1080/09581596.2021.1987385.

Burke, Kelsy. 2023. *The Pornography Wars: The Past, Present, and Future of America's Obscene Obsession*. New York: Bloomsbury.

Burnett, Scott, and John E. Richardson. 2021. "'Breeders for Race and Nation': Gender, Sexuality, and Fecundity in Post-War British Fascist Discourse." *Patterns of Prejudice* 55, no. 4: 331–56.

Butler, Judith. 2021. "Why Is the Idea of 'Gender' Provoking Backlash the World Over?" *The Guardian*, October 23. www.theguardian.com.

Butterfly (Asian and Migrant Sex Workers Support Network). 2021. *Understanding Migrant Sex Workers: Migration + Sex Work ≠ Trafficking*. Accessed December 2022. www.butterflysw.org.

Cabezas, Amalia. 2009. *Economies of Desire*. Philadelphia: Temple University Press.

Calderaro, Chiara, and Claudia Giametta. 2019. "'The Problem of Prostitution': Repressive Policies in the Name of Migration Control, Public Order, and Women's Rights in France." *Anti-Trafficking Review* 12: 155–71.

Califia-Rice, Patrick, and Robyn Sweeney. 2000. *Second Coming*. New York: Alyson Books.

Cameron, Samuel. 2016. "The 'Money for Nothing' Problem in Economics: The Specific Case of Virtual Intimate Exchanges." 22 pages. Available at SSRN: https://papers .ssrn.com.

Campbell, Rosie, Yigit Aydin, Stewart Cunningham, Rebecca Hamer, Kathleen Hill, Camille Melissa, Jane Pitcher, Jane Scoular, Teela Sanders, and Matt Valentine-Chase. 2019. "Technology-Mediated Sex Work: Fluidity, Networking, and Regulation in the UK." Pp. 533–43 in *Routledge International Handbook of Sex Industry Research*, ed. Susan Dewey, Isabel Crowhurst, and Chimaraoke Izugbara. Abingdon, Oxon, UK: Routledge.

Canadian Alliance for Sex Work Law Reform. 2015. "Criminalizing Third Parties in the Sex Industry: Impacts and Consequences." Canadian Alliance for Sex Work Law Reform. Accessed December 15, 2022. http://sexworklawreform.com.

Capous-Desyllas, Moshoula, and Victoria Loy. 2020. "Navigating Intersecting Identities, Self-Representation, and Relationships: A Qualitative Study with Trans Sex Workers Living and Working in Los Angeles, CA." *Sociological Inquiry* 90, no. 2: 339–70.

Capous-Desyllas, Moshoula, Deana Payne, and Meg Panichelli. 2020. "Using Anticarceral Feminism to Illustrate the Impact of Criminalization on the Lives of Individuals in the Sex Trades." *Affilia: The Journal of Women and Social Work* 35, no. 1: 49–72.

Carbado, Devon W. 2016. "Predatory Policing." *UMKC Law Review* 85, no. 3: 545–66.

Carleton, Elliot. 2021. "Recent Locust Swarms Highlight the Importance of Livestock in East Africa." International Livestock Research Institute. Accessed October 8, 2021. www.ilri.cgiar.org.

Carter, Angela M. 2015. "Teaching with Trauma: Trigger Warnings, Feminism, and Disability Pedagogy." *Disability Studies Quarterly* 35, no. 2. http://dsq-sds.org.

Cassidy, Veronica. 2016. "For the Love of Doll(s): A Patriarchal Nightmare of Cyborg Couplings." *ESC: English Studies in Canada* 41, no. 1–2: 203–15.

Celarier, Michelle. 2021. "Bill Ackman Sent a Text to the CEO of Mastercard. What Happened Next Is a Parable for ESG." *Institutional Investor*, June 16. www .institutionalinvestor.com.

Celeste, Luna. 2013. "Grin and Bare It All: Against Liberal Conceptions of Sex Work." The Anarchist Library. Accessed October 10, 2022. https://theanarchistlibrary.org.

Česnulytė, Eglė. 2019. *Selling Sex in Kenya: Gendered Agency under Neoliberalism.* Cambridge: Cambridge University Press.

Chamerlain, Laura. 2019. "FOSTA: A Hostile Law with a Human Cost." *Fordham Law Review* 87, no. 5: 2171–2211.

Chapkis, Wendy. 1997. *Live Sex Acts: Women Performing Erotic Labor.* New York: Routledge.

Chateauvert, Melinda. 2014. *Sex Workers Unite: A History of the Movement from Stonewall to SlutWalk.* Boston: Beacon Press.

Chavez, Leticia. 2020. "The Dynamex Dichotomy and the Path Forward." *Golden Gate University Law Review* 50, no. 2: 147, 149.

Chester, Nick. 2013. "Financial Domination Is a Very Expensive Fetish." *Vice.* Last modified July 2, 2013. www.vice.com.

Chief Elk-Young Bear, Lauren, Yeoshin Lourdes, and Bardot Smith. 2015. "Give Your Money to Women: The End Game of Capitalism." *Model View Culture*, August 10. Accessed May 27, 2021. https://modelviewculture.com.

Chin, John, and Lois Takahashi. 2023. "Illicit Massage Parlors." Pp. 279–303 in *Sex for Sale*, ed. Ronald Weitzer. New York: Routledge.

Chivers, Meredith L., Gerulf Rieger, Elizabeth Latty, and J. Michael Bailey. 2004. "A Sex Difference in the Specificity of Sexual Arousal." *Psychological Science* 11: 736–44.

Chou, R. S. 2012. *Asian American Sexual Politics: The Construction of Race, Gender, and Sexuality.* Lanham, MD: Rowman & Littlefield.

Chow, Kat. 2017. "'Model Minority' Myth again Used as a Racial Wedge between Asians and Blacks." *NPR*, April 19. Accessed October 14, 2022. www.npr.org.

Chu, Sandra Ka Hon, and Rebecca Glass. 2013. "Sex Work Law Reform in Canada: Considering Problems with the Nordic Model." *Alberta Law Review* 51, no. 1: 101–24. https://doi.org/10.29173/alr59.

Chun, Sarah. 1999. "An Uncommon Alliance: Finding Empowerment for Exotic Dancers through Labor Unions." *Hastings Women's Law Journal* 10: 231–52.

Chudyk, Elliot. 2023. "Genderplay: Reclaiming and Reconfiguring Femininity through the Gendered Labor Practices of Transmasculine Sex Workers." *Social Problems*, 2023, spado43. https://doi.org/10.1093/socpro/spado43.

Church, Karly. 2020. "Domestic Sex Trafficking: A Survivor's Perspective." Filmed February 12, 2020. *Tedx Talks* video, 17:33. https://www.youtube.com/watch?v =nh1emIVHy8g.

Clare, Eli. 2017. *Brilliant Imperfection: Grappling with Cure*. Durham, NC: Duke University Press.

Clark, Holly, Aruna Surendera Babu, Ellen Weiss Wiewel, Jenevieve Opoku, and Nicole Crepaz. 2017. "Diagnosed HIV Infection in Transgender Adults and Adolescents: Results from the National HIV Surveillance System, 2009–2014." *AIDS and Behavior* 21, no. 9: 2774–83. https://doi.org/10.1007/s10461-016-1656-7.

Coady, Serena. 2020. "Meet the Findom Goddesses Making Bank from 'Pay Pigs' on TikTok." *I-D* (blog). Last modified November 19, 2020. https://i-d.vice.com.

Cohen, Bernard. 1980. *Deviant Street Markets: Prostitution in New York City*. Lexington, MA: Lexington Books.

Cole, Samantha. 2021a. "The Crusade against Pornhub Is Going to Get Someone Killed." *Vice*. Last modified April 13, 2021. www.vice.com.

———. 2021b. "OnlyFans Says It Will Suspend Porn Ban." *Vice*. Last modified August 25, 2021. www.vice.com.

———. 2021c. "Sex Workers Say Mastercard Ignored Their Concerns about New Regulations." *Vice*. Last modified October 15, 2021. www.vice.com.

———. 2022. *How Sex Changed the Internet and the Internet Changed Sex: An Unexpected History*. New York: Workman Publishing Company.

Collins, Patricia Hill. 1990. *Black Feminist Thought: Knowledge, Consciousness, and the Politics of Empowerment*. New York: Routledge.

Comella, Lynn. 2014. "Studying Porn Cultures." *Porn Studies* 1, no. 1–2: 64–70. https://doi.org/10.1080/23268743.2014.882611.

———. 2017. *Vibrator Nation: How Feminist Sex-Toy Stores Changed the Business of Pleasure*. Durham, NC: Duke University Press.

Commission on Obscenity and Pornography. 1970. *Report of the Commission on Obscenity and Pornography*. New York: Bantam Books.

Craig, Maxine Leeds. 2002. *Ain't I a Beauty Queen? Black Women, Beauty, and the Politics of Race*. Oxford: Oxford University Press.

Crandall, Christian S., Angela Merman, and Michelle Hebl. 2009. "Anti-fat Prejudice." Pp. 46987 in *Handbook of Prejudice, Stereotyping, and Discrimination*, ed. T. D. Nelson. London: Psychology Press.

Crane, Antonia. 2021. "Dispatch from the California Stripper Strike." *n + 1*, February 8. www.nplusonemag.com.

Creasy, Shannon. 2012. "Defending against a Charge of Obscenity in the Internet Age: How Google Searches Can Illuminate Miller's 'Contemporary Community Standards.'" *Georgia State University Law Review* 26, no. 3: 1029–60.

Crenshaw, Kimberlé. 1989. "Demarginalizing the Intersection of Race and Sex: A Black Feminist Critique of Antidiscrimination Doctrine, Feminist Theory, and Antiracist Politics." *University of Chicago Legal Forum* 1989: 139–67.

———. 1991. "Mapping the Margins: Intersectionality, Identity Politics, and Violence against Women of Color." *Stanford Law Review* 43, no. 6: 1241–99.

———. 2017. *On Intersectionality: Essential Writings*. New York: New Press.

Crosby, Andrew C., and Jeffrey Monaghan. 2018. *Policing Indigenous Movements*. Nova Scotia, Canada: Fernwood Publishing.

Cruz, Ariane. 2016. *The Color of Kink: Black Women, BDSM, and Pornography*. New York: New York University Press.

Cunningham, Stewart, Teela Sanders, Jane Scoular, Rosie Campbell, Jane Pitcher, Kathleen Hill, Matt Valentine-Chase, Camille Melissa, Yigit Aydin, and Rebecca Hamer. 2018. "Behind the Screen: Commercial Sex, Digital Spaces, and Working Online." *Technology in Society* 53: 47–54.

Cunt, Rebelle. 2021. "Chicago's Black Sex Workers Hold Each Other Up." *Autostraddle*. Last modified June 2021. www.autostraddle.com.

D'Adamo, Kate, and Spencer Watson. 2021. "Shut Down and Shut Out: Access to Financial Services and Online Payments for Sex Workers in the U.S." Center for LGBTQ Economic Advancement & Research. Accessed October 10, 2022. https://lgbtq-economics.org.

Daniélou, Alain, trans. 1993. *The Complete Kama Sutra: The First Unabridged Modern Translation of the Classic Indian Text*. Original ed. Rochester, VT: Inner Traditions.

Darling, James. 2015. "Blood and Butter." Pp. 196–99 in *Coming Out like a Porn Star: Essays on Pornography, Protection, and Privacy*, ed. Lee Jiz. Berkeley: ThreeL Media.

Davina, Lola. 2017. *Thriving in Sex Work: Heartfelt Advice for Staying Sane in the Sex Industry*. Oakland, CA: The Erotic as Power Press.

———. 2020. *Thriving in Sex Work: Sex Work and Money*. Oakland, CA: The Erotic as Power Press.

Davis, Kingsley. 1937. "The Sociology of Prostitution." *American Sociological Review* 2: 744–55.

DeAngelo, G., J. Shapiro, J. Borowitz, M. Cafarella, C. Re, and G. Shiffman. 2019. "Pricing Risk in Prostitution: Evidence from Online Sex Ads." *Journal of Risk and Uncertainty* 59: 281–305. https://doi.org/10.1007/s11166-019-09317-1.

De Boer, Tracy. 2015. "Disability and Sexual Inclusion." *Hypatia* 30, no. 1 (2015): 66–81.

Decker, Michele, Anna-Louise Crago, Sandra K. H. Chu, Susan G. Sherman, Meena S. Seshu. 2022. "Age of Consent to Sexual Activity." Department of Justice, Government of Canada. Accessed October 15, 2022. www.justice.gc.ca.

Decker, Michele R., Anna-Louise Crago, Sandra K. H. Chu, Susan G. Sherman, Meena Seshu, Kholi Buthelezi, Mandeep Dhaliwal, and Chris Beyrer. 2015. "Human Rights Violations against Sex Workers: Burden and Effect on HIV." *Lancet* (British edition) 385, no. 9963: 186–99. https://doi.org/10.1016/S0140-6736(14)60800-X.

Decriminalize Sex Work. 2022. "The Stripper Strike Goes National." Last accessed June 27, 2022. https://decriminalizesex.work.

Decrim Now. N.d. "Open Letter Opposing the Nordic Model." Accessed October 10, 2022. www.decrimnow.org.uk.

DecrimNY. N.d. "Advocacy." Accessed October 7, 2022. www.decrimny.org.

———. N.d. "Home." Accessed August 22, 2022. www.decrimny.org.

Deer, Ka'nhehsí:io. 2021. "Why It's Difficult to Put a Number on How Many Children Died at Residential Schools." *CBC News.* Last modified September 29, 2021. www .cbc.ca.

Deering, Kathleen N., Avni Amin, Jean Shoveller, Ariel Nesbitt, Claudia Garcia-Moreno, Putu Duff, Elena Argento, and Kate Shannon. 2014. "A Systematic Review of the Correlates of Violence against Sex Workers." *American Journal of Public Health* 104, no. 5: e42–e54.

Delacoste, Frederique, and Asa Akira. 1998. *Sex Work: Writings by Women in the Sex Industry.* Jersey City, NJ: Cleis Press.

Delamont, Sara, and Angela Jones. 2012. *Handbook of Qualitative Research in Education.* Northampton, MA: Edward Elgar Publishers.

Department of Justice, Government of Canada. 2014. "Prostitution Criminal Law Reform: Bill C-36, the *Protection of Communities and Exploited Persons Act.* In force as of December 6, 2014." Department of Justice, Government of Canada. Accessed December 3, 2023. www.justice.gc.ca.

de Vries, Kylan Mattias. 2015. "Transgender People of Color at the Center: Conceptualizing a New Intersectional Model." *Ethnicities* 15, no. 1: 3–27.

Dewey, Susan, Isabel Crowhurst, and Chimaraoke Izugbara, eds. 2018a. *Routledge International Handbook of Sex Industry Research.* London: Routledge.

———. 2018b. "Technologies: An Introduction." Pp. 529–32 in *Routledge International Handbook of Sex Industry Research*, ed. Susan Dewey, Isabel Crowhurst, and Chimaraoke Izugbara. London: Routledge.

Dewey, Susan, and Tonia St. Germain. 2014. "'It Depends on the Cop': Street-Based Sex Workers' Perspectives on Police Patrol Officers." *Sexuality Research and Social Policy* 11: 256–70.

———. 2015. "Sex Workers/Sex Offenders: Exclusionary Criminal Justice Practices in New Orleans." *Feminist Criminology* 10, no. 3: 211–34.

———. 2017. *Women of the Street: How the Criminal Justice–Social Services Alliance Fails Women in Prostitution.* New York: New York University Press.

Dewey, Susan, and Tiantian Zheng. 2013. *Ethical Research with Sex Workers: Anthropological Approaches.* New York: Springer.

Dixon, Rebecca. 2021. "Testimony of Rebecca Dixon, Executive Director, National Employment Law Project. From Excluded to Essential: Tracing the Racist Exclusion of Farmworkers, Domestic Workers, and Tipped Workers from the Fair Labor Standards Act (Subcommittee Hearing)." Hearing before the U.S. House of Representatives Education and Labor Committee, Workforce Protections Subcommittee, May 3. Accessed December 6, 2023. https://s27147.pcdn.co.

Dobson, Amy Shields. 2016. *Postfeminist Digital Cultures: Femininity, Social Media, and Self-Representation.* New York: Springer.

Dodsworth, Jane. 2014. "Sexual Exploitation, Selling and Swapping Sex: Victimhood and Agency." *Child Abuse Review* 23, no. 3: 185–99. https://doi.org/10.1002/car .2282.

Döring, Nicola, M. Rohangis Mohseni, and Roberto Walter. 2020. "Design, Use, and Effects of Sex Dolls and Sex Robots: Scoping Review." *Journal of Medical Internet Research* 22, no. 7.

Döring, Nicola, and Sandra Pöschl. 2018. "Sex Toys, Sex Dolls, Sex Robots: Our Under-Researched Bedfellows." *Sexologies* 27: 1–5.

Driskill, Qwo-Li. 2011. *Sovereign Erotics*. Tucson: University of Arizona Press.

Drolet, Gabrielle, and Shane O'Neill. 2020. "The Year Sex Work Came Home." *New York Times*. Last modified April 10, 2020. www.nytimes.com.

Dr Sue. 2016. "Financial Domination Is DEAD." *The Dr Sue Review* (blog). Last modified March 18, 2016. https://thedrsuereview.com.

Ducatti, Daisy. 2015. "How I Get Men to Give Me Money for No Reason as a Financial Dominatrix: Interview by Cheryl Wischhover." *Cosmopolitan*. Last modified December 22, 2015. www.cosmopolitan.com.

Dufour, Pierre, and Jean Baptiste Thierry. 2014. "Les impasses de l'assistance sexuelle." Pp. 107–21 in *Corps à cœur: intimité, amour, sexualité et handicap*, ed. Yves Jeanne. Toulouse, France: Editions Érès.

Duran, Eduardo. 2019. *Healing the Soul Wound*. New York: Teachers College Press.

Durkin, Keith F. 2007. "Show Me the Money: Cybershrews and On-Line Money Masochists." *Deviant Behavior* 28, no. 4: 355–78. https://doi.org/10.1080/01639620701233290.

Easterbrook-Smith, Gwyn. 2021. "Resisting Division: Migrant Sex Work and New Zealand Working Girls." *Continuum* 35, no. 4: 546–58.

Echols, Alice. 1989. *Daring to Be Bad: Radical Feminism in America, 1967–1975*. Minneapolis: University of Minnesota Press.

———. 2016. "Retrospective: Tangled Up in Pleasure and Danger." *Signs: Journal of Women in Culture and Society* 42, no. 1: 11–22.

Egan, R. Danielle, Katherine Frank, and Merri Lisa Johnson. 2006. *Flesh for Fantasy: Producing and Consuming Exotic Dance*. New York: Thunder Mouth's Press.

Eichert, David. 2020. "'It Ruined My Life': FOSTA, Male Escorts, and the Construction of Sexual Victimhood in American Politics." *Virginia Journal of Social Policy & the Law* 26, no. 3: 202–45.

Ellin, Abby. 2015. "Yes, There Is Such a Thing as a 'Financial Dominatrix,' and It's as Bizarre as You Think." *Observer* (blog). Last modified February 18, 2015. https://observer.com.

Erickson, W., C. Lee, S. von Schrader. 2021. Disability Statistics from the 2018 American Community Survey (ACS). Ithaca, NY: Cornell University Yang-Tan Institute (YTI). www.disabilitystatistics.org.

EricTheYoungGawd. 2020. "Interview with PornStar Sofia Rose and She Talks Race Relation in Porn, Body Image, and More." YouTube video, 40:01. March 24. https://www.youtube.com/watch?v=xkFalNPQrHM.

Fahs, Breanne. 2009. "Compulsory Bisexuality? The Challenges of Modern Sexual Fluidity." *Journal of Bisexuality* 9, no. 3–4: 431–49.

———. 2014. "Freedom To' and 'Freedom From': A New Vision for Sex-Positive Politics." *Sexualities* 17, no. 3: 267–90.

———. 2018. *Firebrand Feminism: The Radical Lives of Ti-Grace Atkinson, Kathie Sarachild, Roxanne Dunbar-Ortiz, and Dana Densmore.* Seattle: University of Washington Press.

———. 2019. "Men, through Women's Eyes." In *Women, Sex, and Madness: Notes from the Edge.* New York: Routledge.

———. 2020. *Burn It Down! Feminist Manifestos for the Revolution.* New York: Verso.

Fahs, Breanne, and Sara I. McClelland. 2016. "When Sex and Power Collide: An Argument for Critical Sexuality Studies." *Journal of Sex Research* 53, no. 4–5: 392–416. https://doi.org/10.1080/00224499.2016.1152454.

Faier, Lieba. 2007. "Filipina Migrants in Rural Japan and Their Professions of Love." *American Ethnologist* 34, no. 1: 148–62.

Fassi, Marisa N. 2015. "Sex Work and the Claim for Grassroots Legislation." *Culture, Health & Sexuality* 17: 74–84.

FBI. 2016. "Violent Criminal Apprehension Program Part 2: The Highway Serial Killings Initiative." *FBI News*, May 6. Accessed October 10, 2022. www.fbi.gov/news.

Febos, Melissa. 2010. *Whip Smart: A Memoir.* New York: Thomas Dunne Publishers.

Ferguson, Cristopher, and Richard Hartley. 2022. "Pornography and Sexual Aggression: Can Meta-Analysis Find a Link?" *Trauma, Violence, and Abuse* 23: 278–87.

The Findom Club. N.d. "The Findom Club." *TheFindomClub* (blog). Accessed May 25, 2021. https://thefindom.club.

———. N.d. "Know Your Findom History." *TheFindomClub* (blog). Accessed May 25, 2021. https://thefindom.club.

———. N.d. "My Personal Findom History." *TheFindomClub* (blog). Accessed May 25, 2021. https://thefindom.club.

Findom Princess Sierra. N.d. "Findom Princess Sierra." Accessed May 25, 2021. www.financialdomination.com.

Flanigan, Jessica, and Lori Watson. 2019. *Debating Sex Work.* Oxford: Oxford University Press.

Flores, April. 2013. "Being Fatty D: Size, Beauty, and Embodiment in the Adult Industry." Pp. 279–83 in *The Feminist Porn Book: The Politics of Producing Pleasure*, ed. Tristan Taormino, Celine Perreñas Shimuzu, Constance Penley, and Mireille Miller-Young. New York: Feminist Press.

Folbre, Nancy. 2002. *The Invisible Heart: Economics and Family Values.* New York: New Press.

Frank, Katherine. 1998. "The Production of Identity and the Negotiation of Intimacy in a 'Gentleman's Club.'" *Sexualities* 1, no. 2: 175–201.

———. 2002. *G-Strings and Sympathy: Strip Club Regulars and Male Desire.* Durham, NC: Duke University Press.

Friedman, Gillian. 2021. "Jobless, Selling Nudes Online, and Still Struggling." *New York Times*, January 13. www.nytimes.com.

Fritsch, Kelly, Robert Heynen, Amy Nicole Ross, and Emily Van Der Meulen. 2016. "Disability and Sex Work: Developing Affinities through Decriminalization." *Disability & Society* 31, no. 1: 84–99.

Gabrielle, Natasha. 2021. "1 in 3 Americans Have a Side Hustle. Here Are the Benefits to Having One." *Nasdaq*, July 24. www.nasdaq.com.

Garofalo Geymonat, Giulia. 2019. "Disability Rights Meet Sex Workers' Rights: The Making of Sexual Assistance in Europe." *Sexuality Research and Social Policy* 16: 214–26.

Garofalo Geymonat, Giulia, and P. G. Macioti. 2016. "Ambivalent Professionalisation and Autonomy in Workers' Collective Projects: The Cases of Sex Worker Peer Educators in Germany and Sexual Assistants in Switzerland." *Sociological Research Online* 21, no. 4: 201–14.

Garofalo Geymonat, Giulia, and Giulia Selmi. 2019. "Feminist Engagements with Sex Work: Imported Polarisations and a 'Feminist Alliance' Model in Jeopardy." *Rassegna Italiana di Sociologia* 4: 783–803.

Gelles-Watnick, Risa, and Monica Anderson. 2021. "Racial and Ethnic Differences Stand Out in the U.S. Gig Workforce." Pew Research Center. Accessed February 18, 2022. www.pewresearch.org.

Gilbertson, Annie, Aaron Mendelson, and Angela Caputo. 2019. "Collateral Damage: How LA's Fight against Sex Trafficking Is Hurting Vulnerable Women." *LAist*, August 7. Accessed October 10, 2022. https://projects.laist.com.

Gillespie, Tarleton. 2018. *Custodians of the Internet: Platforms, Content Moderation, and the Hidden Decisions That Shape Social Media.* New Haven, CT: Yale University Press.

Gilmour, Fairleigh Evelyn. 2016. "Work Conditions and Job Mobility in the Australian Indoor Sex Industry." *Sociological Research Online* 21, no. 4 (2016): 147–58.

Gira Grant, Melissa. 2015. "How Sex Workers' Rights Made the Mainstream." *Rewire News Group*, September 11. Accessed October 10, 2022. http.//rewirenewsgroup.com.

Global Health Justice Partnership and Sex Workers Project of the Urban Justice Center. 2018. "Diversion from Justice: A Rights-Based Analysis of Local 'Prostitution Diversion Programs' and Their Impacts on People in the Sex Sector in the United States." Global Health Justice Partnership of the Yale Law School and Yale School of Public Health in Cooperation with the Sex Worker Project of the Urban Justice Center. September 2018. Accessed March 14, 2024. https://law.yale.edu.

Global Network of Sex Work Projects (NSWP). 2017a. "The Decriminalization of Third Parties." Accessed October 14, 2022. www.nswp.org.

——. 2017b. "The Impact of Criminalisation on Sex Workers' Vulnerability to HIV and Violence." Accessed May 5, 2024. www.nswp.org.

——. 2020. "Briefing Paper: Sex Workers' Lack of Access to Justice." Accessed December 10, 2022. www.nswp.org.

——. N.d. "The Impact of Criminalization on Sex Workers' Vulnerability to HIV and Violence." Accessed October 10, 2022. www.nswp.org.

Glover, Cameron. 2017. "Not Formally 'Coming Out' Didn't Make Me Less Queer." *Glamour*, August 22. www.glamour.com.

Glover, S. T., and J. K. Glover. 2019. "'She Ate My Ass and My Pussy All Night': Deploying Illicit Eroticism, Funk, and Sex Work among Black Queer Women Femmes." *American Quarterly* 71, no. 1: 171–77.

Goddess Macha. 2018. "Financial Domination Is Power." Last modified October 19, 2018. www.goddessmacha.com.

Goldhill, Olivia. 2015. "Inside a Lesbian Escort Agency." *The Telegraph*. Last modified August 2015. www.telegraph.co.uk.

Goldman, Marion. 1981. *Gold Diggers and Silver Miners: Prostitution and Social Life on the Comstock Lode*. Ann Arbor: University of Michigan Press.

Google Trends. N.d. "Findom." Accessed March 4, 2024. https://trends.google.com.

Gordon, Aubrey. 2021. "I'm a Fat Activist: I Don't Use the Word 'Fatphobia.'" *Self*, March 29.

Government of Canada. 2014. Protection of Communities and Exploited Persons Act, S.C. 2014, c. 25.

Graceyswer. 2020. "Looking Up at the Whorearchy from the Bottom." *Street Hooker Blog*, April 20. https://streethooker.wordpress.com.

Graeber, David. 2018. *Bullshit Jobs*. New York: Simon & Schuster.

Grant, Jaime M., Lisa A. Mottet, Justin Tanis, Jack Harrison, Jody L. Herman, and Mara Keisling. 2011. *Injustice at Every Turn: A Report of the National Transgender Discrimination Survey*. Washington, DC: National Center for Transgender Equality and National Gay and Lesbian Task Force. Accessed October 14, 2022. https://transequality.org.

Grant, Melissa. 2014. *Playing the Whore: The Work of Sex Work*. New York: Verso Books.

Gregory, Victoria, Elisabeth Harding, and Joel Steinberg. 2022. "Self-Employment Grows during COVID-19 Pandemic." Federal Reserve Bank of St. Louis. Accessed July 14, 2022. www.stlouisfed.org.

Griffith, D. W., director. 1915. *Birth of a Nation*. 3 hr. 15 min.

Hamilton, Sadie, and Valerie Webber. 2020. "How Sex Workers Take Care of Each Other." *The Independent*. Last modified June 26, 2020. https://theindependent.ca.

Hankins, Sarah. 1998. "'I'm a Cross between a Clown, a Stripper, and a Streetwalker': Drag Tipping, Sex Work, and a Queer Sociosexual Economy." *Signs* 40, no. 2: 441–66.

Hannem, Stacey, and Chris Bruckert. 2016. "'I'm Not a Pimp, but I Play One on TV': The Moral Career and Identity Negotiations of Third Parties in the Sex Industry." *Deviant Behavior* 38, no. 7: 824–36.

Harcourt, Christine, and Basil Donovan. 2005. "The Many Faces of Sex Work." *Sexually Transmitted Infections* 81, no. 3: 201–6.

Hardy, Kate, and Sarah Kingston. 2016. *New Sociologies of Sex Work*. London: Routledge.

Harrington, Carol. 2018. "Gender Policy Models and Calls to 'Tackle Demand' for Sex Workers." *Sexuality Research and Social Policy* 15, no. 3: 249–58.

Harris, LaShawn. 2016. *Sex Workers, Psychics, and Numbers Runners*. Champaign: University of Illinois Press.

Harvard T.H. Chan School of Public Health. 2022. "Poll: High U.S. Inflation Rates Are Having a More Serious Impact on Black Americans Than White Americans." News. August 8, 2022. www.hsph.harvard.edu.

Heckathorn, Douglas. 2002. "Respondent-Driven Sampling II: Deriving Valid Population Estimates from Chain-Referral Samples of Hidden Populations." *Social Problems* 49, no. 1: 11–34. https://doi.org/10.1525/sp.2002.49.1.11.

Heineman, Jenny. 2019. "Pussy Patrols in Academia: Towards a Disobedient, Sex-Worker-Inclusive Feminist Praxis." *Feminist Formations* 31, no. 1: 45–66. https://doi.org/10.1353/ff.2019.0008.

Hendersen, Kaitlyn. 2020. "Why Millions of Workers in the US Are Denied Basic Protections." *Politics of Poverty* (blog), Oxfam. Accessed August 22, 2022. https://politicsofpoverty.oxfamamerica.org.

Hennessy, Rosemary. 2017. *Profit and Pleasure: Sexual Identities in Late Capitalism*, 2nd ed. London: Routledge. https://doi.org/10.4324/9781315270142.

Herrera, Jack. 2020. "How Sex Workers Are Using Mutual Aid to Respond to the Coronavirus." *The Nation*, April. www.thenation.com.

Herrmann, Tess, and Scarlett Redman. 2021. "Payment Rejected." National Ugly Mugs, January 31. Accessed October 10, 2022. www.nationaluglymugs.org.

Hesse-Biber, Sharlene. N. 1996. *Am I Thin Enough Yet? The Cult of Thinness and the Commercialization of Identity*. New York: Oxford University Press.

Hickey, Gary. 2020. "Different Experiences: A Framework for Considering Who Might Be Involved in Research." National Institute for Health and Care Research. Accessed October 10, 2022. www.nihr.ac.uk.

Hill, Mark E. 2000. "Color Differences in the Socioeconomic Status of African American Men: Results of a Longitudinal Study." *Social Forces* 78, no. 4: 1437–60.

HIPS. N.d. "Sex Worker Advocates Coalition (SWAC)." HIPS. Accessed October 14, 2022. www.hips.org.

Hoang, Kimberly Kay. 2011. "'She's Not a Low-Class Dirty Girl!': Sex Work in Ho Chi Minh City, Vietnam." *Journal of Contemporary Ethnography* 40, no. 4: 367–96.

———. 2015. *Dealing in Desire: Asian Ascendancy, Western Decline, and the Hidden Currencies of Global Sex Work*. Berkeley: University of California Press.

Hoefinger, Heidi, Jennifer Musto, P. G. Macioti, Anne Fehrenbacher, Nicola Mai, Calum Bennachie, and Calogero Giametta. 2020. "Community-Based Responses to Negative Health Impacts of Sexual Humanitarian Anti-Trafficking Policies and the Criminalization of Sex Work and Migration in the U.S." *Social Sciences* 9, no. 1: 1–30.

Holston-Zannell, LaLa B. 2021a. "How Mastercard's New Policy Violates Sex Workers' Rights." ACLU. www.aclu.org.

———. 2021b. "PayPal and Venmo Are Shutting Out Sex Workers, Putting Lives and Livelihoods at Risk." ACLU. www.aclu.org.

Hook, J. N., D. E. Davis, J. Owen, E. L. Worthington Jr., and S. O. Utsey. 2013. "Cultural Humility: Measuring Openness to Culturally Diverse Clients." *Journal of Counseling Psychology* 60, no. 3: 353–66.

hooks, bell. 1989. "Choosing the Margin as a Space of Radical Openness." *Framework: The Journal of Cinema and Media*, no. 36: 15–23.

Horn, Tina. 2018. "How Women and Tech Took Over Porn: Inside the 2018 AVNs." *Rolling Stone*, February 12. www.rollingstone.com.

Hosie, Rachel. 2021. "What Is Findom? A Submissive Man Explains the Fetish." *The Independent*, March 24. www.independent.co.uk.

Huber, Lindsay Perez. 2009. "Disrupting Apartheid of Knowledge: Testimonio as Methodology in Latina/o Critical Race Research in Education." *International Journal of Qualitative Studies in Education* 22, no. 6: 639–54.

Human Rights Council. 2020. "Human Rights Violations of Sex Workers, People in the Sex Trades, and People Profiled as Such." Submission to the United Nations Universal Periodic Review of the United States of America. Third Cycle 36th Session. Accessed October 15, 2022. www.bestpracticespolicy.org.

Hummel, Belinda Michele. 2019. "Findom Is Apparently a Thing." TikTok. *@beelieveinyou* (blog). www.tiktok.com.

Hummel, Calla. 2018. "Do Poor Citizens Benefit from Mega-Events? São Paulo's Street Vendors and the 2014 FIFA World Cup." *Latin American Politics and Society* 60, no. 4: 26–48. www.jstor.org.

Humphrey, Malalo. 2011. "Kenya Says Kidnapping Provocation by al Shabaab." *Reuters*, February 12. Accessed October 14, 2022. www.reuters.com.

Hunt, Felicity (@thefelicityhunt). 2021. "Sex Work Has Raised My Standards, Not Lowered Them. If I'm Getting Paid Hundreds of Dollars an Hour to Be Adored, Pampered, and Spoiled, Why Would I Go Out with Your Sweatpant-Wearing, Leave-Me-on-Read Ass for Free." Twitter, May 19, 11:32 p.m. https://twitter.com/thefelicityhunt/status/1395220736759930883.

Hunt, Lola. 2022. "A Tryst with Sydney Escort Edie Lau." *Tryst* (blog), August 15. Accessed March 24, 2024. https://web.archive.org.

Hunter, Marcus. L. 2002. "If You Are Light You're Alright: Light Skin Color as Social Capital for Women of Color." *Gender & Society* 6, no. 2: 175–93.

Hussain, Suhauna. 2022. "Strippers Protesting at North Hollywood Topless Bar Were Unlawfully Fired: NLRB Says." *Los Angeles Times*, December 9.

Huyser, Kimberly R., Arthur Sakamoto, and Isao Takei. 2010. "The Persistence of Racial Disadvantage: The Socioeconomic Attainments of Single-Race and Multi-race Native Americans." *Population Research and Policy Review* 29: 541–68.

Illouz Eva. 2012. *Why Love Hurts: A Sociological Explanation*. Cambridge, UK: Polity.

Impett, Emily A., and Letitia A. Peplau. 2003. "Sexual Compliance: Gender, Motivational, and Relationship Perspectives." *Journal of Sex Research* 40, no. 1: 87–100.

Ipsen, Avaren. 2009. *Sex Working and the Bible*. Sheffield, UK: Equinox Publishing.

Irvine, Janice. 2012. "Can't Ask, Can't Tell: How Institutional Review Boards Keep Sex in the Closet." *Contexts* 11, no. 2: 28–33.

Jackson, Crystal. 2011. "Revealing Contemporary Constructions of Femininity: Expression and Sexuality in Strip Club Legislation." *Sexualities* 14, no. 3: 354–69. https://doi.org/10.1177/1363460711400964.

———. 2016. "Framing Sex Worker Rights: How U.S. Sex Worker Rights Activists Perceive and Respond to Anti–Sex Trafficking Advocacy." *Sociological Perspectives* 59, no. 1: 27–45. https://doi.org/10.1177/0731121416628553.

Jackson, Crystal A., and Jenny Heineman. 2018. "Repeal FOSTA and Decriminalize Sex Work." *Contexts* 17, no. 3: 74–75.

Jackson, Crystal A., Jennifer J. Reed, and Barbara Brents. 2017. "Strange Confluences: Radical Feminism and Evangelical Christianity as Drivers of US Neo-abolitionism." Pp. 66–85 in *Prostitution, Feminism, and the State: The Politics of Neo-abolitionism*, ed. E. Ward and G. Wylie. London: Routledge, 2017.

Jagose, Annamarie. 2003. *Orgasmology*. Durham, NC: Duke University Press.

Jahnsen, Synnøve, and Hendrik Wagenaar, eds. 2017. *Assessing Prostitution Policies in Europe*. London: Routledge.

James, Alsanna. 2018. "The Second Annual BBW Awards Show Is Coming Soon." *Ynot-Cam*, November 20. Accessed October 15, 2022. www.ynotcam.com.

Jameson, Fredric. 1984. "Postmodernism; or, The Cultural Logic of Late Capitalism." *New Left Review* 1, no. 146: 40.

Jeevendrampillai, David, Julia Burton, and Eva Sanglante. 2020. "Objects of Desire: Sexwork and Its Objects." Pp. 89–101 in *Lineages and Advancements in Material Culture Studies*, ed. Timothy Carroll, Antonia Walford, and Shireen Walton. Abingdon, UK: Routledge, 2020.

Jeffreys, Sheila. 2008. "Disability and the Male Sex Right." *Women's Studies International Forum* 31 (2008): 327–35.

Johnson, Bob. 2013. "The Power of Feminist Porn: What Retailers Need to Know." *XBIZ*, July 9. www.xbiz.com.

Johnson, Cyreé Jarelle. 2018. "For Disabled Sex Workers, Congress' Anti-Trafficking Legislation Is Life Threatening." *Rewire News Group* (blog), July 7. https://rewirenewsgroup.com.

Jones, Angela. 2015. "For Black Models Scroll Down: Webcam Modeling and the Racialization of Erotic Labor." *Sexuality & Culture* 19, no. 4: 776–99.

———. 2016. "'I Get Paid to Have Orgasms': Adult Webcam Models' Negotiation of Pleasure and Danger." *Signs: Journal of Women in Culture and Society* 42, no. 1: 227–56.

———. 2019. "The Pleasures of Fetishization: BBW Erotic Webcams Performers, Empowerment, and Pleasure." *Fat Studies* 8, no. 3: 279–98. https://doi.org/10.108/21604851.2019.1551697.

———. 2020a. *Camming: Money, Power, and Pleasure in the Sex Work Industry*. New York: New York University Press.

———. 2020b. "Cumming to a Screen Near You: Transmasculine and Non-binary People in the Camming Industry." *Porn Studies* 8, no. 2: 239–54.

———. 2021a. "Credit Card Companies Investigate While Sex Workers' Livelihoods Still Hang in the Balance." *Peepshow*, May 29. https://peepshowmagazine.com.

———. 2021b. "Sex Work, Part of the Online Gig Economy, Is a Lifeline for Marginalized Sex Workers," *The Conversation*, May 17.

———. 2022a. "FOSTA: A Transnational Disaster Especially for Marginalized Sex Workers." *International Journal of Gender, Sexuality, and Law* 1, no. 2: 73–99.

———. 2022b. "'People Need to Know We Exist!': An Exploratory Study of the Labor Experiences of Transmasculine and Non-binary Sex Workers and Implications for Harm Reduction." *Culture, Health, and Sexuality* 25, no. 1: 48–62. https://doi.org/10.1080/13691058.2021.2018500.

———. 2022c. "'I Can't Really Work Any "Normal" Job': Disability, Sexual Ableism, and Sex Work." *Disability Studies Quarterly* 42, no. 2. https://doi.org/10.18061/dsq.v42i2.9094.

———. 2023a. "Cisgendered Workspaces: Outright and Categorical Exclusion in Cisgendered Organizations." *Social Problems*, April 26. https://doi.org/10.1093/socpro/spad017.

———. 2023b. "'It's Hard Out Here for a Unicorn': Transmasculine and Nonbinary Escorts, Embodiment, and Inequalities in Cisgendered Workplaces." *Gender & Society* 37, no. 5: 665–98.

Jordan, Jan. 2018. "Sex Work: Sex Workers and Clients." *Te Ara: The Encyclopedia of New Zealand*, May 31, 2018.

———. 2010. "Of Whalers, Diggers, and 'Soiled Doves': A History of the Sex Industry in New Zealand." Pp. 25–44 in Taking the Crime out of Sex Work: New Zealand's Fight for Decriminalization, ed. Gillian Abel, Lisa Fitzgerald and Catherine Healy. Bristol, UK: Policy Press.

Joseph, Krupa. 2021. "What Is Trans Joy?" Gaysi, December 8. Accessed December 13, 2023. https://gaysifamily.com.

Joseph, Robert P. C. 2018. *21 Things You May Not Know about the Indian Act*. Toronto: Indigenous Relations Press.

Jungleib, Lillian. 2019a. "Anti-Trafficking and Feminism: Survivors as Movement Activists." Pp. 95–112 in *Nevertheless They Persisted: Feminisms and Continued Resistance in the U.S. Women's Movement*, ed. Jo Reger. London: Routledge.

———. 2019b. "Returning to Grace: Gender and Responsibilization in the State's Management of Sex Work and Sex Trafficking." PhD dissertation, University of California–Santa Barbara.

Kaba, Mariame. 2021. "The System Isn't Broken." *New Inquiry*, June 15. Reprint pp. 6–14 in Mariame Kaba, *We Do This 'Til We Free Us: Abolitionist Organizing and Transforming Justice*, ed. Tmara K. Nopper. Chicago: Haymarket Books.

Kafer, Alison. 2013. *Feminist, Queer, Crip*. Indianapolis: Indiana University Press.

Kamau, Wanjiru C. 2006. "Kenya and the War on Terror." *Review of African Political Economy* no. 107: 133–62.

Karnataka Sex Workers Union. 2018. "About Karnataka Sex Workers Union." KSWU. Accessed August 22, 2022. http://www.sexworkersunion.in.

Katriel, Tamar. 2021. *Defiant Discourse: Speech and Action in Grassroots Activism*. New York: Routledge.

Kempadoo, Kemala, and Joe Doezema, eds. 1998. *Global Sex Workers: Rights, Resistance, and Redefinition.* London: Routledge.

Khuzwayo, Zuziwe. 2021. "'Why Do I Need to Come Out If Straight People Don't Have To?': Divergent Perspectives on the Necessity of Self-Disclosure among Bisexual Women." *Frontiers in Sociology* 6. https://doi.org/10.3389/fsoc.2021.665627.

Kimmerer, Robin. 2013. *Braiding Sweetgrass.* Minneapolis: Milkweed Editions.

Kingston, Sarah, Natalie Hammond, and Scarlett Redman. 2020. *Women Who Buy Sex: Converging Sexualities?* London: Routledge.

Kingtown, Holly. 2019. "Checking in with Karla Lane and the Shape of Beauty." Fleshbot. Accessed December 5, 2023. https://fleshbot.com.

Kipnis, Laura. 1998. *Bound and Gagged: Pornography and the Politics of Fantasy in America.* Durham, NC: Duke University Press.

Kleinman, Arthur, and Joan Kleinman. 1996. "The Appeal of Experience: The Dismay of Images; Cultural Appropriations of Suffering in Our Times." *Daedalus* 125, no. 1: 1–23.

Knoxx, Belle. 2014. "Tearing down the Whorearchy from the Inside." *Jezebel*, July 2. https://jezebel.com.

Kohn, Sebastian. 2017. *The False Promise of "End Demand" Laws.* New York: Open Society Foundation.

Krüsi, Andrea, Jill Chettier, Amelia Ridgway, Janice Abbott, Steffanie A. Strathdee, and Kate Shannon. 2012. "Negotiating Safety and Sexual Risk Reduction with Clients in Unsanctioned Safer Indoor Sex Work Environments: A Qualitative Study." *American Journal of Public Health* 102, no. 6: 1154–59.

Kulig, Teresa C., and Leah C. Butler. 2019. "From 'Whores' to 'Victims': The Rise and Status of Sex Trafficking Courts." *Victims & Offenders* 14, no. 3: 299–321. https://doi.org/10.1080/15564886.2019.1595242.

Ladder, Sophie. N.d. "Site Restrictions." *Google Sheets.* Accessed October 10, 2022. https://docs.google.com.

Lady Emmy. 2014. "I Did Not Consent to Being Tokenized." *Tits and Sass*, September 4. Accessed October 10, 2022. https://titsandsass.com.

Lahav-Raz, Yeela. 2020. "Narrative Struggles in Online Arenas: The Facebook Feminist Sex Wars on the Israeli Sex Industry." *Feminist Media Studies* 20, no. 6: 784–800.

Laite, Julia. 2009. "Historical Perspectives on Industrial Development, Mining, and Prostitution." *Historical Journal* 52: 739–61.

Lake, Ashley, et al. 2018. "Incomplete List of Legal Discrimination against Sex Workers." *Google Sheets.* Accessed October 10, 2022. https://docs.google.com.

Lam, Elene, Elena Shih, Katherine Chin, and Kate Zen. 2021. "The Double-Edged Sword of Health and Safety: COVID-19 and the Policing and Exclusion of Migrant Asian Massage Workers in North America." *Social Sciences* 10, no. 5: 157.

Lau, Nina. 2020. "Memo: Decriminalizing Survival; Policy Platform and Polling on the Decriminalization of Sex Work." Data for Progress, January 30. Accessed December 6, 2023. www.dataforprogress.org.

Law, Tuulia. 2013. "Transitioning out of Sex Work: Exploring Sex Workers' Experiences." Pp. 101–10 in *Selling Sex: Experience, Advocacy, and Research on Sex Work in Canada*, ed. Emily Van der Meulen, Elya Durisin, and Victoria Love. Chicago: University of Chicago Press.

Lee, Jiz. 2012. "Uncategorized: Genderqueer Identity and Performance in Independent and Mainstream Porn." Pp. 273–78 in *The Feminist Porn Book: The Politics of Producing Pleasure*, ed. Tristan Taormino, Celine Parreñas Shimizu, Constance Penley, and Mireille Miller-Young. New York: Feminist Press.

———, ed. 2015. *Coming Out like a Porn Star: Essays on Pornography, Protection, and Privacy*. Berkeley. CA: Three L Media.

Lee, Lorelei. 2021. "The Roots of Modern-Day Slavery: The Page Act and the Mann Act." *Columbia Human Rights Law Review* 52, no. 3: 1200–1239.

Lee, Michael, and Maggie Parkhill. 2022. "Where Searches for Remains Are Happening at Former Residential School Sites." *CTV News*, January 25. Accessed October 14, 2022. www.ctvnews.ca.

Leigh, Carol. 2004. *Unrepentant Whore: Collected Works of Scarlot Harlot*. San Francisco: Last Gasp.

LeRoy, Michael H. 2017. "Bare Minimum: Stripping Pay for Independent Contractors in the Share Economy." *William & Mary Journal of Women & Law* 23, no. 2: 249–70. https://scholarship.law.wm.edu.

Levey, Tania G. 2024. "Race Play: Intersections of Race, Class, and Gender in Dominatrix Work" (unpublished manuscript, January10), Microsoft Word.

Levey, Tania G., and Dina Pinsky. 2015. "A Constellation of Stigmas: Stigma Management and the Professional Dominatrix." *Deviant Behavior* 26, no. 5: 347–67.

Levy, David. 2012. "Robot Prostitutes as Alternatives to Human Sex Workers." *Roboethics*, March. Accessed October 10, 2022. https://homoartificialis.files.wordpress.com.

Levy-Aronovic, Stephanie, Yeela Lahav-Raz, and Aviad Raz. 2021. "Who Takes Part in the Political Game? The Sex Work Governance Debate in Israel." *Sexuality Research & Social Policy* 18: 516–26.

Lindell, Ilda, Maria Hedman, and Kyle Nathan-Verboomen. 2010. "The World Cup 2010 and the Urban Poor: 'World Class Cities' for All?" Nordiska Afrikainstitutet—The Nordic Africa Institute. Accessed October 12, 2022. www.files.ethz.ch.

Lindemann, Danielle. 2011. "BDSM as Therapy?" *Sexualities* 14, no. 2: 151–72. https://doi.org/10.1177/1363460711399038.

———. 2012. *Dominatrix: Gender, Eroticism, and Control in the Dungeon*. Chicago: University of Chicago Press.

Linklater, Renee. 2014. *Decolonizing Trauma Work*. Halifax, Canada: Fernwood Publishing.

Linton, Simi. 1998. *Claiming Disability: Knowledge and Identity*. New York: New York University Press.

Lipsitz, George. 2020. "Conjuring Black Freedom." *Kalfou* 7, no. 1: 155–65.

Lobo, Roanna, Kahlia McCausland, Julie Bates, Jonathan Hallett, Basil Donovan, and Linda Selvey. 2021. "Sex Workers as Peer Researchers: A Qualitative Investigation of the Benefits and Challenges." *Culture, Health & Sexuality* 23, no. 10: 1435–50. https://doi.org/10.1080/13691058.2020.1787520.

Logan, Trevon D. 2010. "Personal Characteristics, Sexual Behaviors, and Male Sex Work: A Quantitative Approach." *American Sociological Review* 75, no. 5: 679–704. https://doi.org/10.1177/0003122410379581.

Louise, Alex. 2021. "Fat Bodies in Sex Work." *Pleasant Danger*, May 31, 2021. https://pleasantdanger.com.

Lowman, John. 2013. "Crown Expert-Witness Testimony in *Bedford v. Canada*: Evidence-Based Argument or Victim-Paradigm Hyperbole." Pp. 230–50 in *Selling Sex: Experience, Advocacy, and Research on Sex Work in Canada*, ed. Emily Van der Meulen, Elya M. Durisin, and Victoria Love. Vancouver: University of British Columbia Press.

Lowrey, Annie. 2017. "Why the Phrase 'Late Capitalism' Is Suddenly Everywhere." *The Atlantic*, May. www.theatlantic.com.

Luo, Nina. 2020. "Decriminalizing Survival: Policy Platform and Polling on the Decriminalization of Sex Work. Data for Progress." Accessed March 22, 2024. www.filesforprogress.org.

Lutnick, Alexandra. 2019. "The 'Prioritizing Safety for Sex Workers Policy': A Sex Worker Rights and Anti-Trafficking Initiative." *Anti-Trafficking Review* 12: 140–54.

Mac, Juno. 2016. "The Laws That Sex Workers Really Want." *TED Talk*, January. 17:41. www.ted.com.

Mac, Juno, and Molly Smith. 2018. *Revolting Prostitutes: The Fight for Sex Workers' Rights*. New York: Verso Books.

Mahdavi, Pardis. 2013. "The Geography of Sex Work in the United Arab Emirates." Pp. 19–42 in *Geographies of Privilege*, ed. F. W. Twine and B. Gardener. Milton Park, Oxfordshire, UK: Taylor and Francis.

Maher, JaneMaree, Sharon Pickering, and Alison Gerard. 2012. *Sex Work: Labour, Mobility, and Sexual Services*. Milton Park, Oxfordshire, UK: Routledge.

Mai, Nicola, P. G. Macioti, Calum Bennachie, Anne E. Fehrenbacher, Calogero Giametta, Heidi Hoefinger, and Jennifer Musto. 2021. "Migration, Sex Work, and Trafficking: The Racialized Bordering Politics of Sexual Humanitarianism." *Ethnic and Racial Studies* 44, no. 9: 1607–28. https://doi.org/10.1080/01419870.2021.1892790.

Makanda, Françoise. 2021. "Rhonelle Bruder: Rising and Making Space in New Places." Dalla Lana School of Public Health, University of Toronto, September 2. www.dlsph.utoronto.ca.

Mandel, Ernest. 1975. *Late Capitalism*. London: Humanities Press.

Marks, Hedy. 2022. "What Is Holistic Medicine?" WebMD. Accessed October 14, 2022. www.webmd.com.

Martinez-Ortiz, Ana. 2017. "The Rise of The College Sugar Baby: New Form of Escorting, Prostitution?" *UMV Post*, April 13, 2017.

Marwick, Alice. 2013. *Status Update: Celebrity, Publicity, and Branding in the Social Media Age*. New Haven, CT: Yale University Press.

Mason, Katherine. 2012. "The Unequal Weight of Discrimination: Gender, Body Size, and Income Inequality." *Social Problems* 59, no. 3: 411–35.

Mastercard. N.d. "Business Risk Assessment and Mitigation (BRAM)." YouTube video. https://www.youtube.com/watch?v=nnOeuMxo3EU.

@Master_Updates. N.d. "The Findom Club." The Findom Club. Accessed May 25, 2021. https://thefindom.club/.

Mauss, Marcel. 2006 [1925]. *The Gift: The Form and Reason for Exchange in Archaic Societies*. Translated by W. D. Halls. Abingdon, UK: Routledge.

McBride, Bronwyn, Kate Shannon, Alka Murphy, Sherry Wu, Margaret Erickson, Shira Goldenberg, and Andrea Krusi. 2020. "Harms of Third-Party Criminalisation under End-Demand Legislation: Undermining Sex Workers' Safety and Rights." *Culture, Health & Sexuality* no. 9: 1165–81. https://doi.org//10.1080/13691058.2020.1767305.

McClelland, Sara I. 2011. "Who Is the 'Self' in Self Reports of Sexual Satisfaction? Research and Policy Implications." *Sexuality Research and Social Policy* 8, no. 4: 304–20.

McCombs, Emily. 2018. "'This Bill Is Killing Us': 9 Sex Workers on Their Lives in the Wake of FOSTA." *HuffPost*, May 11. Accessed October 14, 2022. www.huffpost.com.

———. 2022. "I Gained 70 Pounds during Covid: Here's What Happened on My First Day Back in the Office." *HuffPost*, March 14.

McCracken, Rosey, and Belinda Brooks-Gordon. 2021. "Findommes, Cybermediated Sex Work, and Rinsing." *Sexuality Research and Social Policy* 18, no. 4: 837–54. https://doi.org/10.1007/s13178-021-00609-3.

Mcivor, Alaya. 2017. "Bringing Attention to Canada's Secret Shame: Human Trafficking." *APTN News*. Video, 50:5. https://www.youtube.com/watch?v=qqoBHh-Tpko&t=967s.

McKee, Alan. 2016. "Pornography as a Creative Industry: Challenging the Exceptionalist Approach to Pornography." *Porn Studies* 3, no. 2: 107–19.

McReur, Robert, and Anna Mollow. 2012. *Sex and Disability*. Durham, NC: Duke University Press.

Mears, Ashley. 2011. *Pricing Beauty: The Making of a Fashion Model*. Berkeley: University of California Press.

Meehan, Claire. 2021. "'Lesbian Porn. Anything Girl on Girl': Young Women's Understandings of Their Engagement with Lesbian Porn." *Porn Studies* 8: 21–38.

Mehrotra, Firoza. 2019. "Understanding the Statistical Term 'Dependent Contractor': A Q&A with Firoza Mehrotra." *WIEGO* blog. www.wiego.org.

Mersol, Greg. 2019. "Third Circuit Affirms $4.5 Million Verdict in Favor of Exotic Dancers." Casetext, September 18. Accessed December 4, 2023. www.casetext.com.

Mgbako, Chi Adanna. 2020. "The Mainstreaming of Sex Workers' Rights as Human Rights." *Harvard Journal of Law & Gender* 43, no. 1: 91–136.

Mia, V. 2020. "The Failures of SESTA/FOSTA." *Transgender Studies Quarterly* 7, no. 2: 237–39. https://doi.org/10.1215/23289252-8143393.

Michaels, Kelly. 2017. "Surviving as Working Class after Backpage." *Tits and Sass*. Accessed October 7, 2022. https://titsandsass.com.

Milan Women's Bookstore Collective. 1990 [1987]. *Sexual Difference: A Theory of Symbolic Practice*. Translated and edited by Patricia Cicogna and Teresa de Lauretis. Reprint, Bloomington: Indiana University Press.

Miller-Young, Mireille. 2010. "Putting Hypersexuality to Work: Black Women and Illicit Eroticism in Pornography." *Sexualities* 13, no. 2: 219–35. https://doi.org/10.1177/1363460709359229.

———. 2013. "Interventions: The Deviant and Defiant Art of Black Women Porn Directors." Pp. 105–20 in *The Feminist Porn Book: The Politics of Producing Pleasure*, ed. Tristan Taormino, Celine Parreñas Shimizu, Constance Penley, and Mireille Miller-Young. New York: Feminist Press.

———. 2014. *A Taste for Brown Sugar: Black Women in Pornography*. Durham, NC: Duke University Press.

———. 2015. "Race and the Politics of Agency in Porn: A Conversation with Black BBW Performer Betty Blac." Pp. 359–70 in *New Views on Pornography: Sexuality, Politics, and the Law*, ed. Lynn Comella and Shira Tarrant. Santa Barbara, CA: Praeger.

Minichiello, Victor, and John Scott. 2014. *Male Sex Work and Society*. New York: Harrington Park Press.

Mirchandi, Kiran. 2003. "Challenging Racial Silences in Studies of Emotion Work: Contributions from Anti-Racist Feminist Theory." *Organization Studies* 24: 721–42. https://doi.org/10.1177/0170840603024005003.

Mistress Snow. 2019. "I Told My Mentor I Was a Dominatrix: She Rescinded Her Letters of Recommendation." *Chronicle of Higher Education* 66, no. 19.

Mitchell, David, and Sharon Snyder. 2015. *The Biopolitics of Disability. Neoliberalism, Ablenationalism, and Peripheral Embodiment*. Ann Arbor: University of Michigan Press.

Molla, Rani. 2021. "More Americans Are Taking Jobs without Employer Benefits like Health Care or Paid Vacation." *Vox*, September 3. www.vox.com.

Monto, Martin, and Xtine Mildrod. 2023. "Clients: The Rhetoric and Realities of Sex Buying." Pp. 329–48 in *Sex for Sale*, 3rd ed., ed. R. Weitzer. New York: Routledge.

moon, moses. 2021. "Face-to-Face, Street-Based, or in Cyberspace—We Are All Prostitutes." *peepshowmagazine.com*, May 6. https://peepshowmagazine.com.

Moreno, Nessa. 2022. "Strippers in North Hollywood Are Twerking for Their Rights." *Knock LA*, April 15. https://knock-la.com.

Morgan, Emily. 2020. "On Fosta and the Failures of Punitive Speech Restrictions." *Northwestern University Law Review* 115, no. 2: 503–47.

Morrison, Blake. 2010. "Along Highways, Signs of Serial Killings." *USA Today*, October 5.

Moussawi, Ghassan, and Salvador Vidal-Ortiz. 2020. "A Queer Sociology: On Power, Race, and Decentering Whiteness." *Sociological Forum* 35, no. 4: 1272–89.

Murphy, David. 2014. "Nunavut Inuit Exposed to Human Trafficking, Child Exploitation: Report." *Nunatsiaq News*, February 4. https://nunatsiaq.com.

Musto, Jennifer. 2016. *Control and Protect: Collaboration, Carceral Protection, and Domestic Sex Trafficking in the United States*. Oakland: University of California Press.

Nagle, Jill, ed. 1997. *Whores and Other Feminists*. New York: Routledge.

Nagoski, Emily. 2015. *Come as You Are*. New York: Simon & Schuster.

Nairobian Reporter. 2021. "Sex Workers Operating from Home Will Draw Crime to Estates—Expert." *Naoirobian* (*Standard* e-Supplement), 11–17.

Nash, Jennifer C. 2011. "Practicing Love: Black Feminism, Love-Politics, and Post-Intersectionality." *Meridians: Feminism, Race, Transnationalism* 11, no. 2: 1–24. https://doi.org/10.2979/meridians.11.2.1.

———. 2014. *The Black Body in Ecstasy: Reading Race, Reading Pornography*. Durham, NC: Duke University Press.

National AIDS Control Council. 2011. *HIV and AIDS Situational Analysis of Sex Workers and Their Clients May 2009*. Nairobi, Kenya: Ministry of Health.

Nelson, Alex J., Kathryn Hausbeck Korgan, Antoinette M. Izzo, and Sarah Y. Bessen. 2020. "Client Desires and the Price of Seduction: Exploring the Relationship between Independent Escorts' Marketing and Rates." *Journal of Sex Research* 57, no. 5: 664–80. https://doi.org/10.1080/00224499.2019.1606885.

Nelson, Camille A. 2022. "Racializing Disability, Disabling Race: Policing Race and Mental Status." *Disability Law Journal* 2, no. 1: 321–456. https://escholarship.org.

Nelson, Vednita. 1993. "Prostitution: Where Racism and Sexism Intersect." *Michigan Journal of Gender and Law* 8: 81–89.

Newmahr, Staci. 2008. "Becoming a Sadomasochist: Integrating Self and Other in Ethnographic Analysis." *Journal of Contemporary Ethnography* 37, no. 5: 619–43. https://doi.org/10.1177/0891241607310626.

Noble, Bobby. 2012. "Knowing Dick: Penetration and the Pleasures of Feminist Porn's Trans Men." Pp. 303–19 in *The Feminist Porn Book: The Politics of Producing Pleasure*, ed. Tristan Taormino, Celine Parreñas Shimizu, Constance Penley, and Mireille Miller-Young. New York: Feminist Press.

Nomis, Anne O. 2013. *The History and Arts of the Dominatrix, Collector's Edition*, 1st ed. Auckland, New Zealand: Anna Nomis.

NSWP (Global Network of Sex Work Projects). 2017. "Policy Brief: The Decriminalization of Third Parties." Accessed March 4, 2024. www.nswp.org.

Nuttbrock, Larry. 2018. *Transgender Sex Work and Society*. New York: Harrington Park Press.

Objects of Desire. N.d. "Archive: Objects of Desire." *Objects of Desire*. Accessed April 24, 2022. www.projectofdesire.co.uk.

Olson-Pitawanakwat, Brianna, and Cyndy Baskin. 2021. "In Between the Missing and Murdered: The Need for Indigenous-Led Responses to Trafficking." *Affilia* 36, no. 1: 10–26. https://doi.org/10.1177/0886109920944526.

Omondi, Rose Kisia, and Chris Ryan. 2017. "Sex Tourism: Romantic Safaris, Prayers, and Witchcraft at the Kenyan Coast." *Tourism Management* 58: 217–27. https://doi.org/10.1016/j.tourman.2015.11.003.

Ontario.CA. 2021. "Protection Services for 16- and 17-Year-Olds." Ministry of Children, Community, and Social Services. Accessed December 4, 2023. www.children.gov .on.ca.

Onuoha, Freedom C. 2013. "Westgate Attack Al-Shabaab's Renewed Transnational Jihadism." Al-Jazeera Centre for Studies. Accessed October 14, 2022. https://studies .aljazeera.net.

Orne, Jason. 2011. "You Will Always Have to 'Out Yourself': Reconsidering Coming Out through Strategic Outness." *Sexualities* 14, no. 6: 681–703. https://doi.org/10 .1177/1363460711420462.

Östergen, Petra. 2017. "From Zero Tolerance to Full Integration: Rethinking Prostitution Policies." Available at Research Gate. Accessed December 4, 2023. www .researchgate.net.

Owsianik, Jenna, and Ross Dawson. 2016. "Future of Sex Report." Future of Sex. Accessed October 14, 2022. https://futureofsex.net.

Oxford English Dictionary Online. N.d. "BDSM." Accessed October 7, 2022. www.oed .com.

Paasonen, Susanna. 2011. "Online Pornography: Ubiquitous and Effaced." Pp. 424–39 in *The Handbook of Internet Studies*, ed. Mia Consalvo and Charles Ess. Oxford: Wiley-Blackwell.

Paasonen, Susanna, Kylie Jarrett, and Ben Light. 2019. *NSFW: Sex, Humor, and Risk in Social Media*. Cambridge, MA: MIT Press.

Parisi, Luciana. 2004. *Abstract Sex: Philosophy, Biotechnology, and the Mutations of Desire*. London: Continuum.

Parreñas, Rhacel. 2011. *Illicit Flirtations: Labor, Migration, and Sex Trafficking in Tokyo*. Albany: State University of New York Press.

Paterson, Blake. 2021. "Proposed Laws to Decriminalize Prostitution in Louisiana Shelved over Concerns: Here's Why." *The Advocate*, May 4. Accessed November 22, 2021. www.theadvocate.com.

Pausé, Cat. 2015. "Human Nature: On Fat Sexual Identity and Agency." Pp. 37–49 in *Fat Sex: New Directions in Theory and Activism*, ed. H. Hester and C. Walters. Farnham, UK: Ashgate.

Pausé, Cat, and Kathryn Palmer. 2021. "Weight and the Law in New Zealand." *Fat Studies* 10, no. 2: 172–83.

Pechey, Ben. 2022. *The Book of Non-Binary Joy: Embracing the Power of You*. New York: Jessica Kingsley Publishers.

Peepshow Media. 2019. "Episode 48: Woodhull's Legal Challenge to FOSTA/SESTA." *Peepshow Podcast*, September 16.

———. 2020. "Episode 78: Porn Performers Talk Pornhub and Payment Processing." Audio podcast, *Peepshow Podcast*, December 21.

Pennington, Heather. 2017. "Kinbaku: The Liminal and the Liminoid in Ritual Performance." *Performance of the Real* 1: 42–51.

Perdue, Noelle. 2021. "How Porn's Racist Metadata Hurts Adult Performers of Color." *Wired*, April 28. Accessed October 14, 2022. www.wired.com.

Perry, Adele. 2005. "Metropolitan Knowledge, Colonial Practice, and Indigenous Womanhood: Missions in the Nineteenth-Century British Columbia." In *Contact Zones: Aboriginal and Settler Women in Canada's Colonial Past*, ed. K. Pickles and M. Rutherdale. Vancouver, BC, Canada: University of British Columbia Press.

Perry, Samuel L., and Andrew L. Whitehead. 2022. "Porn as a Threat to the Mythic Social Order: Christian Nationalism, Anti-Pornography Legislation, and Fear of Pornography as a Public Menace." *Sociological Quarterly* 63, no. 2: 316–36. https://doi.org/10.1080/00380253.2020.1822220.

Peterson, Meghan, Bella Robinson, and Elena Shih. 2019. "The New Virtual Crackdown on Sex Workers' Rights: Perspectives from the United States." *Anti-Trafficking Review* 12: 189–93.

Petillo, April. 2019. "Marking Embodied Borders: Compulsory Settler Sexuality, Indigeneity, and U.S. Law." *Women's Studies in Communication* 41, no. 4: 329–34. https://doi.org/10.1080/07491409.2018.1544013.

Pezzutto, S. 2019. "From Porn Performer to Porntropreneur: Online Entrepreneurship, Social Media Branding, and Selfhood in Contemporary Trans Pornography." *AG: About Gender* 8, no. 16: 30–60. https://doi.org/10.15167/2279-5057/AG2019.8.16.1106.

Pharr, Suzanne. 1996. *In the Time of the Right*. Little Rock, AR: Chardon Press.

Pheterson, Gail. 1993. "The Whore Stigma: Female Dishonor and Male Unworthiness." *Social Text* 37, no. 37: 39–64. https://doi.org/10.2307/466259.

Pickett, Andrew C., and George B. Cunningham. 2017. "Physical Activity for Every Body: A Model for Managing Weight Stigma and Creating Body-Inclusive Spaces." *Quest* 69, no. 1: 19–36.

Piepzna-Samarasinha, Leah Lakshmi. 2018. *Care Work: Dreaming Disability Justice*. Vancouver, Canada: Arsenal Pulp Press.

Pilcher, Katy. 2012. "Dancing for Women: Subverting Heteronormativity in a Lesbian Erotic Dance Space?" *Sexualities* 15, no. 5–6: 521–37. https://doi.org/10.1177/1363460712445979.

Pinkesz, Miriam. 2020. "Coerced Sterilization of Indigenous Women: Alisa Lombard Exposes Canada's 'Colonial Hangover.'" Top Class Actions, December 4. https://ca.topclassactions.com.

Pinsky, Dina, and Tania G. Levey. 2015. "'The World Turned Upside Down': Emotional Labor and the Professional Dominatrix." *Sexualities* 18, no. 4: 438–58. https://doi.org/10.1177/1363460714550904.

Piper, Reese. 2019. "The Stripper's Dilemma." *Queer Majority*. Accessed March 16, 2024. www.queermajority.com.

Pitagora, Dulcinea. 2017. "No Pain, No Gain? Therapeutic and Relational Benefits of Subspace in BDSM Contexts." *Journal of Positive Sexuality* 3, no. 3: 44–54. https://doi.org/10.51681/1.332.

Pitcher, Jane. 2019. "Intimate Labor and the State: Contrasting Policy Discourses with the Working Experiences of Indoor Sex Workers." *Sexuality Research and Social Policy* 16, no. 2: 138–50. https://doi.org/10.1007/s13178-018-0323-3.

Platt, Lucy, Pippa Grenfell, Rebecca Meiksin, Jocelyn Elmes, Susan G Sherman, Teela Sanders, Peninah Mwangi, and Anna-Louise Crago. 2018. "Associations between Sex Work Laws and Sex Workers' Health: A Systematic Review and Meta-Analysis of Quantitative and Qualitative Studies." *PLoS Medicine* 15, no. 12: e1002680. https://doi.org/10.1371/journal.pmed.1002680.

Poitras, Andrew. 2015. "What Constitutes Sex Work?" *Hopes & Fears*, November 18. www.hopesandfears.com.

Polsky, Ned. 1967. *Hustlers, Beats, and Others*. Chicago: Aldine.

Porter, Judith, and Louis Bonilla. 2010. "The Ecology of Street Prostitution." Pp. 163–86 in *Sex for Sale*, ed. R. Weitzer. New York: Routledge.

Potter, Gary. 2013. "The History of Policing in the United States, Part 1." *EKU Online*, June 25. Accessed May 5, 2024. ekuonline.eku.edu.

Price, Janet, and Margrit Shildrick. 2002. "Bodies Together: Touch, Ethics, and Disability." Pp. 62–75 in *Disability/Postmodernity: Embodying Disability Theory*, ed. Mairian Corker and Tom Shakespeare. London: Continuum.

Przybylo, Ela. 2019. *Asexual Erotics: Intimate Readings of Compulsory Sexuality*. Columbus: Ohio State University Press.

Puar, Jasbir. 2007. *Terrorist Assemblages: Homonationalism in Queer Times*. Durham, NC: Duke University Press.

———. 2017. *The Right to Maim: Debility, Capacity, Disability*. Durham, NC: Duke University Press.

Public Safety Canada. 2021. "Human Trafficking." Public Safety Canada. Accessed October 10, 2022. www.canada.ca.

Qualls-Corbett, Nancy. 1988 *The Sacred Prostitute: Eternal Aspect of the Feminine*. Toronto, Canada: Inner City Books.

Queen, Carol, and Lynn Comella. 2008. "The Necessary Revolution: Sex-Positive Feminism in the Post-Barnard Era." *Communication Review* 11, no. 3: 274–91. https://doi.org/10.1080/10714420802306783.

Query, Julie, Vicky Funari, and Heidi Rahlmann Plumb. 2001. *Live Nude Girls Unite!* First Run/Icarus Films.

Radačić, Ivana. 2017. "New Zealand Prostitutes' Collective: An Example of a Successful Policy Actor." *Social Sciences* 6, no. 2: 1–12.

Raguparan, Menaka. 2019. "'So It's Not Always the Sappy Story': Women of Colour and Indigenous Women in the Indoor Sectors of the Canadian Sex Industry Speak Out." Doctoral dissertation, Carleton University, Ottawa, Canada.

———. 2020. "Victims of State Violence: Indigenous and Women of Color Sex Workers' Interactions with Law Enforcement in Canada." Pp 165–86 in *Gender Justice: Theoretical Practices of Intersectional Identity*, ed. E. Woods. Lanham, MD: Rowman & Littlefield.

Ramberg Lucinda. 2014. *Given to the Goddess*. Durham, NC: Duke University Press.

Razack, Sherene. 1998. "Race, Space, and Prostitution: The Making of the Bourgeois Subject." *Canadian Journal of Women and Law* 10: 338.

Rekart, Michael. 2005. "Sex-Work Harm Reduction." *Lancet* 366, no. 9503: 2123–34.

Renaissance Diva. 2006. "Punk-Ass Clients." *Renaissance Diva* (blog). Accessed December 2022. http://renaissancediva.blogspot.com.

Rich, Adrienne. 1980. "Compulsory Heterosexuality and the Lesbian Existence." *Signs: Journal of Women in Culture and Society* 5, no. 4: 631–60.

Richardson, Kathleen. 2017. "Slavery, the Prostituted, and the Rights of Machines." *IEEE Technology and Society Magazine* 35, no. 2: 46–53. https://technologyandsociety.org.

Riski, Tess. 2020. "After Demands by Black Dancers, Union Jacks Strip Club Agrees to Cultural Sensitivity Training and Listening Sessions." *Willamette Week*, June 18. www.wweek.com.

Ritchie, Andrea J. 2017. *Invisible No More: Police Violence against Black Women and Women of Color.* Boston: Beacon Press.

Robinson, Brandon Andrew. 2020. *Coming Out to the Streets: LGBTQ Youth Experiencing Homelessness.* Berkeley: University of California Press.

Roos, Julia. 2002. "Backlash against Prostitutes' Rights: Origins and Dynamics of Nazi Prostitution Policies." *Journal of the History of Sexuality* 11, no. 1–2: 67–94. https://doi.org/10.1353/sex.2002.0012.

Roots, Katrin. 2018. "The Human Trafficking Matrix: Law, Policy, and Anti-trafficking Practices in the Canadian Criminal Justice System." PhD dissertation, York University, Toronto, Canada.

Rubin, Gayle. 2011. "Thinking Sex: Notes for a Radical Theory of the Politics of Sexuality." In *Deviations: A Gayle Ruben Reader*, 137–81. Durham, NC: Duke University Press.

Rutman, Margot. 1999. "Exotic Dancers' Employment Law Regulations." *Temple Political and Civil Rights Law Review* 8: 515.

Ryan, Paul. 2019. "Netporn and the Amateur Turn on OnlyFans." In *Male Sex Work in the Digital Age: Curated Lives*, 119–36. London: Palgrave Macmillan.

Sagar, Tracey, Debbie Jones, Katrien Symons, and Jo Bowring. 2015. "The Student Sex Work Project: Research Summary." Centre for Criminal Justice and Criminology. Accessed October 14, 2022. http://thestudentsexworkproject.co.uk.

Sage, Jessie. 2020. "The Future of BBW Porn: An Interview with Lasha Lane." *Peepshow Magazine*, July 14. Accessed October 14, 2022. https://peepshowmagazine.com.

———. 2021. "Sex Working While Fat." *Tryst Blog*, June 17. https://tryst.link.

Salinas, Sara. 2018. "Tumblr's Ban on Adult Content Is Pushing Artists and Sex Workers to Other Sites, Such as Twitter and Patreon." *CNBC*, December 21. Accessed October 14, 2022. www.cnbc.com.

Sanders, Teela. 2005a. "'It's Just Acting': Sex Workers' Strategies for Capitalizing on Sexuality." *Gender, Work and Organization* 12, no. 4: 319–42. https://doi.org/10.1111/j.1468-0432.2005.00276.x.

———. 2005b. *Sex Work: A Risky Business.* London: Willan Publishing.

Sanders, Teela, Barbara Brents, and Chris Wakefield. 2020. *Paying for Sex in a Digital Age: US and UK Perspectives.* London: Routledge.

Sanders, Teela, Peninah Mwangi, and Anna-Louise Crago. 2018. "Associations between Sex Work Laws and Sex Workers' Health: A Systematic Review and Meta-Analysis of Quantitative and Qualitative Studies." *PLOS Medicine* 15, no. 12: e1002680. https://doi.org/10.1371/journal.pmed.1002680.

Sanders, Teela, Maggie O'Neill, and Jane Pitcher. 2009. *Prostitution: Sex Work, Policy, and Politics.* Thousand Oaks, CA: Sage Publications.

Sanders, Teela, Jane Scoular, Rosie Campbell, Jane Pitcher, and Stewart Cunningham. 2018. "Characteristics and Working Practices of Online Sex Workers." Pp. 55–85 in *Internet Sex Work: Beyond the Gaze,* ed. Teela Sanders, Jane Scoular, Rosie Campbell, Jane Pitcher, and Stewart Cunningham. New York: Springer International Publishing. https://doi.org/10.1007/978-3-319-65630-4_3.

Sanders, Teela, Dan Vajzovic, Belinda Brooks-Gordon, and Natasha Mulvihill. 2021. "Policing Vulnerability in Sex Work: The Harm Reduction Compass Model." *Policing and Society* 31, no. 9: 1100–1116. https://doi.org/10.1080/10439463.2020.1837825.

Sankofa, Jasmine. 2016. "From Margin to Center: Sex Work Decriminalization Is a Racial Justice Issue." Amnesty International. Accessed October 14, 2022. www.amnestyusa.org.

Santos, Kristine Michelle L. 2020. "The Bitches of Boys Love Comics: The Pornographic Response of Japan's Rotten Women." *Porn Studies* 7, no. 3: 279–90. https://doi-org.ezproxy.uky.edu/10.1080/23268743.2020.1726204.

Savage, Dan (@fakedansavage). 2021a. "I Would Add . . . the Pandemic Has Led to More People into Power Play Exploring Findom/Finsub—It's Led to More Safely Online Sex Work in All Forms—but I First Noticed Findom Taking off Right after the 2008 Financial Crisis. That's When I Started Getting Calls and Letters about It." Twitter, April 10, 9:39 a.m. https://twitter.com/fakedansavage/status/1380923190667448322.

———. 2021b. "Our Erotic Imaginations Seize on Broad Cultural Events/Traumas and the 2008 Crisis Combined with Growing Awareness of Economic Inequality—IMO—Was the Spark That Set the Findom on Fire. The Pandemic Just Poured a Whole Lot of Gasoline on It." Twitter, April 10, 2021, 9:39 a.m.. https://twitter.com/fakedansavage/status/1380923190667448322.

Sawicki, Danielle, Brienna Meffert, Kate Read, and Adrienne Heinz. 2019. "Culturally Competent Health Care for Sex Workers: An Examination of Myths That Stigmatize Sex-Work and Hinder Access to Care." *Sexual and Relationship Therapy* 34, no. 3: 355–71. https://doi.org/10.1080/14681994.2019.1574970.

Sayers, Naomi. 2014. "Ms. Naomi Sayers (Spokesperson, Canadian Alliance for Sex Work Law Reform) at the Justice and Human Rights Committee." *Open Parliament,* July 7. Accessed October 14, 2022. https://openparliament.ca.

———. 2017. "Canada's 150 and the Decriminalization of Indigenous Sex Workers." AWID, June 17. Accessed January 21, 2022. www.awid.org.

Schaffer, Jennifer. 2015. "We Spoke to Lauren Chief Elk, the Woman behind #GiveYourMoneytoWomen, about the Power of Cold Hard Cash." *Vice,* August 2. Accessed October 14, 2022. www.vice.com.

Schilt, Kristen. 2010. *Just One of the Guys: Transgender Men and the Persistence of Gender Inequality*. Chicago: University of Chicago Press.

Schulte, Brit. 2020. "Ending Violence against Sex Workers Means Abolishing Police and Prisons." *Truthout*, December 17. Accessed December 17, 2020. https://truthout.org.

Schulte, B., and A. Hammes. 2021. "Support Ho(s)e: Sex Work Centered Guide for Health/Wellness Professionals." The Support Ho(s)e Collective. Accessed October 14, 2022. https://sxhxcollective.org.

Sciortino, Karley. 2016. "Sex Worker and Activist, Tilly Lawless, Explains the Whorearchy." *Slutever*, May 23. https://slutever.com.

Scott, John, Denton Callander, and Victor Minichiello. 2014. "Clients of Male Sex Workers." *Male Sex Work and Society* 150 (2014): 77.

Selvey, Linda, Roanna Lobo, Kahlia McCausland, Basil Donovan, Julie Bates, and Jonathan Hallett. 2018. "Challenges Facing Asian Sex Workers in Western Australia: Implications for Health Promotion and Support Services." *Frontiers in Public Health* 6: 171.

Semega, Jessica, Melissa Kollar, Emily Shrider, and John Creamer. 2020. "Income and Poverty in the United States: 2019." U.S. Census Bureau, Current Population Reports, 60–270. Accessed October 14, 2022. www.census.gov.

The Sentencing Project. 2023. "Mass Incarceration Trends." Sentencing Project.org, January. Accessed March 14, 2024. www.sentencingproject.org.

Sepic, Matt. 2019. "Mlps Officials Consider Safety Regulations for Adult Entertainment Workers." *MPR News*, August 12. www.mprnews.org. Accessed July 7, 2021.

Setaro, Shawn. 2017. "The Story behind NYC Stripper Strike." *Complex*, November 8. www.complex.com.

Sexual Trauma and Abuse Care Centre. 2021. "Neurobiology of Trauma." Accessed March 21, 2024. http://stacarecenter.org.

Seymour, Andi. 2019. "The Real Stripper Report: Participatory ACTION Research by and for Sex Workers." Conference presentation, Woodhull Sexual Freedom Summit, Alexandria, Virginia, August 15–18, 2019.

Shakespeare, Tom, Kath Gillespie-Sells, and Dominic Davies. 1996. *The Sexual Politics of Disability: Untold Desires*. London: Cassell.

Shaw, Frances. 2012. "The Politics of Blogs: Theories of Discursive Activism Online." *Media International Australia* 142, no. 1: 41–49. https://doi.org/10.1177/1329878X1214200106.

Shildrick, Margrit. 2012. *Dangerous Discourses of Disability, Subjectivity, and Sexuality*. London: Palgrave.

Shimizu, C. P. 2007. *The Hypersexuality of Race: Performing Asian/American Women on Screen and Scene*. Durham, NC: Duke University Press.

Shirley, Gabrielle. N.d. "I'm a Toronto Sex Worker: Here's Why I Find My Job Empowering." *CBC: The Passionate Eye*. Accessed July 19, 2022. www.cbc.ca.

Showden, Carisa R., and Samantha Majic. 2018. *Youth Who Trade Sex in the U.S.: Intersectionality, Agency, and Vulnerability*. Philadelphia: Temple University Press.

shuster, stef, and Laurel Westbrook. 2022. "Reducing the Joy Deficit in Sociology: A Study of Transgender Joy." *Social Problems*, June 6. https://doi.org/10.1093/socpro/spac034.

Shuttleworth, Russell. 2002. "Defusing the Adverse Context of Disability and Desirability as a Practice of the Self for Men with Cerebral Palsy." Pp. 112–26 in *Disability/Postmodernity: Embodying Disability Theory*, ed. Mairian Corker and Tom Shakespeare. London: Continuum.

Shuttleworth, Russell, and Teela Sanders, eds. 2010. *Sex and Disability: Politics, Identity, and Access*. Leeds, UK: Disability Press.

Silbert, Mimi, and Ayala Pines. 1981. "Occupational Hazards of Street Prostitutes." *Criminal Justice and Behavior* 8, no. 4: 395–99. https://doi.org/10.1177/009385488100800401.

Simpson, Audra. 2014. *Mohawk Interruptus*. Durham, NC: Duke University Press.

Ślęzak, Izabela. 2019. *Social Construction of Sex Work*. Kraków, Poland: Jagiellonian University Press.

S&M Show Podcast Network. 2020. "Adult Star Breana Khalo Interview." *Soundcloud*. Accessed October 15, 2022. https://soundcloud.com.

Smith, Michael, Christian Grov, and David Seal. 2009. "Agency-Based Male Sex Work: A Descriptive Focus on Physical, Personal, and Social Space." *Journal of Men's Studies* 16, no. 2: 193–210. https://doi.org/10.3149/jms.1602.193.

Smith, Molly, and Juno Mac. 2018. *Revolting Prostitutes: The Fight for Sex Workers' Rights*. Brooklyn, NY: Verso Books.

Sobchack, Vivian. 2004. *Carnal Thoughts: Embodiment and Moving Image Culture*. Berkeley: University of California Press.

Spider, Princess. 2006. *Princess Spider: True Experiences of a Dominatrix*. London: VirginBooks.

Srinivasan, Amia. 2021. *The Right to Sex*. London: Bloomsbury.

Staiger, Annegret. 2022. *Legalized Prostitution in Germany: Inside the New Mega Brothels*. Bloomington: Indiana University Press.

Stardust, Zahra. 2014. "'Fisting Is Not Permitted': Criminal Intimacies, Queer Sexualities, and Feminist Porn in the Australian Legal Context." *Porn Studies* 1, no. 3: 242–59.

———. 2018. "Safe for Work: Feminist Porn, Corporate Regulation, and Community Standards." Pp. 155–79 in *Orienting Feminism: Media, Activism, and Cultural Representation*, ed. Catherine Dale and Rosemary Overell. New York: Springer International Publishing.

Stardust, Zahra, Carla Treloar, Elena Cama, and Jules Kim. 2021. "'I Wouldn't Call the Cops If I Was Being Bashed to Death': Sex Work, Whore Stigma, and the Criminal Legal System." *International Journal for Crime, Justice, and Social Democracy* 10, no. 2: 142–57.

Stasz, Cathleen. 2001. "Assessing Skills for Work: Two Perspectives." *Oxford Economic Papers* 53, no. 3: 385–405. https://doi.org/10.1093/oep/53.3.385.

Stegeman, Hanne Marleen. 2021. "Regulating and Representing Camming: Strict Limits on Acceptable Content on Webcam Sex Platforms." *New Media & Society* 0, no. 0. https://doi.org/10.1177/14614448211059117.

Strangio, Chase. 2022. "The Courts Won't Free Us—Only We Can." *Them*, June 1. Accessed October 14, 2022. www.them.us.

Streetnet International. N.d. "Progress Report on World Class Cities for All (WCCA) Campaign." Streetnet International: International Alliance of Street Vendors. Accessed October 15, 2022. https://streetnet.org.za.

———. N.d. "World Class Cities for All: Background." Streetnet International: International Alliance of Street Vendors. Accessed August 22, 2022. https://streetnet.org.za.

Strings, Sabrina. 2019. *Fearing the Black Body: The Racial Origins of Fat Phobia*. New York: New York University Press.

Sun, Chyng, Ana Bridges, Jennifer A. Johnson, and Matthew B. Ezzell. 2016. "Pornography and the Male Sexual Script: An Analysis of Consumption and Sexual Relations." *Archives of Sexual Behavior* 45, no. 4: 983–94.

SUPRIHMBE. 2018. "Sex Work after FOSTA-SESTA: Why the New Wave of Prohibition Has So Many Panicking." Autostraddle, June 11. Accessed June 11, 2022. www.autostraddle.com.

Sutton, Elise. 2007. *Female Domination: An Exploration of the Male Desire for Loving Female Authority*. Accessed October 1, 2022. www.lulu.com.

Swader, Christopher, Olga Strelkova, Alena Sutormina, and Viktoria Syomina. 2013. "Love as a Fictitious Commodity: Gift-for-Sex Barters as Contractual Carriers of Intimacy." *Sexuality & Culture* 17, no. 4: 598–616. https://doi.org/10.1007/s12119-012-9162-1.

Swami, Viren. 2015. "Cultural Influences on Body Size Ideals." *European Psychologist* 20, no. 1: 44–45.

Sweet, Paige. 2019. "The Paradox of Legibility: Domestic Violence and Institutional Survivorhood." *Social Problems* 66, no. 3: 411–27.

Swer, Gracey. 2020. "The Price You Pay for Being an Open Sex Worker." *Street-Hooker.com*, April 1. Accessed October 14, 2022. https://street-hooker.com.

Taekema, Dan. 2020. "Ontario Announces $307M Investment to Take on Human Trafficking." *CBC News*, March 6. www.cbc.ca.

Taormino, Tristan, Constance Penley, Celine Shimizu, and Mireille Miller-Young, eds. 2013. *The Feminist Porn Book: The Politics of Producing Pleasure*. New York: Feminist Press.

Tastrom, Katie. 2019a. "Sex Work Is a Disability Issue. So Why Doesn't the Disability Community Recognize That?" Rooted in Rights, January 4. Accessed October 1, 2022. https://rootedinrights.org.

———. 2019b. "Want to Reduce Sex Trafficking? Decriminalize Sex Work." *Rewire News Group* (blog), July 18. Accessed April 20, 2022. https://rewirenewsgroup.com.

Tate, Shirley Anne. 2009. *Black Beauty: Aesthetics, Stylization, Politics*. Farnham, UK: Ashgate.

Taunton, Esther. 2020. "Sex Worker Wins Six-Figure Settlement in Sexual Harassment Case." *Stuff*, December 14.

Taylor, Drew Hayden. 2008. *Me Sexy*. Vancouver: Douglas & McIntyre.

Thatiah, Joan. 2022. "Why Sex Workers Have Retreated to Working from Home." *Nation*, April 9. Accessed March 21, 2024. https://nation.africa.

Thompson, Mark. 2001. *Leatherfolk: Radical Sex, People, Politics, and Practice*. New York: Alyson Books.

Thukral, Juhu, and Melissa Ditmore. 2003. *Revolving Door: An Analysis of Street-Based Prostitution in New York City*. Urban Justice Center, Sex Workers Project. Accessed October 14, 2022. www.nswp.org.

Tomura, Miyuki. 2009. "A Prostitute's Lived Experiences of Stigma." *Journal of Phenomenological Psychology* 40, no. 1: 51–84. https://doi.org/10.1163/156916209 X427981.

Trautner, Mary Nell. 2005. "Doing Gender, Doing Class: The Performance of Sexuality in Exotic Dance Clubs." *Gender & Society* 19, no. 6 (2005): 771–88.

Treisman, Rachel. 2021. "A 'Relic' and 'Burden': Manhattan District Attorney to Stop Prosecuting Prostitution." *NPR*, April 21.

Tremain, Shelley L. 2017. *Foucault and Feminist Philosophy of Disability*. Ann Arbor: University of Michigan Press.

Tuck, Eve, and K. Wayne Yang. 2014. "R-Words: Refusing Research." In *Humanizing Research: Decolonizing Qualitative Inquiry with Youth and Communities*, 223–48. Thousand Oaks, CA: Sage Publishing.

Turner, Gustavo. 2021a. "Here's What the New Mastercard Rules Mean for Adult Sites, Producers." *XBIZ*, April 15. Accessed October 13, 2022. www.xbiz.com.

———. 2021b. "MasterCard Execs Meet with APAG, FSC over New Processing Rules." *XBIZ*, June 30. Accessed October 12, 2022. www.xbiz.com.

———. 2021c. "The New War on Porn: How Moral Crusaders, Mainstream Media, and Politicians Are Gunning for XXX." *XBIZ*, January 2. Accessed October 14, 2022. www.xbiz.com.

Tusikov, Natasha. 2021. "Censoring Sex: Payment Platforms' Regulation of Sexual Expression." Pp. 63–79 in *Media and Law: Between Free Speech and Censorship*, ed. Mathieu Deflem and Derek M. D. Silva. Leeds, UK: Emerald Publishing.

United Nations: High Commissioner for Human Rights. 2008. "Report from OHCHR Fact-Finding Mission to Kenya, 6–28 February 2008." Office of the High Commissioner for Human Rights. Accessed October 14, 2022. www.ohchr.org.

United States Census. 2021. Quarterly Residential Vacancies and Homeownership, Second Quarter 2021. Accessed March 4, 2024. www.census.gov.

United States Government Accountability Office. 2021. "Sex Trafficking: Online Platforms and Federal Prosecutions." GAO. Accessed June 15, 2022. www.gao.gov.

UN Women. 2019. "Women in Informal Economy." UN Women. Accessed October 15, 2022. www.unwomen.org.

———. 2021. "Violence against Women during COVID 19." *Women Count*, July 1. Accessed October 13, 2022. https://data.unwomen.org.

Upadhyay, Srushti. 2021. "Sugaring: Understanding the World of Sugar Daddies and Sugar Babies." *Journal of Sex Research* 58, no. 6: 775–84.

Urban Dictionary. 2017. "Urban Dictionary: Financial Domination." *Urban Dictionary*. Accessed May 25, 2021. www.urbandictionary.com.

U.S. Equal Employment Opportunity Commission. N.d. "Significant EEOC Race/ Color Cases (Covering Private and Federal Sectors)." Accessed January 29, 2022. www.eeoc.gov.

Van Der Linde, Nadia. 2014. "Nothing about Us, without Us: Reversing the Power Dynamics of Philanthropy." Red Umbrella Fund, March 18. Accessed October 14, 2022. www.redumbrellafund.org.

Van der Meulen, Emily, Elya M. Durisin, and Victoria Love. 2013. *Selling Sex*. Vancouver: University of British Columbia Press.

Verdeschi, John. 2021. "Revised Standards for Adult Content Merchants." *Mastercard Newsroom*, April 14. Accessed October 14, 2022. www.mastercard.com.

Vidal-Ortiz, Salvador. 2014. "Whiteness." *TSQ: Transgender Studies Quarterly* 1, no. 1–2: 264–66.

Wacek, Brittney. 2017. "Factors Which Put Social Workers at a Greater Risk for Burnout." Master's thesis, St. Catherine University, St. Paul, MN. https://sophia.stkate .edu.

Wade, Brandon. 2009. *Seeking Arrangement: The Definitive Guide to Sugar Daddy and Mutually Beneficial Arrangements*. St. Frederick, MD: Bush Street Press.

Wade, Lisa. 2014. "When Whiteness Is the Standard of Beauty." *Sociological Images*, May 16. https://thesocietypages.org.

Walby, Kevin. 2012. "Touching Encounters: Male-for-Male Internet Escorts and the Feigning of Intimacy." In *Touching Encounters: Sex, Work, and Male-for-Male Internet Escorting*, 105–26. Chicago: University of Chicago Press.

Ward, Ellis, and Gillian Wylie, eds. 2017. *Feminism, Prostitution, and the State: The Politics of Neo-Abolitionism*. London: Routledge.

Ward, Jane. 2020. *The Tragedy of Heterosexuality*. New York: New York University Press.

Waxmann, Laura. 2022. "New Rules for Contractors Have Unexpected Consequences for the City's Strip Clubs." *San Francisco Examiner*. Last updated May 24. Accessed December 5, 2023. www.sfexaminer.com.

Weatherby, W. J. 1983. "Hard Times on the Street Walk." *The Guardian*, February 23, 21.

Webber, Valerie, and Rebecca Sullivan. 2018. "Constructing a Crisis: Porn Panics and Public Health." *Porn Studies* 5, no. 2: 192–96.

Weeks, Kathi. 2011. *The Problem with Work: Feminism, Marxism, Antiwork Politics, and Postwork Imaginaries*. Durham, NC: Duke University Press.

Weinberg, Martin S., Frances M. Shaver, and Colin J. Williams. 1999. "Gendered Sex Work in the San Francisco Tenderloin." *Archives of Sexual Behavior* 28, no. 6: 503–21. https://doi.org/10.1023/a:1018765132704.

Weinberg, Thomas S. 1995. "Sociological and Social Psychological Issues in the Study of Sadomasochism." Pp. 289–303 in *S & M: Studies in Dominance and Submission*, ed. Thomas S. Weinberg. Amherst, NY: Prometheus Books.

Weiss, Alexandra. 2021. "Making a Living at Financial Domination Online." *New York Times,* April 10. www.nytimes.com.

Weiss, Margot. 2011. *Techniques of Pleasure: BDSM and the Circuits of Sexuality.* Durham, NC: Duke University Press.

———. 2015. "BDSM (Bondage, Discipline, Domination, Submission, Sadomasochism)." Pp. 113–96 in *The International Encyclopedia of Human Sexuality,* ed. Patricia Whelehan and Anne Bolin. Hoboken, NJ: Wiley. https://doi.org/10.1002/9781118896877.wbiehs043.

Weitzer, Ronald. 1991. "Prostitutes' Rights in the United States," *Sociological Quarterly* 32, no. 1: 23–41.

———. 2007. "The Social Construction of Sex Trafficking: Ideology and Institutionalization of a Moral Crusade." *Politics & Society* 35, no. 3: 447–75.

———. 2009a. *Sex for Sale: Prostitution, Pornography, and the Sex Industry.* New York: Routledge.

———. 2009b. "Sociology of Sex Work." *Annual Review of Sociology* 35, no. 1: 213–34.

———. 2010a. "The Mythology of Prostitution: Advocacy Research and Public Policy." *Sexuality Research and Social Policy* 7, no. 1: 15–29.

———. 2010b. "Sex Work: Paradigms and Policies." Pp. 1–43 in *Sex for Sale,* ed. Ronald Weitzer. New York: Routledge.

———. 2011. "Sex Trafficking and the Sex Industry: The Need for Evidence-Based Theory and Legislation." *Journal of Criminal Law and Criminology* 101, no. 4: 1337–70.

———. 2012. *Legalizing Prostitution: From Illicit Vice to Lawful Business.* New York: New York University Press.

———. 2015. "Interpreting the Data: Assessing Competing Claims in Pornography Research." Pp. 256–75 in *New Views on Pornography,* ed. L. Comella and S. Tarrant. Santa Barbara: Praeger.

———. 2018. "Resistance to Sex Work Stigma." *Sexualities* 21, no. 5–6: 717–29.

———. 2023a. "Criminalization, Decriminalization, and Legalization." Pp. 375–402 in *Sex for Sale,* 3rd ed., ed. R. Weitzer. New York: Routledge.

———. 2023b. "Sex Work: Types and Paradigms." Pp. 3–42 in *Sex for Sale,* 3rd ed., ed. R. Weitzer. New York: Routledge.

———. 2023c. *Sex Tourism in Thailand: Inside Asia's Premier Erotic Playground.* New York: New York University Press.

Welter, Barbara. 1966. "The Cult of True Womanhood: 1820–1860." *American Quarterly* 18, no. 2: 151–74.

White, Elise, Rachel Swaner, Emily Genetta, Suvi H. Lambson, Janell Dash, Isaac Sederbaum, and Ariel Wolf. 2017. "Navigating Force and Choice: Experiences in the New York City Sex Trade and the Criminal Justice System's Response." National Criminal Justice Reference Service. www.ojp.gov.

White, Luise. 1990. *The Comforts of Home: Prostitution in Colonial Nairobi.* Chicago: University of Chicago Press.

WIEGO. 2022. *COVID-19 and Informal Work in 11 Cities: Recovery Pathways amidst Continued Crisis.* July. Accessed March 17. 2024. www.wiego.org.

WIEGO Blog. 2019. "Review of Understanding the Statistical Term 'Dependent Contractor': A Q&A with Firoza Mehrotra." *WIEGO* (blog), February 12. Accessed October 14, 2022. www.wiego.org.

Williams, Linda. 1999. *Hard Core: Power, Pleasure, and the "Frenzy of the Visible."* Berkeley: University of California Press.

Wilmet, Holly J. 1999. "Naked Feminism: The Unionization of the Adult Entertainment Industry." *American University Journal of Gender, Social Policy & the Law* 7, no. 3: 465–98.

Wilson, Ara. 2007. *The Intimate Economies of Bangkok: Tomboys, Tycoons, and Avon Ladies in the Global City*. Berkeley: University of California Press.

Winemaker, Susan. 2007. *Concertina: An Erotic Memoir of Extravagant Tastes and Extreme Desires*. New York: St. Martin's Press.

Witt, Emme. 2020. "What Is the Whorearchy and Why It's Wrong." *An Injustice!*, November 18. Accessed October 14, 2022. aninjusticemag.com.

WLBT. 2019. "Mississippi Strip Club Ordered to Pay over $3.3 Million in Race Discrimination Case." *WLBT News*, May 16. www.wlbt.com.

Women and Gender Equality Canada. 2020. "Backgrounder: National Inquiry into Murdered and Missing Indigenous Women and Girls." Government of Canada. Accessed October 14, 2022. www.canada.ca.

Women's Legal Education and Action Plan. 2020. "IAAW and LEAF Continue to Seek Justice for Cindy Gladue." LEAF: Women's Legal Education and Action Fund. Accessed July 22, 2022. www.leaf.ca.

Wotton, Rachel. 2016. "Sex Workers Who Provide Services to Clients with Disability in New South Wales, Australia." Master of Philosophy thesis, University of Sydney. Accessed August 14, 2023. https://ses.library.usyd.edu.au.

Wyatt, Ben. 2010. "Fact or Fiction: World Cup Woes for Homeless?" *CNN.com*, July 8. Accessed February 14, 2022. www.cnn.com.

yang, nel. 2022. "Ordinary Finance." PhD dissertation, University of Texas at Austin. https://doi.org/10.26153/tsw/41823.

Yang, Nelson. 2018. "Fintech/Findom: On Emergent Sex Publics and the Anthropology of Desire." Thesis, University of Texas at Austin. https://doi.org/10.15781/T2JH3DN19.

Yi, Jacqueline, and Nathan R Todd. 2021. "Internalized Model Minority Myth among Asian Americans: Links to Anti-Black Attitudes and Opposition to Affirmative Action." *Cultural Diversity & Ethnic Minority Psychology* 27, no. 4: 569–78. https://doi.org/10.1037/cdp0000448.

Yuval-Davis, Nira. 2006. "Intersectionality and Feminist Politics." *European Journal of Women's Studies* 13, no. 3: 193–209.

Zelizer, Viviana. 2005. *The Purchase of Intimacy*. Princeton, NJ: Princeton University Press.

Zhou, Yanyan, and Bryant Paul. 2016. "Lotus Blossom or Dragon Lady: A Content Analysis of 'Asian Women' Online Pornography." *Sexuality and Culture* 20, no. 4: 1083+.

Zook, Kristal B. 1990. "Light Skinned-ded Naps." Pp. 85–96 in *Making Face, Making Soul/Haciendo Caras: Creative and Critical Perspectives by Women of Color*, ed. Gloria Anzaldua. San Francisco: Aunt Lute Foundation Books.

Zuboff, S. 2019. *The Age of Surveillance Capitalism: The Fight for the Human Future at the New Frontier of Power*. London: Profile Books.

ABOUT THE CONTRIBUTORS

HOLLIE ANISE is an online FinDomme and graduate student. She is interested in the impacts of economic and social change on male sexuality. Thanks to findom, she has paid off her student loans.

KAYTLIN BAILEY is a sex worker–rights advocate, former sex worker, comedian, writer, and Founder & Executive Director of Old Pros, a non-profit media organization working to change the status of sex workers in society. She also hosts *The Oldest Profession* podcast and created *Whore's Eye View*, a seventy-five-minute mad dash through ten thousand years of history from a sex worker's perspective

BERNADETTE BARTON is Professor of Sociology and Director of Gender Studies at Morehead State University, and author of *The Pornification of America: How Raunch Culture Is Ruining Our Society*, *Stripped: More Stories from Exotic Dancers*, and *Pray the Gay Away: The Extraordinary Lives of Bible Belt Gays*.

AYELLET BEN NER is a researcher, artist, and former sex worker. She has an MA from the Hebrew University of Jerusalem, owns the blog *The True Memories of an Israeli Geisha*, is cofounder of the "when she works" Facebook page, and Chair of ARGAMAN—the Israeli sex workers alliance.

LIZZIE BLAKE is a white settler based in so-called Canada. Lizzie has been working as an escort for seven years and has been struggling as a postsecondary student for even longer. Lizzie is currently working on her PhD with a focus on sex work, digital (in)access, and mutual aid.

LINDSAY BLEWETT is a queer, disabled sex worker and PhD candidate at York University. Her research interests include sexual labor/sex work studies, critical disability studies, disability and sex work histories, sex and death, queer futurities, and feminist theory. Blewett has published in *Briarpatch Magazine, GUTS Magazine, Feral Feminisms*, and anthologies such as *Disability Injustice* (2022).

PEYTON BOND is a Teaching Fellow at the University of Otago in Aotearoa, New Zealand. Her primary research interest is gendered labor, particularly in feminized service industries, affect, commodification, workers' rights, hierarchies, and resistance to neoliberal/capitalist norms. She uses feminist qualitative methodologies in her research and is especially interested in people's stories of their working lives.

BARBARA G. BRENTS is Professor of Sociology at the University of Nevada–Las Vegas. She has been researching sexual commerce for three decades and is the coauthor of *The State of Sex: Tourism, Sex, and Sin in the New American Heartland* (2010), about the Nevada brothel industry, and *Paying for Sex in the Digital Age* (2020), comparing surveys of sex work clients in the United States and United Kingdom.

CHRIS BRUCKERT is Professor of Criminology at the University of Ottawa. She has undertaken research on street-based, in-call, and out-call sex work, erotic dance, clients, and third parties. She is the coeditor of *Red Light Labour* (2018), *Getting Past the Pimp* (2018), and *Sex Work: Rethinking the Job, Respecting the Workers* (2013).

KELSY BURKE is Associate Professor of Sociology at the University of Nebraska–Lincoln and an award-winning researcher of sexuality, culture, and politics. She is the author two books: *Christians under Covers: Evangelicals and Sexual Pleasure on the Internet* (2016) and *The Pornography Wars: The Past, Present, and Future of America's Obscene Obsession* (2023).

MOSHOULA CAPOUS-DESYLLAS is Professor of Sociology at California State University–Northridge. Her research uses transnational, critical feminist, and queer theory, visual and public sociology, community engagement, and arts-based methods to highlight the voices of marginalized individuals, groups, and communities. Over the past fourteen years, she has facilitated numerous community-based photo-voice projects.

AMIE CARR is a graduate student in the MSW program at the University of California–Los Angeles. She has a bachelor's degree in Sociology from California State University– Northridge. Amie has worked with prostitution-diversion groups and hopes to turn her attention to working with children/adolescents who have been sex trafficked.

EGLĖ ČESNULYTĖ is a Senior Lecturer in Politics/International Development at the University of Bristol, UK, specializing in feminist political economy, African politics, gender, and development. She is the author of *Selling Sex in Kenya: Gendered Agency under Neoliberalism* (2019).

LENA CHEN is a PhD student at the University of California–Berkeley in the Department of Theater, Dance, and Performance Studies. Her research explores Asian American sexuality, labor, and performance. Her work has been published in the edited volume, *Curating as Feminist Organizing* (2022).

ELLIOT CHUDYK has been involved in a variety of research projects linked to sexuality, gender, health, criminalization, homonationalism, aesthetic labor, erotic capital, and queer theory. Their current research explores transmasculine sex workers' emotional and embodied labor practices and the gendered negotiation processes they must navigate within the context of genderplay and sexual subversion.

KATE D'ADAMO (they/she) is a partner at Reframe Health and Justice (RHJ). RHJ is a collective of queer people of color working at the intersections of harm reduction, systems change, and healing justice. Kate's background is rooted in community organizing, programming, and direct support and advocacy for people in the sex trades and employing other forms of criminalized survival. Kate's current focus in this work is training and technical assistance for service providers, direct political advocacy, and capacity building for community-led initiatives seeking to impact policy change. They are based in Maryland and hold degrees from California State Polytechnic University and the New School.

BREANNE FAHS is Professor of Women and Gender Studies at Arizona State University and author of six books: *Performing Sex*; *Valerie Solanas*; *Out for Blood*; *Firebrand Feminism*; *Women, Sex, and Madness*; and *Unshaved*. She has also coedited three volumes: *The Moral Panics of Sexuality*, *Transforming Contagion*, and *Burn It Down!*

SHAWNA FELKINS (she/they) is a Faculty/Instructional Consultant at the Center for the Enhancement of Learning and Teaching and a part-time instructor in the Department of Gender and Women's Studies at the University of Kentucky. Her research interests include sex work, labor, disability, and feminist pedagogy.

GIULIA GAROFALO GEYMONAT is a faculty member at the Università Ca' Foscari Venezia, engaging in social research and activism on issues of gender, sexuality, labor, migration, and disability. She has expertise in researching grassroots collective organizing in relation to sensitive and stigmatized topics and identities. She has been an activist for the rights of sex workers in Europe for more than twenty years.

JULIA GIACOMETTI is a trained sexual assistant for people with disabilities based in Italy.

LIA GRAY (she/her) is a white settler based in the Pacific Northwest. Lia began online sex work over five years ago to find greater autonomy, agency, and power during her academic studies. Lia is currently balancing online sex work, her research career, escorting, and building community with other sex workers and allies.

CAITY GWIN worked as a stripper for eleven years in over fifty clubs. She is a Juilliard dance dropout and received her BA from Sarah Lawrence College, where she studied political theory and dance. She is a sex worker–rights advocate and holds a law degree from the University of Nevada–Las Vegas Boyd School of Law.

STACEY HANNEM is a sociologist and Professor in the Criminology Department at Wilfrid Laurier University. Her research examines stigma, marginalization, and the social and symbolic consequences of law for marginalized people. She is coauthor of *Defining Sexual Misconduct: Power, Media, and #MeToo* (2022) and coeditor of *Stigma Revisited: Implications of the Mark* (2012).

KENNETH R. HANSON is an Assistant Professor of Sociology in the Department of Criminal Justice and Sociology at the University of Wyoming. His research examines controversial and underexplored topics relating to sexuality and technology. Most recently his focus has been on various uses of personified sex tech.

YESSICA GARCIA HERNANDEZ is Assistant Professor and Filmmaker in the César E. Chavez Department of Chicana/o and Central American Studies at UCLA. Her research explores Latinx sexualities, performance, and popular culture. She is currently writing a book about the history of Latinas in the pornographic archive and contemporary industry.

KAVITA NAYAR JABLONKA holds a PhD in Communication from the University of Massachusetts–Amherst. Her research interests include feminized labor in cultural industries and the mediation of intimacy and emotion. Her work has been published in the *Journal of Gender Studies*, *Feminist Media Studies*, and the *Communication Review*.

CRYSTAL A. JACKSON is Associate Professor in the School of Social Transformation at Arizona State University. Jackson's research focuses on sex worker–rights activism and advocacy, sex/uality in porn production and consumption, and the impacts of the criminal justice system, immigration control, and social-service practices on sex worker–rights organizing.

ANGELA JONES is Professor of Women, Gender, and Sexuality Studies at Stony Brook University. As a scholar, writer, educator, and activist, Jones focuses their research on African American political thought and protest, sex work, race, gender, sexuality, feminist theory, Black feminisms, and queer methodologies and theory.

ZOEY JONES is a Research Officer at the Alberta Union of Provincial Employees. Her academic work has focused on sexuality, deviance, and stigmatized and criminalized communities. Her research has been published in the *Journal of Symbolic Interaction* and the volume *The Power of BDSM: Play, Communities, and Consent in the 21ˢᵗ Century* (2023).

LILLIAN TAYLOR JUNGLEIB is Assistant Professor of Sociology at the University of Nevada–Las Vegas. Her research is grounded in her commitment to community justice and public sociology and meets at the intersection of criminology, gender, and social inequalities. Using an intersectional approach, she examines how public discourses and legal policies operate within institutions, adversely impacting marginalized communities.

YEELA LAHAV-RAZ is a Senior Lecturer in the Department of Sociology and Anthropology at Ben-Gurion University of the Negev, Israel. She specializes in gender and sexuality, sex work studies, digital anthropology, and the intersections of gender and sexual politics, technological developments, and stigmatized communities. She cofounded the Israeli Association for the Study of Prostitution, Sex Work, and Sex Trafficking in 2019.

TANIA G. LEVEY is Professor of Sociology at York College, City University of New York. Recent publications include "#MeToo in Social Media," in *Institutional Sexual Abuse in the #MeToo Era*, edited by Jason D. Spraitz and Kendra Bowen (2021) and *Sexual Harassment Online: Shaming and Silencing Women in the Digital Age* (2018).

SUMMER LOPEZ COLORADO is a McNair Scholar and doctoral student in Sociology at the University of California–Los Angeles. Her current research centers the sociolegal construction of gender, race, and disability in the policing of sex work. Her dissertation examines mobility, civic engagement, and kinship support networks among Latinx alumni affiliated with Latina-based sororities.

BRONWYN MCBRIDE is a postdoctoral fellow at Simon Fraser University. Bronwyn completed her PhD in 2020 at the Centre for Gender & Sexual Health Equity. Her research investigates the impacts of sex work criminalization and prohibitive immigration policies on health, safety, and labor rights among im/migrant and indoor sex workers in Metro Vancouver.

PENINAH MWANGI is a sex worker–rights activist and the Executive Director of Bar Hostess Empowerment and Support Programme (BHESP)—a Kenyan local sex worker organization created to work toward quality health services, human rights, and economic empowerment for sex workers. Peninah sits on various local and global committees (including WHO and UNAIDS) on health and human rights.

ALEX J. NELSON is Assistant Professor of Anthropology at the University of Indianapolis. He is a sociocultural anthropologist engaged in research on intimacy and gender relations in South Korea and in entrepreneurial and sociolegal strategies of online sex workers.

SOPHIE PEZZUTTO is an activist, trans sex worker, and holds a PhD in Anthropology from Australian National University conducting an ethnographic study of trans pornography. She has written for *TSQ: Transgender Studies Quarterly*, *The Conversation*, and *AG: About Gender*, and her research has been cited in *Forbes*, *Buzzfeed*, and *Mother Jones*.

MENAKA RAGUPARAN is Assistant Professor in the Department of Sociology and Criminology at the University of North Carolina–Wilmington. Her research examines the structure and process of Human Trafficking Courts (HTC) in the United States to understand court-based antitrafficking initiatives and the conflation of sex work and sex trafficking.

TRIP RICHARDS is a transgender man who has been an adult performer for almost a decade. He is also involved in educational and advocacy work, specifically focused on the intersection of gender, sexuality, and labor. His personal website is www.triplextransman.com, and includes other media appearances.

DANIELLA ROBINSON is a Bigstone Cree and Italian sexologist and antiviolence activist. She is a doctoral candidate in Human Sexuality at the California Institute of Integral Studies. Her research is grounded in

Indigenous epistemologies of pleasure, which is central to her work with survivors.

ALEXIS SMILEY SMITH is a writer and cofounder of the Berlin doll brothel, Cybrothel, and the original voice of Kokeshi. As a leader in the sex tech industry, she has contributed to *SX Tech Berlin*, *VR Days Europe*, *The Future of Sex*, and *Playful Magazine*.

KASSANDRA SPARKS is a doctoral candidate in Sociocultural Anthropology at the University of California–Berkeley. Her research examines ritual, exchange, and desire in the commercial BDSM industry in New York City.

JESSICA VAN MEIR is a PhD student in Public Policy at the Harvard Kennedy School of Government researching sex work, informal labor, and the future of work in Latin America and the United States. She earned her MPhil at the University of Cambridge and is the cofounder of MintStars, a content platform to protect creators from financial discrimination using blockchain technology.

VAL WEBBER holds degrees in public health, sexuality studies, and medical anthropology. Their research looks at "health" and "risk" as sites of struggle, particularly for sex workers, queer communities, and other marginalized sexual communities. Val started camming in 2002 and has worked in several areas of the adult industry as a performer, crew member, writer, and voice actor.

RONALD WEITZER is Professor Emeritus at George Washington University. He has conducted research on human trafficking, legal-prostitution regimes, sex tourism, the politics of sex work, client perceptions and experiences, and the social ecology of red-light districts in Europe and Asia.

INKA WINTER is an erotic filmmaker and founder of ForPlay Films, an independent, all-woman porn production company. In addition to erotic filmmaking, Inka is training to be a therapist at the Southern

California Counseling Center and getting certified as an AASECT Sex Educator and Counselor. She also provides desire and arousal coaching.

YEON JUNG YU is Associate Professor in the Department of Anthropology at Western Washington University. She is a cultural and medical anthropologist with a background in Public Health, Women-Gender Studies, and East Asian Studies. She conducts research in social networks, sex work, HIV/AIDS, drug use, and social stigma.

INDEX

Page numbers in italics indicate Figures, Tables, and Photos

www.ingramcontent.com/pod-product-compliance
Lightning Source LLC
Chambersburg PA
CBHW031137020426
42333CB00013B/412